CRITICAL MASS

CRITICAL MASS

Social Documentary
in France
from the Silent Era
to the New Wave

Steven Ungar

University of Minnesota Press
Minneapolis | London

The University of Minnesota Press gratefully acknowledges the generous assistance provided for the publication of this book by the Office of the Vice-President for Research and College of Liberal Arts at the University of Iowa.

Every effort was made to obtain permission to reproduce material in this book. If any proper acknowledgment has not been included here, we encourage copyright holders to notify the publisher.

Portions of chapter 3 were previously published as "Jean Vigo, *L'Atalante,* and the Promise of Social Cinema," *Historical Reflections/Réflexions historiques* 35, no. 2 (2009): 63–83, and as "Toute la misère du monde: Eli Lotar's *Aubervilliers* and a Sense of Place," *Romanic Review* 105, nos. 1–2 (May–November 2013): 37–51; copyright by the Trustees of Columbia University in the City of New York; reprinted with permission. Portions of chapter 4 were previously published as "Whose Voice? Whose Film? Jean Rouch, Oumarou Ganda, and *Moi, un Noir,*" in *Building Bridges: The Cinema of Jean Rouch,* ed. Joram ten Brink (London and New York: Wallflower Press, 2007), 111–23; copyright 2007 Joram ten Brink; reprinted with permission of Columbia University Press; and as "Making Waves: René Vautier's *Afrique 50* and the Emergence of Anti-colonial Cinema," *L'Esprit Créateur* 51, no. 3 (2011): 34–46; copyright 2011 L'Esprit Créateur; reprinted with permission from Johns Hopkins University Press. A portion of chapter 5 was previously published as "Scenes in a Library: Alain Resnais and *Toute la mémoire du monde,*" *SubStance* 41, no. 2 (2012): 58–78; copyright 2012 by the Board of Regents of the University of Wisconsin System; reprinted courtesy of the University of Wisconsin Press.

Published by the University of Minnesota Press
111 Third Avenue South, Suite 290
Minneapolis, MN 55401-2520
http://www.upress.umn.edu

Printed in the United States of America on acid-free paper

The University of Minnesota is an equal-opportunity educator and employer.

24 23 22 21 20 19 18   10 9 8 7 6 5 4 3 2 1

Library of Congress Cataloging-in-Publication Data
Names: Ungar, Steven, author.
Title: Critical mass : social documentary in France from the silent era to the new wave / Steven Ungar.
Description: Minneapolis : University of Minnesota Press, [2018] | Includes bibliographical references and index.
Identifiers: LCCN 2018001921 (print) | ISBN 978-0-8166-8919-4 (hc) | ISBN 978-0-8166-8921-7 (pb)
Subjects: LCSH: Documentary films–France–History and criticism. | Motion pictures–Social aspects–France. | France–Social conditions.
Classification: LCC PN1995.9.D6 U395 2018 (print) | DDC 070.1/8–dc23
LC record available at https://lccn.loc.gov/2018001921

Contents

Introduction

Primal Scenes and Establishing Shots

Attention! Some railroad crossings in France still feature signs warning pedestrians and drivers to look both directions when crossing because one train may hide another on the tracks behind it. The warning comes to mind whenever I think of film culture in France marked between 1925 and 1935 by the transition from silent to sound films. Assessing the impact of this transition—also known as a conversion or a shift—extends from questions of chronology and periodization to the medium specificity of film as it relates to those of painting and photography. Yet this is not really the whole picture until another factor is added. My longtime Iowa colleague Rick Altman has argued that film sound never established its own measure of worth because most approaches to it were grounded in assumptions holding that historically ("films existed without words"), ontologically ("cinema requires an image but not sound"), and practically ("it is the image that sells films"), film was essentially a visual art.[1] From this idea comes my sense that we need to look in more than one way—in more than one direction—at cinema in France during the period in question to see things that preoccupations with the transition to sound may obscure.

The idea for *Critical Mass* began a decade ago with a study of documentaries produced in France between 1945 and 1963, whose engagement with colonialism and postwar modernization I wanted to explore in conjunction with the emergence of the French New Wave. In 1962, film scholar Richard Roud referred to filmmakers Alain Resnais, Chris Marker, and Agnès Varda as a Left Bank group of filmmakers he set apart from Right Bank figures François Truffaut, Jean-Luc Godard, and others associated with the *Cahiers du Cinéma* monthly founded in 1951 by André Bazin, Jacques Doniol-Valcroze, and Joseph-Marie Lo Duca. For Roud, the geographic distinction between Left Bank and Right Bank Paris extended to ideological allegiances among a generation of French filmmakers born from 1921 (Marker) through 1932 (Truffaut). These allegiances positioned individuals along a continuum between progressive (leftist) and conservative (right-wing) values. Film critics and historians continue to ponder and revise these designations and the differences they imply. As I write these lines in early 2018, of this generation only Agnès Varda (born 1928) and Jean-Luc Godard (born 1930) remain alive and active, with Varda now considered godmother of the New Wave and Godard forever its bad-boy genius.

The idea for this book grew after I decided to include early postwar documentaries by Eli Lotar, René Vautier, Georges Franju, and Jean Rouch, whose respective critiques of colonialism and early postwar modernization ranged from denunciation to militancy. Nicole Védrès's 1947 montage film *Paris 1900* warrants special mention because of its adroit use of editing and because Alain Resnais and Chris Marker have cited its treatment of France during the decade and a half leading to the outbreak of World War I as a model for their early films of the 1950s.[2] As I pondered the films in this expanded corpus, I came to see them as delayed responses to Jean Vigo's 1930 call for a social cinema. When Vigo died four years later at the age of twenty-nine, he had completed only four films. The last of the four, *L'Atalante,* was released within weeks of his death under the title of *Le Chaland qui passe (The Passing Barge),* imposed by the Gaumont-Franco-Film-Aubert production company.[3] As I tested the viability of a longer interwar–postwar phenomenon, I began to trace additional trajectories and configurations of social documentary across Europe in films completed from 1930 through 1940 by Joris Ivens, Henri Storck, Luis Buñuel, and Eli Lotar.

The project reached its current form after I came across four late silent-era documentaries in the online collections of the Forum des Images in Paris: Georges Lacombe's *La Zone (The Zone,* 1928), Boris Kaufman's *Les Halles centrales (The Central Covered Markets,* 1928), André Sauvage's *Études sur Paris (Studies of Paris,* 1929), and Marcel Carné's *Nogent, Eldorado du dimanche (Nogent, Sunday's Eldorado,* 1929). I identified these films as precursors of the social cinema Vigo conceptualized in a June 1930 talk at a screening of his *À propos de Nice (Concerning Nice)* at the Théâtre du Vieux-Colombier in Paris.[4] The fact that Kaufman had been cinematographer on all four of Vigo's films strengthened continuities between these examples of late silent-era nonfiction and the socially engaged work that Ivens, Buñuel, Storck, Lotar, and others were to produce during the decade that followed. As a result, my initial postwar project evolved into a longer-duration trajectory, from the late silent era of 1928–30 to the 1959–63 period associated with New Wave practices at the start of France's Fifth Republic.

Caveats concerning film corpus, method, and classifications are in order. While my primary goal here is to explore the emergence and trajectory of social documentary in France from 1928 to 1963, some of the films I consider were shot in Holland, Belgium, Spain, China, Siberia, and West African territories under French colonial rule. Accordingly, the films and practices under consideration are best understood as French-based expressions of a transnational phenomenon. The fact that major documentaries were made by the Russian-born Kaufman, the Dutch-born Ivens, the Spanish-born Buñuel, and the Belgian-born Storck reinforces assumptions concerning practices across national frontiers. The transnational nature of the primary corpus is further supported by the international film and photography exhibition held in Stuttgart, Germany, in 1929 and the international filmmakers' congresses held in La Sarraz, Switzerland, and Brussels, in 1929 and 1930, respectively. All of which is to state as clearly as possible that the critical perspective I take in the chapters to follow should not be understood to equate social documentary in France with a national practice.

In terms of periodization, my starting date of 1928 is marked by Lacombe's *La Zone*. My choice of a 1963 end date is likewise marked by the release of Chris Marker's *Le Joli Mai (The Lovely Month of May)*, which was filmed in May 1962 within weeks of the signing of the Évian Accords, which granted political autonomy to Algeria following 130 years of colonial rule by France. In terms of method, my treatment of the 1928–63 temporal frame borrows from the late *Annales* historian Fernand Braudel's model of event-laden, conjunctural, and long durations whose imbrication challenged the privileging of politics and "great events."[5] I often visualize Braudel's model as a bicycle gearbox whose upward shifts increasing the rate of speed and distance covered are directly related to a decrease in the speed of the rotating pedals. Where Braudel's intent was to account for change on a geological scale over centuries at a time, the modest version I posit in the chart presented here is meant instead to test the explanatory potential of multiple durations over a given period, by which I mean to temper chronology in conjunction with patterns of continuity and change.

A very brief duration near the midpoint of this chronology locates Eli Lotar's *Aubervilliers* within the immediate aftermath of World War II. A somewhat longer duration aligns it with postwar documentaries released in France from 1946 through 1963. A third and final duration—far from anything on the order of Braudel's *longue durée* (long duration)—runs from 1928 to 1963. Starting and end dates are marked by the respective releases of Georges Lacombe's *La Zone* and Chris Marker's *Le Joli Mai*. An alternate end point for the trajectory might have been *Loin du Vietnam (Far from Vietnam)*, a collective project of short films by Joris Ivens, William Klein, Claude Lelouch, Godard, and Resnais filmed in 1967 and released in the United States a year later. This breakdown of my film corpus configures my working thesis that the postwar films reclaim the ambitions and burdens of an interwar corpus of documentaries filmed from 1928 to 1937.

Román Gubern and Paul Hammond have accounted for the transition to sound in France as a four-stage progression, from *films muets* (silent

1928–29	1930–37	1946–50	1953–56	1958	1961–63
Lacombe, *La Zone*, 1928	Vigo, *À propos de Nice*, 1930	Lotar, *Aubervilliers*, 1946	Resnais and Marker, *Les Statues meurent aussi*, 1953	Marker, *Lettre de Sibérie*, 1958	Rouch and Morin, *Chronique d'un été*, 1961
Kaufman, *Les Halles centrales*, 1928	Buñuel, *Las Hurdes*, 1933	Védrès, *Paris 1900*, 1947	Rouch, *Les Maîtres fous*, 1954	Varda, *L'Opéra Mouffe*, 1958	Marker, *Le Joli Mai*, 1963
Sauvage, *Études sur Paris*, 1929	Storck and Lotar, *Les Maisons de la misère*, 1937	Franju, *Le Sang des bêtes*, 1949	Resnais, *Nuit et brouillard*, 1955	Rouch, *Moi, un Noir*, 1958	
Carné, *Nogent, Eldorado du dimanche*, 1929		Vautier, *Afrique 50*, 1950	Resnais, *Toute la mémoire du monde*, 1956		
			Marker, *Dimanche à Pékin*, 1956		

Chronology and periodization of French films, 1928–63.

films), with no sound except for musical accompaniment at screenings, to *films muets et sonores* (silent and sound films), with sound effects and music but no speech, to *films sonores et parlants* (sound and talking films), containing short bursts of synchronized dialogue, to *films parlants* ("talkies"), with extended dialogue.[6] The shift from configuring change as a one-step process (A to B) to an incremental one (A to B to C to D) has immediate consequences that, in line with Altman's remarks on film sound, derive from assumptions concerning the nature of film. Determining whether *Les Trois Masques* (*The Three Masks*, André Hugon, 1929), *La Route est belle* (*The Road Is Beautiful*, Robert Florey, 1930), or *Sous les toits de Paris* (*Under the Rooftops of Paris*, René Clair, 1930) was the first major sound film in France involves more than mere chronology. The explanatory potential of Braudel's model of three durations is especially helpful in accounting for the emergence and disappearance of phenomena whose short- and long-term interactions produce significant change over time.

The 1925–35 decade dominated by the transition from silent to sound film coincided in France with the emergence of documentaries whose aesthetic, narrative, and activist concerns—often building on avant-garde practices of the decade—broke with nonfiction practices of newsreels, travelogues, scientific films, and educational films. Expository forms of nonfiction film had existed as early as 1895, in the films of the Lumière brothers. But it was only during the 1920s that a distinct set of what Tom Gunning calls interpretive practices of nonfiction filmmaking emerged.[7] Bill Nichols accounts for this change by turning to the notion of wave theory *(Wellentheorie)* set forth by the linguist Johannes Schmidt (1843–1901) as an alternative to genetic models of species survival in the form of the family tree *(Stammbaum)* derived from Darwinian notions. Much like Braudel's model of multiple durations, the thesis that Nichols tests through wave theory replaces chronological models grounded in evolutionary progression with patterns of innovation that disclose overlapping relations.[8] Nichols cites the example of Joris Ivens, the lyric poet of *De brug (The Bridge,* 1928) and *Regen (Rain,* 1929), and Joris Ivens, the social advocate of *Misère au Borinage (Misery in Borinage,* with Henri Storck, 1933). I will have more to say about Ivens and this transition following chapter 1.

The remarks by Altman, Braudel, Gunning, and Nichols cited above help to explain why my inquiry concerning the emergence of social documentary in France sets factors of production and distribution related to individual films alongside collective activities in the form of journals, meetings, festivals, and congresses. The latter promoted new collaborations and alliances coincidental with what Nichols has termed a transition from document to documentary. The French noun *documentaire* had appeared throughout the mid-1920s in catalogs produced by film distribution companies to advertise their nonfiction holdings. This early usage was largely descriptive and seldom theorized. Until the 1914 outbreak of World War I, it had also served as a blanket term for newsreels *(actualités)* and travelogues. John Grierson's characterization of documentary as "the creative treatment of actuality" has long remained a point of reference for the emergence of documentary as a discrete form of nonfiction film. Yet the documentary value that Grierson identified in his 1926 review of Robert J. Flaherty's *Moana* was incommensurate with practices of social cinema Jean Vigo grounded four years later on a documented point of view. Grierson's sense of documentary value is therefore less viable in conjunction with practices that Vigo sought to mobilize in the cause of social cinema than as an initial effort to identify necessary and sufficient elements of documentary among a range of nonfiction practices.

When François Porcile referred in 1965 to Lacombe's *La Zone* as the first social documentary in France, he supported his claim by identifying a realist impulse within a cinematic avant garde whose primary concerns were narrative and aesthetic. Citing films completed from 1926 through 1929 by Jean Grémillon, Marc Allégret (with André Gide), Germaine Dulac, Eugène Deslaw, Marcel Carné, and Georges Rouquier, Porcile posited a synthesis of impressionism and realism that culminated in Vigo's *À propos de Nice* (1930), "une dernière bombe" (a last bomb) that he considered nothing less than a social manifesto.[9] Three years earlier, Georges Sadoul had linked *La Zone*'s depiction of ragpickers at work in the streets of Paris to a documentary school of young filmmakers (Carné, Rouquier, Grémillon, Jean Lods) he described as an offshoot of a cinematic avant-garde whose models were Luis Buñuel and Vigo.[10] Some forty years later, Nicole Brenez set *La Zone* alongside László Moholy-Nagy's 1929 *Impressionen vom alten marseiller Hafen (Impressions of the Old Marseille Harbor)* as a pamphlet film generated through an articulation of political demand *(exigence)* and visual exploration anchored in real life and real things.[11]

The remarks by Sadoul, Porcile, and Brenez posit the foundational role of *La Zone* in the emergence of social documentary in France. Yet differences of detail and emphasis pointing to divergent notions of avant-garde and social documentary raise a number of questions. Did Porcile really mean to imply that there was one and only one cinematic avant-garde? If so, what was it, and what place or role, if any, did Lacombe's film have in it? Aside from Lacombe and *La Zone,* how did the work of other filmmakers cited by Porcile, Sadoul, and Brenez contribute to what Sadoul had called a first French school of documentary? Finally, under what circumstances and to what ends did the articulation of political demand and visual exploration referred to by Brenez occur?

My point here is not to dispute the claims Sadoul, Porcile, and Brenez make for *La Zone,* with which I basically agree. Instead, I mean to reconsider these scholars' shared thesis concerning the emergence of social documentary in France by casting *La Zone, Les Halles centrales, Études sur Paris,* and *Nogent, Eldorado du dimanche* within emergent practices for which passing mentions in studies to date only begin to account. At stake in this reconsideration are the various ways in which categories such as period, genre, and corpus inform understanding of social documentary during an early stage in the transition from silent to sound cinema. Accordingly, my primary goal in chapter 1 is to contextualize the four late silent-era films listed above in conjunction with conditions of their production, distribution, and reception. A related goal in chapters 2 through 4 is to account for continuities and differences linking this initial corpus through the 1930s to a postwar corpus of documentaries produced in France from 1945 through 1963. Jean-Pierre Jeancolas provided an initial sense of these continuities when he wrote of a *nouvelle vague documentaire* (documentary new wave) more or less concurrent with Sadoul's first wave.[12] The wave phenomenon invoked in different ways by Jeancolas and Nichols is instructive less as a blanket designation than as a means of positing potential links between interwar and postwar practices.

Models of genealogy run the risk of presupposing outcome or functional end. Strictly in terms of chronology, my postwar corpus constitutes a second life or afterlife of the interwar films whose critical perspectives they elaborate and renew. Central to validating links between interwar and postwar practices are principles that determine individual films' inclusion in or exclusion from a specific corpus as well as the breakdown of period categories such as "interwar" and "postwar" by decade or alternate duration. My corpus of films and flowchart are admittedly constructions from which my analyses of films and institutions will draw out links and patterns that temper difference with continuity.

My approach to documentaries produced in France from 1925 to 1935 draws on additional sources that revise relations between documentary practices and the modernist avant-garde. A first source appears in the form of a question that Nichols raised when he asked how it was that the most formal, abstract, political, and sometimes didactic films "arise, fruitfully intermingle, and then separate in a common historical moment."[13] A second source of my critical approach is a 1953 article in which Henri Langlois identified the advent of the cinematic avant-garde in France in World War I–era discussions among painters and poets including Pablo Picasso, Georges Braque, Léopold Survage, and Guillaume Apollinaire. After noting that Abel Gance's 1915 *La Folie du docteur Tube (The Madness of Doctor Tube)* initially went unnoticed because Gance was neither cubist nor futurist nor Orphist nor Dadaist, Langlois argued that the film received recognition only after it began to be screened:

> Thus the first manifestation of the [cinematic] avant-garde was neither an inner circle, nor a journal, nor a ciné-club nor a school, nor an art house, but a film. What could be more normal? Films are what made an avant-garde, which was not born through artificial insemination, but through cinema itself, through its force and through its content.[14]

Where Nichols approached the relations with a view toward a concept of modernism, Langlois worked from the films toward the avant-garde. Differences between these two trajectories inform the analyses that make up *Critical Mass.*

Chapters 1 and 2 explore the four late silent-era films noted above (Lacombe's *La Zone,* Kaufman's *Les Halles centrales,* Sauvage's *Études sur Paris,* and Carné's *Nogent, Eldorado du dimanche*), whose respective treatments of neighborhoods within and just outside Paris provide examples before the fact of what Vigo would conceptualize in conjunction with his *À propos de Nice* as social cinema. Lacombe's day-in-the-life account of ragpickers *(chiffonniers)* living and working on the city's outskirts traced geographic and social tensions between center and periphery. By contrast, Kaufman's impressionist portrait caught the vibrant pulse of activity at the central produce and meat market that remained invisible to most Parisians, who partook of its offerings on a daily basis. Luc Sante aptly describes Les Halles as a biosphere, "a living embodiment of the chain of production and consumption, an exchange where commerce remained as personal and sensual as it had been before advertising and marketing were invented . . . [not] just the stomach of Paris but its soul."[15]

Where Lacombe and Kaufman provided glimpses of urban periphery and center, Sauvage, in *Études sur Paris,* traced an itinerary of some sixty-five to seventy kilometers through and around the city's neighborhoods and outlying areas. Dividing his film into five sections, he set images of well-known sites associated with picture-postcard images against trajectories that crisscrossed Paris following Métro lines and walking routes. The effect remapped the city following models of urban wandering *(flânerie)* in prose narratives such as Louis Aragon's *Le Paysan de Paris* (*Paris Peasant,* 1926) and André Breton's *Nadja* (1928). Marcel Carné's *Nogent, Eldorado du dimanche* built on the interplay of center and periphery by evoking the day-tripper desertion of central Paris among urban workers looking for a dose of distraction in a riverside village less than an hour by train to the southeast of Paris, where they would dance, drink, and engage in recreational activities on the river. As a set, all four films depicted aspects of daily life that replaced pretty postcard images of the city seen by tourists with reminders of the social and geographic dynamics among marginal populations whose presence more often than not remained invisible.

Chapter 3 is organized around Eli Lotar, whose trajectory from avant-garde and street photography starting in 1927 to his 1946 documentary short subject *Aubervilliers* exemplifies the transition from late silent-era medium-specific experimentation toward committed filmmaking inspired by Vigo's 1930 call for a social cinema. Set at the near midpoint of my extended corpus between 1928 and 1963, *Aubervilliers* bridges interwar and early postwar practices whose mix of social conscience and formal innovation marks the essence of the films I explore in terms of social documentary.

The critiques of French colonial policies in the three films studied in chapter 4—René Vautier's *Afrique 50* (1950), Alain Resnais and Chris Marker's *Les Statues meurent aussi* (*Statues Also Die,* 1953), and Jean Rouch's *Moi, un Noir* (*I, a Black Man,* 1958)—are the most militant within the corpus of postwar films in *Critical Mass.* Those by Vautier and Resnais/Marker are among the first of the early postwar period to adopt openly anticolonial stances. Rouch's *Moi, un Noir* mobilizes observations drawn from anthropology and sociology to portray the complexities encountered by young Africans trying to forge new identities in the Ivory Coast port city of Abidjan under the sway of global economics and mass media. The fact that all three films were subjected to censorship of one kind or another discloses the extent to which they serve as case studies of opposition and resistance to colonial policies and practices extending as far as the 1962 Évian Accords.

Chapter 5 completes the trajectory of social cinema through the early years of the Fifth Republic with analyses of Alain Resnais's *Toute la mémoire du monde* (*All the World's Memory*, 1956) and Chris Marker's *Le Joli Mai* (1963). Both films are rooted in the everyday life of Paris. Resnais depicts France's national library as an institution whose archives of books, prints, and artifacts fulfill its mission as a prime site of cultural heritage *(patrimoine)*. At the same time, sequences in the film that trace the itinerary of a new book being processed convey a sense of the library as a carceral space, along the lines of the World War II concentration and death camps seen in Resnais's previous film, *Nuit et brouillard* (*Night and Fog*, 1955). Marker's *Le Joli Mai* builds on street interviews concerning the expectations of Parisians for the future in the wake of the March 1962 Évian Accords, which granted political autonomy to Algeria. The month is presumably merry because it ostensibly holds promise for a brighter future. More openly pointed than *Toute la mémoire du monde* in its depiction of a France still divided over its political and social future, *Le Joli Mai* also marks an initial moment or phase transition in Marker's militancy over the following fifteen years that culminates in *Le Fond de l'air est rouge* (*A Grin without a Cat*, 1977), his epic account of failed revolution during the decade following 1967.

Three transitions provide critical perspectives on institutions and policies related to individual films. The first places my close readings of late silent-era documentaries by Lacombe, Kaufman, Sauvage, and Carné within the international settings of the May–June 1929 *Film und Foto* (*FiFo*) exhibition in Stuttgart, the September 1929 Congrès International de Cinéastes Indépendants (CICI; International Congress of Independent Filmmakers), held at La Sarraz, and a follow-up CICI held in Brussels in November–December 1930. The three events are notable for their emphasis on efforts to establish networks to promote committed filmmaking on the progressive left among individuals in Europe and North America. Understood as a set, the three exhibitions trace the mutation of avant-garde practices of photography and filmmaking toward explicit engagement with social and political causes through the decade leading to renewed world war.

The second transition is cast as an account of efforts to reform state policies toward film in France during the decade between government reforms following the 1935 bankruptcy of the Gaumont-Franco-Film-Aubert production company and the 1946 creation of the Centre National de la Cinématographie. Crucial to the period is the 1940 creation by Vichy regime officials, under German military control, of the Comité d'Organisation de l'Industrie Cinématographique (COIC; Organizing Committee of the Cinema Industry) to oversee all aspects of filmmaking and film culture.

The third transition is devoted to the Groupe des Trente (Group of Thirty, or G30) collective formed in 1953 to protest proposals by French state officials that group members saw as a threat to the survival of the short subject as an artistic and cultural form. Uniting three generations of directors, producers, and technicians, the G30 modeled itself on similar collectives formed some twenty years earlier during the late Third Republic Popular Front movement and coalition that elected Léon Blum as prime minister in the spring of 1936.

The earliest films made in France were documentary short subjects completed more than a decade before the terms *documentary* and *short subject* were in use. The film often considered among the very first—Auguste and Louis Lumière's 1895 *La Sortie de l'usine Lumière à Lyon (Workers Leaving the Lumière Factory in Lyon)*—ran for about forty-eight seconds and had no camera movement whatsoever. It was a documentary in the sense that it recorded what appeared to be an unrehearsed moment in the daily lives of ordinary people in the real world. This sense aligns with Carl Plantinga's characterization of documentary as an indexical record in which moving photographic images record or trace profilmic scenes.[16]

The majority of men and women shown exiting the Lumière factory on the rue St. Victor appeared oblivious to the camera's presence. (Was this really the case, or had they been prompted in advance not to look at the camera?) They were actors only in the narrow sense of people playing themselves in front of the camera. The French words *tableau* and *vue* used at the time to describe this and other early motion pictures reinforced cinema's debts to painting and still photography. The technical terms for "shot," *prise de vue* and *plan,* and the related expression for "long take," *plan séquence,* did not yet exist. Details complicate standard readings of the film. A horse-drawn carriage seen in two of three extant versions is absent in the third. In the former two versions, one shows one horse, the other two. These and other differences imply that what spectators may have considered a single-take production drawing directly on daily life resulted from multiple takes dictated by the filmmakers. European precursors of the Lumière brothers' first films include Louis Le Prince's motion pictures shot on paper film in and around Leeds in 1888 and Max and Emil

Skladanowsky's images of rooftops of Berlin neighborhoods they had taken with their magic lantern–inspired Bioskop and screened in July 1895.[17]

La Sortie de l'usine Lumière à Lyon was literally a very short subject because the seventeen-meter storage capacity of the *cinématographe*'s reel limited its running time to less than a minute. Increased reel capacity and multireel productions over the following decade resulted in a commercial market for what were later called fiction ("narrative") films, many of them inspired by literary sources. The fifteen-minute running time of Georges Méliès's 1902 *Le Voyage dans la lune (A Trip to the Moon)* was a key factor in its commercial success as a cinematic attraction loosely based on fiction by Jules Verne and H. G. Wells. A decade later, Méliès completed a thirty-minute science fantasy, *La Conquête du Pôle (The Conquest of the Pole, 1912)*, based on Verne's 1866 novel *Les Aventures du Capitaine Hatteras (The Adventures of Captain Hatteras)*. The same year, Victorin-Hyppolite Jasset won the so-called 1,000-meter race with *Zigomar contre Nick Carter (Zigomar versus Nick Carter)*, whose running time at eighteen frames per second was fifty-three minutes.[18] These (relatively) longer films had running times that were short compared to subsequent practices. Even so, they promoted an implicit equation of documentary and short subject that—with notable exceptions—persisted through the advent of television, video, and digital formats.

The rise of feature-length fiction films in France between 1900 and 1915 relegated the documentary to informational modes of newsreel, tourist tableau, sports coverage, and educational film. Consistent usage of the term *documentaire* began around 1910 in the Gaumont production company's catalogs, where it designated short films (*petits films*, literally "small films") whose content was largely informational.[19] A decade later, the term was equated with pedagogical films on topics ranging from natural and physical sciences to the history of art. In a February 1926 review in the *New York Sun*, John Grierson attributed documentary value to what he described as the creative treatment of actuality in Flaherty's *Moana*. Brian Winston writes that a closer reading of the text reveals that what Grierson actually referred to in Flaherty's film was documentary value, which he considered secondary to its value as "a soft breath from a sunlit island."[20] Grierson's sense of documentary was central to the observational practices that he established from 1926 to 1933 at the Empire Marketing Group in Britain. Even so, his evolved sense of documentary as a means of public instruction in the cause of citizenship and democracy was at an ideological remove from the activist practices among documentaries that I explore in the chapters that follow.

A brief example illustrates the radical potential of weekly newsreels that many spectators considered accounts of record on which they based their understanding of what was happening in the world. In *The Camera and I,* Joris Ivens wrote of a didactic switch related to editing practices that occurred just as he was moving away from medium-specific cinematic experiments such as *De brug* and *Regen.* Placed in charge of film programs for a Sunday series of educational films for workers, Ivens would borrow a number of commercial newsreels on Fridays. The next day, he would reedit with colleagues by inserting footage to which they had access in order to give the films a political significance that would have shocked the newsreel companies had they seen the uses to which their "innocent" materials had been put: "After our Sunday morning show was finished we would take the [newly created] film apart again, restore its original form and return it to the newsreel companies who were none the wiser," all of which reinforced an activist potential among nonfiction practices otherwise deemed to be value-free.[21]

The appeal of the early Lumière films is often cast in terms of attraction and wonderment elicited by an illusion that seemed to capture duration in the real world through images projected at sixteen to eighteen frames per second onto a screen or other suitable surface. "How did they do that?" The question conveys the surprise among early spectators, some of whom reputedly wanted to look behind the screen for the outside world behind the flow of images. Yet this impulse to look behind the screen only begins to contend with a new experience of a different order from those to be had in the outside world. Along these lines, Marcel Duchamp once imagined simultaneous projections in front of and behind the screen, with auto headlights turned toward spectators to heighten the experience. For what affected viewers of the earliest silent-era documentaries was often less a matter of assessing the truth claims that these films made concerning the outside world than of contending with the sensations and emotions produced by the motion pictures themselves.[22] As Jennifer Wild notes, the projected exhibition that was the Lumière brothers' supreme invention transformed moving photographic pictures into the collective experience of cinema. What made this transformation so shocking was its "brutal immediacy" and its "intensity of address."[23]

"How did they do that?" Emmanuelle Toulet writes that some viewers of the Lumière brothers' *L'Arrivée d'un train en gare de La Ciotat* (*Arrival of a Train at the La Ciotat Station,* 1895) reputedly shrank into their seats or ran out of the movie theater for fear of being crushed by the train that appeared to bear down on them. Was their reaction sincere, or was it exaggerated for effect? Jean-Louis Comolli notes that spectators knew that a train could not really enter the salon of the Grand Café on the Boulevard des Capucines in Paris where the film was first shown. So what frightened them was perhaps not the representation of reality they were seeing but the reality of the representation equated with the new and unsettling experience of cinema. Tom Gunning adds that the reaction of early film's first audiences that many associate with primitive representation was more directly a reaction to an encounter with modernity.[24] Martin Loiperdinger, for one, has argued that because Louis Lumière staged the *La Ciotat* clip in camera, the reaction should be considered less as proven fact than as a foundational myth of cinema's origins.[25]

Redirecting the primal experience of cinema toward philosophical concepts of being and knowledge helps to explain André Bazin's midcentury views on the ontology of film in conjunction with the photographic image. Despite evident differences, attraction/wonderment and being/knowledge both imply that, as Dai Vaughan argues, what the term *documentary* properly describes is neither a style nor a method nor even a genre of filmmaking but a mode of response to film material grounded in the kinds of claims that documentaries stake upon the world.[26] It follows that what makes a film a documentary is—at least in part—the way it is looked at. As a result, Vaughan continues, the history of documentary can be considered in conjunction with the evolving set of strategies by which filmmakers have tried to make viewers look at films in this way: "To see a film as documentary is to see its meaning as pertinent to the events and objects which passed before the camera: to see it, in a word, as signifying what it appears to record."[27] Francesco Casetti accounts for the receptive dimension of the film experience in his remarks on partial, composite, penetrating, excited, and immersive gazes that open onto the broader phenomenon of a disciplinary gaze. Jonathan Crary tempers spectacle associated with what is seen on screen with a management of attention that arranges bodies in space through "techniques of isolation, cellularization, and above all separation."[28]

The interaction of filmmaker, film, and viewer during the act of watching a documentary as opposed to a fiction film also draws on what Philippe Lejeune has conceptualized with reference to autobiography as a pact between author, text, and reader.[29] Beyond approaches that posit documentary as a distinct genre, Vaughan's foregrounding of experience and interaction is in line with what documentary filmmakers in France have called a *cinéma du réel* (cinema of the real). Since 1978, an annual festival founded by Jean-Michel Arnold and Jean Rouch at the Centre Georges Pompidou in Paris has produced, screened, and discussed documentaries involving as wide a public sphere as possible.[30] This outreach to a public of filmmakers and film lovers builds on populist models of film culture going back in France to post–World War I ciné-clubs and screenings at venues associated with avant-garde literature and theater.

Between 1914 and 1945, documentaries were typically shown in commercial venues as supplements *(compléments de programme)* of feature-length fiction films. In France during the 1920s, articles, reviews, and essays by Robert Desnos, Louis Delluc, Fernand Léger, Germaine Dulac, Jean Epstein, and Elie Faure generated notions of *photogénie* and *cinégraphie* to account for cinema's unique status as a means of creative expression alongside verbal, graphic, and plastic practices from poetry and theater to painting and photography.[31] The mix of verse, tract, and film program advertisements in Epstein's *Bonjour cinéma* (1921) redirected Guillaume Apollinaire's experiments with word, image, and typography in *Calligrammes* (1918) to convey a sense of cinema as a high-energy mass phenomenon.[32] Two years later, Epstein's feature-length fiction film *Coeur fidèle (True Heart)* straddled experimental and realist practices within what Richard Abel has called the narrative avant-garde. Epstein conceived *Coeur fidèle* as a melodrama about a love triangle involving one woman and two men. He and cameraman Paul Guichard shot the film's exterior sequences on location in Marseille and Manosque. Close-ups, extreme close-ups, superimpositions, and variable-duration montage throughout the film illustrated the priority of what Germaine Dulac called an *idée visuelle* (visual idea) over narrative. This priority underscored efforts to explore how film was capable of recasting perceptions of simple experiences—the spinning of an amusement park ride, the wind rippling the surface of water, the steepness of an interior staircase—as uniquely visual moments without precluding a heightened awareness of these moments as a distinctive kind of interaction with the real (profilmic) world.[33] In line with a review by Léon Moussinac that identified the film's realist setting among down-and-out types in working-class Marseille, *Coeur fidèle* has been seen as a precursor of the poetic realism in fiction films of the 1930s directed by Jean Renoir, Julien Duvivier, and Marcel Carné.[34] That realist dimension aligns with similar elements in late silent-era documentaries, including Lacombe's *La Zone*, Sauvage's *Études sur Paris*, and Vigo's *À propos de Nice*.

Outside France, silent-era documentaries of the 1920s, including Walter Ruttmann's *Berlin: Sinfonie der Großstadt (Berlin: Symphony of a World Capital*, 1927) and Dziga Vertov's *Chelovek s kino-apparatom (Man with a Movie Camera*, 1929), featured original treatments of everyday life in urban settings. Both Ruttmann's and Vertov's films mobilized superimposed and kaleidoscopic images that jarred conventional perceptions of contemporary life. Two decades later, Chris Marker noted that the visual energy of Vertov's film in the wake of Sergei Eisenstein's *Bronenosets Potyomkin (Battleship Potemkin*, 1925) conveyed a promise of revolt and revolution that appealed to a growing political awareness among Parisian surrealists.[35] René Clair's 1923 *Paris qui dort (The Crazy Ray)* was a comic science fiction short in which an inventor named Dr. Crase builds a machine that, like the cinema, is able to "arrest, speed up, and slow down movement and time."[36]

Despite location sequences in Marseille, Epstein's exploration of special effects *(trucage)* in *Coeur fidèle* is often considered an end in itself. By contrast, the depiction of the French capital in *Paris qui dort*—especially in sequences looking down on the city from the Eiffel Tower—contained what Grierson would soon refer to as documentary value. The same holds for Clair's *Entr'acte* (*Intermission*, 1924), in which the systematic undermining of narrative continuity by cinematic effects associated with avant-garde practices fails to preclude a nonfiction perspective on locations in and around Paris.

Even the visual content of Luis Buñuel and Salvador Dalí's *Un chien andalou* (*An Andalusian Dog*, 1929), whose sequences of erotically charged violence upset many viewers, included realist sequences set on urban streets. Concerning his intention to do nothing more or other than document facts of thought in their full irrationality, Dalí wrote:

> In effect, documentary and the Surrealist text coincide from the outset in their essentially anti-artistic and more particularly anti-literary process, since not the slightest of intentions, be they aesthetic, emotional, sentimental, etc.,—essential characteristics of the artistic phenomenon— enter into this process. The documentary notes things of the objective world anti-literarily.[37]

Jacques B. Brunius commented that Dalí's receptive stance toward documentary in this passage suggested a major affinity among experimental/ avant-garde filmmakers for the potential among nonfiction elements— even those occurring in the fiction films by Epstein and Clair cited above—to explore the world from multiple angles and directions: "The documentary thus began to uncover both the beauty and the horror of the world, the marvels of the most mundane objects infinitely enlarged, the fantastic of the street or/and of nature."[38] After listing *Entr'acte* and *Un chien andalou* as definitive models of an experimental cinema, Brunius invoked filmmaker Henri Chomette's assertion that because a cinema that he considered pure, absolute, and complete unto itself *(pur, absolu et intégral)* was not limited to the representative world, it could engender unknown visions inconceivable outside the union of the lens and the moving reel of film.[39] The productive tension among late silent-era films that sought to document facts of thought in their full irrationality (Dalí) and others that disclosed new visions of the world (Brunius, Chomette) asserts the role of films that broke with assumptions equating documentaries reductively with nonfiction practices of newsreels and reportage.

In France, the two decades following the 1940–44 German occupation were a period of renewal among young filmmakers, critics, and spectators seeking to make up for time lost under Vichy censorship. Much like the late silent era of the 1920s, this postwar renewal invented its own gaze among self-styled cinephiles with a new eye for consuming films.[40] A full five years before the 1959 Cannes Film Festival brought international acclaim to the French New Wave, film critics François Truffaut, Jean-Luc Godard, Éric Rohmer, and Claude Chabrol took positions in the *Cahiers du Cinéma* that were openly at odds with interwar "tradition of quality" filmmakers who grounded their work in adaptations of literary sources. The "young Turks" (André Bazin's expression) at the *Cahiers* spoke for many postwar cinephiles whose tastes drew on the global history of film as far back as the silent era. The same 1945–68 period produced innovative documentaries by Nicole Védrès, Georges Franju, Jean Rouch, Agnès Varda, and—most of all—Alain Resnais and Chris Marker. Films by these Left Bank filmmakers and by others such as René Vautier and Eli Lotar contributed to short-subject documentary practices that cleared the way for early films by Truffaut, Godard, Jacques Rivette, Claude Chabrol, and Éric Rohmer more readily identified with the French New Wave.[41] As with the new wave of the late silent era, many of these postwar films challenged assumptions concerning distinctions between fiction and nonfiction films, especially when the latter were equated with documentary.

A First Wave

Documentary Paris in the Shadow of the Talkies

> To rove about, musing, that is to say loitering, is, for a philosopher, a good way of spending time; especially in that kind of mock rurality, ugly but odd, and partaking of two natures, which surrounds certain large cities, particularly Paris. To study the *banlieue* is to study the amphibious. End of trees, beginning of houses, end of grass, beginning of pavement, end of furrows, beginning of shops, end of ruts, beginning of passions, end of the divine murmur, beginning of the human hubbub; hence the interest is extraordinary.
>
> — Victor Hugo, *Les Misérables* (1862)

Somewhere Else: Georges Lacombe and *La Zone* (1928)

When it is capitalized and preceded by a definite article, the French word *Zone*—from the Greek ζώνη (zone) and the Latin *zona,* for belt or girdle—refers to a 250-meter-wide strip of land forming a 35-kilometer ring around military fortifications built in 1844 near the former gates of Paris. This usage emphasizes the shape of the area as it might appear on a map of Greater Paris. It persists in the English terms *beltline* and *ring road.* A second usage designates the area's transformation into shantytowns *(bidonvilles)* occupied by poor and transient populations displaced during the 1853 renewal of inner-city Paris by Seine prefect Georges-Eugène Haussmann. The occupation of these peripheral areas thus began two decades before the fortifications fell into disuse following France's 1871 military defeat by Prussia and more than a half century before they were torn down between 1919 and 1932.

The shacks and makeshift structures erected by the area's inhabitants, known as *zoniers,* violated regulations prohibiting all but short-term construction near the fortifications. The fact that the *zoniers* were squatters and thus illegal residents added to the perceptions of *la Zone* as a transitional space between urban Paris and semirural villages *(faubourgs)* that were slowly annexed through urban expansion. The last *zoniers*—whose numbers in 1926 were estimated at 42,000—were formally evicted in the 1940s. Since then, the area has been the site of state-financed high-rise housing projects and two concentric ring roads *(boulevards périphériques)*.[1] Post-1968 *films de banlieue* refer to inhabitants of the housing projects as *zonards.* Translating *films de banlieue* as "suburb films" fails to engage the complexity of a phenomenon that, unlike the concurrent rise of *beur* practices constituted in the main by first-generation Maghrebi immigrants, cannot be reduced to a single ethnic group.[2] Where Mathieu Kassovitz used hip-hop and street slang to convey the area's climate of unrelenting violence in *La Haine* (*Hate,* 1995), Abdellatif Kechiche's *L'Esquive* (*Games of Love and Chance,* 2003) centered on a production of Pierre de Marivaux's 1730 comedy *Le Jeu de l'amour et du hasard* (*Games of Love and Chance*) to stage the complexities faced by teens living in the Parisian equivalent of U.S. inner-city housing projects. Both films cast the Parisian *banlieue* as the antithesis of the postwar U.S. suburbs that television and mainstream films grounded in the nuclear family.[3] In French, the pluralized English term *suburbs* is rendered in the singular as *la banlieue.* More substantial differences are conveyed by the expressions *la banlieue rose* (pink or rosy suburb) for the postwar U.S. model and *la banlieue morose* (morose or gloomy suburb) for the equivalent areas surrounding Paris.

Popular perceptions of *la Zone* cross elite and mass media in word and image. *Zoniers* was the title Eugène Atget chose for a collection of sixty or so photographs of the area and outlying neighborhoods of Paris he took from 1899 to 1913. Some of the photographs included *zoniers*; others did not. The latter may have inspired Walter Benjamin's likening of Atget's photographs of deserted Parisian streets to crime scenes. Benjamin made this assertion twice: first in "A Little History of Photography" (1931) and again in "The Work of Art in the Age of Its Reproducibility" (1935–36). Ian Walker asserts that differences of emphasis in these essays placed the moments captured in the images forward or backward in time, and thus either prior to or following a crime.[4] "Zone" is also the title of a 1913 poem by Guillaume Apollinaire in which the narrator identified with immigrants and outcasts whom he encountered during a twenty-four-hour walk through Paris. Apollinaire's narrator was not a descendant of the *flâneur* (urban stroller), whom Benjamin later explored as a privileged figure in Charles Baudelaire's *Les Fleurs du mal* (*The Flowers of Evil,* 1857). His disaffection following a romantic breakup fashioned him instead as a lone wanderer with no particular place to go.

Two decades later, the first-person narrator of Louis-Ferdinand Céline's *Voyage au bout de la nuit* (*Journey to the End of the Night,* 1932) described the patients at a local dispensary to which he had been assigned on the northern outskirts of Paris as coming mostly from the zone, the village of sorts, which never succeeds in picking itself entirely out of the mud and garbage, bordered by paths where precocious snot-nosed little girls play hooky under the fences to garner a franc, a handful of French fries, and a dose of gonorrhea from some sex fiend. A setting for avant-garde films where the trees are poisoned with laundry and lettuces drip with urine on Saturday night.[5]

The passage displays Céline's sense of the poverty and moral decay that was soon to be seen in poetic realist films of the decade, including Marcel Carné's *Le Quai des brumes* (*Port of Shadows*, 1938) and *Le Jour se lève* (*Daybreak*, 1939). In 1937, the author of the novel on which Carné based his adaptation of the former, Pierre Mac Orlan, wrote that audio records, photography, film, and radio were privileged means of revealing the adventure and romance of a social fantastic encountered along urban streets at certain hours of the night.[6] When Céline's narrator described mud, garbage, and lettuce as a setting for avant-garde films, his point was less to reduce *la Zone* to a cinematic spectacle than to take a jab at those who knew it only from what they had seen on-screen.

Céline's remarks provide an early take on what Adrian Rifkin has described as a persistent dream of semialterity whose expression among petit bourgeois Parisians was often embodied by stars of popular song, from turn-of-the-century figures Fréhel and Maurice Chevalier through the postwar entertainers Yves Montand and Marcel Mouloudji.[7] Looking especially at early sound films, Kelley Conway has analyzed how popular song in Anatole Litvak's *Coeur de lilas* (*Lilac*, 1932) perpetuates *La Zone*'s aura of crime and sexuality through the realist singer Fréhel, who appears alongside Jean Gabin and Fernandel as a character named La Douleur (pain).[8]

David Harvey directs Rifkin's notion of semialterity toward resistance when he writes of efforts to reclaim the city by those displaced in the wake of Haussmann's removal of working-class and "other unruly elements" from the center of Paris.[9] In Harvey's view, the idea of *la Zone* as an urban form resulted from Haussmann's mistaken belief that the beltline fortifications would contain revolutionary movements through surveillance and military control. Rifkin makes a similar point when he writes that Haussmann's reform made *la Zone* into "a place of all that is marginal, a space of the social imaginary, a store of images interleaved with the geographies of the city . . . having at the same time a particular physiognomy and a complex of connotations."[10] Outside France, the term *zone* applies to the Soviet-era network of forced labor camps, whose inmates referred to the world outside in slang as *bolshaya zona*, the "big prison zone."[11] Finally, when Yve-Alain Bois writes that the city as organism and capitalist enterprise continuously invents new ways to recycle waste, he identifies a zonal dynamic that extends from unwanted trash to unwanted humans.[12]

The preceding remarks illustrate how the social and economic realities of *la Zone* are inseparable from constructs that have fashioned perceptions of it in literature, popular song, photography, and film. These constructs recall what the historian Pierre Nora has called *lieux de mémoire* (memory sites).[13] But where Nora associates these sites with republican identities, David Harvey's perception of *la Zone* as a site of resistance populations opposed to the inequalities that isolated them from urban centers aligns with contemporary notions of the "precariat" as a minority population with neither economic nor social stability. This chapter examines *La Zone*, a 1928 documentary short subject whose director, Georges Lacombe, began his career as an assistant to René Clair during the production of the latter's *Paris qui dort* (*The Crazy Ray*, 1923). Lacombe later worked alongside the young Marcel Carné as assistant to Clair on *Sous le toits de Paris* (*Under the Rooftops of Paris*, 1930). *La Zone* was shot in black and white on 35 mm film and was produced by the Société des Films Charles Dullin. It was the first of thirty films, including *Café de Paris* (1938) and *Montmartre-sur-Seine* (1941), that Lacombe directed from 1927 through 1957.[14]

Lacombe's subtitle for *La Zone*—*Au pays des chiffonniers* (*In the Land of the Ragpickers*)—conveys the complexity of the area as geographic reality and collective construct. It does this by association with *In the Land of the Head Hunters* (1914), Edward S. Curtis's fictionalized account of daily life among Kwakiutl peoples on the Queen Charlotte Strait coast of British Columbia. It also recalls the figure of the ragpicker in Baudelaire's *Les Fleurs du mal*, whom Walter Benjamin invoked soon after while working in Paris on what would come to be known as *The Arcades Project*:

> Here we have a man whose job it is to gather the day's refuse in the capital. Everything that the big city has thrown away, everything it has lost, everything it has scorned, everything it has crushed underfoot he catalogues and collects. He collates the annals of intemperance, the capharnaum of waste. He sorts things out and selects judiciously: he collects like a miser guarding a treasure, refuse which will assume the shape of useful or gratifying objects between the jaws of the goddess of Industry. This description is one extended metaphor for the poetic method, as Baudelaire practiced it. Ragpicker and poet: both are concerned with refuse.[15]

Atget had included photographs of ragpickers in *Zoniers*; one driving a horse-drawn wagon is featured throughout Jacques Tati's 1958 *Mon oncle* (*My Uncle*). In line with conventions of the late nineteenth-century illustrated travelogues that were precursors of filmed ethnography such as

Curtis's *In the Land of the Head Hunters,* Lacombe's subtitle cast *La Zone* as a visit to an unknown area, even if the area in question was nearby. The classification is reinforced by the first of nineteen intertitles *(cartons)* in the form of an assertion that some regions on Earth remain little known.

1. Il est sur terre encore des régions peu connues. (There are still regions on Earth that are little known.)
2. Celle que vous allez voir . . . est située à quelques kilomètres de . . . (The one you are about to see . . . is located a few kilometers from . . .)
3. Curieuse population où toutes les races se trouvent mêlées (Strange population where all the races mix)
4. La vie des chiffonniers à 5 heures du matin (The life of ragpickers at 5:00 A.M.)
5. Sept heures (7:00 A.M.)
6. 100 kg de papier (100 kilograms of paper)
7. Le classement en trois categories: chiffons, croûtes, verres (Classification in three categories: rags, food scraps, glass of various kinds)
8. Ce que le chiffonnier a dédaigné, les services municipaux l'enlèvent et . . . (What the ragpicker has rejected, the municipal services pick up and . . .)
9. Dernier triage . . . ce qui peut servir encore, par tapis roulant (Final triage . . . [of] whatever can still be put to use by conveyor belt)
10. Rien ne se perd . . . la poussière sortant de ce tamis servira d'engrais. (Nothing is lost . . . including the dust that, coming up out of the sieve/filter, will be used as fertilizer.)
11. Ce qui reste alimente des chaudières. (Whatever remains feeds the boilers.)
12. Le mâchefer part vers la briquetterie voisine. (The incombustible residue is sent to the nearby brickyard.)
13. La vapeur des chaudières actionne turbines et dynamos. (The steam from the boilers activates turbines and dynamos.)
14. Une personnalité de la zone, la "Mère aux chiens." Âme charitable, providence des chiens abandonnés. (A celebrity of *la Zone,* the "Old Dog Lady," charitable soul and salvation of abandoned dogs.)
15. Parfois un reporter s'aventure chez une ancienne "gloire." (Sometimes a reporter takes a chance with a former celebrity.)
16. Une autre personnalité de la zone, le jars "Coco" fétiche des zoniers de Malakoff (Another celebrity of *la Zone,* "Coco" the gander, mascot of the zone people of Malakoff)
17. Le "Marché aux Puces," centre commercial de la Zone (The "Flea Market," *la Zone*'s commercial area)

18. Fin d'après-midi, l'heure des loisirs (Late afternoon, leisure time)
19. Sept heures, huit heures du soir. Déjà la Zone s'endort . . . (7:00 P.M.,
    8:00 P.M., *la Zone* already drifts off to sleep . . .)

The opening intertitle is followed by nine shots showing a dirt path near a brick wall, a rocky hillside, a mound of earth, boulders, wooden structures, a muddy lane, and a mud-caked boot on the ground near a streetlamp. The location of the shots, which feature soft (lap) dissolves at intervals of five to seven seconds, is indeterminate, with no identifiable landmarks whatsoever. Only one of the nine displays a fleeting human presence in the background. Camera angles vary from a steep upward tilt to horizontal shots at ground level. The final shot is of a six-story brick apartment building, seen at a sharp upward angle from ground level. Its setting in what appears to be urban Paris is a visual precedent for the motif of center and periphery that later sequences will develop.

A second intertitle at 1:22—"The one you are about to see . . . is located a few kilometers from . . ."—in the form of direct address promotes complicity, as though a physically present narrator were inviting spectators to accompany him on a cinematic tour. The detail strengthens associations with the illustrated-format lecture in which photographs and maps contribute to a live account. The intertitle trailing off into an ellipse cuts to an abrupt close-up of hieroglyphs for which the previous shots provide no context. A reverse tracking shot reveals the hieroglyphs to be those of the Obelisk of Luxor, erected on the Place de la Concorde in 1836 after having been offered five years earlier as a gift to King Louis Philippe from the khedive (viceroy) of Egypt. (The obelisk dates from the thirteenth century B.C.; it comes from the temple of Ramses II at Thebes, or Luxor.) The first people to appear in the film are pedestrians seen walking along the Place de la Concorde. Their presence extends uncertainty surrounding relations between the hieroglyphs and the opening sequence, for which no transition has been provided.

A clearer sense of these relations occurs during an approximately half-minute animated sequence that begins with the city limits outlined in white against a black background. Within seconds, major internal thoroughfares marked in white plot what resembles a neural network of streets. Thicker white lines trace the flow of the Seine across the city, with the word "Paris" faintly visible in dotted lettering. After the obelisk rises from a dot on the map into a three-dimensional axis, a beam of light emanating from its top describes two clockwise circles, one after the other, just outside the city's perimeter. The effect recalls the revolving searchlight atop the Eiffel Tower, located on the Seine near the northwestern extremity of the Left Bank. The first circle marks the city's former gates, the second the area of *la Zone* immediately surrounding them. The concentric circles flash briefly—an effect that Charlie Chaplin would reprise in the title credits for *City Lights* (1931)—before the title of Lacombe's film appears in stylized sans serif stick lettering, seemingly contained by the outlined perimeter of the city. Animation serves as an elegant means of conveying a significant amount of visual information. Even so, the effect of the written title at the end is disconcerting because its placement within the city limits contradicts the geographic location of *la Zone* just outside them. Whether by design or not, the layout suggests that the center–periphery motif it introduces is more than a matter of physical location. This is the sense in which the geographic and social marginality of *la Zone* clashes with its status as a collective construct integral to the identity of post-Haussmannian Paris.

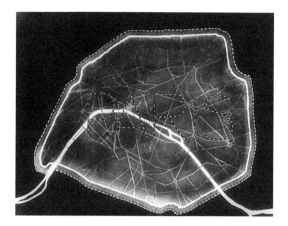

Animated title sequence from *La Zone* (1928).

The close-up of the hieroglyphs and the animated sequence link the first two and a half minutes of *La Zone* with effects in late silent-era avant-garde films produced in France, such as René Clair's *Entr'acte* (*Intermission*, 1924); Georges Antheil, Dudley Murphy, and Fernand Léger's *Ballet mécanique* (*Mechanical Ballet*, 1924); and Marcel Duchamp's *Anémic Cinéma* (*Anemic Cinema*, 1926). As in Jacques-Bernard Brunius's breakdown of a 1920s cinematic avant-garde into four phases culminating in *Entr'acte* and Buñuel and Dalí's 1929 *Un chien andalou* (*An Andalusian Dog*), *La Zone* simultaneously draws on and sets itself apart from practices of the period that explored technical novelty as a self-sufficient end.[16] Programming strengthened this alignment during October 1928–January 1929 screenings at the Studio des Ursulines, where *La Zone* was screened with Man Ray's *L'Etoile de mer* (*The Starfish*, 1928) and Howard Hawks's *A Girl in Every Port* (1928).[17]

The central section of *La Zone* is cast as a day-in-the-life narrative whose seventeen intertitles create continuity with the morning-to-evening chronology Walter Ruttmann had deployed in 1927 in *Berlin: Sinfonie der Großstadt* (*Berlin: Symphony of a World Capital*). A third intertitle—"Strange population where all the races mix"—returns to a level of generalization associated with the travelogue by describing the inhabitants of *la Zone* as a population separate from that living within the city limits. The intertitle once again evokes the center–periphery motif that the animated sequence has cast with visual elegance. Yet it does so without detracting from practical relations that posit the *zoniers'* geographic isolation and containment as a precondition of the day-to-day existence of urban Paris. The words "population" and "race" aligned with assumptions concerning French colonial policies during the decade preceding the 1931 Colonial Exposition, which honored the centennial of French Algeria.[18] If these terms seem intolerable today, their inclusion in 1927 might also have been an indirect way for Lacombe to denounce the material conditions in which the *zoniers* lived and worked by equating them with those of local populations under French colonial rule in Africa, Asia, and the Caribbean. As a reviewer noted at the time of the film's release, "For us, the zone was as unknown as Papua. And like Papua, we know it today because of a documentary."[19]

Following the title sequence, long shots featuring areas of *la Zone* alternate with close-ups of children whose toothy smiles clash with their dirty faces. Three shots of a man playing a glass harmonica in the open air convey the makeshift nature of diversions among inhabitants of the area. Similar sequences appear in Jean Vigo's *À propos de Nice* (1930) and Eli Lotar's *Aubervilliers* (1946). Overhead landscape shots show groups of people appearing and disappearing as though to convey the priority of the area over those who live in it.

Still shots of a woman sewing while seated outdoors recall images of everyday life seen on postcards that French soldiers serving in overseas occupied territories sent home as souvenirs. In discussing turn-of-the-century postcards of Paris, Naomi Schor has contrasted a feminine/feminist model of everyday life emphasizing rituals within a domestic sphere presided over by women with masculinist encounters in public spaces and spheres usually dominated in modern bourgeois societies by men.[20] *La Zone* includes cinematic instances of both models. The day-in-the-life narrative follows a *zonier* family of ragpickers who begin their workday at 5:00 A.M. by scavenging for items set out for trash pickup on sidewalks. Lacombe's depiction of this recycling subculture makes *La Zone* a distant precursor of *Les Glâneurs et la glâneuse* (*The Gleaners and I*, 2000), in which director Agnès Varda depicts scavenging in urban and rural settings within an ethos of environmental awareness.[21]

As the shutters of commercial storefronts rise seemingly on their own at 7:00 A.M. (possibly a nod to a similar segment in Ruttmann's *Berlin*), four ragpickers pull a wooden wagon against the flow of commuters converging on a Métro station entrance for their morning destinations in central Paris. The sequence further blurs the social and spatial divide between center and periphery by illustrating the physical proximity of

Early morning ragpickers in *La Zone*.

salaried and unsalaried labor. The next six minutes of the film revert to instructional reportage by depicting how the ragpickers process what they scavenge. A sixty-second sequence dramatizes the labor necessary to create one-hundred-kilogram blocks of compressed materials to be sold for the manufacture of paper and cloth. Intertitles supply details of a sorting process that recycles as much of the scavenged materials as possible. This hands-on section of the film ends with intertitle 13, whose appearance coincides with a steep upward shot toward the top of a smokestack. (André Sauvage would soon include similarly angled shots of industrial smokestacks in *Études sur Paris,* as would Vigo in *À propos de Nice* and Carné in *Le Jour se lève.*)

Lacombe next enhances expository depictions of labor by featuring vignettes devoted to three local celebrities and a brief visit to a flea market. The first celebrity is introduced in intertitle 14 as *la mère aux chiens* (the Old Dog Lady), known for adopting stray dogs and at least a few cats. A boy sneaks into her front yard to drop off a stray dog. The woman and a friend feign anger by shaking an accusatory finger at the boy as he runs off. They quickly break into smiles, showing their approval of the boy's charity. The second celebrity portrayed is la Goulue (the Glutton), stage name of the noted cancan dancer Louise Weber (1866–1929), whom Henri de Toulouse-Lautrec had featured on posters advertising her appearance at the Moulin Rouge cabaret. In *La Zone,* Weber talks with a reporter, who photographs her standing at one end of the wooden trailer *(roulotte)* in which she lives.

Photographs of Weber as a young woman appear in close-ups as though from a personal collection. A posed portrait shows her around age twenty, wearing a fitted top with sculpted shoulders that resemble military epaulettes. A section of wording at the lower right seems to show the end of the word "Vivienne," presumably the address of the studio where the photograph was taken. A sheet music cover featuring Weber in an equally fashionable outfit carries the caption "La Goulue, danseuse et dompteuse" (The Glutton, dancer and animal tamer). The archival images contrast with the obese older woman, whose grotesque gyrations may—or may not—be self-parody. The third local celebrity is a gander named Coco, described by intertitle 16 as mascot of the Malakoff *zoniers.* The vignettes straddle the perceived foreignness of squalor and local color by exuding an aura of backyard exoticism.

La Zone's evocation of the material conditions of daily life continues in overhead tracking shots of the Saint-Ouen flea market, just beyond the city limits to the north of the Porte de Clignancourt. A sign seen before a wall proclaims *la Zone* as the place for real bargains on used items. Long shots show locals walking back and forth among open-air stalls. In a vignette

Working the streets and compressing the trash in *La Zone*.

filmed in a shot/reverse-shot format, a female hawker intimidates a man into buying an item he had picked up to inspect. A street sign designates the rue Biron, which still exists. Another sign marked "rue Bens" conveys the makeshift efforts at local mapping. The fact that the next shot depicts a small-scale reproduction of paintings by Peter Paul Rubens suggests a playful pairing of the homonyms "rue Bens" and "Rubens." Similar signs for the rue Pin (*rupin,* meaning both "pine street" and "wealthy"), rue Barbe (*rhubarbe,* "beard street" and "rhubarb"), and rue Scie (*Russie,* "saw street" and "Russia") elaborate a string of topographic puns. Whose puns are these? Are they integral to the film, or is this simply a bit of low-grade humor intended to remind spectators that the film they are watching is more than straightforward reportage?

Two additional vignettes complete Lacombe's depiction of a typical day in *la Zone.* The first begins with a medium shot of an outdoor stall where audio records are sold. A close-up shows the Pathé label of a spinning record superimposed on a street shot reflected in the mirror of an item (a dresser?) for sale. The record label reads "Pathé no. 3547" and "Au son de l'accordéon, Java chantée par Allibert" (To the sound of the accordion, Java sung by [Henri] Allibert), with a caption containing the name of composer Vincent Scotto in parentheses on the line below. Passersby stop to listen to the record while a *zonier* walks by eating French fries from a paper cone. (Is she an older relative of Céline's precocious snot-nosed girls? She reappears throughout the rest of the film, finally as a member of the family of streetwise ragpickers.) The sequence stands out because the superimposed image draws attention to passersby united in a moment of collective pleasure. Also notable is the setting of this moment amid the kinds of everyday objects André Breton used to seek out during weekly visits to the area with his friends Jean Dubuffet and Claude Lévi-Strauss.[22] Removed from their instrumental uses, these objects assume qualities of the marvelous and the uncanny. Two decades later, Georges Franju would achieve a similar effect in an opening sequence of *Le Sang des bêtes* (*Blood of the Beasts,* 1949), filmed at an improvised flea market on a barren landscape near the Porte de Vanves on the outskirts of Paris. Philippe Esnault notes the connection when he characterizes the opening sequence of Franju's film as a continuation of *La Zone* and, by extension, of a visual tradition akin to that of photographers Robert Doisneau and Isis Bidermanas.[23]

The second mininarrative involves a young acrobat whose street performance of handstands is interrupted when a teenage girl sprays him with water from a nearby hydrant. When the girl runs off, the acrobat chases her to a grassy slope near an industrial canal. After the two fall to the ground and catch their breath, the man picks up a newspaper page that had blown their way. A close-up of an advertisement for a country house touts an idealized country life *(vie à campagne)* bearing little resemblance to the industrial landscape that surrounds the couple. As a locomotive belching thick smoke passes behind them, the woman grabs the page and throws herself into the man's arms. Only at this point does it become clear that the two are lovers and that the dousing had been a prank staged for their pleasure. Cross-editing with close-ups of a grandly mustached guitarist confirms the moment as a romantic interlude.

The moment is light and sentimental, an instance of fictionalized documentary that blurs distinctions between fiction and nonfiction practices.[24] At the same time, the promise of upwardly mobile happiness implied by the lovers' embrace and the newspaper ad is belied by what *La Zone* shows of their daily lives. Much like the couple Josyane and Philippe at the end of Christiane Rochefort's 1961 novel *Les Petits Enfants du siècle* (translated in 1962 as *Children of Heaven*), the lovers in *La Zone* face uncertain prospects. For Rochefort's Josyane and Philippe, the relevant question is whether they will move to new housing projects in Sarcelles to the north or simply repeat the cycle of their parents' dashed hopes by remaining in the state-subsidized housing towers built after World War II in the very same areas where *La Zone* had been filmed more than three decades earlier.

A bargain marketplace, *la Zone* in *La Zone.*

The final two minutes of *La Zone* return to the family of ragpickers in a fast-forward to the kind of adult life awaiting the young lovers if they remain where they are. As a last intertitle announces the transition from 7:00 to 8:00 P.M., when *zoniers* prepare for bed, the family shares a simple dinner around a table outside their shack. Dinner in the open seems less a pleasure than a routine. The two women in the segment are those seen earlier in the scavenging and flea market sequences. A close-up on the cover of a book the younger woman is reading,

No-man's land in *Le Sang des bêtes* (1949).

Naufrage d'amour (Love's shipwreck), implies a momentary respite from a day-to-day existence seemingly without drama of any kind. The film ends with a shot of barren tree branches against a cloudless sky.

The Ambiguities of Pure Cinema

The innovative contribution of *La Zone* among cinematic practices of the 1920s is best understood in conjunction with films and writings of the decade by Louis Delluc, Germaine Dulac, Jean Epstein, and others associated with impressionist—sometimes known as pure—cinema. For Epstein (1897–1953), the uniqueness of cinema was its capacity to intensify the sensory experiences of the spectators within the movie theater and their relations with the outside world.[25] The insights of medium-specific approaches—those that explored what films could do that novels, poems, or stage plays could not do—depended in large part on the meaning attributed to the concepts of "relation" and "world." *Coeur fidèle* (*True Heart*, 1923) is Epstein's eighty-seven-minute melodrama about a barmaid, Marie (Gina Manès), pursued by two men. The first half of the film was shot on location in and around backstreets near the Marseille waterfront. Close-ups and extreme close-ups of faces, fists, and bottles convey a visual idea of enveloping excess that often trumps narrative. Nowhere in *Coeur fidèle*

is this visual idea more evident than during two carnival *(fête foraine)* sequences filmed on an aerial merry-go-round. In the first sequence, Marie
sits alongside Petit Paul (Edmond Van Daële), a petty crook who has ab-
ducted her to keep her away from Jean (Léon Mathot), an introspective
dockworker whom she loves. Marie's sorrowful facial expressions during
the sequence convey her dejection in a world that oppresses her. At the
film's conclusion, a visibly content Marie rides the merry-go-round alongside Jean in what would be a scene of emotional resolution and narrative
closure if not for the lack of affect on Jean's face.

Epstein first wrote of his desire to shoot a sequence of this kind in *Bonjour Cinéma* (1921): "I long for a drama about a merry-go-round or, more
modern yet, with airplanes. The carnival below and its surroundings would
be progressively confounded. Centrifuged in this way, adding vertigo and
rotation, the tragedy would increase its photogenic quality tenfold."[26]
The idea for the sequence purportedly grew out of conversations with the
painters Pierre Derval and Fernand Léger, possibly prompted by a passage
in which Léger had written of the *fête foraine,* whose brilliance might erupt
unexpectedly.[27] For the art critic Waldemar George, the sequence in *Coeur
fidèle* was an optical poem embodying the potential for cinema to become
an autonomous art with its own laws rather than merely a perfected magic
lantern or a succession of *tableaux vivants.*[28]

As much as the two merry-go-round sequences in *Coeur fidèle* exem-
plify the affective force of a visual and specifically cinematic idea, critical
reception of the film at the time of its release redirected this idea—often
equated with the elusive notion of *photogénie*—toward experiences in the
real world. For Léon Moussinac, once the visual shock of close-ups, rotating cameras, and accelerated montage dissipated, the film became an
effective means of conveying a milieu of crime and squalor.[29] Pierre Leprohon seemed to agree when he wrote that the poetry of port cities and of
misery seen in *Coeur fidèle* reappeared a decade later in poetic realist films
he referred to as "the French school of 1936."[30]

Despite the importance Epstein attributed to formal aspects of the
carnival sequences, spectators and critics responded to the evocation of
the docks, ships, and dives surrounding the old port, which, according to
Henri Langlois, made *Coeur fidèle* "*Le Quai des brumes* of the 1920s."[31] Later
in the same article, Langlois compared the effects of a tracking shot and
agile editing in Epstein's *Les Aventures de Robert Macaire* (*The Adventures of
Robert Macaire,* 1925) to a kind of poetry whose equivalents he found only
in the films of Sergei Eisenstein and Jean Vigo. Langlois's remarks failed to
align completely with those of Moussinac and Leprohon, whose responses
to *Coeur fidèle* straddled formal and realist concerns. At the same time, they
countered Epstein's sense of the priority of the visual idea over narrative
by asserting the impact of film's impressionist perspective on depictions of

Pensive faces in *Coeur fidèle* (1923).

experience that spectators identified with real people, real places, and real objects. Thirty years later, Langlois revived a realist view of *Coeur fidèle* at a remove with Epstein's dismissive characterization of his film as a stripped-down melodrama in which nothing of importance happened. It is unclear whether Epstein's assessment was mere understatement or the expression of his reluctance to recognize the film's referential dimensions.

Starting in the 1940s, the depiction of commonplace objects—fists, bottles, hats, and especially faces—erupting in close-ups also linked *Coeur fidèle* to a mode of experience that Henri Lefebvre and others theorized in conjunction with everyday life.[32] In 1942, the poet Francis Ponge published *Le Parti pris des choses (The Voice of Things)*, a set of thirty-two prose poems he described as *objeux* (word games) created by the interplay of objects such as bread, an orange, or a crate and the words used to describe them. Forty-one years later, Georges Perec wrote that big events made for newspaper headlines precisely because they were extraordinary, as though life revealed itself only through scandal, fissure, or danger. Railway trains likewise existed only when they derailed, airplanes only when they were hijacked. In response to conventional takes on these big events, Perec wrote that coal mines were not scandalous only when they exploded but all the time, because unsafe working conditions increased the likelihood of explosions: "'Social unrest' *[les malaises sociaux]* isn't 'a matter of concern' [only] when there's a strike, [it is] intolerable twenty-four hours a day, three hundred and sixty-five days a year."[33]

For Perec, the real scandal was the daily press's predilection for the extraordinary and its failure to raise questions concerning the banal, the quotidian, the obvious, the common, the ordinary, and the infra-ordinary. As a result, the daily press and mass media that structured relations to a material world on a daily basis rendered vast areas of experience more or less invisible: "What we need to question is bricks, concrete, glass, our table manners, our utensils, our tools, the way we spend our time, our rhythms. To question that which seems to have ceased forever to astonish us."[34]

Perec's corrective to this failure was to question the habitual, especially when this meant making an inventory of what was in one's pockets or handbag, questioning one's teaspoons, wondering what was under the wallpaper in one's room, or thinking about how many motions it takes to dial a phone number:

> It matters little to me that these questions should be fragmentary, barely indicative of a method, at most of a project. It matters a lot to me that they should seem trivial and futile: that's exactly what makes them just as essential, if not more so, as all the other questions by which we've tried in vain to lay hold on our truth.[35]

The mandate to mobilize the infra-ordinary toward a critique of what life had become on an everyday basis clarifies what was at stake in the visual idea that structures *Coeur fidèle.* Epstein's privileging of the close-up—in *Bonjour Cinéma,* he called it the heart of cinema—is crucial to the value he attributed to *photogénie.* In line with Perec's remarks about the infra-ordinary, the force of the visual perspective on people and objects in *Coeur fidèle* points toward the kind of critical engagement with the real world that documentaries starting with Vigo's *À propos de Nice* would soon make explicit. To assert similar claims for Lacombe's *La Zone* would involve accounting in greater detail for the Parisian film culture within which it appeared some two years before Vigo's film. By this I mean to propose that claims to associate *La Zone*'s depictions of daily life on the outskirts of Paris with denunciation and critique take on validity only in conjunction with documentaries by Kaufman, Sauvage, and Carné leading to Vigo's *À propos de Nice* and his statements in the cause of social cinema. Elements of social cinema in *La Zone* are best described as indirect and potential rather than explicit.

A recent counterreading of *La Zone* holds that a slippage from politics to affect precludes the denunciation of class relations that the film's subject and prologue lead the spectator to expect. The proponent of this counterreading, Dimitri Vezyroglou, argues that despite *La Zone*'s status as precursor of a French documentary school with social ambitions, the linearity of its account, the lack of camera movement, and the purely descriptive nature of its few intertitles result in an evocation of dirt and misery that reveals a willful refusal to politicize. Vezyroglou supports his case by citing at length from a 1928 review of Lacombe's film by Jean Marguet:

> The Zone! *What a strange country,* like the Cour des Miracles, *so distant in its particular and exceptional appearance from elegant Paris* and so close in its location to the very heart of the city. Today's *Cour des Miracles* surrounds the city with a belt of filth because it is the home of an irregular population of ragpickers who every morning drag toward picturesque sorting sites the waste that others throw out. This is the life that P.-J. Van Loo [the film's distributor] shows us in a *filmed journey* undertaken with extreme skill. Five A.M.: the pathetic harvest; 9 A.M., *the sorting, even more pathetic.* Bones, paper, rags, and scrap metal flattened by a power hammer to take up less space, everything goes on a conveyor belt toward their respective destinations before coming together again as an eternal return since it will still be of use. Kids in tattered clothing, ragpicker couples in love. La Goulue, grown old, in the flesh. . . . What a surprising procession, high value documentary with its *poetic or moral element!* A fine success awaits this film whose length displays *no excess whatsoever.*[36]

Central to Marguet's remarks is his reference to the Cour des Miracles (Courtyard of Miracles), a Right Bank neighborhood whose reputed lawlessness during the ancien régime played into what the historian Colin Jones describes as bourgeois anxieties about public order.[37] Jones adds that the idea of an urban counterculture of poverty and beggary appealed to the romantic side of Victor Hugo, who drew on accounts of several Cours des Miracles by the historian Henri Sauval (1623–1676) in his 1831 novel *Notre-Dame de Paris.* Marguet targeted a more recent myth when he referred to the presence of La Goulue in Lacombe's film. In both cases, the potential for critique and militancy associated with a longing for popular origins (Adrian Rifkin) and a drive to reclaim the city (David Harvey) is foreclosed through references that absorb this potential within conventional—read here as depoliticized—histories of Paris.

Vezyroglou's claim that *La Zone* skirted social conflicts is the obverse of Moussinac's and Leprohon's assertions that *Coeur fidèle* anticipated practices of poetic realism. Perhaps the issue here has to do less with individual films than with assumptions concerning avant-garde cinema whose political objectives broke with commercial and nonfiction practices of the period. In 1951, Jean-Clarence Lambert challenged readers to move beyond perceived notions of documentaries by looking to short subjects by Alberto Cavalcanti, Jean Painlevé, Buñuel, and Vigo that were to traditional (*vieux*, literally "old") documentaries what poems were to reportage.[38] Even if one concedes Vezyroglou's claim that *La Zone* fails to provide the explicit warning *(mise-en-garde)* against social and economic privilege evident in *À propos de Nice,* Lacombe's film is more than a picturesque description of a different world on the outskirts of Paris.

A decade after *La Zone,* the denunciation of substandard housing in eastern Belgium depicted in Henri Storck and Eli Lotar's *Les Maisons de la misère (The Houses of Misery,* 1937) echoed the militant tone of Storck's 1933 collaboration with Joris Ivens, *Misère au Borinage (Misery in Borinage).* Two decades later, Lotar's *Aubervilliers* made housing a significant motif in postwar French documentaries, extending at least through Édouard Luntz's 1959 short *Enfants des courants d'air (Children Adrift),* Jean Rouch and Edgar Morin's 1961 *Chronique d'un été (Chronicle of a Summer),* and Chris Marker's 1963 *Le Joli Mai (The Merry Month of May).* Yet unlike these later films that it seemed to anticipate if not inspire, *La Zone* stopped short of explicit denunciation.

Documentary short subjects about Paris abound during the period straddling late silent and early sound eras. Lucie Derain's *Harmonies de Paris* (1927) is a twenty-eight-minute tour through Paris organized in thirteen sections, each of which is announced by an intertitle. Its distinctive features include unusual shot compositions and occasional special effects that promote an impressionist take on the city's iconography. The twin towers, stained-glass windows, and flying buttresses of Notre-Dame de Paris—described by an intertitle as "the soul of our city"—are seen in frontal shots. Yet the film's opening sequence of airplanes recalls the opening of René Clair's *Paris qui dort* and includes street shots whose dizzying distortions simulating inebriation result from the use of a special lens.

Pierre Chenal's *Les Petits Métiers de Paris* (*Minor Professions of Paris,* 1932) was an early sound-era complement to *Les Halles centrales* in its depiction of people and places cast in terms of its Balzacian subtitle, *Scènes de la vie parisienne (Scenes of Parisian Life).* The voice-over commentary spoken (perhaps also written?) by Pierre Mac Orlan transformed the film's visual catalog of minor professions, including fortune-tellers, contortionists, fire-eaters, knife sharpeners, outdoor barbers, mattress stuffers, and photographers. These street people contributed not only to the shadow or casual economy of Paris but also to updated versions of local folklore attributed to *la Zone* and its inhabitants starting nearly a century earlier. Mac Orlan referred to horse-drawn carts driven through neighborhood streets as two-wheeled department stores *(grands magasins à deux roues)* and garbage cans as sources of ragpickers' fortunes. The films by Derain and Chenal provide evidence that Lacombe's *La Zone* did not appear in a vacuum.

Paris by Night: *Les Halles centrales* (Boris Kaufman, 1928)

Boris Kaufman (1906–1980) is perhaps best known as a brother of filmmaker Dziga Vertov (born Denys Kaufman, 1896–1954) and for the 1954 Oscar he won for his black-and-white cinematography for Elia Kazan's *On the Waterfront.* Twenty years earlier in France, Kaufman had worked as chief cameraman for the four films Jean Vigo completed from 1930 to 1934. (Credits for Vigo's *À propos de Nice* list Kaufman as codirector.) Kaufman's additional work as a cameraman in France before he settled in the United States in 1942 included *Champs-Élysées* (Jean Lods, 1928); *La Marche des machines* (*The March of the Machines,* Eugène Deslaw, 1928); *Aujourd'hui/24 heures en 30 minutes* (*Today/24 Hours in 30 Minutes,* Lods, 1928); *L'Equipe/L'Etoile du nord* (*The Team/Northern Star,* Lods, 1930); *La Vie d'un fleuve: La Seine* (*The Life of a River: The Seine,* Lods, 1931); *Travaux du tunnel sous l'Escaut* (*Tunnel Works beneath the Escaut,* Lods, with Henri Storck, 1933); and *Zouzou* (Marc Allégret, 1934).

Less well known is *Les Halles centrales,* an eight-minute film Kaufman reputedly shot in 1929 but never released commercially.[39] François Albéra notes that arguments locating the film within the cinematic avant-garde of the period list Kaufman as collaborating with Lods on *Aujourd'hui,* a 1928 film announced for screening at the Théâtre du Vieux-Colombier.[40] The visual style of *Les Halles centrales* was that of a cinematic poem. Whether intentional or not, the absence of title, intertitles, and other indicators of structure, framing, and closure resulted in a film whose cohesion was based in seriality. The effect tempers narrative functions with the kind of visual exploration seen in *Entr'acte* and *Coeur fidèle*. The primacy of the visual idea in *Les Halles centrales* is enhanced by nighttime location shooting in which the interplay of light and shadow approaches geometric abstraction on the order of Georges Antheil, Fernand Léger, and Dudley Murphy's 1924 short subject *Ballet mécanique*.

The film starts with short-duration shots of oncoming and passing automobiles, whose headlights illuminate horse-drawn wagons. The harsh sideways lighting in extreme close-ups of a horse and of wagon wheels is akin to the chiaroscuro effects the photojournalist Weegee obtained a decade later by using flashbulbs at New York City crime scenes.[41] Steam billowing from under the wheels of a locomotive engine is a visual echo of the water vapor surrounding the nostrils of a horse at work in the cold nighttime air. During the first minute, shots of horses and carts prevail over shots of cars and trains. A fuzzy close-up of the face of a railway engineer yields to another, equally fuzzy, of another engineer smoking a cigarette. Shots of a butcher hacking through a side of beef anticipate similar sequences in Franju's *Le Sang des bêtes*. Pans up to and back and forth across the Baltard arches and columns some four minutes into the film are the first visual evidence linking the moving images and the geographic place evoked by Kaufman's title. Brief shots of men unloading sides of beef inside the covered market yield to others of men unloading produce in baskets and of men drinking beer and wine after work. The lighting in both sets is frontal and harsh. A woman sporting a beret and a kiss curl shares the drinks and laughs. A sign on the wall behind her announces the house specialty: *pommes de terre gratinées* (cheese-covered roasted potatoes). Camera movement is minimal except for tracking shots along rows of produce. Many shots are close-ups, others extreme close-ups filmed at a slight tilt enhanced by lighting from the side and back that sculpts profiles into areas of shadow.

The French term *halle* refers to an area—often covered—used for the sale of fresh produce, meats, fish, dairy products, and grains. In Paris, the presence of a covered market in the Right Bank area of what is now the 1st arrondissement dates back to 1183. The twelve pavilions of iron, glass, and cast iron built between 1850 and 1870 from a design by Victor Baltard included spaces for the sale of leather, clothing, linens, and wines. In 1971, the pavilions were torn down and the market operations moved outside the city to Rungis. The end of *Les Halles centrales* features the pavilion setting during an extended interior shot directed out toward

Worker at Les Halles in *Les Halles centrales* (1928).

a daytime street. Shrubs or bushes on the lower left and a row of windows barely visible along the upper right convey a visual heaviness alleviated by daytime light streaming through a tall arch near the top of the frame. The framing and lighting of the shot bear an uncanny resemblance to the sequence midway through Rouch and Morin's *Chronique d'un été* during which Marceline Loridan is shown walking through a Baltard pavilion. As Loridan enters from the daytime street, the camera tracks away from her while the volume of her voice on the sound track remains constant. The effect of Loridan increasingly dwarfed within the pavilion's massive arch conveys a sense of overwhelming confinement. It heightens her voice-over account of deportation to and return from a concentration camp, where she briefly saw her father before he died there. And while I have no hard evidence to support the thought, the cameramen who shot *Chronique*—including Raoul Coutard and Michel Brault—might have had Kaufman's film in mind when they framed the shot of Loridan.

The failure of the interior shot at the end of *Les Halles centrales* to provide narrative closure can be explained by uncertainty surrounding the status of the film, which might never have been completed. As with *La Zone, Les Halles centrales* is a nonfiction film that depicts actions and objects in terms of the kinds of visual details that Lefebvre, Perec, and others later associated with the everyday and the infra-ordinary. But exactly what kind of film is *Les Halles centrales*? As in the sequences in *La Zone* devoted to

Les Halles on film, 1927 and 1961.

the processing of materials collected by ragpickers, *Les Halles centrales* contains sequences of instruction and reportage. But where Lacombe had set such sequences within accounts of daily life, including vignettes of local celebrities and young lovers, the distinctive feature of Kaufman's film is its impressionist evocation of nighttime activities among workers at the central markets, an evocation that—much like Epstein's visual idea—tempers reportage with poetry. At the same time, the images of men at work in Kaufman's film set it alongside populist and proletarian movements, one of whose literary models, Eugène Dabit's 1929 novel *L'Hôtel du Nord,* was a source for Céline's *Voyage.* The mix of poetry and realism in *Les Halles centrales* is thus a precedent for Kaufman's subsequent collaboration with Vigo in *À propos de Nice* and other films more openly identified with social cinema and a documented pointed of view. As in Lacombe's *La Zone,* elements of social assessment *(constat social)* in *Les Halles centrales* remained incipient rather than developed.[42]

Visualizing Paris Anew

Moving In, Moving Out: André Sauvage and *Études sur Paris* (1928)

The toponymic titles Georges Lacombe and Boris Kaufman chose for their respective treatments of Paris assert the priority of the place over population. They also promote associations with city symphony films of the period, including Walter Ruttmann's *Berlin: Sinfonie der Großstadt* and Dziga Vertov's *Chelovek s kino-apparatom (Man with a Movie Camera)*. These associations persist despite the fact that *La Zone* and *Les Halles centrales* invoked specific sites within and just outside Paris rather than the city as a whole. *La Zone* also followed the city symphony model through a narrative structure organized loosely as a day in the life of a ragpicker family. *Les Halles centrales* deployed editing techniques resembling those used by Vertov to capture the rhythm of nighttime activities at the produce market in central Paris.

Both films are listed in a 2004 article surveying seventy-three nonfiction films shot on location in Paris from 1919 through 1929. The article's author, Myriam Juan, argues that these silent-era treatments of Paris fashioned a symbolic geography of the city.[1] The films Juan surveys, including *Paris-Express* (Marcel Duhamel and Pierre Prévert, 1928) and Lucie Derain's *Harmonies de Paris* (1927), feature commercial and residential neighborhoods as well as postcard views of the Champs-Élysées, the Place de la Concorde, and the Eiffel Tower.[2] Juan's corpus also includes the twenty-one titles of the Films de l'Encyclopédie Gaumont that were produced for educational use. The priority of local geography in these street films that purportedly record Paris "in the raw" *(sans artifice)* is visible in a motif of movement through urban spaces for which film constitutes an especially apt medium.

The symbolic geography that Juan identifies in nonfiction films of Paris in the 1920s also draws on Atget's turn-of-the-century photographs of central Paris. Juan further illustrates the priority of place over population when she singles out *La Zone* (1928) as the only film in her corpus whose primary objective is to locate the "black belt" of *la Zone* as precisely as possible within an overview of Parisian space. In this instance, the designation expresses an unintentional variant of leftist voting in the same area of Paris that the historian Tyler Stovall later referred to as the "red belt." Where Juan's black connotes the hazardous health conditions of areas known as *îlots insalubres*, Stovall's red implies allegiance to the French Communist and Socialist Parties. Stovall resumes the point when he writes that the political history of the Paris suburbs seems to rest on a paradox that suburbanization had created the red belt encircling the city that no longer had room for its working-class inhabitants.[3]

Juan's article also raises questions concerning relations between the part and the whole that the films in her corpus illustrate through topographic detail. By far the fullest treatment of these relations appears in *Études sur Paris*, a set of five nonfiction short subjects filmed by André Sauvage in 1928 under the titles of *Paris-Port (Paris Port)*, *Nord-Sud (North-South)*, *Petite Ceinture (Little Beltline Railway)*, *Les Îles de Paris (The Islands of Paris)*, and *De la Tour Saint-Jacques à la Montagne Sainte-Geneviève (From the Saint Jacques Tower to the Montagne Sainte-Geneviève)*. The five shorts were released individually in Paris between January and April 19, 1929, at Parisian venues including the Caméo (on the Boulevard des Italiens), the Studio Diamant (on the Place Saint-Augustin), and the Vieux-Colombier (in the Saint-Germain des Prés neighborhood), where they were programmed as openers for feature-length fiction films.[4] A year later, Hans Richter selected *Paris-Port* for screening at the *Film und Foto* exhibition organized by the Deutscher Werkbund in Stuttgart. After all five fragments—as Sauvage called them—were released, they were screened either individually or as a single feature-length film. (Running times listed for the long version vary from eighty to ninety-five minutes. The 2012 Carlotta Films DVD is eighty minutes long.)

The five short studies that make up *Études* trace an itinerary of some thirty-five kilometers (more than twenty-one miles) across and surrounding the city. *Paris-Port* starts along inland waterways north of Paris, moving south through the Bassin de la Villette and the Canal Saint-Martin as far as the Seine before turning west toward the Pont de l'Alma. Images of daily life on and alongside the waterways anticipate sequences in later documentaries such as Jean Lods's *La Vie d'un fleuve: La Seine (The Life of a River: The Seine*, 1931) and Joris Ivens's *La Seine a rencontré Paris (The Seine Met Paris*, 1957). Sequences featuring lock systems on the Canal Saint-Martin likewise anticipate moments in narrative films of the 1930s such as Jean Vigo's *L'Atalante* and Marcel Carné's *Hôtel du Nord*. Subsequent sections that jump across nonadjacent neighborhoods drop geographic continuity in favor of thematic and narrative concerns. The *Petite Cein-*

ture short on the railway that circles the city just inside its limits includes segments in and around the fortifications seen a year earlier in *La Zone* as well as others of the Parc Montsouris and the Cité Universitaire in the 14th arrondissement, the Tourelles swimming pool in the 19th arrondissement, and the suburban commune of Le Pré-Saint-Gervais. The trajectory traced in the fifth and final section stays close to central Paris, moving from Right Bank to Left Bank locations before ending with a five-minute sequence in the Jardin du Luxembourg (Luxembourg Gardens).

If the aggregate itineraries traced in the five studies were placed end to end, they would extend some seventy kilometers (about forty-three miles) in the shape of ever-tightening circles. Transposed onto a map of the city, the initial movement south from the northeast might be likened to the weighted plumb line used by artists, architects, and engineers to trace large circles on horizontal surfaces. Variations among trajectories in the short studies mark minor differences recast by the longer version as a grand cinegraphic tour of the city as a whole.[5] These differences persist within the eighty-minute version as traces of productive tensions between the part and the whole. One can best understand these tensions by looking closely at the individual studies before recasting them as segments within a larger whole.

Paris-Port, the first of the short studies, opens with a five-and-a-half-minute series of tracking shots and pans alternating between port and starboard aboard a barge. Barges seen in passing carry place-names such as the Congo and Himalaya. Others seen later along the Canal Saint-Martin are named in honor of the writer Victor Hugo and the painter Jean Dominique Auguste Ingres. Waterway shots edited at intervals between five and seven seconds each convey sensations of continuous movement on canals and along their banks, as when the camera tracks or pans from left to right while a barge, rowboat, or sailboat is seen going in the opposite direction. Shots taken near the surface of the water and the use of soft dissolves enhance effects of visual fluidity. Intertitles are infrequent throughout the five short *études,* with a total of only fifty-two over the eighty-minute duration. Of these, forty-seven are descriptive, stating the titles of individual segments, naming geographic areas, or noting trajectories. The remaining five are assertions, two of which are cast as direct addresses in the first person plural.

Minor moments of daily life in rural settings recorded at the start of *Paris-Port* include shots of recreational fishermen and of a man driving a horse-drawn cart along a canal-side path. However, additional shots of industrial cranes, of smokestacks, and of a seaplane point to a technological and industrial modernity associated with urban expansion toward rural and semirural areas surrounding Paris. Dark smoke billowing upward into the sky appears at first to come from a factory chimney until a downward pan discloses a tugboat chimney. An overhead shot of laundry flapping on the open deck of a barge recalls Vigo's depiction of daily life on a canal barge in *L'Atalante* (1934). Is there evidence that Vigo knew Sauvage's film? If so, when and where did he see it?

Shots of industrial cranes, of smoke from a barge chimney set against distant trees in front of a storage tank, and of a train crossing an arched bridge over the water record the approach southward toward urban spaces. The framing and mise-en-scène of many shots temper their referential value with effects that recall openly photogenic sequences in Jean Epstein's *Coeur fidèle* (1923). An illustration of this mix of formal and referential concerns occurs in a striking shot (time stamp 3:10) of a tall brick building featuring a larger-than-life graphic advertisement for Cadum soap on its windowless side wall. This gigantic commercial image—the smiling face of a baby known as Bébé (Baby) Cadum—breaks with the iconography of rural and semirural spaces. The effect recalls the mix of the old and the new that surrealist leader André Breton used to write *Nadja* (1928) as a chronicle of urban encounters. The numerous illustrations in *Nadja* include a reproduction of Jacques-André Boiffard's photograph of an illuminated billboard advertising Mazda brand lightbulbs. Perhaps Sauvage's Bébé Cadum shot was a cinematic reply to Breton's Mazda billboard.

Barge life in *Études sur Paris* (1929).

Attention to editing and average shot length reveals the visual complexity in the opening segments of *Paris-Port.* One segment edited in slow
tracking shots and in pans that dwarf workers among steam shovels and
warehouses is broken by rapid shots of a speedboat going upstream and of
three women walking along a waterside path. All three wear dark outfits
and fashionable cloche caps. A shot of two horses pulling a barge on a long
rope records the presence of humans and animals in settings increasingly
subjected to mechanized labor. This presence stands out in time-lapse
shots of pedestrians zipping across a canal lock's footbridge over a barge,
of a woman seen walking (too) quickly on a barge deck, and of two barges
moving jerkily through locks. All three instances break with verisimilitude
as a result of acceleration and time-delay effects *(trucage)* that manipulate
time and space. Less comic than disorienting, the effects attest to documentary practices beyond pure reportage.

Segments along the Bassin de la Villette and the Canal Saint-Martin
feature locales in which human and spatial density heightens the complexity of information within the visual frame. A half-minute segment
(9:32–10:04) shows women performing the slow manual labor of unskilled
workers scavenging for materials to be recycled for a profit. In a second
plane behind the women, a man monitors a conveyor belt unloading crates
from a barge. At the dockside end of the belt, two or three men transfer
the crates onto a horse-drawn cart. The frame grab only begins to capture

Larger-than-life
advertisement
*(Études sur
Paris).*

Stop action on the Canal de l'Ourcq *(Études sur Paris)*.

the interactions of visual planes, activities, and speeds, all of which are heightened by the immobile urban architecture in a distant rear plane. Diagonal lines from the left margin of the frame suggest a minor example of gender-specific labor roles in which the movement downward toward the women in a frontal plane contrasts with the movement upward from barge to truck among men seen in a middle plane.

A follow-up segment (10:37–11:01) beneath a lifted canal bridge shows one barge moving downstream from left to right along a frontal plane while another—the *Victor Hugo*—crosses from right to left behind it. A man standing on deck turns his head from right to left and left to right. Perhaps he is checking to make sure that the barge does not bump into the sides of the narrow passage. On the bank behind the canal, a pedestrian walks back and forth as he waits for the bridge to lower. Two lap dissolves heighten a sense of simultaneous movement of barges and people adjacent to the ever-present surface of the flowing water of the canal.

These urban canal segments contrast with others featuring inactivity and stasis. A man hunched over in broad daylight appears oblivious to a horse-drawn milk wagon that crosses behind him. Is he a drunkard *(ivrogne)* or perhaps a bum *(clochard)*? Another man is shown drinking

Manual labor in *Études sur Paris*.

from a wine bottle and eating something wrapped in newspaper. He barely moves aside as workers haul a rope pulling a barge around him. The comic staging of the episode and the fact that no one in the frame looks into the camera reassert the ability of film to capture the ephemera and details of human experience that Georges Perec would later theorize as the infra-ordinary. They also suggest Sauvage's intention to depict individuals isolated within the human and objective environment surrounding them. The "faces in a crowd" phenomenon is also present in sequences of *La Zone* during which the ragpickers walk against the flow of morning commuters making their way to the Métro station. Vigo would reprise it in *À propos de Nice* (1930) in the incongruous presence of the beggar and the Gypsy woman, whose shabby clothing—the beggar's cloth cap and the woman's head scarf—stands out against the fancier garb of the affluent boardwalk crowd.

The most stunning visual effects in *Paris-Port* occur during a five-minute segment marked by an opening intertitle—"Nous allons passer sous la colonne de la Bastille" (We are going to pass beneath the column of the [Place de la] Bastille)—that is one of only two in the entire film expressed as a direct address to the spectator. A shot forward along the bow of a tugboat shows a male worker manipulating heavy chains that pull

Spirit of Liberty in *Études sur Paris.*

the boat through the tunnel. A countershot toward the aft of the tugboat in the tunnel outlines workers in silhouette against the daylight behind them. Visual alternation of various sorts over the next minute begins with a long shot of a sculpted human figure atop the round cap of what appears to be a column. The winged figure, known as the Génie de la Liberté (Spirit of Liberty), sits atop the Colonne de Juillet (July Column), completed in 1840 to commemorate Louis Philippe's July 1830 ascension to the monarchy. (Shots of the Spirit of Liberty appear briefly in Carné's *Nogent, Eldorado du dimanche* [*Sunday's Eldorado*, 1929], Cédric Klapisch's *Chacun cherche son chat* [*When the Cat's Away*, 1996], and Hou Hsiao-Hsien's *Le Voyage du ballon rouge* [*Flight of the Red Balloon*, 2007].)

A slow pan to the left animates the figure that seems to move across the screen against a blank sky above the covered section of the Canal Saint-Martin directly below. Shooting the gilded figure in black and white adds to the visual contrast while preparing for the images in the tunnel to follow that exploit a striking depiction of tugboat and barge smoke swirling along the tunnel's roof. The smoke is illuminated by diffused light streaming down through skylights—some opaque, some grated—located along boulevards above. The effect of the swirling smoke below the skylights simulates the space of a cathedral or a prison. Equally striking effects occur in long shots of light from above on the surface of the water. These are followed by a close-up of the uneven surface of the water churned by the passage of the tugboat and barges. The latter distorts the circular shape of the skylights above, creating a visual moment one might imagine recycled from Abel Gance's *La Folie du docteur Tube* (1915) or Epstein's *Coeur fidèle.* An extreme long pan upward from the southern opening of the tunnel shows the July Column in the distance before the barge turns westward onto the Seine. The sequence closes with shots from under the river's bridges and along its banks. Long shots of movement along the Seine disclose vignettes of a man receiving a shave at the foot of a stone staircase, a club of fishermen, and a painter wearing a beret. The last four minutes of *Paris-Port* include an upwardly tilted medium shot of the lower leg and flexed foot of a sculpted figure sticking out from below the stone arch of a bridge. The incongruous detail is a minor distraction, as though Sauvage wanted to break momentarily from the arrival in central Paris for which the entire sequence has been preparing.

The second fragment of *Études sur Paris, Nord-Sud,* takes its name from the company that financed Métro line A, the 1910 completion of which linked a northern terminus at the Porte de la Chapelle to another at Issy-les-Moulineaux to the south. Known today as line 12, some of its current stations retain the original decor of white tiles and signs over the tracks at either end marking directions toward Montmartre or Montparnasse.[6] The

Underground passage along the Canal Saint-Martin (*Études sur Paris*).

engineer Jean-Baptiste Berlier had first thought about building a new line between Montmartre and Montparnasse via the Gare Saint-Lazare and the Gare d'Orsay by constructing parallel tunnels in the shape of metal hoops, along the lines of the London Underground's "tubes." *Nord-Sud* was also the name of a short-lived but influential literary journal founded in 1917 by Pierre Reverdy along with fellow poets Max Jacob, Vicente Huidobro, and Guillaume Apollinaire. In the 1924 *Manifesto of Surrealism,* André Breton cites Reverdy's notion that the more distant the semantic differences between two realities, the greater the emotional power and poetic force created from the juxtaposition of those realities.[7]

Paris-Port follows a continuous itinerary southward along inland waterways leading to the Seine. In *Nord-Sud,* jumps from one urban neighborhood to another extend the directional associations generated by the title toward images of daily life in areas on either side of the Métro line that bisects the city along a north–south axis. Because the new line illustrates the impact of electrified transportation technologies on the rhythms of daily life in the city, *Nord-Sud* comes closest among the five fragments to evoking the aesthetics of speed and acceleration that literary publications such as Reverdy's *Nord-Sud* explored through poetry. Technology as a visual motif appears in opening shots of the Eiffel Tower that culminate in a 360-degree pan whose nearly vertical tilt upward from ground level adopts the same perspective as that in a 1926 painting by Sonia Delaunay.[8] Shots that render the tower's gridwork as geometric shapes likewise recall photographs in Germaine Krull's 1928 collection *Métal* as well as sequences filmed on the Eiffel Tower in René Clair's *Paris qui dort* (1923).

Follow-up shots of commuters entering the Nord-Sud station at the Porte de Versailles station summon up images of the commuters seen at the beginning of *La Zone* as they filed down through a street-level Métro entrance. A sequence filmed in the Montparnasse neighborhood a bit north along the new Métro line displays the vitality of mass culture affected by technologies of visual and audio recording. A poster outside a movie theater lists showtimes for *Les Mystères de Paris (The Mysteries of Paris),* Charles Burguet's 1922 adaptation of Eugène Sue's 1842–43 serialized novel. Posters for *Les Frères Karamazov (The Brothers Karamazov,* Carl Froelich and Dimitri Buchowetzki, 1921) and a U.S. Western starring Buck Jones display the range of available cinematic product. Audio reproduction receives creative treatment in a shot showing a woman seated at a Pathé song palace and another of a spinning disk superimposed onto the head of a man. Time-lapse footage in the former makes pedestrians flash by the song palace entrance between the woman and the camera. Six years later in *L'Atalante,* Vigo and Kaufman would dramatize the isolation of Juliette (Dita Parlo) in the city by placing her in a similar mechanized setting.

Listening in *(Études sur Paris)*.

The framing and canting of overhead shots of vehicles and pedestrians on cobblestone streets border on compositional exercises. A poster ad for Zig-Zag brand cigarette papers on a Morris column is the basis of a visual pun. Do the angles formed by the tilted column and its shadow on the sidewalk form a zig or a zag? The uncanny effect of a dress-form mannequin rotating in a storefront window is enhanced by a hairdo featuring a lightning-traced streak of blonde curls similar to those Elsa Lanchester would sport in *The Bride of Frankenstein* (James Whale, 1935). A mile or so to the north in Saint-Germain des Prés, two men gaze at a collage through an art gallery window. Did they just happen to be standing apart, or is the shot staged to allow a clear view of the artwork on display inside?

On the Right Bank across the Seine, overhead views from atop the Garnier Opera yield to street-level tracking shots along the Grand Boulevards where two well-dressed men sitting at an open terrace at the Café de la Paix smile directly into the camera. Toward Montmartre, a playful trick effect of cars moving backward reminds spectators that the film they are watching is something more than reportage. A second oversize ad for Cadum soap shares space on a building wall with others for Cinzano vermouth and Sigrand & Company clothiers. A shot of the Moulin Rouge cabaret at the

Zig-Zag and tilted shot (*Études sur Paris*).

Window shopping (*Études sur Paris*).

Place Clichy centers on its trademark windmill while the cabaret's marquee touts performances by the realist chanteuse Mistinguett. These sequences feature creative framing and brief vignettes whose editing rhythm is often faster than that in *Paris-Port*. The loss of geographic continuity in *Nord-Sud* is supplemented with minor jolts of unexpected images—the rotating mannequin, the oversize Cadum soap ad—amid more conventional treatments of the ephemera of the urban infra-ordinary.

Nord-Sud illustrates that the visual style first seen in *Paris-Port* is neither casual nor isolated. Instead, it results from Sauvage's experience as a writer and painter aware of modernist poetry, painting, and photography of the period. This visual style, which ranges from mise-en-scène to montage and content, is especially evident during a sequence in Montmartre (18th arrondissement) that starts with a shot of an elderly woman seen from behind arranging produce on an open cart at an outdoor market. The woman moves slowly and with deliberation, oblivious to the traffic swarming on either side of her. The sequence is filmed on the rue Lepic, whose onetime inhabitants included Vincent and Théo van Gogh (at no. 54) and Louis-Ferdinand Céline (at no. 98). (The Café des 2 Moulins, at no. 15, serves as a location setting for Jean-Pierre Jeunet's 2001 *Le Fabuleux Destin d'Amélie Poulian [Amélie]*.) Older buildings on both sides of a deserted street in a follow-up sequence evoke Montmartre's earlier place among the towns *(communes)* and villages *(faubourgs)* slowly absorbed by urban expansion. *Nord-Sud* records traces of these exurban areas in outlying areas of the city integrated into the greater whole of Paris, much as the five short subjects that make up *Études* are integrated into a feature-length whole.

Midway through Céline's *Voyage au bout de la nuit*, the protagonist, Ferdinand Bardamu, walks across central Paris from the Latin Quarter to his apartment in Rancy, just north of the city. On the rue Lepic just off the Place Blanche, he sees a crowd tormenting an enormous pig that a local butcher has tied up in front of his shop: "Everyone was laughing. The butcher back in his shop was exchanging signs and jokes with his customers and gesticulating with a big knife."[9] The moment stages an urban variant of ritualized violence—everyone knows that the pig will soon be slaughtered—among area residents and passersby, many of whom might have experienced similar moments firsthand in rural childhoods. Somewhat to the east of Métro line A, Bardamu's trek bisects a Paris whose neighborhoods retain their local identities as parts within a greater urban whole. Sixty years after *Nord-Sud*, François Maspero and Anaïk Frantz published a written and photographic account of daily life along the Réseau Express Régional (RER; Regional Express Network) line B, whose trajectory through Paris runs almost directly north–south from the Gare du Nord to the Cité Universitaire.[10] The minor drama Bardamu witnesses on the rue Lepic is another antecedent of the ephemeral actions and moments Perec and Virilio would theorize as the infra-ordinary, as well as of those that *Nord-Sud* displays through a visual style based in effects of temporal and spatial manipulation more readily associated with avant-garde films of the 1920s such as Epstein's *Coeur fidèle* and Clair's *Entr'acte*.

Nord-Sud ends with upward pans of the Sacré-Coeur Basilica, time-lapse shots and dissolves of horse-drawn carts on wide cobblestone streets, and shots of areas near the Thiers fortifications seen two years earlier in *La Zone*. Longer average shot lengths depart from the editing pace of previous sequences filmed closer to central Paris. This pace persists in the fifteen-minute *Îles de Paris* fragment filmed mainly along riverside *quais* (docks) on and surrounding the Île Saint-Louis and the Île de la Cité. The segment abounds in long shots and slow pans that combine vertical and horizontal movements. A man and a woman are seen painting behind easels set up facing each other beneath the arches of a bridge. Do they know each other, or is the tableau set up for the film? A couple picnicking on the river bank is filmed from directly overhead. A dog sits immobile and sphinxlike on a windowsill. These and other moments are staged with visual economy, as when a well-dressed man and woman look at each other from opposite staircases, separated by the flooding waters from the Seine. Are they lovers who have come to meet each other? The woman in the foreground has her back to the camera. The posture of the man on the far staircase and a follow-up shot of him trudging up toward the street suggest his disappointment. The overhead angle of the latter accentuates the angles

Getting together
(*Études sur Paris*).

formed by cut rocks set along one side of the staircase. The effect isolates the man, whose form in black stands out just to the right of center.

A presumably happier outcome occurs minutes later on the Îles des Cygnes—an island south of the Eiffel Tower—in a series of close-ups of a man and a woman whose leg and foot movements from the knees down suggest an embrace if not also a kiss. A follow-up shot shows the couple looking at each other as they walk away from the camera. The man's right arm

Getting together (*Études sur Paris*).

is around the woman's waist. A concluding sequence alternates between postcard views of the Notre-Dame de Paris cathedral taken from the Left Bank across the Seine and overhead shots whose perspective from atop the cathedral's twin steeples simulates what the gargoyle sculptures might be seeing as they look outward across the city below. The bird's-eye panorama these overhead shots afford is the closest Sauvage and cameramen Jean Le Miéville and Georges Sprecht come to an aerial take on the city.

The fourth fragment short, *Petite Ceinture*, takes its title from the thirty-two-kilometer-long railway that circles Paris just within the city limits. Segments filmed at the Parc Montsouris and the Cité Universitaire near the railway's tracks on the Left Bank are followed by others filmed on the Right Bank across the Seine. The latter abound with images of locomotives chugging through switching yards, industrial areas with factory chimneys churning smoke, and street traffic in gritty outlying districts. These segments are filmed mainly as extreme long shots, with movement often visible in more than one plane. Occasional medium close-ups vary in visual scope. Minimal camera movement once again enhances framing and mise-en-scène, much on the order of photographic stills. Pans and tracking shots at a Right Bank amusement park adopt the point of view of a passenger on a roller coaster and a water slide. The visual treatment of a merry-go-round is lively, even if it fails to rival its equivalent in Epstein's *Coeur fidèle.* A long sequence in the Bois de Boulogne toward the western edge of the Right Bank includes time-lapse shots of cars and bicyclists on wide paved *allées* (paths) as well as a parallel-edited vignette of a carriage driver with a prominent handlebar mustache making his way toward the Arc de Triomphe. The fourth fragment ends with an intertitle, "Nous voici revenus vers le Sud, après un tour de 35 kilomètres" (Here we are, back in the southern part of the city after a 35-kilometer spin).

The southward trajectory of the fifth and last fragment, *De la Tour Saint-Jacques à la Montagne Sainte-Geneviève,* duplicates that of *Paris-Port.* But it does so on a reduced geographic scale in the 1st, 5th, and 6th arrondissements on either side of the Seine in central Paris. A shot tilted upward through a protective window from within the tower contrasts with panoramic pans across the city from atop the tower. Extended pans range from steep downward shots of the nearby Place du Châtelet and the Sainte-Chapelle on the Île de la Cité to more horizontal shots of the Left Bank dominated by the eighty-three-meter-tall Panthéon. Anemometers and related meteorological equipment filmed in close-up stand out alongside flamboyant Gothic architecture and sculptures on upper portions of the fifty-two-meter-tall tower. (The latter is all that remains of the Church of Saint-Jacques de la Boucherie, completed in 1523 and destroyed following the French Revolution.) A closing iris shot of a circular "window"

The rue du Chat-qui-pêche *(Études sur Paris)*.

within the square frame finishing in complete darkness is the first of seven wipes or fades to follow.

Building on sequences in *Nord-Sud* taken from below and atop Notre-Dame, Sauvage's visual idea in this final fragment alternates between high and low perspectives as complements to conventional alternations between long shots and close-ups. In line with the fragment's title, four long-shot panoramas sutured by lap dissolves form a 360-degree turn around the Tour Saint-Jacques. The first starts as an overhead shot tilted downward almost vertically to street level before turning toward the rue de Rivoli directly to the west and then left toward the Seine, with a second lurch upward. A slow 90-degree sweep left shows the Eiffel Tower far to the west before cutting to areas directly south dominated by Notre-Dame on the Île de la Cité and the dome of the Panthéon in the Left Bank's Latin Quarter. Street-level shots near the Place du Châtelet afford a brief glimpse of a group of horse-mounted Garde Républicaine soldiers, whose shiny helmets would be seen some thirty years later reflected in mirrors at a hat shop in Agnès Varda's *Cléo de 5 à 7* (*Cleo from 5 to 7*, 1962).

A brief street scene segment depicts areas of the rue Saint-Séverin and rue de la Huchette just to the east of the Boulevard Saint-Michel. Time-lapse shots down the rue du Chat-qui-pêche show pedestrians walking along the Quai Saint-Michel. They are taken from the rue de la Huchette near a police station that would be photographed in 1930 by the Hungarian-born Brassaï (born Gyula Halász). Sauvage's treatment of the Panthéon farther to the south includes time-lapse shots and an alterna-

Three takes on the Panthéon (*Études sur Paris*).

tion of interior and external shots of visitors dwarfed by epic Corinthian columns and the rotunda of this eighteenth-century church turned secular mausoleum of France's great men.

The mise-en-scène of a long shot taken from the rue Soufflot makes it appear as if a streetlamp were bisecting the building straight down the middle. Others show monuments honoring the revolutionary figures

Mirabeau and Georges Danton as well as members of the 1792–95 National Convention. The long duration of these still shots *(plans fixes)* conveys an ironic take toward heroic figures akin to that Georges Franju would adopt toward France's national war museum in his 1952 documentary *Hôtel des Invalides*. A pan from atop the Panthéon down the rue Soufflot toward the Jardin du Luxembourg ends with an iris-out before cutting to a frontal shot of the building on which Sauvage superimposes an extreme close-up of a long, curly beard being stroked by its owner, presumably a street person. The playful deflation of the seriousness typically associated with the Panthéon as a site honoring revolutionary and republican heroes anticipates a similar strategy in Franju's *Hôtel des Invalides* and Alain Resnais's 1956 short subject on the French national library, *Toute la mémoire du monde (All the World's Memory)*.

At first glance, Sauvage's treatment of the Jardin du Luxembourg during the final five minutes of the fragment seems seldom to venture beyond animated—that is, moving—versions of postcard tableaux. A woman pushes a baby stroller; another sits reading a book on a wrought-iron chair. Children riding in a cart pass in front of a palm tree set into a giant wooden box near the garden's north end. A segment filmed near the Fontaine Médicis (Medici Fountain) features statues of literary figures George Sand, Paul Verlaine, and Charles-Augustin Sainte-Beuve. A pan upward toward the rue Soufflot and the Panthéon from a pool where children launch toy sailboats with long wooden sticks is a visual reply to an earlier shot from atop the Panthéon. Surprisingly, the final minutes of the film provide neither flourish nor narrative closure. At the most, what unites the visual sobriety of the final fragment are five shots of a curly-haired toddler playing with a toy truck amid pedestrian traffic on one of the park's dirt paths.

In Thrall to the Silent Image

A year after the release of *Études sur Paris,* Sauvage wrote a series of articles for the Parisian weekly *L'Ami du peuple* in which he set forth his views on documentary and the advent of new sound technologies. The weekly, founded in 1928 by the perfume manufacturer François Coty, took its name from the 1789–92 weekly edited by the revolutionary figure Jean-Paul Marat. Despite this nominal source, the weekly's political orientation was decidedly reactionary. In 1933, Coty founded the fascist league known as Solidarité Française. Isabelle Marinone characterizes the ideological orientation of *L'Ami du peuple* as fascistic and anti-Semitic, but she adds that Sauvage was likely unaware of this ideological orientation.[11]

A major motif in Sauvage's 1930 articles in *L'Ami du peuple* addresses what the loss of creative control among individual filmmakers implied concerning the fate of documentary practices. For Sauvage, the loss had already been evident in large-budget silent films such as Robert Flaherty's *Moana* (1926), Ernest Schoedsack and Merian Cooper's *Chang* (1927), and Martin and Osa Johnson's *Simba, King of the Jungle* (1923), in which conventions of the travelogue were overlaid with narrative elements of romance and adventure.[12] (Schoedsack and Cooper soon exploited a similar formula while collaborating on *King Kong,* 1933.) The transition to sound thus matched the financial clout of big-studio budgets with the interests of movie theater owners ready to capitalize on profits generated by sound recording technologies. In sum, the advent of these technologies coincided with the ongoing transformation of cinema into a financial transaction *(opération)* in which filmmakers like Sauvage and documentaries on the order of *Études sur Paris* had little or no place.

The critique of studio-produced documentaries in Sauvage's articles for *L'Ami du peuple* positioned his efforts among those of independent filmmakers who worked with minimal budgets, little or no supporting crew, and no commercial guarantees. At times, Sauvage's romantic notion of the outsider struggling against an intransigent system bordered on the spiritual, as when he compared the origin of a film project to a miraculous birth affecting the filmmaker with a kind of madness that the *revelation* of the cinema alone was able to provoke.[13] It also helped to explain the difficulties Sauvage encountered while trying to finance *Fugue,* a film project he had undertaken with help from Man Ray soon after seeing Germaine Dulac's *La Coquille et le clergyman* (*The Seashell and the Clergyman,* 1928). Sauvage had thought of *Fugue* as a foray into cinegraphic writing modeled on surrealist poetry. On April 13, 1928, Marc Chavannes, a banker who was a stockholder in Sauvage's fledgling production company, wrote to him after receiving a synopsis of the new project. Casting himself as a realist equipped with the powers of reason available to people in touch with reality, Chavannes dismissed the synopsis as nothing more than haphazard images he found unshowable and a clear step down from Sauvage's 1928 *Portrait de la Grèce (Portrait of Greece).* Chavannes's conclusion was direct: "I will not follow you, under any circumstances, in this direction."[14] Sauvage tried to move forward on *Fugue* but soon abandoned the project. To date, no material traces of it have been located.

In July 1928, Sauvage began work on *Études sur Paris* with support from financial backers who included Chavannes and his brother, Ferdinand, to whom he had offered walk-on roles. Later the same year, he set forth the idea of cinema he meant to carry out in *Études sur Paris* in an article titled "Panoramiques" (Panoramic shots or pans). His idea can be summarized in the assertion that cinema was a mode of popular expression whose physical form *(matière)* was singularly clean, healthy, and sparkling *(propre, saine, et étincelante),* but not vulgar. Sauvage began by defending a conception of cinema as an art and a profession against those for whom it was primarily a business:

> Never before have our pride and the feeling of our impotence been carried together as far as this. Cinema exalts us as much as it humiliates us. . . . We find ourselves confronted with so much that is absurd that we need to see things clearly. Most of the time, we mumble excuses whenever we are asked to "explain ourselves." Cinematic argumentation is, in general, a singular act of trickery. (Of course, I omit any mention whatsoever of advertising's unbearable excesses.) Most films can be defended only by travelling salesmen. Super Leonard and Super Courbet [movie cameras] are not the way for us to work things out. Yet we feel within ourselves a love being irresistibly born and establishing itself.[15]

The passage asserted Sauvage's love of cinema, and he went on to note that the intensity of two silent films from 1928 had brought him to tears— Carl Theodor Dreyer's *La Passion de Jeanne d'Arc (The Passion of Joan of Arc)* and Charles Vidor's *The Crowd.* Of the latter, Sauvage wrote that, as though for the first time, the soul of the American city and the drama of the middle and working classes offered themselves to the spectator. Sauvage's passion for these films was also the counterpoint of his disdain for the cheapened emotions of an uncultured viewing public. Once again, cinema was popular (literally "of the people"), but it was not vulgar in the sense of a commodity created expressly to maximize profit.

Reviewers of *Études sur Paris* at the time of its release were understandably drawn to the underground sequence in *Paris-Port* in which Sauvage had composed an absolutely new spectacle with a visual force that, in the words of Paul Gilson, made explanation unnecessary.[16] Writing in the neo-Royalist daily *L'Action française,* J. P. Gelas supported his positive assessment of the sequence as follows:

> I want to talk about the crossing of the underground section of the Canal Saint-Martin by a special tugboat that pulls barges back and forth between La Villette and the Arsenal. Air and light enter the tunnel only through street-level openings along the Boulevard Richard Lenoir. In the darkness, one can see a line of luminous columns that, depending on the moment, reveal on the train of barges crossing them the work and the movement of passengers on board. This round trip journey is so well treated in *Paris-Port* that the spectator cannot fail to be moved by images that are mysterious yet perfectly simple and natural.[17]

The adjectives "mysterious," "simple," and "natural" at the end of the passage provide a key to the singular appeal of the Paris seen in *Études* in close-ups that disclosed physical qualities of objects perceived—the grid pattern of a chain-link fence, the rough surface of a brick wall, the lustrous facial features of a shopwindow mannequin—simultaneously within and apart from their instrumental uses. The same disclosure understood in temporal terms recorded swirls of engine smoke caught by daylight diffused through street-level vents above or a man enjoying an outdoor shave on the banks of the Seine. As filmed by Sauvage, these objects, people, and moments were the ephemera of the everyday and the infra-ordinary that drew artists, writers, and photographers associated with the period's Parisian surrealism down into the streets of the city. But where Breton had described such objects and moments in *Nadja* as a means of access to the marvelous, Sauvage's use of visual understatement generated an evocative force of images throughout all five sections of *Études sur Paris*. A measure of what Breton and Sauvage were trying to do appears in their respective treatments of interactions between word and image. In *Nadja*, Breton relied on frequent illustrations and photographs—forty-four plates in all—to supplement his written account of urban encounters starting on October 4, 1926. In *Études sur Paris,* Sauvage integrated fifty-two intertitles in an eighty-minute film.

An excursus in the form of a comparative study points to relevant crossovers and differences involving Breton's and Sauvage's respective projects. About a third of the way through *Nadja*, Breton's first-person narrator chronicles a ten-day period during which a chance encounter leads to a liaison with a woman who calls herself Nadja "because in Russian it's the beginning of the word hope, and because it's only the beginning."[18] André's initial encounter with Nadja occurs shortly after he leaves the Humanité bookshop, where he had gone to buy a copy of Leon Trotsky's latest work. A photograph by Jacques-André Boiffard shows the bookshop, which was located at 120 rue Lafayette, from across a cobblestone street. In the photo, a man in the street is leaning on a wooden cart. His cap and boots suggest that he is a worker. (What is the man doing there? Is he, like André, waiting to buy a book? Is he perhaps an upscale version of the ragpickers Georges Lacombe had filmed in *La Zone*?) Portions of storefronts visible on the street level include the capital letters "RIE" to the left of the number 120. It is likely that the letters end the word *librairie* (bookshop), despite the fact that the words *chapeau rouge* (red hat) visible in white lettering just below an awning suggest also that they might end the word *chapellerie* (hat shop). The word *Cartes* (maps) and the letters "TA" on the awning of the next storefront suggest that the bookshop might be—so to speak—on the right. ("TA" could be the start of Taride,

the name of a company that started out in 1895 selling street maps of Paris
for use by bicyclists.) The storefronts are separated by a decorated iron
doorway, in which one of the two doors is open.

Of particular interest in the photograph is a large sign attached to the
side of the building, one floor above and slightly to the left of the doorway.
The sign reads, "On signe ici," a literal translation of which as "One signs
here" fails to account for the interpellation expressed by the impersonal
construction as "This is where you sign up." The latter translation makes
more sense in light of the fact that the name of the bookshop is also that
of the daily newspaper published by the French Communist Party (Parti
Communiste Français, or PCF). The inference is that one can sign up for

PCF membership by entering the doorway. (An alternative reading might hold that the message refers to a place where one would go to endorse a petition.) The message is enhanced by the larger font of the word *ici* (here) and by an arrow pointing down from the sign to the doorway. The curved shape of the arrow is a decorative flourish emphasizing the sign's function as a spatial marker. The mix of word and graphic design invites a more colloquial translation along the lines of "This is the place."

Breton joined the PCF in January 1927, some three months after the auspicious walk through Paris that begins at the Humanité bookshop. His term as a formal member—which is sometimes described as more of a flirtation than a commitment—was volatile and short-lived because Breton's radical sensibilities were closer to the permanent revolution of Leon Trotsky than to party orthodoxy.[19] All of this suggests that the primary message conveyed by the sign—"This is the place to sign up for the PCF"—is overlaid with a more personalized reading on the order of "This is where it all begins." In this case, the geography of urban Paris coincides with a personalized topography generated by the narrator's efforts after the fact to understand the fuller consequences of the encounter. While *Nadja* prioritizes the value Breton's narrator places on the latter geography, the indexical value of the arrow pointing to a determinable place in the real city of Paris is undeniable. The resulting mix of topographies fashions a variant of the processes of relay, inscription, picture, and enigma that Tom Conley has explored in conjunction with the graphic display of writing in early modern France.[20] Where Conley demonstrates how pictorial and lexical montage mediated between vernacular and learned cultures, Breton's inclusion of photographs by Boiffard and Man Ray transposed graphic montage toward urban topography and architecture. Mass-circulation advertising recast the symbolic letter into a component of a spatial poetics whose vernacular expressions in newspapers, flyers, and outdoor signs held special appeal for modernist figures such as Pablo Picasso and Guillaume Apollinaire.[21]

Two shots of oversize outdoor advertisements for Cadum soap display instances of the urban unconscious in *Études*. The first, in *Paris-Port* (reproduced earlier in this chapter), marks the move toward semiurban areas on either side of the inland waterways north of Paris. The second, in *Petite Ceinture*, is a long shot of oversize billboard ads painted on the sides of two buildings near Montmartre. The building on the left sports on two of its walls two ads dominated by the smiling face of Bébé Cadum. Power lines cutting horizontally and diagonally across the shot indicate an upward tilt from street level. Scaffolding at the very top of the building suggests that the ads may have been completed shortly before the sequence was filmed. Unlike the single portrait of Bébé Cadum on the poster based on a 1912

Monstrous Bébé
Cadum (*Études
sur Paris*).

drawing by the painter Arsène-Marie Lefeuvre, one of the ads uses linear perspective to show rows of the Bébé Cadum character extending back toward an implied horizon line. The multiplication effect stages a dream or nightmare image associated with the product's smiling embodiment, whose outsize scale borders on the monstrous. Is it a coincidence that the name of the clothing company Sigrand, painted on the wall of the building seen on the right in the shot, is a homonym of *si grand*—literally "so large" or "so big"? What about the second Cadum soap ad painted high on an adjacent wall of the same building, facing outward to the left? Was this simply an effort to maximize wall space to increase commercial effect? Or did it illustrate the proximity of the everyday and the marvelous as parts of an experience Breton explores throughout *Nadja*?

The presence of Bébé Cadum as an element of Parisian topography extends to the practice of pasting posters side by side on walls and fences, approximating frames of a filmstrip. The posters that A. M. Cassandre designed for Dubonnet vermouth revised the format of the strip ad from repetition of a single image toward a primitive form of animation. These strip ads were often pasted on the walls of Métro tunnels to simulate a motion picture effect as passengers viewed the images flashing by between stations. Among the core of future surrealists gathered around

Breton starting in 1919, these urban graphics exuded the mix of familiarity and strangeness Sigmund Freud had theorized in terms of the uncanny *(Unheimlich)*. It is therefore worth noting that Bébé Cadum appears as a character in Robert Desnos's 1927 novel *La Liberté ou l'amour! (Liberty or Love!)*. Three years earlier in the *Manifesto of Surrealism*, Breton had referred to Desnos as the (only?) one who *"spoke Surrealist"* (Breton's emphasis) at will.[22] In *Nadja*, Breton reproduced two photographs of Desnos by Man Ray and wrote that Desnos continued seeing what he (Breton) saw only after Desnos showed it to him.[23] A year later, Desnos had fallen out with Breton after contributing to the new journal *Documents*, edited by the onetime surrealist and "anti-Breton" Georges Bataille. By the end of 1929, Breton's remarks on Desnos in the *Second Manifesto of Surrealism* were openly harsh.[24]

Liberty or Love! is a cross between a novel and prose poem. Its second chapter or section, "The Depths of Night," begins with a sentence— "When I reached the street, the leaves were falling from the trees"— whose concision and first-person mode would not be out of place at the start of a detective novel. It ends by setting this concision within images worthy of a dream report or a screenplay:

> From the top of a building, Bébé Cadum, magnificently illuminated, announces better times ahead. A man peers out from a window. He is waiting. What is he waiting for? An alarm rings and wakes a corridor. On the street, a door shuts. A car goes by.[25]

Some ten pages later, a twenty-one-year-old Bébé Cadum fights with Bibendum Michelin, a messianic figure whose name is based on an animated figure designed in 1898 by the cartoonist O'Gap (born Marius Rossillon) as a mascot for Michelin tires. The battle between Bébé Cadum and Bibendum Michelin begins one morning in June as a soapy rain accompanied by thunder and lightning covers Paris with lightweight foam dispersed by the wind to create innumerable rainbows. On the street, a kind of fragrant snow reaches up as far as the knees of passersby, some of whom engage in soap-bubble fights.

> Then a charming madness settled on the town. The inhabitants tore off their clothes and ran through the streets, rolling on the soapy carpet. The Seine was full of lumpy, white sheets which clotted against the supports of the bridges and dissolved into milky clouds.[26]

The vision of upheaval expressed a tenet among Parisian surrealists that romantic love is a privileged means of personal redemption and revolutionary change. Desnos may have had this tenet in mind when he chose the title *La Liberté ou l'amour!,* which echoed the expression *La liberté ou la mort!* (Liberty or death!), first associated with revolutionary-era Paris. Motifs of love and death thus converge in this "soap star" figure of a smiling baby boy whose face was so ubiquitous that Parisians might have failed to recognize in it the symbolic value that Desnos exploited in a novel he was reputed to have written with his eyes closed.[27]

The convergence of surrealist prose (Desnos) and late silent-era documentary (Sauvage) around the figure of Bébé Cadum acquires added meaning in light of the fact that the major antagonist in *Liberty or Love!* has the same name as the central character of a film, *Bibendum,* that Sauvage undertook in February 1929 after completing *Études sur Paris.* The project began as a commercial short commissioned for the Michelin tire company and financed by a Michelin family friend, the manufacturer Charles Peignot, whose daughter, Colette (aka Laure), was a literary collaborator of Georges Bataille as well as his lover. For the title role, Sauvage chose the singer-dancer Georges Pomiès, known for his performance the previous year in Jean Renoir's *Tire au flanc (The Sad Sack).* Entries in Sauvage's personal papers of the period mention withdrawn financial commitments and creative differences over the film's scenario, as well as evenings out with Renoir, the painter Tsuguharu Foujita, and . . . Robert Desnos "in blue boxer shorts."[28] Eric Le Roy describes a print titled *Bibendum* found in the collections of the Archives Françaises du Film containing a filmed ("documentary") segment of a man dressed as Bibendum walking in a working-class neighborhood on the outskirts of Paris. A second segment features animated footage describing the evolution of the Bibendum character. When Sauvage's daughter, Agnès, saw the two segments, she remained unconvinced that they corresponded to family photographs taken during a 1929 shoot. Le Roy explains that he did not include the segments in the 2012 DVD release of *Études* because "anything is possible *[tout est envisageable],* including a total mistake in attributing this film to Sauvage."[29]

By the fall of 1929, Sauvage had abandoned *Bibendum* in favor of *Pivoine,* a fiction short subject in sound starring Michel Simon, René Lefèvre, and Line Noro. *Pivoine* was filmed from October to December 1929 on the Île Saint-Louis as a production supported by Charles Peignot and Jean Tedesco's Studios du Vieux-Colombier. Sauvage had hopes that it would launch a series of fictional sequels to *Études* modeled on scenes of Parisian life inspired by Honoré de Balzac's multivolume series of novels, *La Comédie humaine (The Human Comedy).* As with *Bibendum,* the absence of consensus surrounding the status of existing prints makes it uncertain that the seventeen-minute footage included on the 2012 DVD is part of the film Sauvage intended to complete. Michel Simon's title character was cast as a bearded hobo, a role he would soon repeat to even stronger effect in Jean Renoir's 1932 feature-length sound film, *Boudu sauvé des eaux (Boudu Saved from Drowning)*. Might the beard superimposed over the facade of the Panthéon in *Études sur Paris* have belonged to Simon?

Desnos's and Sauvage's respective treatments of Bébé Cadum and Bibendum illustrate the copresence of elite cultures of literature and film and their mass-oriented ("lower") expressions in advertising and the popular press. Michel Ciment notes that there was one Desnos who wrote *for* the cinema and another who wrote *on* it.[30] The former was the author of screenplays (some filmed, others not) including *Minuit à quatorze heures (Midnight at Two P.M.)* and *Les Mystères du Métropolitain (The Mysteries of the Métro)*; of a poem, "L'Etoile de mer" ("The Starfish"), that Man Ray made into a 1928 film; and the voice-over commentary for two films—*Records 37* and *Sources noires*—by Jacques B. Brunius in the 1930s.[31] From 1923 to 1930, Desnos wrote film reviews and articles for dailies and weeklies such as *Paris-Journal, Le Journal littéraire, Le Soir*, and *Paris-Matinal*. His name was listed among contributors to *La Revue du Cinéma*, the 1928–32 monthly edited by Jean-George Auriol and Denise Tual.[32]

The short pieces Desnos devoted to films such as *The Thief of Bagdad* (Raoul Walsh, 1924), *Das Cabinet des Dr. Caligari (The Cabinet of Dr. Caligari*, Robert Wiene, 1920), *Paris qui dort, Fantômas* (Louis Feuillade, 1913), *Moana*, and *Battleship Potemkin* (Sergei Eisenstein, 1925) display an openness to film cultures on both sides of the Atlantic. Most of all, the articles Desnos wrote on topics ranging from musical scores to censorship show him as ready to debate the use of subtitles (which he favored) as he was to confessing his preference for films with Harold Lloyd and Alla Nazimova over musical compositions by Edvard Grieg and Jules Massenet.[33]

Desnos did not hesitate to name directors and actors whose self-serving efforts in the cause of a cinematic avant-garde he found pretentious and emotionally empty. Those whom he singled out included Marcel L'Herbier, for *L'Inhumaine (The Inhuman Woman*, 1924); Jean Lods, for *Aujourd'hui/24 heures en 30 minutes (Today/24 Hours in 30 Minutes*, 1928); and Arthur Robison, for *Schatten—Eine nächtliche Halluzination (Warning Shadows*, 1924). Against these pretenders, Desnos asserted a preference for what he took for authentic practices:

> Let me be clear. When René Clair and [Francis] Picabia made *Entr'acte*, Man Ray *L'Etoile de mer*, and Buñuel his admirable *Un chien andalou*, it was not a matter of creating a work of art or a new aesthetic, but only of obeying deep and new energies *[mouvements]* that required new forms.[34]

Later in the same piece, Desnos took a position against the convolutions, the hodgepodge, the murkiness, and the disorder in films that working-class spectators of good taste would not fail to see as failed imitations of films by Alberto Cavalcanti and André Sauvage.

The point here is not merely one of having come full circle, from Sauvage to Desnos and back again to Sauvage, but also of plotting significant relays across verbal and visual media among onetime and continuing surrealists with affinities for film that extended from recognized projects by Clair, Picabia, Man Ray, Buñuel, and Dalí to lesser-known efforts such as Sauvage's *Études sur Paris*. These relays characterize the decade following World War I as a period in Paris and, by extension, Europe when the proliferation of pictures, illustrations, and photographs in the form of postcards, posters, the illustrated press, films, and even postage stamps created an unparalleled concentration of visual media.[35] In Germany, a new kind of visual culture, from elite ("high") practices of graphic and plastic arts to mass ("low") practices of advertising and caricature, prompted a shift in attitude toward the picture *(Bild)* among readers of the illustrated press, whose tendency was to see life "through the eye," the newspaper editor Kurt Korff explained in 1927 with reference to the parallel development of the *Berliner Illustrirte Zeitung* (Berlin illustrated newspaper) and the cinema.[36] A year later, Lucien Vogel launched the illustrated Parisian weekly *Vu,* whose photomontages by Germaine Krull, André Kertész, and others it made a direct precursor of the photojournalism that inspired Henry R. Luce to launch the U.S. weekly *Life* in the mid-1930s.

In May 1929, the film critic, actor, and director Jacques-Bernard Brunius praised Sauvage's *Nord-Sud* for its lucid and original treatment of Paris that captured the city's picturesque singularity and movement: "For the first time, because of *Études sur Paris,* one is able to recognize a personal element through the document itself. A humor that . . . reveals a perfectly lucid intelligence as it discloses the poetry of a large city by means of an acute sensitivity."[37] Even if this personal element was not yet a full formulation of what Vigo would refer to a year later as a documented point of view, Brunius understood it as an advance in documentary practices. Two decades later, Brunius described *Études* as unjustly forgotten and grouped it with Vigo's *À propos de Nice* and Buñuel's *Las Hurdes (Land without Bread,* 1933) as model films for a generation of film enthusiasts, including Marc Allégret, Georges Lacombe, Marcel Carné, and Pierre Chenal, all of whom had found in the documentary a means of self-assertion that came close to forcing open the doors of major studios. These filmmakers and the corpus they completed from 1925 to 1929 were central to a third period of the 1920s cinematic avant-garde that Brunius aligned with protocinematic projects of the 1880s by Jules-Etienne Marey and his disciples:

The experiments and discoveries of the avant-garde, even those that stood out like hair in the soup during certain fiction films, should have a natural application in documentaries in which narrative action did not risk being slowed down, in which no dramatic action hindered the freedom to explore the world from every angle and in all directions. Documentaries began to discover the beauty and the horror of the world, the marvels of the most banal of objects infinitely enlarged, the fantastic elements of the street and in nature.[38]

Brunius's remarks express his ongoing sense of the place of *Études* in the late silent-era avant-garde. They are also noteworthy because their temporal frame between 1929 and 1947 supports a major thesis concerning continuity among interwar and postwar practices of documentary to be tested throughout the chapters to follow. Equally astute was the 1930 assessment of *Études* by Jean-Georges Auriol, who wrote that whatever difficulties one encountered in talking about Sauvage's films resulted from his efforts to make films that more or less precluded commentary.[39] It was as though Sauvage had decided to avoid anything that might flatter fashions of the moment in order to pursue a visual style whose freshness and lucidity some filmmakers and spectators might predictably perceive as untimely. For Auriol, the term "lucidity," which Brunius had also used a year earlier, gave the occasional departures from it in the underground segment—in *Paris-Port*, the vignette of the lovers separated across flooded staircases in *Les Îles de Paris*—all the more impact by showing that the urban everyday contained the overlap of the marvelous and the unexpected precipitated by encounters such as those with Nadja (Breton) and Bébé Cadum (Desnos and Sauvage).

Sauvage's pursuit of outlets that might allow him to develop a visual style in line with what he wanted cinema to become received a definitive setback in conjunction with his work on *La Croisière jaune* (*The Yellow Cruise*, 1934), a documentary commissioned by automobile manufacturer André Citroën to chronicle a 1931–32 motorized expedition across Asia. The project was the third in a series of films that drew on conventions of the travelogue to promote the Citroën Corporation's half-track vehicles. Sauvage was hired after Léon Poirier, who had directed a documentary on the October 1924–June 1925 Expedition Citroën Central Africa, declined Citroën's offer to accompany the expedition across Asia. When Citroën expressed misgivings about a rough edit of *La Croisière jaune*, Sauvage summarized the former's response as "not enough Citroën and too many naked women."[40] The failure to resolve what had started as minor differences with Citroën and the Pathé-Natan production company led to Sauvage's dismissal and his replacement by Poirier.

Letters from Jean Renoir and Antoine de Saint-Exupéry, with whom Sauvage had hoped to remake *La Croisière jaune* filmed from an airplane, as well as expressions of support from Desnos and the poet Henri Michaux, document Sauvage's failed struggle with Citroën and the Pathé-Natan production company. A virulent account of this failure appeared in a brief 1934 notice by the onetime surrealist René Daumal, who compared Citroën to the title character of Alfred Jarry's 1896 play *Ubu roi (King Ubu)* and described Poirier's version of *La Croisière jaune* as "a work of Franco-Citroïc propaganda."[41] The outcome of the Citroën-Poirier collaboration, expressed by the title of Daumal's text, was *un film assassiné* (an assassinated film). Footage from the Citroën expedition salvaged by Sauvage but not seen in Poirier's redacted version of *La Croisière jaune* included a twenty-minute segment on Indochina, "Dans la brousse annamite" (In the Annamite bush). In 1937, Sauvage sold his last movie camera. Five years later, he left German-occupied Paris and abandoned filmmaking definitively.

Sauvage's position concerning the transition to sound in his 1930 articles in *L'Ami du peuple* was less dismissive of the transition itself than of the priorities of big production companies, whose focus on commercial concerns precluded consideration of the changes in spectatorship that the transition would generate. When Sauvage wrote that spectators were reluctant to sacrifice the magnetic draw of the silent image, the spectators whom he targeted were an idealized projection of a film public he modeled on himself.[42] And when Sauvage asserted in the same article that the challenge for sound film practices was to find a new sensory balance capable of enriching the spectator's sensory experience, the idea of film underlying his assertion aligned with activities among poets, writers, and painters associated with Parisian surrealism. This congruence drew less on formal or casual affiliation than on the sensibility of a cinematic analogue of the poetic arrangement of individual images into a developed whole. To this end, Sauvage's articles in *L'Ami du peuple* developed a humanistic vision of film within which the preeminence of documentary was a tacit and unquestioned *(indiscutable)* given.[43]

Sauvage's writings on documentary crystallized in two articles in *L'Ami du peuple* in which he inscribed documentary within a broader program. The aptly titled "L'Homme de documentaire" (The documentary man) embodied the values on which Sauvage based his own practice in the figure of a man for whom making a documentary was more than taking the kinds of shots *(vues)* that amateur photographers brought back from seaside visits. The distinctive trait of the documentary man was that he tolerated only what he took to be real. By which Sauvage meant first an engagement at the level of content with the natural world and, in particular, what he called the full complexity of human elements. This engagement was already evident in Sauvage's 1923 documentary *La Traversée du Guépon,* whose images of the ascent of the Mont Blanc chain's Grépon Needle reduced climbers into dark dots on snowfields or dangling figures on rocky cliffs. Close-ups of sailors, fisherman, and villagers in *Portrait de la Grèce* likewise alternated with long shots of the Aegean Sea, Mount Athos, and the islands of Delos, Santorini, and Mykonos. Even when Sauvage showed people as dwarfed by natural environments, a human presence persisted.

In terms of film style, what Sauvage meant by "the real" was the integration of tone, form, and continuity within a unified whole, for which he cited Walter Ruttmann's 1929 *Melodie der Welt (Melody of the World)* as a striking counterexample:

> All my pleasure, despite the extreme interest of individual shots, is spoiled by the deep and fundamental opposition I sense between these images: an opposition of form, of author, of light sources, of force. . . . These images seem to me irreducible to each other, and this makes me shout. I recall a scene showing a small boat transporting a child's casket covered by a white cloth along an astounding river Styx. This passage continues to haunt me, but my memory frames it with distressing and destructive images.[44]

The integration Sauvage found lacking in *Melodie der Welt* clarifies that the transition from the five short fragments to the feature-length *Études sur Paris* resulted less from the real and immediate circumstances of production than from a continuous attention to how what was seen in the individual images, segments, sequences, and shorter studies contributed to an integrated whole.

Montage editing was thus the hands-on dimension of a broader phenomenon of integration. Sauvage's remarks on the gap between individual images and continuity in *Melodie der Welt* may have recalled the oppositional (dialectical) montage associated with Sergei Eisenstein. They also pointed to Sauvage's treatment of the human milieu continuum for which the dominant presence of nature in his earlier documentaries on mountain climbing and Greece evolved in *Études* from the segments of *Paris-Port* set in rural and semirural spaces to the urban settings of Paris and its immediate surroundings. Extreme long shots of the visual scale seen in *La Traversée du Grépon,* where mountain climbers were depicted as overwhelmed by the natural surroundings of the Mont Blanc range, were less frequent in *Études.* Even so, the alternation of long shots with close-ups expressed the integration into a unified whole that Sauvage had found lacking in Ruttmann's *Melodie der Welt.* The changes in visual scale between *La Traversée du Grépon* and *Études* disclosed an increased human presence of individuals and groups in the spatial environments in and just outside Paris.

The last of Sauvage's 1930 *L'Ami du peuple* articles reproduced by Marinone was a defense of silent film against the transition to sound in the voice-over Sauvage embodied as *le speaker.* Sauvage began by characterizing silence as a reality and a state *(état)* rather than a mere abstraction. By "state," Sauvage meant a moment of pure and harmonious existence that even the noblest of Johann Sebastian Bach's musical compositions failed to attain. A sense of what the transition to sound implied for this harmony was evident in a passage in which Sauvage described himself as someone who wanted to believe deeply in the union of the world of sound and the world of images:

> I saw on-screen incomparable images, images that call for and command silence. We were shown aerial shots of flooded areas, floating houses, miniature trees, debris on a sea of silver. Not only a ridiculous noise of airplane juxtaposed after the fact in a sound studio interfered with the emotion we felt by reminding us of the infernal accompaniment of a journey through the skies, but also the voice of a man, a so-called speaker, imposed on us technical explanations concerning the unexpected swelling of the Seine and its tributaries. I saw magnificent images become, through these sound accompaniments, a sort of amusing demonstration for people who live on the top floor in the area around the Sacré-Coeur.[45]

Later in the same article, Sauvage described the return to the word imposed on newsreels and narrative features as dreadful. For the documentaries he hoped to continue making, Sauvage considered it even more violent, concluding that because life occurs without voice-over, cinema ought to do the same.

The sharp tone of the December 1930 article expressed Sauvage's frustration as a spectator who self-identified as a film worker *(travailleur du cinéma)* less and less able to make the kinds of films he wanted to make. An ongoing defense of silent film also framed Sauvage's stance toward the transition to sound within an assertion of the primacy of the image throughout the individual and integrated versions of *Études sur Paris.* This stance set Sauvage alongside avant-garde documentarians of the period such as László Moholy-Nagy and Ruttmann, who, in the apt words of Nicole Brenez, directly interrogated the worldly presence of objects mediated through visual and/or sound technologies.[46] Specifically, the primacy of the image linked to the presence of the real world accounted for Sauvage's comparison of "the mystery, the unexpectedness, the beauty, and the humanity" of Paris with those of the North Pole and the Sahara as the expression of something more than the exotic and the picturesque.[47] The supplement—the "something more" in the previous sentence—results from a confidence in the image Sauvage addresses throughout his 1930 articles on documentary and the transition to sound.[48] Yet the aesthetic appeal of individual images integrated into a whole should not occlude what their content displays. Emphasis on reportage among silent documentaries filmed in Paris during the 1920s—including many of those surveyed by Myriam Juan in her 2004 article—asserted the priority of content over presentation. Spectators drawn to see *La Zone* by what the film's title led them to believe they might learn about the geographic area to which it referred may have considered the animated sequence of the obelisk in the Place de la Concorde a distraction or brief entertainment.

By the time *Études sur Paris* was released two years later, the visual styles of films by Lacombe and Kaufman had approximated cinematic equivalents of poetic composition for which previous models of reportage-based documentary no longer sufficed. Even here, the poetic effects of visual style and editing in films by Lacombe, Kaufman, Carné, and Sauvage failed to account for how spectators linked what they saw on-screen to their lives once they left the movie theater. Poetic composition enhanced cinematic images of people, objects, and actions displayed on-screen with heightened attention to material detail. Only in retrospect—that is, only after Jean Vigo's films and writings expressed the basis, scope, and range of a social cinema—was the full significance of these late silent-era documentaries acknowledged in the postwar writings by Epstein, Sadoul, Porcile, and Brenez mentioned previously.

Sunday in the Country: Marcel Carné and *Nogent, Eldorado du dimanche* (1929)

"Atmosphère! Atmosphère!" Alongside Julien Duvivier's *Pépé le Moko* (1937) and Jean Renoir's *La Bête humaine* (*The Human Beast*, 1938), the three films Marcel Carné directed in 1938 and 1939—*Le Quai des brumes, Hôtel du Nord,* and *Le Jour se lève*—form the core of a poetic realism later associated with postwar melodrama and film noir on both sides of the Atlantic. Carné's *Les Enfants du paradis* (*Children of Paradise*, 1945) likewise remains a perennial favorite in France, with a status of epic romance in France akin to that of Victor Fleming's *Gone with the Wind* (1939) in the United States. The adulation of these four films obscures eighteen others Carné made during a career of nearly fifty years. Carné's first film, *Nogent, Eldorado du dimanche (Nogent, Sunday's Eldorado),* was a silent nonfiction short whose March 1929 premiere at the Studio des Ursulines in Paris coincided with that of the *Petite Ceinture* fragment of Sauvage's *Études sur Paris*. Rather than approach *Nogent* as anticipating the poetic realist films Carné made a decade later, I want to locate it instead among first-wave silent documentaries of the late 1920s by Lacombe, Kaufman, and Sauvage.

Edward Baron Turk has described *Nogent* as an affectionate tribute to the working class of Paris that recorded the simple pleasures of Sunday outings to Nogent-sur-Marne, southeast of Paris.[49] Whether or not Carné made the film with an eye to issues of social class, the activities seen in *Nogent* share little with the sailing, sunbathing, automobile racing, and tennis among affluent visitors to wintertime Nice that Vigo would depict a year later in *À propos de Nice*. An initial sense of what Carné was trying to do was conveyed in the film's title by the word *Eldorado* (the Gilded One), whose evocation of the idealized "golden" land in Voltaire's 1759 philosophical tale *Candide* suggested something closer to a poor man's paradise. Carné filmed *Nogent* some eight years before the May 1936 election of the leftist Popular Front coalition government that legislated two-week paid vacations for two million workers. *Nogent* was less a vacation film than a Sunday film in the sense that it recorded activities of ordinary people—salaried workers in a broad sense—on their weekly day off. Even so, shots throughout the film anticipated Henri Cartier-Bresson's 1938 photograph *Sunday on the Banks of the Marne*. In contrast to the monumental elements of the Seine's bridges and bridges filmed by Sauvage in the *Paris-Port* fragment of *Études sur Paris*, the Marne seen in *Nogent* was very much the people's river.

A second approach to *Nogent* sets it alongside Carné's articles on film published in *Cinémagazine, Hebdo-Film, Cinémonde, Film-Sonore,* and *Vu* from 1929 to 1933.[50] An early piece for *Cinémagazine* was cast as a review of Ivens's *De brug* (*The Bridge*, 1928), and others were devoted to films by Jacques Feyder, Fritz Lang, René Clair, and Marcel L'Herbier.[51] Carné began his training as a filmmaker in night school, with courses on photography and filmmaking at the École des Arts et Métiers. He later worked as an assistant to the director Jacques Feyder. After he impressed Feyder's wife, Françoise Rosay, with his knowledge of and love for films, the couple provided him with a movie camera, film, and some seed money. Jean Mitry recalled years later that Carné had immediately wanted to make a documentary on Nogent by using his free time on Sundays to shoot in the waterside dance halls *(guinguettes)*: "I want to make a film without a story, recording 'true life' and 'authentic reality.'"[52] The idea to make a film without a story echoed Gustave Flaubert's statement that he had written his 1856 novel *Madame Bovary* as a book about nothing. But where Flaubert had wanted his novel to depend on nothing external to itself, the authentic reality Carné wanted to record took form as a cinematic account of ephemeral moments united by time (Sunday) and place (Nogent). The result mixed elements of impressionist cinema associated with films such as Epstein's *Coeur fidèle* with a depoliticized version of Dziga Vertov's 1924 statement that he wanted to film life unawares in order to show people "without masks, without makeup, to catch them through the eye of the camera in a moment when they [were] not acting."[53]

The first ninety seconds of *Nogent* feature shots edited in intervals of two to five seconds in order to convey speed. Much of the sequence was filmed straight ahead as a phantom ride aboard a moving train traveling eastward from the Bastille Métro station. Immobile shots of a bus and a tram extend the motif of motorized mass transit. Carné's rapid cuts may have been intended to express a visual strategy, as in Vertov's *Man with a Movie Camera* (1929). Or they may have resulted from the simple fact that the capacity of Carné's movie camera allowed him to film no more than six seconds of footage at a time. A shot of the Spirit of Liberty atop the July Column at the Place de la Bastille might have been inspired by the *Paris-Port* fragment of *Études*. A twenty-second sequence aboard a train presumably leaving Paris alternates between forward shots along the roofline and tilted upward toward power or telephone lines, overhead bridges, and railroad signals and perpendicular shots straight down through couplings between train cars to the tracks below. The editing recalls the opening

Abstracted effects in *Nogent, Eldorado du dimanche* (1929).

phantom ride sequence aboard a train in Ruttmann's *Berlin* (1927). The effect of accelerated movement continues in a follow-up sequence of three stills filmed in Paris. The first is of the steps leading to the stock exchange (the Paris Bourse) and the second of some closed shutters outside a shop. The third shows the interior of an unoccupied office with a diagonal row of typewriters. The transition from exterior to interior shots links emptiness and slowness, casting the shot of typewriters with shroud-like covers as one of dead space and dead time. Arrival at Nogent, to the east of the Bois de Vincennes, is marked by a sign at the local railroad station, where men and women alight before walking in groups toward the banks of the Marne.

The next ten minutes of *Nogent* alternate between segments of water activities (canoeing, swimming, diving, fishing, sailing, crew) and segments filmed in and around casinos and riverbank dance halls. A long shot (time stamp 6:18) of people in the water is notable for the shimmering sunlight bouncing off the water's surface. Filming directly into the intense sunlight darkened human figures into abstract silhouettes. A striking underwater shot of fish might well have inspired Vigo's underwater experimentation in his 1931 documentary short subject *Taris, ou la natation (Taris, or Swimming)*. Pans and low-angle shots of dancing couples inside a dance hall contrast with occasional still shots of seated figures drinking alone. An exterior sequence of a musical trio playing while a woman hawks sheet music of a piece called "Séduction" extends the previous dance-hall sequence toward ephemeral street spectacle.

The staging of musical performance—seen but not heard (*Nogent* is a silent film)—displays a populist dimension that Turk and others have noted in conjunction with the urban sets Alexandre Trauner would design a decade later for *Le Quai des brumes, Hôtel du Nord,* and *Le Jour se lève.* Toward the end of *Nogent,* a blind accordionist is shown seated and playing on a deserted street. The musician is framed from the left, with his physical form hunched over his instrument, distorted by an elongated shadow. A close-up of the accordionist's hands shows his fingers placed delicately on the instrument's treble register and bass buttons. The musician's head is visible in soft focus in the upper left corner of the shot. Inlaid above the bass buttons is an address, presumably of a musical instrument shop, at 29 rue de Reuilly in the no-frills 12th arrondissement, which runs south and east on the Right Bank from the Place de la Bastille and the Place Daumesnil toward the Bois de Vincennes. Children seen playing on a seesaw and on a slide of wooden slats are a minority among adults of all ages. Formal policies across Europe soon replaced the voluntary togetherness recorded in *Nogent* with organized leisure for the masses in the form of annual paid vacations.[54]

The accordionist sequence resumed Carné's evocation of a Sunday in the country just outside Paris as a moment during which urban workers shared space and time away from their workday environments and schedules. This was the sense in which the accordion player embodied the ephemeral nature of idealized togetherness, presumably to be renewed the following Sunday, all of which supported the idea of Nogent—as both place and film title—as a variation on and counterpart to *la Zone*. When Turk refers to *Nogent* as an affectionate tribute to the simple pleasures of Paris's working classes, he adds that it was first and foremost the

Character studies in *Nogent, Eldorado du dimanche.*

documentation of a festive ritual of repression.[55] The implied equation of the simple pleasures with ritualized repression aptly disclosed the ambiguities associated with notions of distributed free time (time off from work). Yet the equation only began to account for claims concerning what might have been at stake for Carné ideologically when he made *Nogent*. Commentators have approached the film primarily in terms of form and visual style. Jean Quéval characterized it as an amateur effort at making an

Instrument of the people *(Nogent, Eldorado du dimanche).*

atmospheric silent film while praising Carné's sincerity toward the people he was portraying and the film's attempt to break away from the more elaborate avant-garde manner of the time.[56]

Carné's take on *Nogent* in his 1975 memoir was mixed. He rejected the tag of fictionalized documentary *(documentaire romancé)* sometimes attributed to the film while conceding the presence of a thematic motif in the round-trip railway journey between Paris and Nogent:

> It began at the Bastille station, where an old steam engine, puffing and dirty but filled with the joyous screams and songs, led away its cohort of young people hungry for the pleasures of the great outdoors—and ended at the melancholic moment of return when, having quickly forgotten the songs and singing, one no longer thought of anything except the work to be done the next day.[57]

Carné's dismissal of fictionalized documentary made it clear that the kind of attention he had wanted *Nogent* to elicit from spectators was closer to that associated with an experience they might have had in real life than to that prompted by a developed narrative with individualized characters.

Lacombe's and Sauvage's inclusion of vignettes—the young couple along the canal in *La Zone* and the lovers separated on staircases flooded by the Seine in *Études*—punctuated expository segments with minor elements of narrative. Along with *Nogent*, these films shared a number of elements with Robert Siodmak's 1930 silent feature *Menschen am Sonntag (People on Sunday)*, whose screenplay by a twenty-two-year-old Billy Wilder centered on a Sunday outing among four young adults on the shores of Nikolassee, to the southwest of Berlin. Renewed interest in Siodmak's film has tempered the priority of narrative with documentary values targeting details of daily life in late Weimar-era Berlin. As in *Nogent*, the young adults in *Mennschen am Sonntag* were cast as ordinary people and only indirectly as workers on their day off. Yet even here, the full title of Siodmak's film—*Menschen am Sonntag, ein Film ohne Schauspieler (People on Sunday, a Film without Actors)*—and the indication in an opening intertitle that the five people on-screen were appearing in front of a camera for the first time in their lives suggested a complex interplay of narrative and documentary concerns. Raymond Bellour notes that this information implied from the start that everything these characters *(personnages)* did on-screen occurred both in the purportedly real lives to which their physical presence bore witness and in the fictional narrative the camera created out of those lives.[58]

When Armand Tallier and Laurent Myrga proposed programming *Nogent* at the Studio des Ursulines movie theater, Carné was astonished, because he had not counted on the film receiving a commercial release. Along with the Théâtre du Vieux-Colombier and the Studio 28, the Studio des Ursulines was a prime Parisian venue for experimental and avant-garde films.[59] *Nogent* premiered in March 1929 to mixed reviews. It was programmed between a documentary by Jean Painlevé, Man Ray's *Les Mystères du Château du Dé (The Mysteries of the Chateau of the Dice)*, and a feature-length American import, *Romance of the Underworld* (Irving Cummings, 1928), starring Mary Astor as a moll who tries to make a straight life for herself. It ran at the Ursulines for two months. One critic challenged readers to see *Nogent* and try to take something from it. A second praised its "intelligent and sensitive" treatment of Parisian crowds *(la foule parisienne)* spending their Sundays on the banks of the Marne. A third noted its potential contribution to the film-essay.[60]

The last of the three reviews was the only one to engage *Nogent* with any degree of critical seriousness. Yet it seemed to announce the notion of film that Carné would soon formulate in 1932 and 1933 articles written after sound films had more or less supplanted silent productions. The three reviews are striking in the proximity of the positions they formulated to those taken by Sauvage in articles he had written for *L'Ami du peuple* in 1929 and 1930. What might Carné's early film criticism disclose after the fact concerning his ideas on film at the time he made *Nogent*? How might the positions Carné took toward film in 1932 substantiate or detract from claims linking *Nogent* to the incipient practices of social cinema in late silent-era documentaries by Lacombe, Kaufman, and Sauvage? How might they mediate relevant differences and continuities between *Nogent* and Carné's poetic realist films of the late 1930s?

Through the Window

Carné wrote "Cinema and the World" (November 1932), a polemical summary of French film, in 1931–32. The polemic appeared early on when Carné dismissed vaudeville entertainments and fantasy films, whose pretty stories and tiresome effects had betrayed the hopes many had held for talking film. The dismissal was heightened by Carné's resentment concerning cinema's failure to address "the profound unrest of our time," to which literature and theater were increasingly committed: "Some of us feel ashamed that the cinema, such a young art and modern medium, contents itself with banal, infantile little stories, shopworn entertainments, instead of subjects of real substance."[61] Anticipating a notion André Bazin would defend a decade later, Carné wrote that the screen had been compared to a window open to the world, with Life—capitalized in French as *la Vie*—passing before it. But where Bazin would write in the context of a cinematic realism with no clear ideological basis, Carné complained that recent cinema in France—which he equated with the transition to sound—had displayed absolutely no serious engagement with social issues.

In direct contrast to what was happening in France, Carné cited examples of films from Germany and the Soviet Union—*Kuhle Wampe* (Slatan Dudow, 1932) and *Putyovka v zhizn* (*The Road to Life*, Nikolai Ekk, 1931)—which he characterized as vast frescoes of the life and struggle of entire nations:

> *Kuhle Wampe*: the unemployed masses' struggle for life in Germany. *The Road to Life*: the forward march of an entire people. In these films society and the pride of the masses are both given expression. But how many more revelations could we have through our "window"! What spectacle might we see by turning the lens toward Asia? What would the Hindu masses tell us? What might we learn from the American farmer, lost among the fruits of his land accumulated in heaps and no longer marketable?
>
> Finally, what might we ourselves express, moved by so many fears and hopes? Who will evoke for us the true face of France in 1932?[62]

The strident tone of Carné's call to pass through the open window of the screen into the world of social and political urgency expressed the perspective of someone for whom cinema was—or could become—more than an entertainment focused on individual drama. The mention of films from Weimar Germany and the Soviet Union combined with the challenge to turn the camera lens to Asia projected a global perspective at odds with the turn to individual drama that Carné had deplored in French films of the early sound era. Even more striking was the proximity of this (nominally) global perspective to a leftist vision of social and collective struggle that devolved in Carné's poetic realist trilogy later in the decade toward an ideologically ambiguous populism. The "forward march of a people" that Carné lauded in *The Road to Life* bore little resemblance to Jean Gabin's doomed working-class heroes in Carné's *Le Quai des brumes* and *Le Jour se lève* or to the unstable community of transient boarders in *Hôtel du Nord*.

The vision that Carné formulated in "Cinema and the World," of film as an active presence in the world of social and political struggle, clashed with Jean Renoir's alleged characterization of *Le Quai des brumes* as a counterrevolutionary film of fascist propaganda. Carné's account of the episode in his memoir is terse and sour. Perhaps Carné still held a grudge against Renoir for failing to acknowledge the contributions he had made to the editing of *La Vie est à nous* (*Life Is Ours*, 1936).[63] *Le Quai des brumes* was awarded the 1939 Prix Louis Delluc in competition with Renoir's *La Bête humaine*. Even so, Carné's persistent sense of resentment toward Renoir may be attributed to his responses to critiques of his films in anything other than personal terms. Jonathan Driskell explains the Carné–Renoir episode in terms of personal rivalry framed by the harsh reception of *Le Quai des brumes* by critics on both the radical left and the right.[64] In his memoir, Carné listed critiques of the film by Georges Sadoul (in the French Communist Party daily *L'Humanité*) and Lucien Rebatet (in the neomonarchist and protofascist *L'Action française*) before noting that Sadoul eventually retracted his initial assessment. It was as though Carné found it difficult to break his tendency to see relations with colleagues and friends, even those with Jacques Prévert during their work together from 1936 to 1951, as threatening.

"When Will the Cinema Go Down into the Street?" When, indeed? By casting the title of his oft-cited November 1933 article in the form of a question, Carné sharpened the tone of "Cinema and the World" toward a direct challenge. Was the question to be understood rhetorically as an expression of impatience? Or was it closer to asserting a move to the streets as inevitable and necessary? The difference might have been nothing more than a matter of emphasis on the word "when" or "will." Instead, Carné immediately disappointed expectations of a move from words to action when he assured readers that his title was intended to convey nothing revolutionary. It simply reasserted his irritation with cinema in France that had turned its back on life by locking itself in an airtight chamber, the better to admire sets and artifice.[65]

Yet even if Carné wrote "When Will the Cinema Go Down into the Street?" merely to reiterate his 1932 take on the transition to talking films, he did so with some notable twists. A first twist was rhetorical, expressed by an engaging title whose rapid deflation from promise to disappointment disclosed more ambivalence than Carné might have realized. And this to the point where aligning this initial disappointment with his films through *Les Enfants du paradis* traced a clear move away from the revolutionary vision in "Cinema and the World." A second twist concerned the target of Carné's irritation. "Cinema and the World" had measured the failures of early talking films made in France against socially and politically engaged films from Germany and Soviet Russia. A year later, Carné singled out directors Jacques Feyder and René Clair, with whom he had worked as assistant cameraman on the set of (Feyder's) *Les Nouveaux Messieurs* (*The New Gentlemen*, 1929) and as assistant director of (Clair's) *Sous les toits de Paris* (*Under the Rooftops of Paris*, 1930).[66] After praising both directors for having used pre-talkie technology—a single handheld camera and several meters of film stock—to reinvest the deep, hidden faces of familiar sites of Paris with authenticity, Carné added that the accurate, stirring, and sensitive Paris seen in *Sous les toits de Paris* was in reality a Paris of wood and stucco reconstructed on a soundstage at Éclair-Menchen Studios in Epinay.

Carné's perspective on French films whose claims to authenticity resulted from skillful artifice took full expression in the closing lines of

"When Will the Cinema Go Down into the Street?" in the form of a second direct challenge:

> Populism, you say. And after that? Neither the word nor the thing itself frightens us. To describe the simple life of humble people, to depict the atmosphere of hard-working humanity which is theirs. Isn't that better than reconstructing the murky and inflated ambience of night clubs, dancing couples, and a nonexistent nobility, which the cinema has kept on doing as long as they've been so abundantly profitable?
>
> Paris, the two-faced city. Is there any other name better able to generate a multitude of images out of the ground of popular sentimentality?[67]

"Populism" was the key term around which Carné formulated his critique of films that substituted the "murky and inflated" ambience conveyed by studio sets for the "atmosphere of hard-working humanity" he equated with location ("street") shooting. But taking Carné at his word would mean that the studio sets Alexandre Trauner subsequently designed for *Le Quai des brumes, Hôtel du Nord,* and *Le Jour se lève* would fail to meet the prime criterion of location shooting he asserted against Clair and Feyder in 1933. The populism in Carné's poetic realist trilogy was generated at least as much by fatality and melodrama as by humble workers and humanity. The *atmosphère* prescribed in 1933 acquired a decidedly harder edge five years later in *Hôtel du Nord,* when Arletty snarled the word in her famous riposte, "Atmosphère, Atmosphère. Est-ce que j'ai une gueule d'atmosphère?" (Atmosphere, atmosphere. Do I look like an atmosphere kind of girl?)[68]

Carné wanted things both ways. On the one hand, he admitted that the authenticity of Lazar Meerson's sets for *Sous les toits de Paris* had moved him, perhaps even more than if Clair had been filming on location. On the other, he countered that there were still many things to be said about Paris. And for this, Carné turned from film to literature, describing the writers Pierre Mac Orlan, Jules Romains, and André Thérive as having seized the spirit hidden under the familiar facade of the streets of Paris. Carné also singled out Eugène Dabit, whose 1929 novel *L'Hôtel du Nord* he commended for its depiction of the picturesque, restless world of workers surrounding the Canal Saint-Martin. The reference to Dabit's novel was especially telling because Carné organized his 1938 film adaptation of the book around an elaborate reconstruction of the Canal Saint-Martin that Alexandre Trauner designed and built at the Billancourt Studios.[69]

Carné's conclusion that Paris was a two-faced city is arguably double. In geographic terms, the Paris seen at the start of *Nogent* was a workplace and point of departure for a spatial environment structured by salaried labor, all of which made it the antithesis of Nogent as a destination where urban day-trippers spent time together away from the workplace. In terms of the challenge Carné directed toward cinema, Paris was split again between the evocative force of studio sets and the location shooting Carné had invoked in his 1933 article as a measure of authenticity. *Nogent* had upheld this measure in 1929. But the same did not hold for *Hôtel du Nord* almost a decade later, in which Trauner's studio set was the backdrop for a sentimental populism bolstered by the box-office appeal of the movie stars Annabella and Jean-Pierre Aumont.

Despite Carné's call for cinema to go down into the streets, the populism he invoked in 1933 paled by comparison to literature by and for workers that sought to heighten class consciousness. In the words of the onetime anarchist, dissident Communist, and self-declared champion of proletarian literature Henri Poulaille, populism was a label invented by critics to conceal the existence of a true proletarian writing at a time when literature was still dominated by bourgeois ideology.[70] Carné's call for a cinema of the streets likewise fared badly when compared to Jean Renoir's *Toni* (1935), whose production in the South of France displayed none of the stylized elements of milieu Carné would showcase, starting with Trauner's studio sets for *Le Quai des brumes*.[71] Differences here point to realism understood as an engagement with social realities (Renoir) rather than a realism of style and atmosphere (Carné). Dudley Andrew notes that Dabit's *L'Hôtel du Nord* was not a novel that the hotel's real clientele would naturally have read.[72] By extension, the film Carné adapted from Dabit's novel was directed less at the hotel's clientele than at middle-class spectators looking for momentary identification with the working-class authenticity associated by Adrian Rifkin, Kelley Conway, and David Harvey with collective perceptions of *la Zone.*

Carné's trajectory between *Nogent* and *Le Jour se lève* is complex to the point of contradiction. His depiction of a Sunday on the banks of the Marne mobilized location shooting through a visual style beyond reportage held together by vignettes and minor motifs. A decade later, his poetic realist trilogy would deploy the very elements of melodrama and studio set he had denounced in his 1932 and 1933 articles as symptoms of French film's decline in the new era of the talkies. Where Turk and others cite "When Will the Cinema Go Down into the Street?" as a populist manifesto, the admiring nods to German and Soviet films in "Cinema and the World" come as close as anything Carné would do or say to an activism on a par with that of André Malraux, André Gide, Léon Moussinac, and Eugène Dabit, all of whom were involved at the time with the leftist Association des Écrivains et Artistes Révolutionnaires (Association of Revolutionary Writers and Artists).

The chronological progression from location shooting and filmed facts to filmed tableaux marks Carné's ideological regression from remarks supportive of socially engaged film to his use of the stylized authenticity of studio sets in his poetic realist trilogy. Framed between *Nogent* and *Le Jour se lève*, Carné's *Cinémagazine* articles of 1932 and 1933 posit the promise of a cinema committed to social and political critique that is nowhere evident in his poetic realist films, which revert to dramatic set pieces and to tableaux filmed in Trauner's studio sets. At the same time, the unfulfilled promise charted in Carné's evolution from 1929 *(Nogent)* to 1939 *(Le Jour se lève)* fails to diminish the potential for cinema as an instrument of activism that other filmmakers working in France and in northern Europe took up as early as 1930. Carné's trajectory thus resumes the productive tensions between exposition and narrative in modes of poetic and observational documentaries by Lacombe, Kaufman, Sauvage, and Carné's late silent-era documentaries that would crystallize a year later in Vigo's *À propos de Nice* and "Toward a Social Cinema."

Transition I

Networking, 1929–1930

I want to add to my remarks on specific films and filmmakers by considering the role of what film scholar Malte Hagener has referred to as "ephemeral instances" (congresses, screenings, and exhibitions) whose convergence of individuals, groups, and institutions is instructive as a measure of transformative potential.[1] The instances I have in mind—an exhibition and two congresses—occurred over nineteen months in 1929 and 1930, culminating in the 1930 Congrès International de Cinéastes Indépendants, held from November 27 through December 1 at the Palais des Beaux-Arts in Brussels. The Brussels congress followed a September 1929 congress of the same name at La Sarraz, Switzerland, and the May–June 1929 *Film und Foto* exhibition organized in Stuttgart on behalf of the Deutscher Werkbund. Looking at these three events concurrent with the four silent films by Lacombe, Kaufman, Sauvage, and Carné reframes the silent documentaries within a transnational setting. In addition, these events mark a specific phase in the history of what Peter Wollen has described as the long history of two cinematic avant-gardes dating back to the mid- to late 1920s.[2] In keeping with the motif of critical mass, I will argue that the three instances are best understood less in and of themselves than as a series adumbrating a trajectory from the late silent era toward socially engaged practices of the 1930s.

Film und Foto (aka *FiFo*) was a retrospective of new photography of the 1920s organized by László Moholy-Nagy, Alexander Rodchenko, and Germaine Krull in thirteen rooms at Stuttgart's Neue Städtische Austellungshalle. Its catalog listed 977 titles, but Beaumont Newhall has written that a number of unitemized groups of photographs brought the total to many more.[3] Photographs by Krull, André Kertész, Man Ray, Berenice Abbott, Eugène Atget, Florence Henri, and Eli Lotar were arranged in a *salon de l'escalier* (staircase salon). Other rooms organized by nationality included a Russian section curated by El Lissitzky, an American section by Edward Weston and Edward Steichen, and a Dutch section by Piet Zwart.[4] Individual photographers were represented by ten to twenty-two works each. The selection of works by *FiFo* organizers and consultants resulted in personal and ideological tensions. These were especially evident in fifteen screenings organized by Hans Richter over two weeks in June 1929, which included films by Walter Ruttmann, Viking Eggeling, Vsevolod Pudovkin, and Richter himself. Films from France at *FiFo* included Germaine Dulac's *La Coquille et le clergyman* (*The Seashell and the Clergyman*, 1928), Henri Chomette's *Jeux des reflets et de la vitesse* (*Plays of Reflections and Speed*, 1925), René Clair's *Entr'acte* (*Intermission*, 1924), Man Ray's *L'Étoile de mer* (*The Starfish*, 1928), Fernand Léger's *Emak Bakia* (*Leave Me Alone*, 1928), and Fernand Léger et al.'s *Ballet mécanique* (*Mechanical Ballet*, 1924). The selection was notable for the inclusion of *Chelovek s kino-apparatom* (*Man with a Movie Camera*, 1929), screened in person by director Dziga Vertov. Equally notable was the absence of Luis Buñuel and Salvador Dalí's *Un chien andalou* (1929). Was this absence intentional and the equivalent of an exclusion? Documents show that the film was to be screened at La Sarraz three months later. Even with minimal evidence to resolve matters, questions surrounding which works were included and which were not target rifts that would resurface in the two follow-up meetings over the next eighteen months.

The first CICI, held three months after *FiFo* at La Sarraz, centered on independent films. Documentation related to the meeting's planning belied what one of its major organizers, Robert Aron, described as an event whose goal was to promote direct contact among filmmakers from several countries, "with no political dimension whatsoever."[5] Aron's remark appeared in a July 22, 1929, letter to Dziga Vertov, whom he and congress sponsor Hélène de Mandrot were courting to participate as part of a Soviet delegation that included Sergei Eisenstein. By the time border guards denied the Russian delegation entry at the German–Swiss border in September, Vertov had decided not to attend. Mandrot eventually obtained authorization for Eisenstein to enter Switzerland, but only with a stipulation that he and his colleagues Edouard Tissé and Grigory Aleksandrov restrict their movements to the conference site. Out of deference to his hosts, Eisenstein complied and screened only two sequences from *Staroye i novoye* (*The General Line*, 1929).

Twenty-five participants representing eleven national delegations at La Sarraz included Béla Balázs, Richter, and Ruttmann from Germany; Aron, Jean-Georges Auriol, Alberto Cavalcanti, and Léon Moussinac from France; Eisenstein, Aleksandrov, and Tissé from the Soviet Union; Mannus Franken from the Netherlands; and Ivor Montagu from England. The sole American participant, Montgomery Evans, was listed as director of the Fifth Avenue Playhouse in New York City. The first of four plenary sessions was devoted entirely to reports by delegates on the situation of independent film in their countries. Auriol acknowledged the equation of "independent" with "avant-garde" while speaking in positive terms of movie theaters and ciné-clubs within and outside Paris that programmed domestic and foreign films. He also described police censorship of screenings of films from Soviet Russia and called on colleagues to strategize about financing independent productions outside the studio mainstream. Balázs and Richter described the dire condition of independent film in Germany, where filmmakers had little support from state and private sources.[6] Subsequent plenary sessions included delegate reports on proposed resolutions opposing censorship and establishing a cooperative in Paris to collect, promote, and distribute works by congress participants and like-minded colleagues.

The second major activity at La Sarraz involved four screenings for participants, with a fifth organized for the local public. As reconstituted by Roland Cosandey and Thomas Tode, one program mixed films from England and the United States (presumably brought by Montagu and Evans), including *The Fall of the House of Usher* (James Sibley Watson and Melville Webber, 1928), *The Love of Zero* (Robert Florey, 1928), and *Rachmaninoff's Prelude in C Sharp Minor* (Castleton Knight, 1927). A second program, this one devoted to avant-garde shorts, featured Man Ray's *L'Étoile de mer*, Buñuel and Dalí's *Un chien andalou,* and two films by Joris Ivens, *De brug* and *Regen*. A third program included three documentaries by Ulrich K. T. Schultz produced in Germany by the Universum Film AG (also known as UFA). The screenings provided attendees of the congress access to recent films under viewing conditions that promoted exchange and networking. They failed to fulfill what Tode describes as a primary mission among organizers to launch an "Internationale of new film" without providing any kind of clear orientation.[7] At the same time, CICI at La Sarraz marked an initial phase in the development of social documentary that could be seen both at Brussels a year later and in films that Ivens, Storck, Buñuel, and Lotar were to make over the next decade and a half.

Some fifteen months later, the mandate to organize undertaken by participants at La Sarraz persisted in Brussels in the form of resolutions and strategic planning among delegates from France, Britain, the Netherlands, Germany, Italy, Czechoslovakia, and Belgium. (An observer from Hungary was present but did not vote. Delegations from Switzerland and Poland dropped out at the last moment.) According to Henri Storck, the Brussels congress resulted from collaborations among the Belgian Sept Arts (Seven Arts) group of artists and writers, Auriol and Aron, editors of *La Revue du Cinéma,* and Léon Moussinac, whose support Storck described as crucial (*déterminant*).[8] The involvement of individuals in planning the congress extended to a delegation of fourteen participants from France that included Jean Painlevé, Jean Lods, Jean Vigo, Robert Aron, Jean-Georges Auriol, Georges Altman, Germaine Dulac, Claude Autant-Lara, Boris Kaufman, and Pierre Bost. Participants from other delegations included Charles

Dekeukeleire and Storck (Belgium), Hans Richter (Germany), and Joris Ivens (Netherlands).[9]

Delegates' reports on the state of avant-garde cinema addressed conditions in their respective home countries. Dulac spoke of the range of activities made possible by a growing number of movie theaters in France that screened avant-garde films such as her *La Coquille et le clergyman* and *Étude cinégraphique sur une arabesque* (*Arabesque*, 1929). In Italy, one company was said to hold a near monopoly on production and distribution, while efforts by Luigi Pirandello, Filippo Tommaso Marinetti, and Enrico Prampolini had resulted in the projected opening of Rome's first avant-garde movie theater.[10]

A program of six screenings ranged in format from mixed short subjects and montage films to so-called galas of silent and sound films. One screening paired films by Jean Painlevé and Hans Richter, while a second programmed Jean Lods's *Champs-Élysées* (1928) alongside Alexander Dovzhenko's *Zemlya* (*Earth*, 1930). A third featured short and midlength films by Storck, Vigo, Vertov, and Man Ray. Other films screened included Walter Ruttmann's *Melodie der Welt* (*Melody of the World*), William Nigh's *Thunder*, a sequence from King Vidor's *Hallelujah*, Robert Florey's *Gratte-ciel* (*Skyscraper Symphony*), and John Grierson's *Drifters*, all from 1929, and a series of montage films by Jean-Georges Auriol.

The Brussels screenings made it possible for congress attendees to see and discuss recent films from both sides of the Atlantic. The showcasing of recent work by local filmmakers Storck and Dekeukeleire promoted pride among Belgians, who no longer felt they were lagging behind their French, German, and Soviet colleagues. Journalist André Cauvin described Storck as a promising beginner already adept at conveying true forms of life in their most banal expressions and Dekeukeleire as skilled at camera movement and rapid montage.[11] Dekeukeleire noted in the magazine *Le Rouge et le noir* that the paucity of sound films screened—*Melodie der Welt*, *Hallelujah*, and *Thunder*—failed to convey the tendencies of this emergent genre.[12] The Brussels conference was also where Germaine Dulac recruited Jean Vigo to make *Taris* (1931) and Henri Storck to assist Pierre Billon at the Buttes-Chaumont production studio in Paris.[13] Shortly after the Brussels congress, Dulac wrote that Vigo's *À propos de Nice* (1930) "leads us to make a biting social critique, without a word, through the simple opposition of images gathered and formed in their substance by life itself."[14] Tami Williams notes that Dulac's efforts to bring together independent and commercial talents at the 1930 Brussels congress marked a significant juncture in the history of cinema that contributed to the emerging social documentary movement.[15] Beyond simple cosmopolitanism, the Stuttgart exhibition and the conferences at La Sarraz and Brussels during 1929 and 1930 recast the efforts of individual filmmakers in Europe, Britain, and the United States toward a network of like-minded activists ready to align their filmmaking over the long decade of the 1930s to social and political issues of the moment.

Did Eli Lotar attend the CICI in Brussels? To date, I have found no evidence to respond to this question. Ivens remains a key figure as an intermediary through whom Lotar might have first met Storck, with whom he would work seven years later on *Les Maisons de la misère* (*Houses of Misery*, 1937). Whether or not Lotar was in Brussels, his work with Ivens, Painlevé, Jacques-Betrand Brunius, Buñuel, and Storck over the following decade was grounded in the very kind of collaboration that the congresses at La Sarraz and Brussels were organized to promote.

Writing in 1975 about avant-garde filmmaking, film scholar Peter Wollen identified a split between the North American co-op movement and European directors such as Jean-Luc Godard, Jean-Marie Straub, Danièle Huillet, Marcel Hanoun, and Marcel Janco. In order to understand this split, Wollen argued, it is necessary to go back into history to consider a similar split in the 1920s between film practices that attempted to extend the scope of painting beyond the canvas and others that were inspired by theater and sound poetry. Among the former group, Wollen included Fernand Léger, Dudley Murphy, Francis Picabia, René Clair, Viking Eggeling, Hans Richter, Man Ray, and László Moholy-Nagy. Among the latter, Wollen grouped Russian directors Sergei Eisenstein, Alexander Dovzhenko, and Dziga Vertov. The only real contact between the two groups, Wollen added, was at the very end of the decade, when El Lissitzky first met Vertov to discuss the *FiFo* exhibition and when Eisenstein met Richter on his first trip out of the Soviet Union to La Sarraz, "which turned out to mark the end rather than the beginning of an epoch."[16]

Where Wollen goes on to assess the priority of painting in a shift or break (he cites Louis Althusser's notion of *coupure*) he associates with the beginning of modernism, I want instead to see *FiFo* and the two CICIs as precursors of the socially engaged filmmaking whose trajectory over the following decade and a half in the Ivens–Storck collaboration *Misère au Borinage* (*Misery at Borinage,* 1933), the Storck–Lotar collaboration *Les Maisons de la misère,* and Lotar's *Aubervilliers* (1946) forms the basis of chapters to follow. If *FiFo* marked the end of certain practices of photography associated with *Die Neue Sachlichkeit* (The New Objectivity), the congresses at La Sarraz and Brussels marked a new start for documentary filmmaking increasingly committed to social activism.

3

"All the World's Misery"

Paris, the center; the *banlieues,* the circumference; to these children, this is the whole world. They never venture beyond it. They can no more live out of the atmosphere of Paris than fish can live out of water. For them, nothing exists beyond the city gates. Ivry, Gentilly, Arcueil, Belleville, Aubervilliers, Ménilmontant, Choisy-le-Roi, Billancourt, Meudon, Issy, Vanvres, Sèvres, Puteaux, Neuilly, Gennevilliers, Colombes, Romainville, Chatou, Asnières, Bougival, Nanterre, Enghien, Noisy-le-Sec, Nogent, Gournay, Drancy, Gonesse; these are the end of the world.

—Victor Hugo, *Les Misérables* (1862)

The End of the World

Place-names align experience with measurable space. The fact that those listed above still appear on maps of Greater Paris enhances their evocative force a century and a half after Victor Hugo cited them in *Les Misérables.* Maps indicate where, for example, to find Billancourt, now known as Billancourt-Boulogne, across the Seine to the west of the 15th arrondissement. But geography alone fails to disclose the extent to which place-names spawn associations that evolve ("thicken") according to context and duration. Belleville thus conjures up generations of immigrants newly arrived from Europe, Asia, and Africa; Ivry, an asylum where the poet, playwright, actor, and theater director Antonin Artaud spent the last two years of his life; and Nanterre, the site of February 1968 student demonstrations at the University of Paris X campus. Aubervilliers, just north of the city limits of Paris, provides the title for Eli Lotar's 1946 documentary around which this chapter is organized. Like the other places named above, its history extends to literature and film. A detour makes the scope of this extension explicit.

The novels that Didier Daeninckx (born 1949) has written since the late 1970s have fashioned a singular take on the subgenre of socially engaged detective fiction known as the *néo-polar.* Typically translated as "detective novel" or "crime novel," *polar* is a shortened form of *roman policier* (police novel), a term that is sometimes condensed to *rompol*. Its origins in France go back at least as far as Charles Baudelaire's translation of Edgar Allan Poe's 1841 short story "The Murders in the Rue Morgue." Other French antecedents include the Nouveaux Mystères de Paris (New Mysteries of Paris), a series of crime novels, each of which writer Léo Malet (1909–1996) planned to set in a different one of the capital's twenty arrondissements. For Jean-Patrick Manchette (1942–1995), the *néo-polar* and *roman noir* (literally, "black novel") contributed to a self-styled literature of crisis among young leftists and anarchists whose writings directed conventions of crime fiction toward social critique in the aftermath of May 1968.[1]

A key motif in Daeninckx's novels is the disclosure of a crime's origins— often those of a murder committed in one of the seedy neighborhoods on either side of Paris's northern ring roads *(boulevards périphériques)*—a generation or more before the fact. Daeninckx's early fiction often featured investigations *(enquêtes)* into seemingly minor crimes that opened onto historical explanation: "There is of course a murder, but it is motivated, and becomes in a way a pretext: what's more important than the crime is the road that leads to the crime, and its implications."[2] Daeninckx's early novels repeatedly raised pointed questions about France's wartime and colonial pasts, so much so that his work as a novelist approximated that of a prosecutor looking at cold cases with a historian's eye.[3] A brief example is in order.

Daeninckx's 1984 novel *Meurtres pour mémoire (Murder in Memoriam)* centers on the 1982 shooting death of twenty-year-old Bernard Thiraud in Toulouse, where Thiraud had gone to consult World War II documents he hoped would shed light on his father's death during the October 17, 1961, demonstrations in Paris supporting an end to French colonial rule in Algeria. The demonstrations had been organized as a peaceful show of solidarity with the Front de Libération Nationale (National Liberation Front), a group with which, to the chagrin of those in France and Algeria opposed to self-determination for Algeria, President Charles de Gaulle had recently opened negotiations. Things turned violent when local and riot police clubbed pedestrians throughout central Paris, ostensibly for violating a curfew that applied specifically to individuals whom police officials referred to as "French Algerian Muslims." Many of the alleged violators were taken to the Vélodrome d'Hiver, a bicycle stadium in Drancy on the northern outskirts of the city where, from 1942 to 1944, some 67,000 Jews and other perceived enemies of the German occupation forces had been interned en route to concentration and death camps east of the Rhine. Dozens of demonstrators—estimates range from seventy to more than two hundred—died in areas of central Paris. Many drowned when they were thrown into the Seine with their hands tied behind their backs. Most victims were North Africans who had come to France to fill demands for cheap labor, often at construction sites.[4] Bernard's father, Raymond, was white and taught history at a local lycée. His death by a pistol shot through the temple at close range pointed to murder and premeditation. By the end of the novel, the Toulouse police inspector assigned to the case has traced the murders of son and father to the Paris police chief of criminal affairs, André Veillut.

Veillut is Daeninckx's fictional stand-in for Maurice Papon, a high-level administrator during the Vichy regime who oversaw the deportation of Jews from the Bordeaux region from 1942 to 1944. As Paris police prefect in 1961, Papon authorized the October 17 crackdown. In *Meurtres pour mémoire*, Veillut orders the killing of Raymond Thiraud in 1961 after learning from a colleague in Toulouse that Thiraud has inquired about documentation dealing with the wartime deportations that Veillut oversaw. This is the sense in which Veillut uses the October 1961 demonstrations as a cover for premeditated murder. Twenty-one years later, Veillut drives from Paris to shoot the younger Thiraud himself when the same archivist reports that the son is following in his father's footsteps. In both instances, seemingly random murders are committed in order to prevent disclosure of past crimes for which Veillut/Papon was responsible.

By the time *Meurtres pour mémoire* was published in 1984, Papon had resigned from public service following allegations related to his activities under Vichy and during the 1954–62 conflict in Algeria. Three years earlier, the satirical French weekly *Le Canard enchaîné* had published documents implicating him directly in the deportation of 1,690 Jews to the Drancy internment camp just outside Paris. (Drancy is another place-name listed by Victor Hugo in *Les Misérables*.) Even so, no formal charges were filed until 1995. Convicted in 1999 for complicity with Nazi crimes against humanity, Papon served three years of a ten-year sentence. He died in 2007 at the age of ninety-six.

Like the film critic André Bazin a quarter of a century earlier, Daeninckx spent time as a young adult in the early 1970s screening films in schools and youth centers on the outskirts of Paris. Recalling the stint, Daeninckx has stated that he often introduced feature-length films by Fritz Lang, Joseph Losey, and Jean Renoir by showing Eli Lotar's *Aubervilliers,* which he considered a tribute to the town where he had attended primary and secondary schools.[5] Because Lotar's film depicted the gritty atmosphere that Daeninckx would later evoke in his own fiction, he wondered why it was not better known among the town's inhabitants. The historian Tyler Stovall begins his study of Bobigny, just to the east of Aubervilliers, by noting that turn-of-the-century Parisians considered areas in and around the 18th, 19th, and 20th arrondissements as either terra incognita or the citadel of "an organized and vengeful proletariat, the barbarians waiting outside the gates of the city."[6] What Stovall calls the "red belt" of working-class neighborhoods in northeast Paris included some of the same locales in which Daeninckx later set his novels and novellas. It also overlapped with sections of *la Zone* that Victor Hugo had described in *Les Misérables* as the end of the world. This sense of the area as foreign and threatening persisted as late as 2001, when Stephen Barber referred to Aubervilliers as a vast "noncity of noncitizens" beyond Paris.[7]

In the pages that follow, I trace Eli Lotar's involvement with Parisian cultures of photography and film from 1928 through 1931 before exploring formal and narrative elements of his first solo-directed film, *Aubervilliers* (1946). I also work outward from Lotar's photography and initial film activities toward radical filmmaking of the 1930s by Jean Vigo and Joris Ivens. I conclude the chapter by considering a series of still photographs by Lotar whose publication in three print venues from 1929 to 1931 coincides with his evolution from photojournalism and art photography toward an engagement visible over the following decade that culminated in his directorial debut in the immediate aftermath of the 1944–45 liberation of France. Concerning questions of method, I take a first cue from efforts by many of Daeninckx's fictional narrators to retrace the causal trajectory of a crime that appears initially to be a minor incident. A second cue comes from Michel de Certeau's assertion that every story is a travel story and thus a spatial practice.[8] How, then, does Lotar's cinematic treatment of place in his 1946 film draw on his transition from street, art, and reportage photography to cinema? And how might a clearer understanding of this transition provide insight into the films I have designated as a discrete set or cycle of social documentaries in France from 1928 to 1963? A second excursus is needed.

The inception of social documentary in France is often equated with filmmaker Jean Vigo's 1930 call for a social cinema whose treatment of provocative subjects would move spectators in ways that only cinema could move them.[9] Vigo made only four films before he died in 1934 at age twenty-nine. The first of the four, *À propos de Nice* (*Concerning Nice*, 1930), followed the wave of silent-era documentaries that depicted what an intertitle in Georges Lacombe's *La Zone* (1928) had referred to as "a strange population where all the races mix" on the outskirts of Paris. This was the case despite the fact that Vigo and codirector Boris Kaufman shot their film on the Mediterranean coast some 550 miles southeast of Paris. It is unclear to what extent Vigo was aware of these first-wave films. His collaboration with Kaufman suggests that he knew the latter's depiction of the central Paris produce and meat market in *Les Halles centrales* (1928). Yet Buñuel and Dalí's *Un chien andalou* (1929), on which Vigo claimed to model his vision of social cinema, could hardly be called a documentary. This is the sense in which Vigo's notion of social cinema drew on but was not at all equated with documentary practices, even if elements and/or perceptions of it continue to be associated with them.

A Kick in the Pants to Open Our Eyes: *À propos de Nice* (Jean Vigo, 1930)

Vigo first presented the remarks later published as "Toward a Social Cinema" to introduce a June 14, 1930, screening of *À propos de Nice* organized for the Spectateurs d'Avant-Garde ciné-club at the Théâtre du Vieux-Colombier in Paris. Venue and format warrant attention. The theater actor, director, and literary critic Jacques Copeau launched the Théâtre du Vieux-Colombier in 1913 to stage experimental productions at a remove from realist conventions and the theatrical star system of the period. When Jean Tedesco succeeded Copeau as the theater's director in 1924, he expanded programming to include avant-garde films by Abel Gance, D. W. Griffith, Louis Delluc, Jean Epstein, and Marcel L'Herbier.[10] Four years later, Tedesco and Jean Renoir built a small production studio in the Vieux-Colombier's attic, where they shot Renoir's *La Petite Marchande d'allumettes* (*The Little Match Girl*, 1928), which had its premiere downstairs in the main theater. The ciné-club format promoted by Tedesco brought Vigo into contact with the filmmaker Germaine Dulac, former secretary and future president of the French Federation of Ciné-Clubs, founded by Louis Delluc.[11] In 1930, Dulac used her influence as vice president of Gaumont-Franco-Film-Aubert to commission Vigo's second film, a portrait of the swimming champion Jean Taris. The techniques of underwater shooting that Vigo and Kaufman developed while making the Taris film reappeared three years later during a key sequence in *L'Atalante*.[12]

"Toward a Social Cinema" provided an opportunity for Vigo to assert a critical stance opposed to those of filmmakers whose preoccupations with profit and entertainment, he argued, kept them isolated from social realities. To aim at a social cinema was thus to free oneself "from the two pairs of lips that take 3,000 meters to come together and almost as long to come unstuck."[13] Positioning his work within the cinematic avant-garde associated with Parisian surrealism and its offshoots, Vigo cited Luis Buñuel and Salvador Dalí's *Un chien andalou* as exemplifying the qualities of a film with social implications. Vigo's devotion to the film extended to December 13, 1931, screenings at Les Amis du Cinéma in Nice, where he programmed it along with *À propos de Nice* and René Clair's *Entr'acte* (1924).

After offering a figurative kick in the pants to conventional films, Vigo described his predilection for documentary practices that "cut into the flesh" when he distinguished the type of filmmaking that interested him from practices of conventional documentaries and weekly newsreels: "This kind of social documentary demands that one take a position because it dots the *i*'s. If it doesn't persuade an artist, at least it will compel a man."[14] The emphasis Vigo placed on documentary grounded it less in genre apart from fiction films than as a value or function potentially present in all films. This grounding is close to what Grierson had identified in his 1926 remarks on Robert Flaherty's *Moana.* The assertive tone of "Toward a Social Cinema" recalls that of the *Second Manifesto of Surrealism* (1930), in which André Breton ascribed a political mission to experimental practices exploring the potential of poetic images to disrupt daily habits. In the *Manifesto of Surrealism* (1924), Breton had understood such practices in more metaphysical terms as a means of attaining self-knowledge. Six years later, he reframed this project of self-knowledge within social and political issues of the period.

Vigo's distinction between the artist and the man in "Toward a Social Cinema" followed the Breton of the second surrealist manifesto by ascribing a social function to documentary beyond purely aesthetic concerns. The consequences of this perspective had direct bearing on Vigo's sense of the term *document,* which derived in this instance less from nonfiction films such as newsreels or an artistic avant-garde than from the capacity of social cinema to express a vibrancy that films grounded in realist concerns failed to achieve. "Vibrancy" here refers to life animated by the force of passion conveyed in *Un chien andalou.* It also recalls Émile Durkheim's notion of the sacred linked to contagion and to activist effervescence such as the representations of social structures studied by members of the 1937–39 Collège de Sociologie founded by Georges Bataille, Roger Caillois, and Michel Leiris.[15] In what was likely an allusion to the notorious opening sequence in *Un chien andalou,* Vigo suggested that, as Dudley Andrew notes, "French producers and spectators needed their eyes slashed. In 1930 they needed the energy of direct, even adolescent, visions."[16] Six months later, Buñuel wrote to Vigo after seeing *À propos de Nice* at the Studio des Ursulines. In a letter dated December 19, 1930, he described the film as a poetic documentary whose "monuments to the dead" in obscene slow motion he found quite touching.[17]

À propos de Nice aligned with practices of image composition and editing that maximized the evocative potential of film as a silent medium. The film's title conveyed an initial expectation of the documentary subgenre of travelogue, with which Vigo tampered as a means of expressing what he called a "documented point of view." Opening aerial shots mobilized a totalizing perspective in line with other documentaries that depicted the city and its inhabitants as a single massive entity. These images tapped into a more politicized depiction of urban spaces in other documentaries of the late silent period, such as Jean Lods's *Aujourd'hui/24 heures en 30 minutes* (*Today/24 Hours in 30 Minutes,* 1928), Joris Ivens's *De brug* (*The Bridge,* 1928), and Henri Storck's *Images d'Ostende* (*Ostend Images,* 1930). It was as if, in the words of Michael Temple, "the new social order, to which [these films] aspired, could already be foreseen through their artistic transformation of everyday life."[18]

The cameraman for the location shoot in Nice was Boris Kaufman, whom Vigo had met in Paris in 1929. Though *Les Halles centrales* was his only film credit at the time, Kaufman offered hands-on technical advice that contributed significantly to a visual style more often associated with Vigo. In 1949, Kaufman provided a concise account of his collaboration with Vigo and the structure of *À propos de Nice*:

> Nice was preparing for the carnival. The palm trees along the promenade were being painted, the enormous floats and plaster figures were being constructed. The obvious focal point was the Promenade des Anglais, which was the center of activity (or inactivity) for international sloth. Our method consisted of taking facts by surprise, actions, attitudes, expressions and of stopping the camera as soon as the subject became conscious of being photographed. . . . We rejected without fail everything that was picturesque but without meaning, facile contrasts. The story was to be understood without subtitles or commentary. We therefore filmed by counting on the evocation of ideas by the association of images alone.[19]

Kaufman's admission that they had worked without a shooting script confirmed Vigo's characterization of *À propos de Nice* as a rough draft and first attempt at a social cinema for which postproduction editing was crucial. Interestingly, the emphasis Kaufman placed on editing suggests that he and Vigo also recognized that their initial collaboration was an attempt to generate and develop a cinematic style suitable to conveying a critical vision that moved beyond outward appearances to put a certain world on trial:

> In fact, no sooner is the atmosphere of Nice and the kind of life one leads there—and elsewhere, alas,—sketched out, than the film moves to generalize the gross festivities situating them under the sign of the grotesque, of the flesh and death, which are the last spasms of a society so little conscious of itself that it is enough to sicken you and to make you an accomplice of a revolutionary solution.[20]

The initial aerial sequence in *À propos de Nice,* cutting between overhead and low-angle shots, is a visual metaphor for the high/low division between leisure and working classes. The opening segment builds on point of view, changes in perspective, and editing without the support of intertitles, presumably excluding music as well.[21] Where the opening sequences follow conventions for travelogues of the period by locating the city topographically along the Mediterranean coast, Vigo quickly undercuts realist expectations with a sequence that draws on period techniques of animation in its depiction of a toy train and miniature dolls dressed as tourists. The contrast establishes an ambiguity that persists in sequences mixing realism and the grotesque. Two dolls dressed as a tourist couple, presumably just descended from the toy train seen behind them, are literally swept with their suitcases onto a casino's gaming table by the kind of rake used by croupiers to manipulate gambling chips. Subsequent shots show individual workers painting the nose of a large carnival figure wiping a café table, setting up a parasol, and braiding palm leaves in preparation for the carnival parade. These shots allegorize the construction of bourgeois spectacle, whose underside the film reveals in shots of labor performed by the poor.

Doll-like tourists in *À propos de Nice* (1930).

Getting ready (*À propos de Nice*).

Misfits along the boardwalk (*À propos de Nice*).

Shots of the Grand Hôtel de la Promenade, the Palais de la Méditerranée, and the Negresco at forty-five-degree tilts introduce a segment devoted to the Promenade des Anglais boardwalk as a venue where affluent tourists can walk, watch, and be seen. Fade-ins and close-ups vary the visual rhythm, while isolated shots of a shabbily dressed man and a woman beggar dressed in Gypsy attire reveal the presence of poverty among men in three-piece suits and women in furs. Images of sailboats, racing cars, and tennis players likewise clash with others of men in rolled-up shirtsleeves playing a modest game of *boules.* A montage of well-dressed strollers and animals—a dog and an ostrich—introduces touches of satire that sharpen in a series of five stop-action shots (time stamp 9:19 to 9:29) of a young woman in various outfits. The series ends with a shot of her sitting naked in a chair. Less than a minute later, a close-up of a man's face turned skyward to bask in the winter sun suddenly depicts the face as badly sunburned before yielding to a shot of crocodile, a visual form of metonymy that identifies wrinkled facial skin as the result of immoderate exposure to the wintry sun. The sequences recalled visual pranks seen in films such as Clair's *Entr'acte.* Both illustrated how the documented point of view undermined conventions associated with the travelogue. In particular, they supported Vigo's and Kaufman's efforts to alternate direct critique and/or denunciation with humor and irony as a softer form of the more violent juxtaposition Buñuel and Dalí had adopted a year earlier in *Un chien andalou.*

The ambiguities of scale and perspective developed through the initial alternation of aerial and low-angle shots reach fuller thematic expression in the second half of the film during a segment Temple has aptly tagged

Grotesque parade figure in *À propos de Nice.*

"two worlds apart."[22] Changes in visual scale during the film's first four minutes already objectify this ambiguity in the giant papier-mâché figures. Their preparation for the carnival parade is interspersed with images depicting the city as a site of distraction for the idle rich and brief shots of sweepers and others who make their living on the streets. The parade figures become satirical props that workers turn against the rich whom they ostensibly entertain. Yet even this rhetorical appeal to the grotesque is

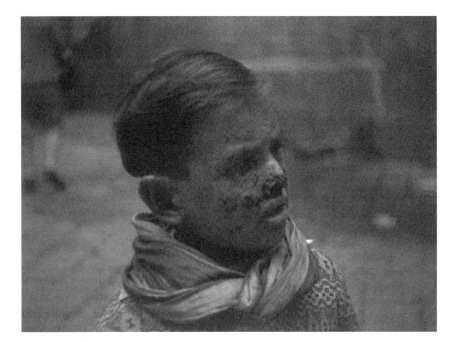

Inner-city inhabitants (*À propos de Nice*).

ideologically ambiguous, hovering between potential protest by the poor and the carnivalesque deployment of ritualized symbols in a moment of licensed, politically controlled disorder.[23] Critique here depends less on open denunciation than on a progressive collapse of distinctions between affluent visitors and workers occupying the same geographic space under the wintry sun of the Riviera.[24]

Vigo next portrays class difference in images of daily life in which women wash clothes around a communal washtub while others cut slices of pizzalike *pissaladière* to be sold on the streets. These images record routine aspects of daily life, with emphasis on Italian immigrant minorities in residential sections of the city seldom frequented by affluent tourists. They also strip the representation of working-class poverty of romantic treatment. A boy with a pockmarked face looks directly into the camera, as does a stray cat drinking water from a garbage-strewn gutter. The gazes are neither aggressive nor hostile. Their openness conveys an absence of artifice at odds with the tightly edited sequences of the carnival parade during which Vigo and Kaufman crosscut images of oversize papier-mâché figures with others of scantily dressed women dancing on a float amid a shower of confetti. Vigo and Kaufman consistently shot the women from below at speeds varying from slow to fast motion. The effect—already present in Clair's *Entr'acte*—abstracted their movements into something mechanical and uncanny. (This was the use of slow motion to which Buñuel referred in his December 1930 letter to Vigo.)

A second key element of the parade involves the use of flowers thrown to spectators by those riding parade floats. The tossing soon turns into a minor battle, showering all parties involved and introducing the motifs of violence and death subsequently expressed through images of a military procession, long panning shots of offshore naval ships, and cemeteries. Shots of a heavily made-up elderly woman grimacing skyward alternate with industrial chimneys belching black-and-white smoke. An elderly woman's grimaces clash with the warmer smiles of laughing men dressed in working-class attire. Images of ovens inside a steel smelting plant evoke an inferno, marking the culmination of a seven-minute death dance that renders the distractions of the idle rich grotesque and morbid. Vigo's montage in *À propos de Nice* moves from caricature in the form of the doll-size couple to grotesque images of the elderly rich unable to ward off death. The visual tone and editing rhythm of *À propos de Nice*'s final three minutes mark a transition from travelogue toward something more aesthetically complex and politically ambivalent. The crosscutting of aerial shots and off-scale shots of the doll-size tourist couple draw the viewer's attention to subsequent techniques of contrapuntal montage, disclosing the underside of labor, exploitation, and poverty seldom seen in standard travelogues. *À propos de Nice* thus served as an exercise in the

Smiling faces (À
propos de Nice).

rhetorical possibilities of silent film grounded in point-of-view framing
and montage (editing).

À propos de Nice turned out to be something more than or different from
the documentary travelogue it started out to resemble. Even so, Vigo's
stance was less openly political in this first film than it would become
two years later, when he joined filmmakers Buñuel, Jean Lods, Pierre
Unik, and Man Ray in the antifascist Association des Écrivains et Artistes

Révolutionnaires (AEAR).[25] Even in terms of documentary practices, Vigo's use of montage to contrast the idle rich and the workers whose labor sustained this idle lifestyle was less unsettling than that in Buñuel's *Un chien andalou* and *Las Hurdes (Land without Bread, 1933)*.[26] If even the most pointed moments in Vigo's films failed to attain the level of dark satire, this failure added to their humanity and thus to their ongoing appeal. Bathélemy Amengual has noted that the more often he watched Vigo's films, the more he was astonished not to find in them—especially in *À propos de Nice* and *Zéro de conduite (Zero for Conduct, 1933)*—the elements of sarcasm, coldness, and aggressiveness that he had sensed at first and that were replaced by a kind of fairy-tale atmosphere whose ferocity never approached desperation.[27] In sum, *À propos de Nice* redirected the first wave of late silent-era Parisian documentaries by Lacombe, Kaufman, Sauvage, and Carné toward the explicit vision that "Toward a Social Cinema" held out as both promise and challenge. It marked a necessary phase in the transition to social documentaries of the 1930s by Ivens, Renoir, Malraux, Storck, and Lotar.

Aubervilliers is a twenty-four-minute black-and-white documentary shot on location during the summer of 1945 in the commune of the same name just north of the municipal slaughterhouse complex at La Villette. This is the same location Georges Franju would feature four years later in *Le Sang des bêtes (Blood of the Beasts)*.[28] It was the first film directed by Eli Lotar (born Eliazar Lotar Teodoresco, 1905–1969), whose involvement with the Parisian literary and visual avant-garde began in 1926 in the form of an apprenticeship under the German-born photographer Germaine Krull (1897–1985). Within a year, Lotar's photographs appeared in art journals and galleries alongside those of Krull, Man Ray, André Kertész, Jacques-André Boiffard, and Berenice Abbott. Twelve of Lotar's photos were shown at the landmark 1929 *FiFo* exhibit in Stuttgart.

From 1929 to 1932, Lotar and Boiffard operated Studios Unis, a photography studio financed by Charles de Noailles and Georges-Henri Rivière. An aristocrat with avant-garde tastes, Noailles had been so taken with Buñuel and Dalí's *Un chien andalou* that he offered to bankroll their follow-up film, *L'Âge d'or (The Golden Age, 1930)*. He had done the same for Man Ray's *Les Mystères du Château du Dé (The Mysteries of the Chateau of the Dice, 1929)* and Jean Cocteau's *Le Sang d'un poète (The Blood of a Poet, 1930)*. Along with Georges Bataille and Michel Leiris, Rivière edited *Documents*, an upscale illustrated review of the arts that was the original venue for Boiffard's notorious close-up of a big toe and for a series of photographs that Lotar shot at the La Villette slaughterhouses. In 1930, Lotar contributed a three-part photomontage to Antonin Artaud and Roger Vitrac's tract *Le Théâtre Alfred-Jarry et l'hostilité publique* (The Alfred Jarry Theater and public hostility). The same year, he assisted Boiffard with the doctored

Paris street scene (by Eli Lotar). Courtesy of the Art Institute of Chicago / Art Resource NY.

cover photo of *Un cadavre* (A corpse), a pamphlet in which Bataille, Leiris, Robert Desnos, Jacques Prévert, and Raymond Queneau confirmed their respective breaks with surrealists under the leadership of André Breton.[29]

Lotar's early street photographs display motifs of the urban marvelous evoked in illustrated prose narratives by surrealists Breton, Desnos, and Louis Aragon.[30] The arrangement of objects in an untitled 1927 photo draws attention as much to the images, fonts, and surfaces surrounding a wooden construction site fence as to the products and events that the posters and signs on the fence advertise. The effect derives from cropping that creates vertical cuts across all but two of the posters in the shot. The larger of the two—seen in full at the center of the photograph—is an advertisement for the Nicolas chain of wine and liquor stores. It features a company mascot named Nectar, who was also seen in print and movie theater ads of the period as a deliveryman able to carry as many as thirty-two bottles at a time. Seated on a bench, Nectar sports his blue worker's apron but is without his customary supply of wine bottles.

The second poster, whose dimensions make its text almost indecipherable, calls for mass demonstrations during the annual May 1 Fête du Travail (Labor Day), the modern origins of which go back to the 1886 labor union strikes in Chicago that culminated in the Haymarket riot. The initial sense of the photo displaying Lotar's predilection for isolated areas and an almost painterly attention to surfaces is tempered by the smaller

Somewhere in Paris (Eli Lotar, 1929). Copyright CNAC/ MNAM/Dist. RMN–Grand Palais / Art Resource NY.

poster's call to social action. The copresence of aesthetic, commercial, and activist concerns persisted in Lotar's photography and film work through the 1930s.

In the photograph *Somewhere in Paris* (1929, English in the original title), the whiteness of laundry on a makeshift clothesline pops out against the darker tones of a decrepit stone wall and the wooden shutters behind it. The shadow of a chair atop a pole forms an acute angle on a dirt surface. The image of the chair seemingly impaled by the rod adds a jolt of violence to the mundane setting. The photograph aligns expository reportage with Lotar's predilection for unattractive subjects and arresting details. Ian Walker notes that the ordinary genre scene, resonant by virtue of its indeterminacy as a no-man's land *(terrain vague)*, situates Lotar's work at the conjuncture of New Objectivity and surrealist approaches to photography.[31] *Somewhere in Paris* transforms a visual record of banal objects such as

La Zone, Billancourt (Eli Lotar, 1933). Copyright CNAC/ MNAM/Dist. RMN–Grand Palais / Art Resource NY.

bedsheets, a clothesline, and a wooden chair into an unexpectedly lyrical evocation of squalor. For the writer and critic Jean Galloti, "There are—in the laundry, on the wall, on the ground—subtleties of light that draw the spectator directly to elements of physical density. And this time, the excellent choice of light compensates for the unfortunate choice of subject."[32]

Lotar's 1933 photograph *La Zone, Billancourt* features parallel diagonals formed by rooftops, posts, the right shoulder and back of a man pushing a wheelbarrow, and bicycle wheels. Utility lines sagging against a blank sky connect the man and wheelbarrow in the lower left to an industrial storage tank in the upper right. Smoke rising from a chimney forms yet another diagonal linking foreground and background planes. On the left side of the photo, the letters BAC on a wall above a tobacco shop *(tabac)* reassert Lotar's attraction to the kinds of desolate sites to which photographers of Paris from Charles Marville to Brassaï were drawn.[33] With their absence of human subjects, two of the three photographs I have described exude the aura Walter Benjamin identified with crime scenes in Eugène Atget's turn-of-the-century photo albums. In *La Zone, Billancourt,* the man in the lower left is a nondescript presence within an evocation of place on the southwestern outskirts of Paris.

From 1928 to 1935, Lotar's photographs appeared on a regular basis in *Vu*, an illustrated weekly whose covers featured photomontages and an art deco logo by Adolphe Mouron Cassandre. The magazine's sepia-tinted images conveyed a softer look than grayscale illustrations while referencing an earlier stage of photographic reproduction. The prominence of *Vu* among interwar weeklies drew in large part on founding editor Lucien Vogel's taste for photo stories and striking layouts that set his weekly apart from its German predecessors, including the *Berliner Illustrirte Zeitung* and the *Allgemeine Illustrirte Zeitung.*[34] Vogel (1886–1954) began as an art director and later served as editor in chief of fashion, art, and gardening magazines. After Vogel's wife, Cécile de Brunhoff, was named editor of French *Vogue* in 1920, he became its art editor. *Vu*, which the American publisher Henry Luce cited as the model for the pictorial weekly *Life* that he founded in 1934 to exploit a growing market for news in a visual form. Vogel even stated that he had designed his weekly to provide readers with an experience approximating that of the millions of filmgoers who watched syndicated newsreels at movie theaters.[35]

The photographers who contributed to *Vu*, including Denise Bellon, Ilse Bing, Brassaï, Robert Capa, Henri Cartier-Bresson, David Seymour (aka Chim), Alfred Eisenstaedt, Gisela Freund, and Man Ray, straddled photojournalism and art photography. André Kertész was featured in forty-three photo essays, Germaine Krull in thirty, Lotar in seventeen, and Vogel himself in ten. Some photographers hired by Vogel were grateful for the extra income; others simply welcomed the opportunity to pursue commissioned assignments. Nighttime photos taken by Lotar on the set of Francis Carco's *Paname* appeared in *Vu*'s first issue (March 21, 1928). His last major project for the weekly accompanied Pierre Unik's article "Ten Hours from Paris, at the Home of the Sultan of Las Hurdes" in issue 364 (March 6, 1935). Photography was Lotar's initial means of access to film studios, where his production stills led to occasional walk-on roles in commercial releases by Marcel L'Herbier, René Clair, and Alberto Cavalcanti.[36] In 1929, Lotar assisted Jean Painlevé with still photography on two shoots of sea animals in Brittany. Enlargements of the stills appeared in *Documents* and *Photo-Graphie*. In 1932, Lotar was on the production crew working with Pierre Prévert on *L'Affaire est dans le sac* (*It's in the Bag*, 1932) and with Yves Allégret on *Prix et profits, la pomme de terre* (*Prices and Profits, the Potato,* 1932), for which Jacques Prévert wrote the commentary and acted. The same year, Lotar accompanied Allégret to the Las Hurdes region in southwestern Spain before Spanish officials threw them out of the country as suspected agitators. Heading south, Lotar and Allégret explored the Canary Islands, which served as the basis of a film, *Ténérife* (1933), for which Jacques Prévert once again wrote the commentary.[37] The next year, Lotar returned to the region as one of three cameramen working with Buñuel on *Las Hurdes.* In the summer of 1936, shortly after the election of the Popular Front coalition government under Léon Blum, he was set photographer for Jean Renoir's *Une partie de campagne* (*A Day in the Country,* 1936).[38]

Despite his sympathy for the Republican cause, Lotar did not accompany Ivens, John Ferhout, and Henri Cartier-Bresson on the front lines of the Spanish Civil War. Instead he worked with the filmmaker Jacques-Bernard Brunius and producer Pierre Braunberger on projects including *Records 37* and *Violon d'Ingres.* The former was a montage film inspired by the notion of human achievement. It was screened in competition at the 1937 International Exposition of Arts and Techniques in Modern Life before being distributed commercially later the same year as a short feature programmed in a number of Parisian movie theaters with Jean Renoir's *La Grande Illusion (Grand Illusion).*[39] Best described as an artistic documentary on the theme of amateur inventors, *Violon d'Ingres (Hobbies across the Sea)* was commissioned by Braunberger (with a musical score by Marcel Jaubert) for the 1939 World's Fair in New York City, where it was shown in the Palais de la France alongside documentaries by René Clair, Abel Gance, Jean Epstein, and Marcel Ichac.

Starting in 1930, Lotar collaborated on a concurrent series of film projects after the Dutch-born filmmaker Joris Ivens invited him to assist on two documentaries, *Wij bouwen* (*We Are Building,* 1930) and *Zuydersee*

(1930).[40] The impact of Ivens (1898–1988) on social documentary based in Europe during the 1930s cannot be overstated. Less than a year after completing his 1929 experimental short *Regen,* Ivens was in Moscow, where his work evolved from silent-era medium-specific exercises toward a more pointed "accusatory aesthetics" that mobilized the film image to document and overturn suffering.[41] In 1933, Ivens and a Belgian colleague, Henri Storck, shot *Misère au Borinage (Misery in Borinage),* a reenactment film about degraded living conditions afflicting coal miners following 1932 strikes in eastern Belgium. In April 1934, Ivens returned to Moscow to film a screenplay that he and André Malraux had based on *La Condition humaine (Man's Fate),* Malraux's 1933 Goncourt Prize–winning novel about a failed 1927 Chinese Communist insurgency in Shanghai. While in Moscow, Ivens also worked on a Russian version of *Borinage,* a documentary about Soviet aviation, and a major film on the Kamchatka Peninsula in Siberia. But when Malraux arrived in Moscow in June 1934, he had replaced Ivens with Sergei Eisenstein on the *Condition humaine* collaboration, which failed to materialize. Perhaps the government-run Mezhrabpom (International Workers' Relief) studio collective withdrew support from a project that it considered out of line with Soviet cultural policy under Stalin.[42]

Ivens left Moscow in January 1936 for what his Russian sponsors described as a "creative vacation." A month later, he was in New York City, ostensibly still on assignment. By the summer, Ivens was in Spain filming *The Spanish Earth* (1937) near Madrid in support of the Republican cause. A year later, he was in China shooting *The 400 Million* (1939). By 1940, he was back in the United States working for the U.S. Film Commission to shoot *Power and the Land* (1940), a documentary on electrification in rural Ohio. Ivens's personal trajectory from 1929 to 1940 illustrated the transnational context of leftist filmmakers active in what Thomas Waugh has called the emergence of radical documentary among cotravelers of the Comintern's global ambitions.[43] Ivens had lived on and off in Paris, where, in 1927, he filmed a silent short, *Études des mouvements à Paris (Study of Traffic Circulation in Paris),* whose iconography recalled that of early interwar documentaries of the city by Lucie Derain, André Sauvage, Eugène Deslaw, and Jean Lods. Three decades later, Ivens and Jacques Prévert collaborated on *La Seine a rencontré Paris (The Seine Met Paris,* 1957), a twenty-eight-minute short that Michèle Lagny has astutely linked to realist documentaries by members of the Groupe des Trente (Group of Thirty) collective.[44] In sum, the peripatetic Ivens embodied the geographic and cultural diversity of European social cinema between the wars as a phenomenon of what Kathleen Newman has described in a more recent context as "above the level of the national, but below the level of the global."[45]

A 1927 screening of Robert Flaherty's *Moana* at the Brussels Cinema

Club convinced Henri Storck (1907–1999) to organize a similar group in his hometown of Ostend and to experiment with a 9.5 mm Pathé Baby movie camera. Three years later, he released eight short subjects under the title *Images d'Ostende.* At the second Congrès International de Cinéastes Indépendants, held in Brussels in November–December 1930, Jean Vigo and Germaine Dulac invited Storck to France. His experience there as an unpaid apprentice at production studios in Paris and Nice convinced him to return to Belgium, where he established his own production company, Ankerfilms. In 1933, Storck accepted Vigo's invitation to assist him in France on the set of *Zéro de conduite.* The same year, he asked Ivens to codirect *Misère au Borinage* with him. Commenting on the latter project, Storck wrote that he and Ivens had wanted to reveal the infernal world of workers: "We felt close to the lives of these people, knowing that the document itself would suffice by conveying its horrified message to spectators who had no idea whatsoever of such existence."[46] While in the Soviet Union in 1931, Ivens had first used reenactment as a narrative technique in *Pesn o Gerojach (Komosol, or Song of Heroes),* produced by the Mezhrabpom-Film agency in Moscow. In *Borinage,* the technique established a porous frontier between documentary and narrative film.[47]

Lotar's major film project of the 1930s was a collaboration with Storck

Young victims (*Les Maisons de la misère,* 1937).

Garden apartments (Les Maisons de la misère).

on *Les Maisons de la misère* (*The Houses of Misery*, 1937), a thirty-minute film commissioned by the Société Nationale des Habitations à Bon Marché (National Society of Inexpensive Housing), a regional housing authority, to promote planned communities of controlled-rent garden apartments and low-rise towers. Despite its location shooting and elements of reportage, *Les Maisons de la misère* was a reenactment film whose depiction of substandard housing was enhanced by a people's chorus consisting of actors and actresses from the Théâtre de l'Équipe, an agitprop troupe with ties to the Belgian Communist Party and a tradition of working-class theater.[48]

Reviewing *Les Maisons de la misère* in 1939, the American photographer and filmmaker Paul Strand described it as the most devastating visual account of a slum he had ever seen:

> Nothing in British or American films dealing with similar material approximates the understanding and sensibility which those who made this film brought to the task. For they have dramatized not only the horror of the slum filth, all the inhuman living conditions of a steel town street, but they have also revealed the people living there with a profound sense of their dignity and worth. We come very close to these people as the texture of their lives is woven from moments which the

camera discovers: the hurried call for the midwife and the funeral of the new-born child; the eviction of a family as the neighbors watch from their windows, unable to help. These and other visits into the houses of this one street which take the audience into the intimate lives of these slum-dwellers never allow us to be disinterested spectators.[49]

By aligning *Les Maisons de la misère* with the international leftist film culture in which Ivens circulated throughout the decade, Strand saw the film as a follow-up between the militancy of *Misère au Borinage* and the more main-stream vision of Arthur Elton and Edgar Anstey's 1936 *Housing Problems.* Even before completing *Borinage* with Ivens, Storck had been asked by Louis Aragon to head a cinema section of the AEAR in Belgium. In sum, the crossed trajectories of Ivens, Storck, and Lotar from 1927 to 1937 display a shared commitment to documentary practices grounded in what the film-maker Chris Marker referred to in the early 1960s as societies in transition. But where Marker was thinking specifically of Cold War China, Siberia, and Cuba, the mission to document the struggles of workers in local, national, and international contexts was already evident in collaborations among Ivens, Stork, Lotar, and Vigo some twenty to twenty-five years earlier.

Sweet Children of Misery: *Aubervilliers* (Eli Lotar, 1946)

Aubervilliers was commissioned by Charles Tillon, a French Communist Party member who was elected mayor of the town in 1945 after represent-ing it for nine years in the Chambre des Députés. Tillon's predecessor as mayor for the previous twenty-two years was Pierre Laval, whose cabinet posts during the Vichy regime resulted in his postwar arrest, trial as a traitor, and execution by firing squad. Much as Nazi officials had under-stood the importance of controlling the French film industry within weeks of their arrival in Paris in June 1940, *Aubervilliers* is a key reference for understanding what Georges Sadoul once called "the battle for French film" immediately following the 1944–45 liberation.[50] Within this brief duration, Lotar's film served as a test case for understanding the place of film—in particular, documentary—among Gaullists and others who wanted to outdo French Communist Party efforts to transform wartime solidarity against German occupying forces into postwar allegiance to partisan doctrine. Where Communists promoted a vision—some saw it instead as a myth—of a postwar France unified under a single class and a single party, Gaullists foresaw a Fourth French Republic unified beyond class and partisan divisions. Which was perhaps a myth of another kind.[51]

Critical attention on *Aubervilliers* at the time of its February 1946 re-lease was heightened by its initial run as a *complément de programme* (com-panion or accompanying film) to René Clément's *La Bataille du rail (The*

Battle of the Rails, 1946) and Paul Grimault's animated ten-minute short *Le Voleur des paratonnerres* (*The Lightning Rod Thief,* 1944). The inclusion of a documentary short or newsreel as part of a commercial program complied with regulations instituted by the French film industry in 1940.[52] (This was the programming model Daeninckx inadvertently followed when he screened *Aubervilliers* in schools and youth centers in the early 1970s.) Yet some movie theater owners were so concerned that Lotar's depiction of substandard living conditions would upset spectators that they lobbied to have *Aubervilliers* dropped from the bill. A compromise limited its screenings to weekdays, when its negative impact on attendance was likely to be lower.[53] Was the threat of films like *Aubervilliers* simply a matter of economics, or did it extend to such films' perspective on social and political issues of the moment?

Seven months after its release, *La Bataille du rail* won the Grand Prize as best film at the 1946 Cannes Film Festival. (*Aubervilliers* was screened at Cannes under the heading of social documentary.) Clément mixed sequences of reportage and reenactment centered on efforts by workers of the state-run Société Nationale des Chemins de Fer Français railway system to sabotage transports under control of German occupying forces. André Bazin praised the film for its fusion of the moralities of art and history. Jean-Pierre Bertin-Maghit has compared it to the cinematic equivalent of an epic poem. Sylvie Lindeperg characterizes it as a valuable piece of ideological capital inhabiting a "chaotic space" between contradictory projects whose interweaving has become the stuff of legend.[54] Some of this capital extended to Lotar's film.

One production element that many spectators took away from *Aubervilliers* was Joseph Kosma's title song, with lyrics by Jacques Prévert that burnished the unofficial title of "people's poet" he had earned a decade earlier on the basis of his tart dialogue for films by Renoir and Carné. As early as 1929, Lotar had frequented the Prévert gang at the Café Les Deux Magots on the Boulevard Saint-Germain. The music critic Alex Ross notes that an insidiously hummable melody is an especially effective vehicle for conveying a serious message.[55] The assertion holds for the Kosma–Prévert composition, whose plaintive performance by Germaine Montero and Fabien Loris sharpened Lotar's depiction of substandard living conditions that were especially hard on children and the elderly. (The so-called children's song was one of the film's three Kosma–Prévert compositions. The others were the song of the river Seine and the song of the water.)

Aubervilliers begins with a credit sequence whose first panel in the form of a photomontage draws directly from Dziga Vertov's 1929 *Man with a Movie Camera.* The upper half of the panel—borrowed from Vertov—features three frames of a man looking away from the camera, apparently

through the lens of a movie camera. A fourth frame on the right shows a tripod tilting upward and back toward the left. Following the images from left to right along slight variations in framing simulates a form of flip-book animation. The name of the Uni/ci/té production company in the lower right corner of the frame sets the primary meaning of the noun (uniqueness) against homonymic wordplay matching *unité* (unity) and *cité*, which could be translated as "city," "town," or "housing project." The word "Ciné-France" superimposed over a close-up of a brick wall in the second panel reinforces the ideological dimension of the film because it is the name of the French Communist Party's production company known between the wars as Ciné-Liberté. The ties to the PCF point to Lotar's desire to align himself on the postwar cultural left. They also reinforce the PCF's desire following the 1944–45 liberation to cast itself as the chief party of French film.[56] The third panel features a scrolling text stating that the goal of the film shot in the suburbs of Paris during the summer of 1945 is to draw attention to the living conditions in urban slums. The fourth displays the film's title in italicized lettering superimposed over an image of the outside wall of a structure whose broken windows suggest a tenement or abandoned factory. As a set, the four panels provide visual cues of a sober realism tempered by another cue that references practices of openly ideological filmmaking associated with Soviet Russia during the 1920s.

Lotar samples Vertov (*Aubervilliers*, 1946).

A follow-up sequence features additional credits over moving post-cardlike images of central Paris. Long shots of barges on the Seine moving eastward past the Pont-Neuf, Notre-Dame, and neighboring bridges alternate with medium shots of sailors and lock attendants at work that recall the depictions of daily life on an inland waterway barge in Vigo's 1934 feature *L'Atalante*. Shots of the churning river surface recall sequences filmed on the Canal Saint-Martin at the start of Marcel Carné's 1938 feature *Hôtel du Nord*. Visual effects of liquidity are heightened by Kosma's orchestration for strings and reeds. Lyrics kick in after a minute and a half to assert that the Seine is lucky and worry-free as it flows calmly toward the Atlantic, as though a dream amid the mysteries of Paris. The images and sound track continue to tap into poetic realist films of the late 1930s, such as Julien Duvivier's 1937 *Pépé le Moko*, in which the one-time music hall and cabaret star Tania (played by the former music hall and cabaret star Fréhel) sings longingly of the Paris of her youth.[57] Yet, as Prévert's voice-over commentary asserts at a later point, the ruins of Aubervilliers were not caused by the war. They are old ruins, everyday ruins, the simple ruins of working-class misery only a short distance from the Place Vendôme and the Champs-Élysées.

The main section of *Aubervilliers* is structured as the cinematic equivalent of a ballad in five stanzas, each with a refrain that has come to be known as the children's song:

> Sweet children of Aubervilliers
> Sweet children of the working class
> Sweet children of misery
> Sweet children of the whole world.[58]

The narrative device of the refrain in *Aubervilliers* taps into Storck and Lotar's collaboration a decade earlier on *Les Maisons de la misère*, which included a recitation by a people's chorus matched with close-ups of the sober faces of workers:

> We're dying of cold, hunger, and poverty
> The sky is heavy on this fragile roof
> We sleep day and night in this train carriage
> We sleep day and night with lice, disease, and dust.[59]

Shifting collaborations enter the picture as the Storck–Ivens project in *Borinage* evolves to the Storck–Lotar team in *Les Maisons de la misère* and the Lotar–Prévert work on *Aubervilliers*.

The Kosma–Prévert song returns during a sequence that features chil-

dren swimming in the Canal de l'Ourcq amid dockside work and factories in full swing. A montage of shots featuring industrial machinery and
gridwork, workplace conditions, decrepit housing, and local outdoor markets alternate with sketch vignettes of individuals and families, often with
pointed voice-over commentary. José Pereira is described as fifty-three
years old but looking older. Former nurse Madame Rochaud displays a

On the job
and at play in
Aubervilliers.

certificate honoring a boy under her charge for winning a baby beauty contest. But when the same baby turned seventeen, former mayor Laval had him sent to Germany to perform forced labor. Eighty-seven-year-old Madame Carouget is likewise proud of a certificate and family medal she received in 1929 from French president Gaston Doumergue. Yet Carouget and her sixty-six-year-old daughter, Laurence, live in constant fear that they will be forced to vacate the hovel they have occupied as squatters for years.

The vignettes were not chosen as visual evidence to pressure administrators and legislators to improve living conditions in the area. This denunciation had already occurred before the film was shot. Instead, they were aimed at inner-city spectators for whom the geographic proximity of Aubervilliers did nothing to lessen its invisibility. To this end, Lotar reverted to narrative strategies deployed a decade earlier in *Borinage* and *Les Maisons de la misère,* in which reenactment and vignettes personalized conditions affecting larger—and essentially anonymous—groups of victims. Additional vignettes depict living conditions among those accustomed to misery. Looking as though they might have stepped out of Buñuel's *Las Hurdes,* an elderly couple shot in stark high-contrast black and white are seen in their hovel to which they have become accustomed. The voice-over adds that this is normal among those for whom life amid ruins and slums begins badly and will likely end the same way. A cobbler at work in his tiny shop is seemingly oblivious to the camera crew. A young woman pulling a cart piled high with rags glares at the camera as she passes by. A blind accordionist, truck farmers *(maraîchers),* ragpickers atop a horse-drawn wagon, and women on their way to outdoor markets complete this evocation of populist dignity amid misery on the northern edge of Paris that few spectators of the film were likely ever to have seen in person. The milieu barely differs from that seen twenty years earlier in Lacombe's *La Zone.*

The five-minute sequence at the end of *Aubervilliers* sketches a different kind of family portrait. Four children of the Izy family are introduced by name and age—Jeanne (ten), Denise (eight), Pierre (seven), and Solange (twelve)—followed by their dog, Bobbi, and their mother, whom the voice-over politely refers to as Madame Izy. A sharp cut shows the father, Monsieur Izy, returning from work, accompanied by his fifteen-year-old son, Roger, described as an apprentice typesetter. The eldest child, sixteen-year-old Alexandre, works at the post office. Prévert's commentary pokes fun at the father: "Monsieur Izy looks unpleasant, but don't trust your first impression. He is good-natured and cheerful. The trouble is that his eyeglasses give him a harsh look; it's not his fault."

The prominence of the children within the family unit sets the Izy family apart from the elderly and the dispossessed seen earlier in the film. Much as he and Storck had done a decade earlier in *Les Maisons de la misère,*

Family portraits in *Aubervilliers*.

Lotar gives names and faces to working-class children for whom a supportive family and education offer the prospect of upward mobility. But because this future is not yet a reality, Prévert's concluding commentary states what needs to occur first:

> And who might think while looking at the family portrait hanging on the wall that this wall, as well as everything that supports all the other walls surrounding it, might collapse, literally collapse at any moment? . . . Possible or not, this is how it is. And despite their involuntary charm, these images of Aubervilliers present only minor aspects of distress in the world in which war has once again returned nearly everywhere to add its ruins to those of the past to make things difficult for those who need to clear away, reconstruct, and repair everything.
>
> And as always, it is at the foot of the wall that the bricklayer is to be found and the hands of workers that come once again to the aid of this paralyzed and depressed world, this world which must absolutely change and which will change in the end.

In his 1912 novel *Aubervilliers*, Léon Bonneff describes the town's liminal status: "Adjacent to the boulevards of this town, the most fertile countryside in the Île-de-France provides strong and sturdy wheat. The town has two faces: the old and the modern, the cauldron of hell and the basket of springtime."[60] The passage sets the future evoked at the end of Lotar's film within a longer series of verbal and visual accounts that go beyond straightforward reportage. Bonneff's remarks prophesy a cinematic realism casting Lotar's *Aubervilliers* as a corrective to softer depictions of Paris in poetic realist films of the 1930s by Jean Renoir and Marcel Carné.[61] Commenting on *The Long Night*, Anatole Litvak's 1947 remake of Carné's 1939 *Le Jour se lève (Daybreak)*, André Bazin wrote that the French original was a tragedy at Aubervilliers that could not be the same thing in the suburbs of San Francisco. As Didier Daeninckx has put it, all roads do lead to Aubervilliers, where, in 2001, the local government created Parc Eli Lotar, whose green spaces between a canal and the rue Marcel Carné are a testament to the city's cinematic past.[62]

The release of *Aubervilliers* in early 1946 occurred near the midpoint of the twenty or so social documentaries completed from 1928 through 1963 that constitute the corpus under study in this book. Lotar's early work in photography and his transition to film from 1928 to 1931 set his personal trajectory alongside those of the Dutch-born Joris Ivens, the Russian-born Boris Kaufman, the Spanish-born Luis Buñuel, the Belgian-born Henri Storck, and the French-born Jean Vigo, whose respective activities evolved from medium-specific experiments of the late silent era toward activist documentary in early sound-era documentaries in the 1930s. *Aubervilliers* extended these interwar practices toward postwar documentaries by Georges Franju, Nicole Védrès, René Vautier, Chris Marker, Alain Resnais, Jean Rouch, and Agnès Varda. Some of the postwar films—Vautier's *Afrique 50* (1950), Resnais and Marker's *Les Statues meurent aussi* (*Statues Also Die*, 1953), and Rouch's *Moi, un Noir* (*I, a Black Man*, 1958)—responded to French colonial policies and, in the case of *Nuit et brouillard* (*Night and Fog*, 1955), the memory of wartime concentration camps. Others, such as Franju's documentary on Paris slaughterhouses and Resnais's short on the

Slaughterhouse photograph (from *Documents*, November 1929). Photograph copyright the Metropolitan Museum of Art. Source: Art Resource NY.

French national library, overlaid reportage treatments of postwar Paris with critiques of Fourth Republic modernization policies. Still others, such as Marker's *Dimanche à Pékin* (*Sunday in Peking*, 1956) and *Lettre de Sibérie* (*Letter from Siberia*, 1958), Rouch and Edgar Morin's *Chronique d'un été* (*Chronicle of a Summer*, 1961) and Marker's *Le Joli Mai* (*The Merry Month of May*, 1963), addressed transitional societies in Asia and Africa as well as domestic topics of youth cultures, racism, sexuality, and the war without a name in Algeria.

Aubervilliers attests to Lotar's evolution as a photographer turned film-maker and committed artist on the cultural left, in keeping with Damarice Amao's assertion that *Aubervilliers* is above all a photographer's film, with striking shots that display the sensitivity and training of an image maker *(faiseur d'images)* in sync with what amounts to an interrupted—or per-haps even delayed—history of interwar avant-garde cinema going back as far as Lacombe's *La Zone* and André Sauvage's *Études sur Paris* (1929).[63]

The Slaughterhouse Photos

Nowhere is the significance of Lotar's early work in mass circulation and art venues more striking than in his photograph of twenty-eight severed hooves lined up against a wall at the municipal slaughterhouse at La Vil-lette. The photo first appeared in the November 1929 issue of the noncon-formist art journal *Documents* as one of three illustrations accompanying a brief entry, "Abattoir," by the journal's codirector, Georges Bataille.[64] The reproductions in *Documents* were made from glass plate negatives of thirty-four shots Lotar had taken a month earlier during a visit to the slaughter-house complex in the company of the painter André Masson. A year later, the same photograph was among eight from the series reproduced as a four-page portfolio, "La Viande" (Meat), published in the Belgian jour-nal *Variétés*.[65] In 1931, the hooves shot appeared a third time in a montage of nine photos accompanying Carlo Rim's article "La Villette rouge" in issue 166 (May 20, 1931) of *Vu*. A closer look at the three sets of slaugh-terhouse photos suggests how their publication venues and formats an-ticipated Lotar's evolution over the following decade from art photos and photojournalism toward social documentary in collaborations with Ivens, Buñuel, and Storck that culminated in his directorial debut in *Aubervilliers*.

The formal austerity of the full-page reproduction of the hooves pho-tograph in *Documents* enhances the shock value of its subject matter. Hard lines along the mineral surfaces of three walls set off a curved border be-tween bricks and a patch of earth at the foot of a large tree trunk. Depth of field in a rear plane is marked by a shade of medium gray that contrasts with darker gradations of walls in middle and frontal planes. The name

"Pichard" written in chalked capital letters on the wall in the upper right asserts ownership of the work space. Its repetition in faded chalk toward the center of the photograph and other marks on the same wall counter broader effects of symmetry. The marks on the wall also recall photos of graffiti that photographer Gyula Halász (aka Brassaï) began to shoot in Paris around the same time.

The arrangement of hooves is neat, so much so that in recent years it has inspired one online commentator to compare the appearance of the animal hooves to a line of young women in white dresses facing the wall. The comparison is in poor taste, but it conveys unseen violence as a precondition of what Ian Walker calls a bureaucratic process placing animal remains in a row, as though on an assembly line.[66] The comparison is strengthened in the same issue of *Documents* by a photo of female dancers whose legs are figuratively cut just below the hips by the lower edge of a curtain. (The photo is from *The Movietone Follies of 1929.*) The effect borrows from the rhetorical figure of synecdoche. Readers of *Documents* see the severed limbs that stand for the slaughtered animal, some of whose remains have been cleaned up for display.

The full-page photo in the December 1929 issue of *Documents* appeared opposite a page containing Bataille's "Abattoir" entry and a second entry by him, "Cheminée d'usine" (Factory smokestack). The latter included a Keystone agency shot of a sixty-three-meter-tall industrial smokestack

Two-page spread, I (*Documents*, November 1929).

Aux abattoirs de La Villette. — Photo. Eli Lotar.

Chute d'une cheminée haute de 60 mètres
Banlieue de Londres.

Photo Keystone

CHRONIQUE

DICTIONNAIRE

ABATTOIR. — L'abattoir relève de la religion en ce sens que des temples des époques reculées, (sans parler de nos jours de ceux des hindous) étaient à double usage, servant en même temps aux implorations et aux tueries. Il en résultait sans aucun doute (on peut en juger d'après l'aspect de chaos des abattoirs actuels) une coïncidence bouleversante entre les mystères mythologiques et la grandeur lugubre caractéristique des lieux où le sang coule. Il est curieux de voir s'exprimer en Amérique un regret lancinant : W. B. Seabrook (1) constatant que la vie orgiaque a subsisté, mais que le sang de sacrifices n'est pas mêlé aux cocktails, trouve insipide les mœurs actuelles. Cependant de nos jours l'abattoir est maudit et mis en quarantaine comme un bateau portant le choléra. Or les victimes de cette malédiction ne sont pas les bouchers ou les animaux, mais les braves gens eux-mêmes qui en sont arrivés à ne pouvoir supporter que leur propre laideur, laideur répondant en effet à un besoin maladif de propreté, de petitesse bilieuse et d'ennui : la malédiction (qui ne terrifie que ceux qui la profèrent) les amène à végéter aussi loin que possible des abattoirs, à s'exiler par correction dans un monde amorphe, où il n'y a plus rien d'horrible et où, subissant l'obsession indélébile de l'ignominie, ils sont réduits à manger du fromage. — G. BATAILLE.

(1) *L'île magique*, Firmin-Didot, 1929 (cf., plus loin, p. 334).

CHEMINÉE D'USINE. — Si je tiens compte de mes souvenirs personnels, il semble que, dès l'apparition des diverses choses du monde, au cours de la première enfance, pour notre génération, les formes d'architecture terrifiantes étaient beaucoup moins les églises, même les plus monstrueuses, que certaines grandes cheminées d'usine, véritables tuyaux de communication entre le ciel sinistrement sale et la terre boueuse empuantie des quartiers de filatures et de teintureries.

Aujourd'hui, alors que de très misérables esthètes, en quête de placer leur chlorotique admiration, inventent platement la *beauté* des usines, la lugubre saleté de ces énormes tentacules m'apparaît d'autant plus écœurante, les flaques d'eau sous la pluie, à leur pied, dans les terrains vagues, la fumée noire à moitié rabattue par le vent, les monceaux de scories et de mâchefer sont bien les seuls attributs possibles de ces dieux d'un Olympe d'égout et je n'étais pas halluciné lorsque j'étais enfant et que ma terreur me faisant discerner dans mes épouvantails géants, qui m'attiraient jusqu'à l'angoisse et aussi parfois me faisaient fuir en courant à toutes jambes, la présence d'une effrayante colère, colère qui, pouvais-je m'en douter, allait devenir plus tard ma propre colère, donner un sens à tout ce qui se salissait dans ma tête, et en même temps à tout ce qui, dans des états civilisés, surgit comme la charogne dans un cauchemar. Sans doute je n'ignore pas que la plupart des gens, quand

321

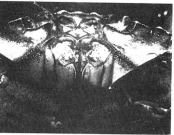

Aux abattoirs de La Villette (cf. p. 329). — Photo Eli Lotar.

1. Tête de crevette ; 2. Tête de crabe. (cf. p. 332). — Film Jean Painlevé (1929).

Two-page spread, II (*Documents*, November 1929).

collapsing in a London suburb. Two additional photographs from the slaughterhouse series appeared on the following page opposite shots of a shrimp head and a crab head that Lotar had taken in Brittany on location with filmmaker Jean Painlevé. (The latter two accompanied Jacques Baron's dictionary entry "Crustacés" [Crustaceans] on the following page.) The four-photo spread in parallel (mirror) layout on facing pages illustrates the attraction to brutal processes of life and death that Bataille and his colleagues at *Documents* explored in the critical dictionary. The attraction persisted later the same decade in the journal *Acéphale*—five issues appearing from 1936 to 1939—and among others such as Michel Leiris, Roger Caillois, Pierre Klossowski, and André Masson, all of whom participated with Bataille in the Collège de Sociologie collective (1937–39).[67]

The two photographs on page 330 record moments of bloody violence that the full-page photograph on page 328 leaves unseen. The upper shot centers on what appears to be a roll of cloth in front of two closed wooden doors. Lines on the floor in a gentle curve are likely traces of blood, making the cloth an index of the violence imposed on animals. Doors lead to scalding vats *(échaudoirs)* inside the complex that facilitate skinning the hide from carcasses of larger animals. Georges Didi-Huberman argues that the formless heap *(tas informe)* may not be a rolled cloth but rather the remains of a slaughtered animal with "its own skin rolled onto itself, like a crude cloth."[68] The lower photo on page 330 is an overhead shot of three slaughterhouse workers cutting up a small animal. Blood and fat fill a gutter in front of them. In the upper left corner, a third worker stands facing the wall near a downed animal tied to the wall by a cord or a rope. The slatted wooden platform behind the two men is a dissecting table. A small metal tub for collecting blood is visible on the floor at one end. As in the upper photo, the swirls on the floor and entrails at the lower left and center are traces of animal remains dragged through the doors. The overhead angle and layout support Didi-Huberman's characterization of the shot as a slaughterhouse choreography of butchers.[69]

The graphic depictions of slaughterhouse processes in the two photos on page 330 clash with the understatement of the full-page photo. Those of crustaceans on page 331 likewise elicit a visceral response by enlarging their subjects to the point of grotesque abstraction. This is especially the case in the photo of the crab head, in which the carapace resembles the body armor an extraterrestrial might wear in a science fiction movie. The placement of the four-photo spread two pages after the full-page photograph seems calculated. Yve-Alain Bois notes that the two-photo spread on page 330 belies the flat horror of the initial image by disclosing—if only in part—the essential violence of a meat factory.[70]

The photo spread in *Documents* raises a number of questions. Who chose the photographs that were reproduced? Who was responsible for

Montage layout (*Variétés*, 1930).

L a   V i a n d e

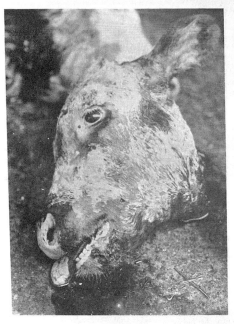

*H u i t   p h o t o s   p r i s e s   à   l' a b a t t o i r
p a r   E l i   L o t a r*

their layout and placement in the journal issue? Was it Lotar, Bataille, or someone else? In a 1979 interview with Ian Walker, Michel Leiris stated that the photos, which Lotar had titled rather flatly as *La Villette, Abattoir,* had inspired Bataille's text rather than been used to illustrate prose that Bataille had written beforehand. Walker adds that the passion and sarcasm of Bataille's entry are at odds with the dispassionate mood of Lotar's photographs, "which offer no such judgments."[71] Bois writes that even if Lotar's photos contain nothing of the mythic mysteries and lugubrious grandeur conveyed by Bataille's prose, the lie that they might be seen as giving to Bataille's entry is not one because Lotar's photos fail to express concern for the slaughtered animals. Are the slaughterhouse photos an iconographic climax in which the desire to see is stronger than horror or disgust? Or does Bataille's predilection for base materialism overwhelm Lotar's project to record (document) the workplace and labor process at the La Villette complex?[72]

The full-page photo in *Documents* only begins to display the violence that the two follow-up photos disclose. Yet the same photo reproduced five months later in *Variétés* has lost its formal starkness among eight that are laid out two photos per page over four pages as a portfolio titled "La Viande," with the caption "Huit photos prises à l'abattoir par Eli Lotar" (Eight photos taken at the slaughterhouse by Eli Lotar). The hooves shot appears on the first page of the *Variétés* portfolio alongside a close-up of a dead calf. Photos, title, and caption are laid out with their left edges toward the bottom edge of the page so that the reader has to turn the journal copy ninety degrees in order to see the images upright. This is not the case for the following six photos, which are placed in pairs, one image on top of another, with lower edges parallel to those of the pages on which they appear. As in the *Documents* spread, the second page provides details of the slaughterhouse process. The upper photo, an overhead long shot, shows a worker standing to the left behind a cow held by a chain attached to a large door. Another worker standing to the front and right of the animal might be holding a long knife or similar tool. Visible in the upper right corner of the shot are carcasses of slaughtered animals neatly suspended from long poles. Detritus on the floor appears to include blood and offal. The lower shot shows two slaughtered animals placed on low benches. Blood from the animals' cut throats is collecting in a metal tub. No workers are visible.

The absence of human subjects extends to the photos on the third page, whose layout constructs a composite entity dominated by the lower shot, a close-up featuring four hooves with other hooves presumably behind. The subject of the photo may be the same row of hooves seen in the full-page *Documents* photo. The photo above it provides an additional take on a shot in the initial series recast in *Variétés* as a close-up of six rolls of

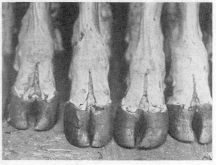

flesh arranged in two rows near a curb. A wheel belonging to an appara- Two-page
tus of some sort is visible in soft focus in a rear plane. The ground-level spread (*Variétés*, 1930).
angle of the shot complicates any stable sense of scale, making the exact
content of the image initially difficult to identify. Taken together, the two
photos depict end products of the slaughterhouse process whose status as
unfit for consumption conforms to what Bataille would later theorize as
the accursed share *(part maudite)* that is both marginal and necessary to
the economy of general circulation.

The final pair of shots in *Variétés* further documents phases of slaughterhouse operations divided visually between human presence and absence. The upper photo is a medium shot of a man skinning an animal,
whose flesh and skin in two tones stand out against the darker tones of the
worker's hands, forearms, and clothing. It is unclear whether the man is
using a knife to skin the animal or if he is tugging at a carcass that has been
scalded. The lower shot returns to the work area outside the large wooden
door seen throughout the series. Once again, no workers are present, and
the only objects visible are a bench, the dissecting platform leaning against
a wall, and a pile of entrails/offal. (An object behind the bench may be
another roll of animal hide.) Where the two earlier shots of rolled hides
record the reduction of a live animal to a formless mass, the final image in
the *Variétés* portfolio is a grisly reply to the full-page shot of hooves at the
start of the *Documents* series. With no written text except for the opening

title and caption, the documentation of slaughterhouse operations provided by the eight shots in *Variétés* is purely visual.

The third venue for the hooves photo was a three-page (698–700)
photomontage in issue 166 of *Vu* (May 20, 1931). This time around, the
photos accompany an article, "La Villette rouge" (Red Villette), by Carlo
Rim. The first two pages of the article are cast as a double-page spread
with images at all four corners. In all, six photos are arranged around a text
laid out in four columns. The title and credit top a layout whose symmetry
is broken by a photo cutout (page 699) of a butcher looking directly into
the camera. The man's posture and upper body exude strength. The knives
he carries in a holster strapped across his hips make him look like a gun-
slinger in a western feature film. A blood-stained apron and leather boots
enhance the effect. The worker's cap on the man's head barely softens this
portrait of the demeanor that the poet Charles Baudelaire evoked in *Les
Fleurs du mal* (*The Flowers of Evil*, 1857) when he wrote, "Je te frapperai sans
colère / Et sans haine, comme un boucher" (No rage, no rancor: I shall
beat you / As butchers fell an ox).[73]

Four of the six photos reproduced in *Vu* include workers. Moving clockwise from the upper left corner of page 698, the first photograph is of a
workplace area, taken from a near-horizontal perspective. A splash of
water frozen in midair by the shot on the right side of the frame suggests

Two-page
spread (*Vu*,
1931).

a cleanup. Water droplets hanging in the air are just about to break up the surface reflection of slaughterhouse architecture and open sky on water already on the floor. While the caption for the shot—"Ici tout est rouge" (Everything here is red)—implies that the liquid on the floor might be blood, the surface tension of the liquid suggests something closer to water. A close-up in the upper right corner of the spread shows a worker using a knife to skin an animal. The proximity of human and animal flesh is conveyed by the posture of the worker leaning his head on the carcass of the animal he is skinning with one hand while tugging at it with the other. The man appears to be the same one seen standing in the cutout.

A photo reproduced in smaller dimensions in the lower right corner shows a woman in boots, skirt, and short-sleeved top bent over astride a carcass. A scarf on her head is the only visible concession to occupational safety. Straw spread on the surface below and a brick wall in a rear plane to her left are minimal indicators of a workplace. The caption explains that the woman is using a small knife to scrape pig hides. The photo in the lower left reprises the overhead shot on the second page of the *Variétés* layout. One man holds the tub used for collecting blood from the animals while a slaughtered animal lies on its right side. Chains visible in front of and behind the carcass suggest how the trace lines of blood are formed when the animal is dragged through the door. A second worker standing just inside an open wooden door toward the rear of the shot prepares another animal for blood draining. Carcasses suspended from rods on the right, a large tub, and a sizable puddle complete the iconography of tools used in the skinning process. The caption for the shot reads, "A torrent of blood flows from the slit throat of the animal." The photo placed just above the center and across the two pages of the spread shows sheep being bled, presumably from a low wooden platform such as the one seen in other photos. The close-up depicts the sheep placed close together with their heads hanging. Their legs, stiffened in death, appear almost to intertwine. The caption reads, "The sheep live and die in flocks."

The layout on page 700 includes two columns of prose and three photos. The top photo is circular and the others rectangular. Their juxtaposition at opposite corners adumbrates the visual continuity of a scan. The photo in the upper left reprises the overhead angle of other shots showing workers in an open area near the scalding vat doors. The middle photo, which breaks up the right column of text, is a cropped version of the hooves photo seen earlier in *Documents* and *Variétés*. Cropping centered on the hooves and the wall behind them excludes elements of architecture seen in the previous two venues. The third photo, at the bottom of the left column, likewise crops the shot of six rolls of hide first seen in *Variétés*. Where the two-page spread adheres to Lucien Vogel's penchant for the

Revised layout (*Vu*, 1931).

photo-essay, the layout of the third and final page conforms to conventional practices in which images illustrate a prose text. In the absence of documentation indicating how Lotar and Rim collaborated on "La Villette rouge," a closer look at Rim's text identifies how Lotar's photos in *Vu* can be understood in contrast to those from the slaughterhouse series published eighteen months earlier in *Documents*.

Carlo Rim (born Jean Marius Richard, 1905–1989) was a caricaturist and cartoonist before serving as editor in chief of *Vu* and the right-wing daily *L'Intransigeant.* In 1934, he wrote screenplays for the Josephine Baker–Jean Gabin vehicle *Zouzou* (Marc Allégret) and for Maurice Tourneur's *Justin de Marseille* (1935). At the time he wrote "La Villette rouge," Rim was editor of *Jazz*, an illustrated monthly of current intellectual life *(l'actualité intellectuelle).* "La Villette rouge" was cast as a walk-through visit by a first-person narrator who invited his readers to accompany him. In keeping with Vogel's desire to make *Vu* an illustrated print equivalent of a weekly newsreel, Rim assumed a tone of good-natured storytelling: "I visited the slaughterhouse at La Villette starting at the end, as one might project a film from end to start. And I advise you to follow my example if you want to fully partake of this magnificent and alarming spectacle."[74]

References to characters in Émile Zola's novels early in Rim's account evoked the period of the La Villette complex's completion, which coincided with the 1867 Exposition Universelle. These origins were the basis for Rim's description of operations among slaughterhouse workers, whose specialized skills extended artisanal (hands-on) traditions:

> I enter a work area. Outside, colors and shapes merge in the gray dawn. Inside, everything is red: walls, floor, carts, tables, chains, hands, animal horns. . . . A bull enters, docile yet majestic. He sniffs at the littered floor and spreads a calm gaze on the blood that has spread itself everywhere. A black leather mask is placed over its head, followed by a stem and a chute over its paws. A man approaches, carrying a poleax in his hand. Direct and precise, the blow falls. . . . The butchers proceed with their follow-up. They grasp the stiff feet and cradle the bull's carcass until every last drop of blood flows into the tub that is already close to overflowing. The beast is now skinned with a prodigious dexterity. . . . Capital punishment turns into gastronomy. The torturer has become the top chef. And on his head, Escoffier's white toque has replaced the executioner Deibler's top hat.[75]

Rim's attention to detail humanized his portrait of the workers by placing them within a professional environment whose categories of animal specialization and job function extended beyond the blanket term *bouchers* (butchers).[76] Accordingly, *veautiers* worked with calves, *bouviers* with cows and bulls, *moutonniers* with sheep, and *porciers* with pigs. The order reflected a casual hierarchy, with *veautiers* at the top and *porciers* at the bottom. The terms invoked by Rim derived from traditional usage designating herders of different species. (As documented twenty years later in Franju's *Le Sang des bêtes,* horses were typically processed at the Vaugirard

Close-up worker in *Vu.* Copyright CNAC/MNAM/ Dist. RMN– Grand Palais / Art Resource NY.

Looks of pride in *Vu*. Copyright CNAC/MNAM/ Dist. RMN– Grand Palais / Art Resource NY.

slaughterhouse located in 15th arrondissement, at the southern extremity of the Left Bank.) In terms of job function, drivers *(conducteurs)* herded the animals from the market or sales area to the actual slaughter areas, where killers *(tueurs)* killed them and cut them up before wholesalers *(chevillards)* prepared them for sale by hanging the dissected carcasses on large hooks or pikes. The only passage in which Rim approached Bataille's nonconformist take on the slaughterhouse occurred in his comparison of butchers to bearded priests whose short-bladed knives evoked the sword of the Zoroastrian divinity Mithra.

The detail and tone of Rim's prose in "La Villette rouge" recall those of "Ici, on ne s'amuse pas" (This is no place to have fun), a text Lotar wrote in November 1929 while assisting Joris Ivens on location filming of *Wij bouwen*. Notably, Lotar's emphasis on the activities of workers at La Villette expresses concerns with labor conditions at a remove from Bataille's perspective, animated by interests in collectives and myth:

We are somewhere, very far away, in a region that resembles no other and to which one has no desire to give a name. I know for a fact that Amsterdam is only a few hours away and that Amsterdam is in Holland.

But it is so hard to try to imagine after spending a week here in this country that is not, in truth, yet one, but which will have taken shape when one will be able to walk in wooden shoes on its surface. We are in the Gulf of the Zuydersee, where painstaking efforts to drain the sea are taking place. . . .

The area currently resembles a deportation site. Life is reduced to exhausting labor. More than 200 workers working like convicts also display the resignation of convicts. It is neither in two years, nor in five nor in ten years that "this" will be done, but in 50. They know this and yet they think of the goal: hard labor for a lifelong sentence.

Nothing matters here but the work. When night falls, these men trudge off to sleep. They awaken with the sunrise, ready to do the same thing again for ten hours. And they know that this can last for 50 years. I confess that the frightful simplicity of this life without surprises, the perfect beauty of this mechanical existence, is one of the most distressing things one might ever see, and also one of the most beautiful.[77]

Lotar adopts an eyewitness perspective by casting his remarks in the first person singular. The effect recalls the opening words of Chris Marker's 1958 *Lettre de Sibérie*: "Je vous écris d'un pays lointain" (I am writing to you from a distant country). As in Marker's film, Lotar's reportage is tempered by critique that targets working conditions that are compared to those of convicts. Six years later, Lotar's collaboration with Henri Storck on *Les Maisons de la misère* would combine critique with reenactment to humanize the substandard living conditions of workers in Eastern Belgium. Sensitivity to this plight was already evident in 1929, both in the slaughterhouse series of photos and in the prose that Lotar wrote while assisting Ivens while on location with *Wij bouwen*.[78]

Two photographs from *Variétés* capture the essence of the slaughterhouse series by showing the activity and humanity of the workers. In the first, a medium close-up of a man skinning an animal uses a shallow depth of field to focus on his effort and concentration. As he leans against the carcass, the flesh tone on his face and bare upper arm bears an eerie resemblance to the animal flesh in close proximity to it. An accompanying shot is more posed, but the pride in the two workers' gazes toward the camera likewise conveys their ease with and pride in what they are doing. As such, the two photographs anticipate shots of the inhabitants that Lotar will feature fifteen years later in conjunction with the more explicit engagement with misery in *Aubervilliers*.

Transition II

Popular Front—Vichy—Postwar

Documentary filmmaking in France from 1944 through 1946 was marked by the lifting of restrictions imposed by Vichy regime officials during the 1940–44 German occupation. Curiously, these restrictions drew on reforms proposed a decade earlier by French state agencies whose oversight of the film industry ranged from financing to censorship. The regulatory authority of these agencies often set them at odds with individual filmmakers, labor unions, and film industry entities. Continuities in reforms across the interwar, wartime, and early postwar periods appeared in the occupation-period Comité d'Organisation de l'Industrie Cinématographique (COIC; Organizing Committee of the Cinema Industry), which spawned the post-war Centre National de la Cinématographie (CNC; National Center of Cinematography) and the national school for filmmakers and technicians known as the Institut des Hautes Études Cinématographiques (IDHEC; Institute for Advanced Cinema Studies). The origins and evolving roles of these agencies clarify what was at stake in debates surrounding state involvement with documentary filmmaking in France from the mid-1930s to the mid-1950s.

The impetus for postwar reforms affecting documentary practices is best understood in conjunction with government reports commissioned a decade earlier in the wake of two scandals. A first set of reforms was initiated in the aftermath of the Gaumont-Franco-Film-Aubert production company's 1935 fall into receivership. A second was prompted by allegations of fraud against Pathé-Cinéma's Bernard Natan that implicated state officials.[1] A June 1935 report by National Assembly deputy Maurice Petsche proposed the creation of a national credit organization to finance film production under the aegis of a state ministry with authority over all public services related to cinema. A year later, a report to the Conseil National Économique (National Economic Council) supported efforts among film industry professionals who had responded to the Petsche report by proposing a patchwork confederation of production, distribution, and exhibition companies.[2] The author of the follow-up report, Ministry of Finance inspector Guy de Carmoy, outlined the prototype of an industry-based entity with significant autonomy. A major difference be-tween the Petsche and de Carmoy proposals was the latter's restriction of state intervention to approving decisions adopted by the film industry confederation.[3]

The same year, the newly appointed minister of education, Jean Zay, took a hard line concerning what he described as the ongoing disarray of the French film industry: "In these conditions, I don't think that anyone can expect the classic principles of a liberal market to continue present op-erations, or the state to preserve a noninterventionist stance."[4] Zay spent a year drafting legislation that called for tighter government regulation of film financing and the creation of a national film school. When his proposal came before the Chamber of Deputies in March 1939, no action was taken. Six months later, the international film festival that Zay had scheduled for September 1–13 in Cannes was canceled following France's general mobilization against Germany.

It is no small irony that major reforms affecting France's postwar film industry drew heavily on policies enacted during the 1940–44 Vichy re-gime under German military rule. Alan Williams notes that the sorry state of cinema in the summer of 1940 offered the new Vichy government under Philippe Pétain a privileged arena in which to demonstrate the virtues of the National Revolution through quick and decisive action based on groundwork that Zay and other technocrats of the hated Third Republic had established nearly a decade earlier.[5] The point is well-taken, even if the push and pull surrounding the film industry under Vichy resulted less from partisan politics or tensions between government agencies and pro-fessional trade groups than from circumstances that set all of the above against an occupying foreign power.

A second irony is the fact that the groundwork for the recovery (as-sainissement) of the film industry that took place under Vichy and the oc-cupying German military had been laid by Petsche, de Carmoy, and Zay during the 1930s. The French term assainissement—which also translates into English as "cleansing"—is semantically dense (additional trans-lations include "streamlining" and "stabilization"). The adjectival and nominal forms sain and santé denote a distinct sense of health. Vichy offi-cials turned that sense toward a mission targeting Jews and other minori-ties who were cast as unhealthy for the new France that Vichy's National Revolution sought to establish. Evelyn Ehrlich translates assainissement as "housecleaning," in conjunction with the mandate for reform in the wake of the Gaumont and Pathé scandals, before concluding that credit for the COIC's successes must be balanced by recognition of its responsibility for perpetuating the most obnoxious of the Vichy regime's policies and goals.[6]

German oversight of the French film industry began within weeks of the June 1940 fall of France, when German military authorities enlisted local support to reopen movie theaters and control programming while managing a broad range of day-to-day operations. Parallel to its initiatives affecting literary publishing and the large-circulation press, the German military's propaganda section (Propaganda Abteilung) in Paris launched a program to promote a return to prewar conditions of activity while it exercised tight control over all aspects of the film industry. By October 1940, more than five hundred movie theaters were operating within the zone under German military command in Greater Paris. Among them, the Rex and the Marignan in Paris were transformed into *Soldaten-kinos* (soldier movie theaters) reserved for recreational use by the German military.[7] The Propaganda Abteilung drew on local professionals of all kinds—filmmakers, technicians, movie theater operators, actors, actresses, and producers—who were willing to enforce policies it implemented in the name of the Vichy regime. German policies mobilized strategies of indirect rule adopted by Hubert de Lyautey while he was resident governor-general of the protectorate in Morocco from 1912 to 1925. As a result, German military officials could be seen as redirecting French colonial practices to occupy the native film industry. In November 1940, the German initiative enacted a major advance when the Vichy government's counterpart to the Propaganda Abteilung, the Services du Cinéma (Cinema Services), authorized creation of the COIC with a mandate to oversee film industry activities and personnel through a structure of subcommittees dealing with producers, artistic and technical personnel, distributors, exhibitors, and technology.[8] To direct this new committee, Vichy officials appointed Guy de Carmoy, whom they might have seen as being credible among his peers thanks to his 1936 report supporting oversight of the French film industry by professional groups.

The December 2, 1940, edition of the Vichy government's *Journal Officiel* authorized the COIC to regulate "the totality of the cinematographic industry and its personnel, and to take all measures which it deemed indispensable concerning technical, economic, and social matters, and in particular recruitment, employment, training, and allotment of personnel to ensure their maximum use."[9] Yet because the COIC was a trade-based entity accountable to the Vichy Services du Cinéma and to the German military Propaganda Abteilung for the issuing of certificates *(visas)* of approval for production, exhibition, and export, its autonomy was minimal.[10] Under such conditions, it is fair to ask why de Carmoy—whom available sources describe as openly opposed to collaborating with the occupying authorities—and subsequent COIC directors Raoul Plonquin and Louis-Émile Galey agreed to collaborate with Vichy and the German military's propaganda section. Alan Williams grasps the complexity of the situation when he writes that, despite the fact that the dangerous double game de Carmoy was playing ended with his arrest and deportation to a prison camp, there is little doubt that the COIC and Vichy's Services du Cinéma rescued the French film industry from near collapse.[11]

De Carmoy and his successors might have agreed to work in the film industry during Vichy because they saw their actions as a viable means to ensure the industry's survival. What some took for compromise and collaboration, others saw as various kinds and degrees of resistance. Ehrlich maintains that, because the French industry needed to prove to itself and to the world that it and France were not dead, "to go on making movies of substance and stature was to affirm that the French spirit had survived."[12] She concludes that for many in the French film industry, collaborating with Vichy in 1940 was preferable to surrendering governance to German authorities by default. The Jewish producer Pierre Braunberger (1905–1990) wrote with generosity that he held no grudges against those who were doing only what they knew how to do to earn a decent wage: "Why reproach [Jacques] Prévert for having continued to write screenplays? It would be absurd."[13]

German military authorities exploited this generosity in conjunction with their efforts to sustain, produce, and distribute quality French films in the "new Europe" they were waging war to create. It would be reductive and unfair to judge COIC supporters in absolute terms as proponents of a collaborationist cinema. Even so, there is no doubt that the COIC applied racial laws passed as early as October 1940 that isolated and excluded numerous professionals from working within the French film industry. Among Vichy policies whose implementation fell to the COIC was a seemingly harmless law requiring anyone working in the film industry to obtain and carry a professional identity card. Far less harmless was the requirement that, along with evidence of commercial probity and professional recognition, applicants for the card had to provide evidence that they were not Jewish.[14] The French word *Israélite* appearing in the law was a synonym of *Juif*. Its use by non-Jews during the 1871–1940 Third Republic referred to the Jewish community as a collective entity within a French society that was largely Catholic. As a substitute for *Juif*, the term *Israélite*, which dates back to the revolutionary period of the Consistoire, often conveyed assumed or explicit assimilation of Jewish identity within republican values. The latter qualification extended an October 1940 law prohibiting Jews from participating in a number of professions. Jean-Pierre Bertin-Maghit notes that the COIC's implementation of the law in the film industry, which barred hundreds of individuals from work, exceeded the law's application in other professions.[15]

Allegations of anti-Semitism on the part of the COIC remain subject to debate. Colin Crisp lists Pierre Braunberger, Bernard Natan, Raymond Bernard, Robert Siodmak, Pierre Chenal, Marcel Dalio, and Jean-Pierre Aumont among those directly affected by prohibitions against Jews.[16] Elsewhere, he asserts that the identity card required to work in the film industry was not exclusively racist and that the criterion of technical competence further guaranteed "a quality product" by eliminating from the system the multitude of fly-by-night firms that had characterized the 1930s.[17] Jewish émigré directors who had worked in France in the 1930s and who were targeted by German ordinances of September and October 1940 included Fritz Lang, Anatole Litvak, Max Ophüls, and Billy Wilder. A year later, the Filmprüfstelle compiled separate lists of Jewish and non-Jewish personnel whom it sought to proscribe from the industry.[18] The consequences of the policy changes implemented by the COIC varied. While new laws supported programming of short subjects within a wider cleansing and streamlining—that loaded term *assainissement* again—of the film industry, their implementation by the Vichy government under German military authorities did not sit well with many film professionals.

Ideology bested practical concerns in late 1943, when the prospect of an Allied victory motivated journalist René Bleck to organize a resistance group among film actors and directors. The result was the clandestine Comité de Libération du Cinéma Français (CLCF; National Committee for the Liberation of French Cinema), which merged five small resistance groups affiliated with the film industry, trade union movements under the Confédération Générale du Travail (General Confederation of Labor), and the cinema section of the French Communist Party's Front National.[19] Others involved in the CLCF included the actor Pierre Blanchar and directors Jean Painlevé, Jean-Paul Le Chanois, Louis Daquin, Jean Grémillon, André Zwoboda, Jacques Becker, and Pierre Renoir. The CLCF distributed leaflets to industry workers and published a clandestine journal, *L'Écran français.* It also militated for active intervention on the part of the incoming French government to provide the film industry with the means to defend itself against individual and international interests.[20] The CLCF tried to overcome partisan and trade union rivalries by casting itself as an active agent in the short- and longer-term purge *(épuration)* of alleged wartime collaborators. As with reforms proposed by Jean Zay a decade earlier, the CLCF based its mission on the prospect of an eventual return to self-governance for film industry workers. This time around, administrative reform—*assainissement* of a different kind—meant a purge of COIC personnel whom the CLCF accused of collaborating with Vichy government and German military authorities.

In April 1944, some two hundred CLCF demonstrators occupied the

Buttes-Chaumont studios on the rue de Belleville before marching to the Place de la République, where they distributed leaflets informing film industry workers of the new group's existence. Four months later, the CLCF participated in the general uprising throughout Paris by occupying the German-run production studios Tobis and Continental, labor union offices, and the COIC headquarters at 92 avenue des Champs-Élysées. Street fighting resulted in fifteen wounded and three killed, including the noted character actor Raymond Aimos.[21] Two years later, the formal demise of the COIC occurred under the terms of a law passed on April 26, 1946, that dissolved all professional organizations created by an August 16, 1940, Vichy-era law regarding control of French industries. It was an additional six months before the National Assembly authorized creation of a new CNC, with financial autonomy under an executive director and an administrative council made up of industry professionals and ministerial representatives. The CNC's functions were to (1) study legislation and regulation proposals, (2) control financing and income (receipts), (3) provide financial support for French film productions in general, (4) ensure the distribution of documentaries and the development of a noncommercial (i.e., educational) sector, (5) organize professional and technical training, and (6) coordinate outreach and charitable activities associated with the film industry.[22]

Assessments of the COIC-to-CNC transition divide over tensions between state and professional control going back as far as the interwar reforms undertaken by Petsche and Zay. Crisp views efforts to reform the film industry during the decade following 1936 as displaying significant continuity, with the notable exception of the postwar prioritizing of market concerns over political programs and policy.[23] Bertin-Maghit characterizes the CNC as more authoritarian—more bureaucratic?—than the COIC. He notes that the CNC's increased dependence on state support over the first decade of its existence made it clear that government officials were less and less willing to share power with film industry professionals: "The hopes of 1944 are buried once and for all. Cinema became a government affair, but not in the way technicians understood this in 1945."[24]

Where Crisp sees ongoing efforts to unify the industry in the interests of commercial solvency, Bertin-Maghit sees a rigid hierarchy under state control. Financial stability remained a top priority for all concerned parties. This was a holdover from the aftermath of the Gaumont-Franco-Film-Aubert and Pathé-Natan scandals of the mid-1930s through the 1946 Blum-Byrnes agreement that made the French film industry a pawn in negotiations to secure loans from the United States in exchange for removing restrictions on the importation of American films.[25] The Blum-Byrnes agreement, the terms of which were revised in 1948, catalyzed debate within the French film industry involving various configurations of corporate bosses, workers, trade unions, political parties, ad hoc groups, and government agencies. Suddenly, longtime adversaries found themselves united by their resistance to major Hollywood studio efforts to infiltrate European markets after the extended interruption caused by World War II.

A measure of efforts to stabilize filmmaking in France during the immediate aftermath of Vichy was the creation of a national film school, IDHEC, the origins of which once again dated back to interwar and wartime reforms. Jean Zay's 1937 proposals had included creation of a national cinema institute to supplement the activities of the École Technique de Photographie et Cinématographie (ETPC), whose founding director, Paul Montel, had hired none other than Louis Lumière in 1926 to establish a curriculum specializing in sound engineering and cinematography. Started as a private school, the ETPC went public in 1937. Its students included future New Wave–period directors Jacques Demy and Philippe de Broca.[26] The technical training provided by the ETPC and by state-funded correspondence schools had not prevented filmmaker Marcel L'Herbier and others from militating as early as 1927 for a national film institute with a balance of theoretical and practical training. L'Herbier foresaw support for the institute from box-office receipts, an approach that interwar reforms proposed by Petsche and Zay would adopt a decade later.

IDHEC's immediate precursor was the Centre des Jeunes (Youth Center), also known as the Centre des Jeunes du Cinéma (Cinema Youth Center), established on the Mediterranean coast near Cannes following the June 1940 exodus from Paris. Within a year, the center moved to Nicem, where it became the Centre Artistique et Technique des Jeunes du Cinéma (CATJC; Artistic and Technical Youth Center for Cinema), supported by prominent film industry professionals Henri Alékan, Jean Lods, René Clément, Claude Renoir, Louis Page, and Roger Leenhardt. Hands-on experience among students supervised by director René Clément in 1942 and 1943 led to completed sections of his subsequent releases *La Bataille du rail* (*The Battle of the Rails*, 1946) and *Les Jeux interdits* (*Forbidden Games*, 1952). The CATJC's main activity was screening films, including Marcel Carné's *Quai des brumes* (*Port of Shadows*, 1938) and Jean Vigo's *L'Atalante* (1934), both of which the Vichy government had banned. Its after-screening discussions and debates developed a format later adopted by the postwar ciné-club movement.[27]

In September 1943, the groundwork to create IDHEC was laid through a merger of the CATJC and a school in Paris for stage acting directed by film director Henri Fescourt. On January 6, 1944, a new school began operations in Paris under the presidency of Marcel L'Herbier, with authority from the COIC to oversee the technical and artistic training of filmmakers; promote experimental film; distribute scholarships for study, invention, and research; and mobilize outreach in the form of publications, lectures, and public screenings.[28] Out of some one hundred applicants, thirty students, including twenty-one-year-old Alain Resnais, were selected to form the initial entering class. Applications were restricted to French citizens between eighteen and twenty-seven years of age who had passed the *baccalauréat* exams marking successful completion of the secondary level in the national system of public education.[29]

IDHEC designed its curriculum to produce film industry professionals with specialized competence in direction, production, cinematography, sound editing, scriptwriting, set design, and costume design. Enrollment varied from two to three years, depending on individual plans of study, completion of which earned the successful candidate a diploma and—more important on a practical basis—the professional card required for working in the film industry. The card soon lost its associations with wartime anti-Semitism under the COIC, but its practical and symbolic status persisted. Agnès Varda was granted a professional card by the CNC only in 1964 after she had completed three long features and three short subjects during the previous ten years.[30] Continuing education included evening courses for professionals already working in the industry. René Vautier, Paulin Soumanou Vieyra, and Adonis Kyrou joined Resnais in IDHEC's early *promotions* (cohorts or entering classes). Other early IDHEC students with significant careers in the film industry included the cinematographer Sacha Vierny, the set and costume designer Bernard Evein, and directors Henri Colpi, Claude Sautet, Jacques Rozier, Serge Bourguignon, Louis Malle, and Constantinos Costa-Gavras.[31] By 1950, many of the school's graduates were opting for careers in television.

IDHEC developed curricula geared toward two-year programs with specialization areas in production *(production-régie)*, directing *(réalisation)*, set design *(architecture-décoration)*, cinematography, and sound and music. Complementary areas of technical training included screenwriting *(scénario)*, editing *(montage)*, television, and culture. Courses on cinema and literature, film analysis, film culture, and introduction to so-called primitive arts were taught by historians and critics Henri Agel, Michel Leiris, Jean Mitry, and Georges Sadoul. General History of Cinema, a two-part course taught by Mitry and Sadoul, included units on Georges Méliès, the beginnings of the Pathé production company, early Scandinavian cinema, D. W. Griffith, film comedy from Max Linder to Charlie Chaplin, the Soviet school, and the growth of the Hollywood system during the 1920s.[32] Prospective applicants to IDHEC were often channeled through a preparatory class offered at the Lycée Voltaire in Paris.

Marcel L'Herbier's vision of a national film school that would produce competent technicians who were also trained as artists mobilized filmmaking as a cultural practice in the public interest. His mission to train professionals to bring new technologies to a broad public resonated with cultural policies that the Popular Front had sought to implement from 1936 to 1938 in programs aimed at the working class. Yet as early as 1922, L'Herbier was already running his Cinégraphie production company along the lines of an art school, whose apprentices—including Claude Autant-Lara, Jean Dréville, and Alberto Cavalcanti—might have thought they were in a painters' studio.[33] Within a year of its creation, IDHEC had become a cultural brokerage house with an outreach program—led successively by Claude Roy, André Bazin, and J. R. Debrix—that published the *Bulletin de l'IDHEC* and forged ties with the Cinémathèque Française, the Fédération Française des Ciné-Clubs, and the Jeunesses Cinématographiques that Bazin had founded with help from IDHEC.[34] By 1948, the school had built a collection of research materials of more than 22,000 catalog entries *(fichiers)*, with information on individual films, French and foreign periodicals, and documents related to film production. These materials, which IDHEC promoted as the nucleus of an exhaustive bibliography of cinema to be found nowhere else in France, were available to IDHEC students, applicants for admission, members of the film industry (who were required to show their professional cards), members of the ETPC, journalists, and university students preparing dissertations devoted to film studies.[35]

Under L'Herbier's leadership, IDHEC worked with Henri Langlois to revive the Cinémathèque Française and with André Bazin to screen films in factories and labor union halls on behalf of the Travail et Culture (labor and culture) group.[36] Both initiatives aligned with wartime reforms implemented by the COIC minus the crucial factor of Vichy and German military oversight. The Petsche, de Cambroy, and Zay reforms of the mid- and late 1930s likewise set relevant precedents by balancing state control of the French film industry with the self-governance advocated by professional groups and labor unions. This give-and-take evolved during the wartime COIC among film industry professionals who remained active under constraints imposed by Vichy and German authorities. By 1944, the prospect of a German defeat recast the missions of the CNC, IDHEC, and Cinémathèque Française within a postwar phenomenon known as cultural radiance *(rayonnement culturel)*. Two years later, the initial exhilaration that had followed the August 1944 liberation of Paris had lapsed as a result of purges by the CLCF and other groups that coincided with the onset of the Fourth Republic.[37] Over the next two decades, the prospects for documentary filmmaking would result in what Dominique Bluher and François Thomas have called a golden age of the French short subject.[38]

4

Colonial Cinema and Its Discontents

Eugène Delacroix's 1834 oil painting *Les Femmes d'Alger dans leur apparte-ment (Women of Algiers [in their Apartment])* is among early contributions to an image archive whose expressions under French colonial rule ranged from photographs and postcards to advertisements and films. In terms of mass-produced images, this archive was especially rich in North Africa, where French soldiers stationed in Morocco, Algeria, and Tunisia often wrote home to family and friends on picture postcards showing places and people *(scènes et types)* deemed typical of the region. By the 1920s, film pro-duction studios within and outside France exploited a market demand for so-called exotic romance and adventure with features such as Jacques Feyder's *L'Atlantide (Lost Atlantis,* 1921), Josef von Sternberg's *Morocco* (1930), and Julien Duvivier's *Pépé le Moko* (1937). Intended mainly to dis-tract and entertain, colonial cinema depicted overseas territories and their local populations as both alluring and dangerous. David Slavin notes that racial and sexual subtexts in these feature films fostered blind spots that camouflaged the injustices of the social order depicted on-screen.[1] Be-tween world wars, French colonial cinema extended to nonfiction prac-tices of newsreels and educational films. In line with Slavin's identification of the blind spots in silent and early sound features, Peter Bloom argues that the power of documentary images was intimately connected to a pho-tographic construction of truth that sought to justify the imposition of French colonial authority.[2]

Reappraisals over the past thirty years have teased out ideological dimensions of fiction and nonfiction films that positioned French colo-nial cinema in the service of state policies and commercial interests. As a result, these colonial films have come to be seen as complicit with soft diplomacy that fashioned public perceptions grounded in Orientalist as-sumptions. A measure of these revised approaches can be seen in Pierre Boulanger's 1975 monograph *Le Cinéma colonial.* Looking again at the book recently, I realized the extent to which Boulanger's industrial-commercial perspective on mainstream features from Feyder's *L'Atlantide* to David

Lean's *Lawrence of Arabia* (1962) reduced colonial cinema to something on the order of what Graham Greene had called entertainments. While this commercial perspective made sense for the mainstream studio corpus on which Boulanger drew, the result skirted serious engagement with colonial policies during the period in question.[3]

Equally of note was Boulanger's exclusion of a small but influential number of documentaries whose respective critiques helped to consolidate opposition to French colonial policies, from the May 1945 massacre of anticolonial demonstrators in Sétif and Guelma through the March 1962 Évian Accords, which granted political autonomy to Algeria. My goal in what follows is to explore three films—René Vautier's *Afrique 50* (1950), Alain Resnais and Chris Marker's *Les Statues meurent aussi* (*Statues Also Die,* 1953), and Jean Rouch's *Moi, un Noir* (*I, a Black Man,* 1958)—whose absence in Boulanger's monograph I take to be a significant blind spot that more recent approaches to colonial cinema in France have brought toward fuller disclosure. The films align with postwar practices of engaged and militant filmmaking associated with the short subject and documentary in France from 1945 to 1968.[4]

While the three films are often linked to a broad phenomenon of decolonization, I prefer to frame their respective and collective critiques in more modest terms as anticolonial, with type and degree of critique varying by specific circumstances of production, distribution, and reception. It is likewise no small detail that each of the three met with censorship and sanctions of one kind or another. Since the mid-1960s, the early postwar films by Vautier, Resnais and Marker, and Rouch can be seen as precursors of the revised depictions of former colonies in postindependence documentaries and fictional features from Gillo Pontecorvo's *La battaglia di Algeri* (*The Battle of Algiers,* 1966) and Ousmane Sembène's *La Noire de . . .* (*Black Girl,* 1966) to Claire Denis's *Chocolat* (1988), Brigitte Roüan's *Outre-mer* (*Overseas,* 1990), and Moufida Tlatli's *Les Silences du palais* (*The Silences of the Palace,* 1994).

Making Waves: *Afrique 50* (René Vautier, 1950)

Those who cite René Vautier's *Afrique 50* as the first anticolonial film in France likely take their cue from Vautier, who makes the claim in his 1998 memoir before adding that he was not thinking along such lines when he undertook the film.[5] The claim is consistent with the persona of renegade or rogue filmmaker (*cinéaste à contre-courant*) that Vautier (1928–2015) cultivated while completing more than twenty films on topics including the struggle for Algerian autonomy, racism in France and South Africa, pollution, the extreme right, feminism, and Breton identity.[6] *Afrique 50* was

Vautier's first major film project. Three years after enrolling in the initial entering class of France's national film school, the Institut des Hautes Études Cinématographiques, Vautier accepted a commission from an educational group called the Ligue d'Enseignement (Teaching Association) to make a film about the daily lives of villagers in what was then known as Afrique Occidentale Française, or French West Africa. The completed film was to be part of a traveling exhibition intended for secondary-level institutions throughout the French school system. The crew assigned to the shoot included an ethnographer, a doctor, a teacher, a photographer, a fine arts student, and a political science student.

Vautier's relations with local authorities in Niger deteriorated after a representative of the colonial governor warned him about filming Africans who were using their arms and shoulders to operate the sluice gates of a local dam. When Vautier answered that he planned to film whatever he wanted, an emissary of the governor ordered Vautier to sign a form acknowledging that he had received notice requiring him to conform to existing legislation on shooting motion pictures in French West Africa. Vautier was also ordered to surrender the film that he had shot earlier that day in violation of legislation of which he had been informed only after the fact. It is no small irony that the legislation in question was a 1934 decree instituted under Pierre Laval, then France's minister of colonies. The decree in question authorized the ministry to examine scripts and individuals involved with production as a prerequisite of authorization to film in colonial territories. Anyone who wanted to shoot a film or make sound recordings needed to file a written request with the lieutenant governor of the colony. The request needed to specify relevant information concerning the applicant's civil status and professional references, any extant or planned script, and the text of any extant or planned musical accompaniment.[7] Vautier wrote that he pointed out to colonial officials that the very same Laval had been executed by firing squad four years earlier because of his wartime collaboration with occupying German forces and that he—Vautier—had been decorated the same year for his active opposition to policies that Laval had endorsed during the Vichy regime. Once Vautier clarified his stance toward colonial authorities, things took a turn toward farce:

> In 1949–1950 and by the force of my conviction, I chose to defy censorship in the form of onetime Minister of the Colonies Pierre Laval, but enacted under the acting Secretary of Overseas France. The result was *Afrique 50*. Forty years later, the Intermédia company, an offshoot of the French Ministry of Foreign Affairs, bought my rights to *Afrique 50*, which had never formally been censored—and rightly so, because

the negatives had been seized and destroyed—in order to distribute and project it among the network of French embassies abroad and, in particular, those in Africa; and this because it is especially important today to send out a message that an anticolonial sentiment existed in France during the immediate postwar period. A detail of note: French policy in Africa is currently the domain of President François Mitterrand. And the Minister of Overseas France who applied the Laval Decree was the same François Mitterrand. All of which simply proves that censorship is closely linked to short-term policy.[8]

Vautier's recapitulation conveys what he considered long-term continuities of government policies from the 1934 Laval decree to limits on immigration enacted under the presidencies of Valéry Giscard d'Estaing and François Mitterrand from 1974 to 1995. After colonial officials ordered Vautier to remain in Bamako, he fled north, where underground groups helped him to send his film footage to France by breaking it down into thirty-three separate shipments. Once back in Paris, Vautier had the film processed by sympathetic technicians who spliced his footage onto the ends of pornographic films. Despite the fact that the processed footage was seized on police order as soon as Vautier took it to the Ligue d'Enseignement offices, he was able to salvage twenty-one out of sixty reels during a lengthy inspection at which he was ordered to acknowledge responsibility for making, importing, and processing a film in violation of orders he had received from colonial authorities in French West Africa.

Vautier edited the salvaged reels at his mother's apartment in the Jean-Jaurès area of the 18th arrondissement and enlisted African musicians who volunteered their services. He recorded *Afrique 50*'s music track during an outdoor screening before some six hundred spectators in Argenteuil. In preparation for the public screening, Vautier first screened the seventeen-minute film three times for the musicians: once to watch it "cold" without playing, a second time to accompany it, and a third time to record the music. Gérard Philipe had agreed to do the voice-over narration, but Vautier wound up doing it himself. Confrontations with police and government authorities related to these illegal screenings earned Vautier thirteen months in jail over the next five years, during which *Afrique 50*—whose official status remained that of a seized film prohibited from commercial distribution—was shown at political rallies and film festivals throughout Europe.

Legal judgments of the period surrounding the film paled in Vautier's estimation alongside that of a film critic for whom *Afrique 50* provided a viable account of violence and resistance during a series of 1949–50 repressions instituted by French colonial officials against local peoples in the Côte d'Ivoire:

The originality of this film is to have accentuated the true causes of this genocide. It shows us that behind every rifle stuck in front of a face, every bullet that kills, every kick that slashes a stomach, there is an economic fiefdom. This film shows clearly that imperialism was at the forefront of these massacres and that in order to suppress them with a view toward eventual freedom, it was necessary to suppress imperialism. Therefore, to triumph with regard to capitalist coalitions, *Afrique 50* emphasizes solidarity among those whom the coalitions exploit. The film's demonstration is intransigent. An argument-based film *[film à thèse]*, indeed, but what an argument! The argument of a reality transcended by evident facts that are nearly palpable, and not at all an abstract vision.[9]

The review appeared in *Présence Africaine,* the same journal whose director, Alioune Diop, had commissioned Resnais and Marker in 1950 to make *Les Statues meurent aussi.* Its author, Paulin Soumanou Vieyra (Vautier misspells the name variously as Viajra and Vinjra), was the first black African student at IDHEC. His 1955 documentary short *Afrique sur Seine (Africa on the Banks of the Seine)* portrayed young Africans in Paris, much along the lines of what Jean Rouch tried to convey through the character of Landry in his 1961 feature-length documentary *Chronique d'un été.*[10]

The censorship to which *Afrique 50* was subjected left Vautier with bitterness toward colleagues who, he felt, could have done more to align themselves with his plight. In *Caméra citoyenne,* he recounts an exchange with "the great Africanist" Jean Rouch in which Vautier (self-cast in the role of "small-time filmmaker") suggests that Rouch's films had been supported by the Musée de l'Homme's Comité du Film Ethnographique (Committee of Ethnographic Film) because they upheld policies that French colonial authorities in Africa were expected to maintain. And so, Vautier recounts more than forty years after the fact, the great Africanist and the small-time filmmaker had an initial falling out, after which they were able to work things out. By contrast, Vautier recalls his ongoing admiration for his onetime IDHEC classmate Alain Resnais, whose collaboration with Chris Marker on *Les Statues meurent aussi* was censored in 1953.

Full circle or vicious circle? In 1992, Jack Lang, then France's minister of education, distributed some five thousand cassettes of *Nuit et brouillard* (*Night and Fog,* 1955) for use in state-run public schools. He did this under the authority of French president François Mitterrand, who thirty-six years earlier, in his role as minister of justice, had his delegate to the Centre National de la Cinématographie's censorship commission vote against the commercial release of *Nuit et brouillard.* Vautier writes that the state censorship imposed on these two films by Resnais was an object lesson. Most pernicious in the suppression of *Les Statues meurent aussi* and *Nuit et brouillard* was the warning given to a young and talented director at the start of his career: "If you do not bend, we'll break you."[11] Censorship thus became a default criterion for determining what constitutes anticolonial cinema, not only in the specific cases of *Afrique 50* and *Les Statues meurent aussi* but also with reference to other documentaries, including Rouch's *Les Maîtres fous* (*The Mad Masters*, 1954) and *Moi, un Noir,* both of which colonial authorities in sub-Saharan Africa refused to authorize for screening.

Exactly what was it, then, about *Afrique 50* that prompted such vigorous resistance from government authorities in Africa and in France? What made it so inflammatory that it could not be screened openly in public for years after its completion? The first five minutes of *Afrique 50* conform to conventions of exotic-pedagogic documentary by featuring sequences of the kinds of sustenance labor—weaving, rope making, fishing— associated with daily life in a rural village.[12] Vautier casts his voice-over in the familiar second-person *tu,* which marks a departure from practices of the illustrated travel lecture dating back to the end of the nineteenth century.[13] Use of the second person singular simulates a logbook or set of field notes, while direct address promotes complicity with the spectator. This complicity abruptly acquires a critical edge during the film's second minute when the voice-over states, "You will see surely very picturesque things but, little by little, you will realize that the picturesque hides signifi- cant misery."[14] What begins as a personalized description of an experience quickly becomes the account of a conversion.

Returning to images seen at the very start of the film, Vautier adds

Welcome glances in *Afrique 50* (1950).

Workers in jungle brush (*Afrique 50*).

that the games the village children play in which they imitate local adults are among the few options they have to learn under a colonial regime in sub-Saharan ("black") Africa, where the 4 percent of school-age children who attend school do so mainly to provide administrators with clerks and accountants. Further complicating the tone of the first five minutes is Vautier's assertion that the village is fortunate because it is not (yet?) under attack.

The remaining twelve minutes of the film complete the transformation from description and critique to accusation and militancy as Vautier calls on Africans to join fellow travelers around the world to resist forms of colonial oppression. He begins this call by listing atrocities in villages such as Palaka in the northern part of Côte d'Ivoire, where colonial troops appeared at 5:00 A.M. on February 27, 1949, to burn and kill after the village chief was unable to pay outstanding taxes; Sikali Wattara, another village chief, was smoked out of his home and shot in the neck by a French bullet. The voice-over leaves no doubt concerning Vautier's—and presumably the spectator's—surprise: "You are shocked, the burned huts, the population massacred, the slaughtered cattle rotting in the sun; this is not the official image of colonization."[15] Vautier continues by denouncing missionaries of commerce (his expression) who boast of colonial Africa's economic and technological progress while failing to acknowledge the exploitation of native workers whose cheap labor builds roads for commercial transport and provides electricity for white neighborhoods. His choice of the term "missionaries" is a pointed reference to the self-appointed mandate among early French explorers who sought to establish Christian beliefs and values in the region. The implication is that the newer missionaries are complicit with what Vautier calls a rule of vultures consisting of colonial administrators and trading entities such as La Compagnie Française de l'Afrique Occidentale, Le Niger Français, and Le Prince Anglo-Saxon Unilever.

Stills of European-based banks and investment houses alternate with sequences of black Africans whose work under the sun Vautier compares to the dung beetle rolling its ball to stock supplies. Images of physical labor shown earlier in conjunction with subsistence activities become images depicting such labor as a cheap alternative to mechanization. Sequences of workers seen earlier are likewise recast in the film's second half alongside others showing violence imposed on villages and their inhabitants

Banks as vultures
(Afrique 50).

by colonial forces. In the film's closing three minutes, these images yield to a montage of blacks and whites marching together in solidarity. Visual treatment of the progression from critique and denunciation to resistance occurs repeatedly in close-ups of protesters exercising their rights under the French constitution to demand restitution of lands and property appropriated ("stolen") by colonial companies. With the prospect of constitutional rights still an abstraction, Vautier details the relentless violence of colonial billy clubs and rifles used previously by colonial administrators to put down demonstrations in Madagascar and Vietnam.

The film concludes with tributes to two individuals: M'Bog Um, who was killed by a blow from a rifle butt during a police search, and Mamba Bakayoko, a seventy-year-old woman who fought so that schools and hospitals might replace prisons such as the one at Bassam in which she died. Vautier casts both as martyrs who helped to lay the groundwork for a new war so that kids *(gosses)* such as those seen at the start of the film might live in peace, freedom, and pride. A slow and steady drumbeat grounds the sound track underlying Vautier's final call to arms over a montage of images showing demonstrators for whom the death of Mamba Bakayoko has generated a new solidarity:

> The entire population of Africa has taken its place alongside the people of France, in the broad shoulder to shoulder of people united in the name of peace and happiness. . . . From Abidjan to Nimaey, from Dakar to Brazzaville . . . the people of France and of Africa stand shoulder to shoulder in a common struggle. And the African people will hold their ground until the battle of life is won.[16]

Afrique 50 satisfies several criteria of a *film à thèse* by documenting and denouncing incidents of violence perpetrated during 1949 and 1950 in conjunction with colonial policies in French West Africa, especially in Côte d'Ivoire. The fact that Vautier films what he has witnessed firsthand opposes his film not only to state-funded documentaries such as the 1938 *La France est un empire* (*France Is an Empire*, Emmanuel Bourcier et al.), which sought to recruit soldiers among native populations of occupied territories, but also to informational films produced from 1945 to 1962 by the Section Photographique et Cinématographique des Armées (SPCA) to support French efforts to thwart decolonization in Algeria.[17] The montage that Vautier creates during the film's closing call to arms broadens the context of resistance toward human rights. In retrospect, this progression anticipates the evolving vision of resistance, rebellion, and revolution in Africa in Frantz Fanon's writings over the following decade, from *Peau noire, masques blancs* (*Black Skin, White Masks*, 1952) to *Les Damnés de la terre*

(*The Wretched of the Earth*, 1963) and the posthumous *Pour la Révolution afri-caine* (*Toward the African Revolution*, 1964).

Afrique 50 fulfills its mandate to record daily life in French West Africa by framing Vautier's cinematic record of his experience within a denunci-ation of political and commercial interests associated with colonial occu-pation. Recalling the fate of André Sauvage's initial version of *La Croisière jaune* (*The Yellow Cruise*, 1934) that was reedited (cut) by Léon Poirier, it is plausible that Vautier might have considered relinquishing his claim to having made the first anticolonial film. Whether or not *Afrique 50* is the first anticolonial film matters less than its pivotal role within the full tra-jectory of French colonial cinema from which we have yet much to learn.

A second measure of *Afrique 50*'s ongoing contemporaneity *(actualité)* derives from the evolution of France's political and economic involvement with North and—especially—sub-Saharan African territories that it had once occupied as colonies or protectorates. For what Vautier had referred to in 1950 as the rule of vultures among commercial enterprises and in-vestment houses extends through the 1958–74 presidencies of Charles de Gaulle and Georges Pompidou to policies of economic cooperation known after the fact as Françafrique (sometimes spelled as "France-à fric," a homonymic play on the French term *Afrique* that links France and Africa on the basis of cash, or *fric*).[18] The fact that this phenomenon remains an object of scrutiny as a major yet barely acknowledged scandal of Fifth Re-public neocolonialism supports Vautier's early postwar vision of daily life in French West Africa as an object lesson that has lost little, if any, of its relevance more than sixty-five years later. This is not all. For as much as Vautier prided himself on a lifelong militancy grounded in denouncing in-justice perpetrated on minorities of various kinds, *Afrique 50* is also moving by virtue of its focus on the faces of individual men, women, and children. This sense of the human face—no faces of colonial administrators or the human "vultures" with whom they collaborate are ever seen—points to a humanist dimension of Vautier's militancy that *Afrique 50* initiates.

A third measure of *Afrique 50*'s place within Vautier's lifelong militancy appears in a 2003 interview with Nicole Brenez during which he enumer-ated five basic principles for a committed cinema: "1. Try to bring back true images rather than tell false stories; 2. [Ensure that] governments are not the only ones to write history; all peoples need to work at this; 3. Write history images . . . right away; 4. Create a dialogue of images during wartime; 5. Against official disinformation, practice and distribute counterinformation."[19] As surely as the first principle's viability hinges on the meaning one attributes to the term "true," the remaining principles set forth a clear sense of what Vautier was trying to do in his very first film. Reconsideration of *Afrique 50* is not limited to salvaging its role within

Faces of resistance, I (*Afrique 50*).

a general phenomenon of decolonization. For if Vautier's film is, as he claims in *Caméra citoyenne*, a precedent on which subsequent films by Resnais, Marker, and Rouch build, the phenomenon of anticolonial cinema is isolated within a postwar film culture that is markedly conservative. As Jean-Pierre Jeancolas has observed, the dossier on the war waged on black Africa by French colonial policies is thin when compared to those on the wars in Indochina and Algeria.[20]

"We Martians of Africa": *Les Statues meurent aussi* (Alain Resnais and Chris Marker, 1953)

The timeliness of a novel, poem, painting, or film draws not only on circumstances surrounding its genesis and reception but also on its capacity to speak to the present long after the fact. This is certainly the case concerning the production and afterlife of Alain Resnais and Chris Marker's 1953 film *Les Statues meurent aussi* as a test case for understanding social documentaries of the period. Alongside those by René Vautier and Jean Rouch, *Les Statues* contributes in distinct ways to the sphere of influence *(mouvance)* exercised by a corpus of anticolonial activities among writers, artists, and intellectuals during the 1954–62 war without a name in Algeria.

Les Statues meurent aussi is a thirty-minute black-and-white documentary commissioned in 1950 by the Présence Africaine group, whose founder, Alioune Diop, wanted to provide a cinematic account of what some referred to at the time as *l'art nègre* (black art). Born in Senegal, Diop (1910–1980) moved to Paris in 1937, where he completed studies in classics at the Sorbonne. With support from Albert Camus, André Gide, Michel Leiris, Jean-Paul Sartre, and Richard Wright, he launched the periodical *Présence Africaine* in 1947 as a cultural review of the black world. According to Marker, the title of the film was chosen in homage to Fritz Lang and Bertolt Brecht's *Hangmen Also Die*, a 1943 feature released in France only four years later.[21]

By the time Marker asked Resnais to assist him with the commission for the film, Présence Africaine had grown into an organization whose enterprises included a bookstore and a publishing house. (Both still exist at 25 bis rue des Écoles.) Bennetta Rosette-Jules describes the publishing house as the equivalent of a cultural broker that organized lectures and promoted the work of unpublished writers.[22] In 1950, Marker contributed to *L'Aube noire* (Black dawn), a radio program broadcast on France-Inter; published articles, poems, and short fiction in the left-wing Catholic monthly *Esprit*; and written a novel, *Le Coeur net (The Forthright Spirit)*.[23] Resnais had completed a short film on Vincent van Gogh, a second on Paul Gauguin, and a third on Pablo Picasso's 1937 painting *Guernica*. Marker and Resnais first met in 1947 in the office of the film critic André Bazin at the Catholic activist group Travail et Culture, located at 5 rue des Beaux-Arts.[24]

Présence Africaine commissioned the film to raise awareness among Europeans concerning the figurative death of black art on display at museums in France, England, and Belgium, three countries with significant colonial histories. The film was a cinematic response to the question of why artworks from China and Greece were displayed at the Louvre while those from sub-Saharan Africa were displayed at France's anthropological museum, Le Musée de l'Homme. The Tadié-Cinéma production company, working with Présence Africaine, followed standard practices when it submitted a copy of the completed film to a government commission in charge of issuing the certificate (known in French as a *visa*) required for commercial release. A July 31, 1953, letter from the CNC stated that, while its commission had no problems with the film's first twenty minutes, sequences in the final ten minutes had raised objections of such seriousness that the commission had decided to defer its decision because it seemed unlikely *(peu probable)* that the version of the film it had reviewed would be authorized for commercial release. The author of the letter, Henry de Segogne, added that the commission had not found it possible to suggest cuts of certain sequences without running the risk "in its own eyes" of being reproached for substituting itself for the authors of the film. For this reason, Segogne suggested that Resnais and Marker modify the film as they saw fit before resubmitting it. Simply stated, no commercial visa would be issued until Resnais and Marker had practiced a self-censorship whose scope and degree they were free to specify.[25]

Was Segogne's letter written in good faith, or was it a way of imposing self-censorship on Resnais and Marker without any explicit guidance? Either way, direct or indirect censorship fueled controversy when what had begun as a commissioned film became a cause célèbre. Because Présence Africaine and Tadié wanted the film to be released, Resnais and Marker allowed them to edit a shortened version on the condition that it would open with a disclaimer about the cut sequences. When Resnais and Marker saw that the shortened version prepared for release in 1957 failed to include this disclaimer, they had the film withdrawn from consideration for commercial release. Only in 1964—more than a decade after its completion and after the independence of territories in sub-Saharan Africa formerly occupied by the French—was the film in its original version approved for distribution. Even then, it was not until November 1968 that the first commercial screening of the uncut film occurred at the Studio Gît-le-Coeur in Paris, where one of the films on the same program was Jean Vigo's *À propos de Nice* (1930).[26]

No clear consensus exists concerning what happened between the commissioning of *Les Statues meurent aussi* in 1950 and its completion some three years later. Did Resnais and Marker intentionally plan a project that they knew from the start would be rejected by the government commission? If so, did Présence Africaine endorse this provocation? Statements by Marker suggest that the organization supported the completed film; others point to a rift after the government commission refused to issue the required visa. Alternatively, did Marker and Resnais decide at some point to implement a logic whose subversive potential they exploited?

The logic in question derives from the French term *détournement,* the meanings of which include the diversion of funds, the misuse of authority, and hijacking. As conceptualized by the Situationist International group as early as 1956, *détournement* referred to acts that reconfigured, misused, or distorted elements of an aesthetic object in order to undermine its former meaning.[27] Situationist *détournement* derived, in part, from Parisian Dada and surrealism of the 1920s. It was also linked to the phenomenon known in French as *bricolage,* in which circumstances prompt improvised repurposing of an object. To state the essential question pointedly, did Marker and Resnais hijack the commission they were given by Diop in the name of Présence Africaine? Or would almost any depiction of the death of black art on display in European museums have led to government censorship?

As early as 1961, Marker introduced the film's voice-over, reprinted in the first volume of his *Commentaires,* by pondering what he characterized as its untimeliness:

> Here is a film about which much has been said. Perhaps even a bit too much. And it is probable that set free from a censorship that has been keeping it under lock and key for ten years, it might easily disappoint. The "colonialism" that it questions in its final section, who defends it in the enlightened and decolonized times in which we live? As a matter of fact, even at the time it was made, the reasons for prohibiting [the release of] this "Grandeur and Decadence of Black Art" were never very clear. They seemed to target the form of the film rather than its content and, in particular, a certain rule of the game, a certain code that was not respected. . . . Now it is well established that acceptance and honor of the literary genre of the pamphlet does not extend to film, when the latter is understood as nothing more than mass entertainment.[28]

Marker's assertion of the film's untimeliness was an ironic overstatement, especially because his closing reference to film as nothing more than entertainment did not align with what he and Resnais had accomplished in their first and subsequent collaborations and in numerous films that each made afterward. Perhaps the assertion was yet another ironic *détournement* meant to befuddle those who had kept the film from circulating in its entirety.

Resnais consistently asserted that the controversy surrounding *Statues* was unexpected. In a 1972 interview with René Vautier and Nicole Le Garrec, he stated that, because he knew practically nothing at the time about the notion of colonialism, he and Marker could not have started out on a given ["a priori"]:

And then, in our eyes, it was totally outside what we had been asked to do: that is, make a film saying that African art is as important as other arts. . . . And this became immediately evident to us after some visits to the Musée de l'Homme in Paris, to Tervuren [Belgium], and to the home of the collector and specialist Charles Ratton. We had seen such beautiful things that overwhelmed us. . . .

While working on the film, we saw that we needed a structure, a subtler construction than a simple series of images of African art. This is how we began to mix in a bit of African reality, some true documents, taken either from newsreels or from short subjects shot in Africa. . . .

At first, it was a kind of proof that this nonfigurative art was also realist and, bit by bit, we came upon this construction of the film in which African art is progressively seen as diminishing, replaced by cinematic images taken by whites. . . .

This structure may be what gives the film its anticolonial flavor [parfum]. Even at that moment, were we perfectly aware of it? I don't think so: our vision [optique], our presentation was born while we were working. The result clearly surprised the producer Tadié; it surprised us, as well.[29]

From the perspective of Présence Africaine, its commissioning of the film was fully in line with a project of cultural affirmation in which literature consistently took priority over visual arts. Despite denials of one kind or another by Diop, Resnais, and Marker, *Statues* and its censorship are inseparable from the broad phenomenon of decolonization understood with reference to cultural resistance and militancy among writers, artists, and intellectuals opposed to French colonial policies from 1945 to 1962.[30]

Les Statues meurent aussi is an account of aesthetic decline cast as a figurative movement toward death that the very first words of commentary formulate in terms of a parallel: "When men die, they enter history. When statues die, they enter art. This botany of death is what we call culture."[31] This death is immediately identified as that of a black art whose display in Western museums removes it from the living culture in which it was created. The break with origins is deemed fatal because it opposes the unity of art and life that these objects were made to ensure within African communities. Museum display reduces the value of these objects to the aesthetic pleasure that they provide to mainly (white) Western spectators in what amounts to a classic shift from use to exchange value. Resnais and Marker spoof the museum gaze by creating a phony exhibition space in which the mundane contents on display are reduced to the labels that kill them by inserting them into objects for display: "And then they die in turn. Classified, labeled, conserved in the display case windows and collections, they enter the history of art."[32] Accordingly, the gaze of a woman of color in the film who looks at these objects in a Western museum is understood as registering a loss of unity that the makers of the film deplore. The same holds for the intent gaze of another woman of color looking at objects from the street outside a gallery window. The effect is enhanced by earlier shots showing purported artifacts that look more like curiosities.

The first thirteen minutes of *Les Statues* include numerous tracking

Gazing in (*Les Statues meurent aussi,* 1953).

shots—occasionally in rapid succession but more often at slow and dirge-like speed—that focus on individual pieces of African art on display. The alternation between throbbing percussion and softer melodies in Guy Bernard's original musical score conveys perpetual motion, with the sounds of swirling flutes, reeds, and strings likewise suggesting wonder and enigma. Three extended sequences—including one almost four minutes long—contain no voice-over narration whatsoever, as though Resnais and

Dubious artifacts on display (*Les Statues meurent aussi*).

Marker wanted the objects to be seen as much as possible on their own. The first two sentences of voice-over at the start of the film are spoken against a black screen. Image, voice-over commentary, and sound track promote a back-and-forth editing of ear to eye (André Bazin's expression) that deprives the image of its traditional primacy.

One could thus read *Les Statues* in at least two ways. Based on the first thirteen minutes or even the unreleased twenty-minute version prepared by Présence Africaine and Tadié-Cinéma, the film could be seen as a superb poem on the glory of black art, "a poem in which statues and masks seen through the lens of Ghislain Cloquet's movie camera seem to divulge their secrets to us through Chris Marker's words."[33] In 1963, Resnais stated that, despite an appearance of self-sufficiency, Marker's texts have an emotional force that is seemingly inseparable from the images they accompany:

> There is an interaction between the emotions conveyed by the plasticity of the image and those conveyed by the rhythm and balance of the text. . . . At first, people were especially struck by the lyricism and refinement of Marker's texts without taking into account the perfect fusing [*soudure*] of word and image.[34]

Alternatively, and in conjunction with the original thirty-minute version, it is as though Resnais and Marker's ability to mobilize the emotional force of word and image toward critique brings *Statues* closer to a pamphlet or tract documented by film.

One critique formulated early in the film targets the misunderstanding among European museumgoers, whose projections of intention and meaning reveal as much about them as about the objects on display. The effect borders on a category error in which the function of objects in their original context is replaced with an aesthetic value attributed to the objects by spectators who view them displayed under glass in European museums:

> We want to see suffering, serenity, and humor there, but we really know nothing about it. Colonizers of the world, we want everything to speak to us: animals, the dead, statues. And those statues are silent. They have mouths and do not speak. They have eyes and they don't see us. And they are not idols, but really closer to toys, serious toys that have worth only in terms of what they represent.[35]

The pronoun "we" here should not be equated with the "royal we," known in French as *le nous magistral*. Instead, it is part of an indictment from which Resnais and Marker do not exempt themselves, and this from an initial formulation in the commentary's opening passage equating death and culture. The indictment is repeated with greater intensity some twenty-one minutes into the film, when the voice-over states:

> We are the Martians of Africa. We arrive from our planet with our ways of seeing, our white magic, our machines. We will cure the black man of his illnesses, this is certain. And he will catch ours, this is certain, too. Whether he is better or worse off in the end, his art will not survive.[36]

Especially by inverting conventions, making Westerners aliens in the eyes of Africans, these lines likely stood out among the final ten minutes of the film that government censors wanted cut in 1953.

Les Statues meurent aussi asserts in no uncertain terms that European understanding of black art mediated by comparisons among European scholars and curators softened the impact of a black art whose difference would otherwise be disconcerting. Accordingly, the voice-over states that Europeans "recognize" Greece—or India, or Sumerian idols, or Romanesque Christs, or modern art—in a two-thousand-year-old African sculpture of a head. Alternatively, objects created specifically for sale in non-African venues transform black art into knickknacks such as flowerpots, paperweights, and souvenir penholders.

Resnais and Marker structure this initial critique, which dominates the first half of the film, around tracking shots of objects that they often illuminate to enhance material surfaces and three-dimensionality. Archival footage of desert landscapes and travel are continual reminders of how and where the objects were encountered and acquired in conjunction with colonial expansion. Only after some thirteen minutes into the film do spectators first see living Africans. Images of a dead orangutan shown as a fact of life within this environment thus parallel the figurative death of black art appropriated by European and other collectors who then fill the vacuum they have created with products of a degraded native. Peter Bloom notes that the image of the human hand touching that of the orangutan provides an ironic interpretation of Michelangelo's 1511–12 fresco *The Creation of Adam,* in which God gives life to Adam by touching his hand. In *Statues,* the orangutan's death represents a sacrificial gift *(don)* that is spiritually transformed into a procession of appearances capable of repairing the tissue of the world.[37] Marker's commentary inflects conventions of the educational art film toward practices of the film-essay modeled on what Jean Vigo had referred to in 1930 as a documented point of view. Yet at the time of the Resnais–Marker collaboration, almost all films shot on location in Africa drew on exotic images from painting, photography, postcards, and travelogues. Because *Statues* was filmed outside Africa with passages of archival footage often set in ironic contrast to the voice-over text, it was less a colonial film than a film about colonial Africa.

Human body in motion (Les Statues meurent aussi).

A sense of the initial critical responses to *Statues* when it was first screened in noncommercial venues such as ciné-clubs and festivals can be gauged in conjunction with at least one other film of the period. *Afrique sur Seine*, a portrait of young Africans living in Paris, is a twenty-one-minute film directed by Paulin Soumanou Vieyra (1925–1987), who was a graduate of IDHEC as well as a film critic and historian. Two of Vieyra's early books published by Présence Africaine, *Le Cinéma et l'Afrique* and *Le Cinéma africain*, were long considered standard references.[38] In a 1969 text on the state of African cinema, Vieyra echoed the anticolonial stance taken by Resnais and Marker when he lamented how so-called exotic films had exploited stereotypes of Africans as background in stories made for Europeans. Assessing options for an African cinema by and for Africans, Vieyra distinguished among four groups: the racists, who assumed the essential inferiority of all Africans; the ideologues, who claimed to plead the cause of Africans but held on to prejudices of all kinds; the idealists and dreamers, who had good intentions but whose paternalism had disfigured Africa by reducing its problems to abstractions of humanity; and the realists, who understood that politics was the only viable context through which to address Africa's problems. He concluded that "short films *[courts métrages]* alone speak at present of Africans in ways that we would like to see more often."[39]

Later in the same collection, Vieyra acknowledged the insights that Resnais, Rouch, Vautier, and Joris Ivens had attained through the skillful ordering of images and through commentaries that, in the case of Vauti-

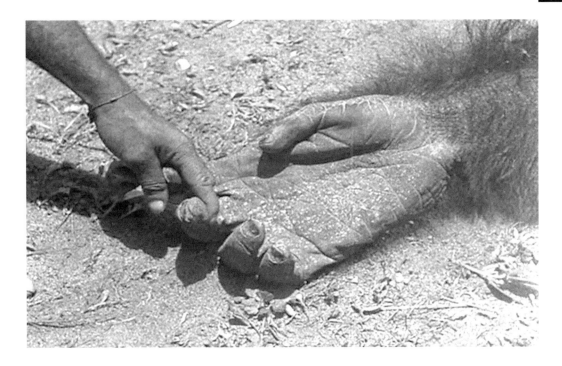

er's *Afrique 50*, targeted "those who are truly responsible for the atrocities that are nothing other than economic feudalism."[40] Vieyra remained firm in his mission to promote films made by Africans for Africans, but he also valued the contributions of these realist documentarians. Alongside *Statues* and Vautier's *Afrique 50*, Vieyra's *Afrique sur Seine* and his critical writings constituted initial efforts to correct misperceptions of Africans and African culture grounded in Orientalist assumptions that more conventional colonial cinema continued to support through the 1960s.

Connection *(Les Statues meurent aussi).*

The ideal way to see *Les Statues meurent aussi* would be to view the cut-down twenty-minute version followed by the uncut thirty-minute original. What count here are the differences between what can be seen today and what a general public was prevented from seeing between 1953 and 1968. The physical break between the two versions involves a cut of some ten minutes. The cut occurs during the twenty-first minute of the original with a forward jump to the final thirty seconds of the original, showing a man locking a storage box in what may be understood as a minor allegory of the act of censorship. The first words of commentary heard after a four-second gap in the sound track, "car il n'y a pas de rupture" (because there is no break), clearly contradict the cut that viewers of the censored version have just experienced. Is this simple coincidence? Or are Resnais and Marker adding another *détournement* by cutting the film "under erasure"—that is, by showing the act of erasure they have been compelled to implement?

The nine sequences deleted from the original thirty-minute version of

Statues can be summarized as follows: (1) from black art to bazaar craft; (2) Martians of Africa, seeing, magic, machines; (3) black soldiers for France; (4) colonial Africa as a laboratory to produce the compliant black man *(le bon nègre)*; (5) the failed hybrid *(métissage)* of Negro-Christian art; (6) problems of the African subject that colonial rule does not raise; (7) daily life recast as exotic spectacle; (8) emergence of the black sports figure (track, basketball, boxing) as performing puppet *(guignol)*; (9) saying yes, saying no—confronting violence and racism, jazz drumming as symbolic resistance. The content and presentation of these sequences constitute a clear departure in tone from that of the film's first twenty minutes. Predictably, these are the sequences that led state censors to deem the film unfit for commercial release in 1953. Resnais once noted in an interview, "The censorship commission said to us: 'If you write a book or an article, the reader maintains self-control. . . . But because in the movie theater, the spectator is passive, believing all that she or he sees, you do not have the right to exert your influence in this manner.'"[41] More of an alibi than anything else, the assertion also acknowledges the potential of film to inform audiences as well as to move them.

A final word on timeliness involves issues of cultural patrimony raised in *Les Statues meurent aussi* seventeen years before the United Nations Educational, Scientific and Cultural Organization (UNESCO) adopted the 1970 Convention on the Means of Prohibiting and Preventing the Illicit Import, Export and Transfer of Ownership of Cultural Property, which stipulates that "cultural property constitutes one of the basic elements of civilization . . . and that its true value can be appreciated only in relation to the fullest possible information regarding its origin, history, and traditional setting."[42] Kwame Anthony Appiah has argued that such questions are especially relevant with reference to objects acquired—often by theft—in conjunction with European colonial expansion. When he writes that "people die when their bodies die; cultures, by contrast, can die without physical extinction," the echoes with *Les Statues meurent aussi* assert the capacity of the significant work of art to speak to successive generations and to us today, more than seventy years after the fact.[43]

Whose Voice? Whose Film? *Moi, un Noir* (Jean Rouch, 1958)

Can one flee the West? Can one flee oneself? Gilles Deleuze has described the problems faced by the filmmaker—presumably a white European male—among Africans colonized by those who imposed their stories from elsewhere while appropriating local myths to their own ends. In answer to these two questions, Deleuze cites trance sequences in Rouch's *Les Maîtres fous* in which characters on-screen become others through storytelling and the filmmaker becomes another by using his camera to fashion characters drawn from real life: "It may be objected that Jean Rouch can only with difficulty be considered a third world author, but no one has done so much to put the West to flight, to flee himself, to break with a cinema of ethnology and say 'Moi, un Noir.'"[44] The passage discloses the complexity of interactions under conditions of colonial rule that imposed social roles inflected by perceptions of race and difference. Some three decades earlier, Jean-Luc Godard referred to Rouch's 1958 film *Moi, un Noir* as "audacious and humble because it showed a free Frenchman freely setting his free gaze on a free world."[45] If, in terms of this composite portrait, Rouch was a free Frenchman (Godard) who tried more than anyone to flee himself (Deleuze), it remains unclear what *his* freedom and *his* ability to become another implied concerning those whom he portrayed in his film.

Rouch once described *Moi, un Noir* as an ethno-fiction based on the type of observational research he had conducted in conjunction with two migratory studies that he had documented in the form of the films. *Jaguar* (shot in 1954–55, definitive version released in 1968) can be seen as a road film based on Rouch's interactions with the three protagonists—Damouré Zika, Lam Ibrahim, and Illo Garoudel—whom he had befriended four years earlier. The three call themselves "jaguars," a slang term for fashionably hip or cool young men. Returning home after months on the road, they distribute goods that they have acquired along the way before returning to the lives of subsistence labor they had led before leaving. Rouch's voice-over at the start of the film is followed by commentary that two of the three protagonists, Zika and Ibrahim, improvised while watching a silent work print of the film. If, as Paul Henley notes, *Jaguar* is sometimes cited as an example of reverse anthropology in which the Other of the European imaginary meets its own Other, it is worth noting that the others whom the three jaguars meet in the luxuriant tropical forest (Kourmi) along the Guinea coast and in Accra do not include any Europeans.[46] As Godard and others would soon note, Rouch's ethno-fictions of the period were striking instances in which, as if for the first time, Africa and Africans were speaking directly to non-Africans.

Undertaken a year before *Jaguar, Les Maîtres fous* depicts an initiation ritual held during a weekend retreat outside the Gold Coast (now Ghanaian) Accra. Participants in the ritual are members of the Hauka (new gods) cult, who, like the three jaguars, have come to the coastal city in search of jobs. Along with *La Pyramide humaine (The Human Pyramid,* 1961), about white and black teenagers at an elite lycée in Abidjan, the model of ethno-fiction based on real-life observations that began with *Les Maîtres fous* and *Jaguar* remained central to Rouch's films through *Chronique d'un été (Chronicle of a Summer,* 1961).

Moi, un Noir is an ethno-fiction account of day-to-day life among six young Africans living in the black Treichville section of Abidjan. The bulk of the film is narrated in a first-person voice-over by Oumarou Ganda, a Zerma-Songhay who had been a day laborer *(bozori)* when he and Rouch first met a year earlier. An early title of the film, *Le Zazouman de Treichville,* strengthens continuities with *Jaguar.* (The terms *zazou* and *zazouman* refer to French and African versions of the American zoot-suiter phenomenon of the 1940s. It was thus a loose synonym of the slang term *jaguar.*) Finally, *Moi, un Noir* is a direct antecedent of and prod to *Cabascabo,* a 1968 film that Oumarou Ganda (who played the role of Edward G. Robinson) made as a retort to *Moi, un Noir.* It thus fulfills the function of what the anthropologist and filmmaker Jean-Pierre Colleyn has described as the way a film almost requires a follow-up film to throw light on it in its full specificity.[47]

In 1958, Rouch was very much a white French male—"free," in Godard's choice of term—collaborating with Africans in urban settings to record their daily lives under colonial rule.[48] But exactly what images of modernity and urban Africa in 1957 did *Moi, un Noir* disclose? How did its narrative and structure fashion its singular place in the history of film in late colonial Africa? My intention in what follows is not to judge Rouch ad hominem on the basis of circumstances that empowered him as a free French male who benefited from privileges under colonial rule. Considering *Moi, un Noir* instead within this colonial condition is a productive means of assessing the status of this ethno-fiction within the corpus of social documentaries explored throughout this book.

Moi, un Noir centers on a group of six young Africans from Niger, four of whom have adopted nicknames to mark their evolving identities. The nicknames—Edward G. Robinson, Eddie Constantine, Tarzan, and Dorothy Lamour—are the names of actors and characters in feature films made in the United States and France. They illustrate the impact of global film as a commodity of mass consumption that fashions identities and stories tailored to "the new universe of the young Africans moving almost without transition from the griot to Hollywood, from tribal myths to the mythologies of contemporary societies."[49] Nicknames are also a means of remaining anonymous in a labor market that exploits those who work illegally and for minimal pay. The encounter with modernity staged in the film extends from motif to method—that is, from scenes of daily life in Treichville grounded in Rouch's efforts to relocate filmed ethnography from "folkloric" rural settings to urban spaces. This is the sense in which *Moi, un Noir* constitutes a case study of colonial modernity in which migrant workers involve themselves in new sociopolitical formations between evolving Western institutions and their African counterparts.[50] Whether or not the six protagonists are aware of it, the new formations to which they try to adapt point to the phenomenon of transition that Henley and others have called migration studies.

Of particular note throughout the film is the use of voice-over commentary, the function of which approaches a cinematic equivalent of stream of consciousness.[51] This is especially true for words spoken by Ganda (hereafter Ganda-Robinson) in his role as Edward G. Robinson as he fantasizes first about becoming a world champion boxer like Sugar Ray Robinson and later about marrying the woman who calls herself Dorothy Lamour. Consistent with the film's emphasis on role-playing, Ganda-Robinson is never referred to as anything other than Edward G. or Sugar Ray Robinson. The adoption of a stage or professional name is often at odds with the lived origins of the individual whom the name purports to identify.[52] The stakes for Ganda-Robinson in contending with this split identity— who he was before he left to serve in the French army and who he has become in Treichville—increase during the course of the film.

The opening sequence of *Moi, un Noir* includes twenty-one shots before credits of any kind appear. The first of the twenty-one—hardly conventional as an establishing shot—shows a young African man sitting on the curb of an urban street, with moving traffic visible in the background. Successive shots show him alongside two acquaintances stretched out on the same curb. Ambient sound enhances this initial take on urban Africa, with gas-powered motors, automobile horns, and background conversations accompanying an extended voice-over that continues from shots 1 through 14:

Each day, young people . . . such as the characters of this film arrive in the cities of Africa. They have left school . . . or the family home in order to try to enter the modern world. They know at the same time how to do nothing and everything; they are one of the illnesses of the new African cities . . . unemployed youth. This youth caught between tradition and the machine world, between Islam and alcohol, has not renounced its religious beliefs, but devotes itself to the modern idols of boxing and cinema. For six months, I followed a small group . . . of young immigrants from Niger living in Treichville, on the outskirts of Abidjan. I offered to make a movie about them in which they would play their own roles, in which they would be able to say and do whatever they wanted. This is how we improvised this film. One of them, Eddie Constantine, was so true to his character, U.S. federal agent Lemmie Caution, that he was sentenced to three months in prison while we were still shooting the film. For another, Edward G. Robinson, the film became a mirror in which he discovered who he was, the army veteran of Indochina, chased away by his father because he had lost the war. He is the hero of the film; it is time for me to let him speak.[53]

Only after this initial voice-over does Ganda-Robinson speak: "Ladies and gentlemen, here is Treichville." Only after the first voice-over ends might the spectator infer that the voice heard had been that of the filmmaker, Jean Rouch. The transition personalizes practices of ethnography in which a primary investigator—typically a white European male—recruits local informants to help him interpret words, gestures, and actions whose full meaning he might otherwise fail to understand. Some spectators might have recognized the first voice right away as that of Rouch, even though he is never identified by name. But since others might have associated the unidentified voice with anonymous and omniscient narration, it is fair to ask in which mode Rouch meant to speak. Is the framing "I" heard in the initial voice-over personalized and identifiable? Does Rouch speak as a white French "insider" collaborating on an equal basis—that is, in Deleuze's formulation, "becoming another"—with those whom he films? Or does he speak instead as a sympathetic outsider nonetheless removed from the subjects whom he films?

Even in the intermediate role of participant observer, Rouch discloses his identity and status only progressively in the opening sequence. The initial ambiguity derives both from technical constraints of the period that required the sound track to be recorded in postproduction and from a nar-

Urban Abidjan in *Moi, un Noir* (1957).

rative model at a remove from the conventions of the travelogue and/or informational documentary. As in his other ethno-fictions of the period, in *Moi, un Noir* Rouch blurs received distinctions between documentary and fiction film, with ethno-fiction arguably a mode of fiction built on images and effects that, in the words of Jacques Rancière, mobilize point of view, depth-of-field editing, and sound on a par with practices of fiction film.[54]

Welcome to Treichville *(Moi, un Noir)*.

The arrest of Petit Touré-Eddie Constantine toward the end of the initial film shoot is acknowledged in the final sequences of the film when Ganda-Robinson, Tarzan, and Petit Jules are turned away from the prison (shots 683–89), where they had gone to visit him. In practical terms, the arrest led to a three-month delay before Petit Touré, Ganda, and others among the group of six were able to record their voice-overs while watching a rough cut Rouch had made in the interim. In a 1996 interview with Colette Piault, Rouch described the interval as formative because it underscored how he and his collaborators were able to integrate unforeseen aspects of real life within the filmmaking process:

This imprisonment changed the tone of the film. At first, it was somewhat like "The Treichville Zazouman," the initial title chosen, except that because of this interruption, the narrative became much more

> dramatic. . . . It should be said that the film was reconstructed only after the initial shooting because the need to rewind our little movie camera manually [meant that] hardly any one shot lasted more than 25 seconds. As a result, the art of editing completely re-created continuity in a film narrative, an operation that was simultaneously a stimulus and a hindrance for the actors, who were often unable to say everything they wanted to say because we had to move on to the following shot.[55]

This passage shows the extent to which Rouch openly acknowledged how unexpected circumstances added to the narrative function of the recorded voice-overs. Yet his remarks only begin to explore what was at stake in voice-over commentary that often approached the cinematic equivalent of free indirect discourse. With no screenplay of any kind, it is fair to question the extent to which the rough cut limited in advance the voice-over that literally commented on images that Rouch had assembled into a visual from the longer filmed footage. The voice heard most often in the film is that of Ganda-Robinson, but the larger question to be addressed is to what extent he was speaking for himself and/or through Rouch's images, which might have limited what he said.

One approach to engaging the complexity of Rouch's visual treatment and Ganda-Robinson's commentary involves three sequences, two of which stage fantasy in the form of wish fulfillment. The first sequence (shots 304–29) occurs after Ganda-Robinson and his friends spend an afternoon swimming on the Atlantic coast. As Ganda-Robinson sits across from Dorothy, he confesses his sadness: "Dorothy Lamour, you see, I need a wife and—later on—children, too. I, too, need to be happy like everyone else."[56] Over the lilting song about Abidjan and its lagoon heard at the start of the film, Ganda-Robinson enters a boxing ring dressed in a striped robe on the back of which can be seen the words "Edward Sugar Ray Robinson." A ninety-second sequence that follows shows him fighting an opponent in the ring as the sound track switches to fast-tempo drumming on a jazz kit until Ganda-Robinson raises his hands in victory amid crowd sounds of jubilation. A return to the lilting lagoon tune brings the fantasy back to reality. Ganda-Robinson comments, "This is what I'd like to be, champion of the world Ray Sugar [sic] Robinson. I ain't no boxer, it's only a dream and here's the real boxer."[57]

A brief clip of the real Sugar Ray Robinson in the ring further discloses the sequence as Ganda-Robinson's fantasy. It also recalls footage of black athletes—including the Olympic track star Jesse Owens, the real Sugar Ray Robinson, and the Harlem Globetrotters exhibition basketball team—seen during the final ten minutes of Resnais and Marker's *Statues*. Ganda-Robinson's words to Dorothy are a plea. The two had planned to marry in Niamey but were unable to do so before Ganda-Robinson left for the French army. By the time he returned, Dorothy had broken the betrothal. In Treichville, Ganda-Robinson's relations with Dorothy have devolved to a point where his fantasy about becoming a champion boxer is inseparable from his (ill-founded) hopes of regaining the affection of his ex-fiancée.

The second sequence (shots 620–28) occurs while Ganda-Robinson wanders drunk at night through the city streets, just after he passes a theater poster of Marlon Brando advertising a French-dubbed version of László Benedek's 1953 outlaw biker film *The Wild One*. (The French title, *Le Gang descend sur la ville*, translates roughly as "The gang blows into town.") While Dorothy Lamour is seen standing in a doorway, Ganda-Robinson says in voice-over:

> And Dorothy Lamour will be my wife, and I'll be an actor like Marlon Brando . . . and Dorothy Lamour will wait for me in front of our door because the house could belong to me and I could be master of the house . . . with Dorothy Lamour as my wife. She will always wait for me and at night, she will close the door. We don't want anything to bother us, we want to be at ease . . . in our very own house. I have my Dorothy Lamour! The radio is turned on, she speaks words of love to me, she will take off her dress because I like to see her breasts, she is thirsting for love; there on our bed, what we do is our business alone.[58]

In fact, Dorothy has agreed to spend the night in the company of an Italian who paid for the privilege after picking her up while she sat next to Ganda-Robinson in the ironically named Bar de l'Espérance (Bar of Hope). When Ganda-Robinson bangs on her door the next morning, the Italian emerges hurling insults, provoking a fight between the two men. When Ganda-Robinson walks away after losing this physical encounter, he also loses the fantasy of marriage to Dorothy that he had based on the virility and fame embodied in the figure of Sugar Ray Robinson.

Ganda-Robinson's bitterness following his fight with the Italian, the loss of Dorothy Lamour, and the arrest of Petit Touré-Eddie Constantine leads to a final sequence—not at all a fantasy—in which he laments his decision to leave Niger. The sequence takes the form of a monologue addressed to Petit Jules:

> What the hell are we doing here in the Ivory Coast? We really made a big mistake. See, we are sleeping on the streets, in the market, on the sidewalks. Other people are happy! Look how they live! While for us, there is nothing except prison and for three whole months, at that![59]

This monologue extends over thirty-five shots lasting a total of four minutes. Unlike the earlier sequences that project wish fulfillment toward the future, the images accompanying this final sequence evoke a past of lost innocence in Niger. Rouch added this sequence after the initial shoot to enhance the force of Ganda-Robinson's disenchantment, conveying a picturesque Africa—pastoral setting, smiling children swimming naked—at odds with the realities of his life in Treichville. Where did this sequence come from? Even if it was intended as an idyllic counterpart to Ganda-Robinson's state of mind in Treichville, the sequence's reversion to images seen in interwar colonial films such as Léon Poirier's silent-era *La Croisère noire* is troubling and at odds with almost all other narrative elements of the film—unless, as with a similar sequence at the start of Vautier's *Afrique 50*, these images of an idyllic Africa were meant to serve as a prelude to critique.

Ganda-Robinson is first seen in a medium-long shot walking with Petit Jules near a lagoon or waterway. A lone water skier passing from right to left in the distance is one of the few white Europeans seen in the film. Suddenly, Ganda-Robinson heaves a stone that he has picked up before dropping supine to the ground, standing up, and jumping again, as though he were sprawling into a trench. He repeats the gesture as he begins his lengthy voice-over:

> I'm in a mess, a fuckin' mess. . . . In my life, I have done it all, I mean everything. You know, Petit Jules, I served in the war, the war in Indochina. I killed the Vietminh with a submachine gun, with a knife, with anything I could find, even a hand grenade. And here's how you do it with a hand grenade, you throw it straight out and you hit the ground flat. I stayed in Ceylon. It wasn't worth a damn, Petit Jules. I did it all! Anything and everything! But nothing worked out. Listen, old buddy, I don't know; I did it all; everything that a man should do, I did it. . . .
>
> But it doesn't matter, I am always the same. Here's how you throw a grenade standing up, lying down, crawling forward. . . .
>
> Don't let this scare you, Petit Jules! I'm telling you that's how it is. Everything! Killing people! A thousand! Five thousand! You hide deep in the woods, far back, and you set up ambushes. We did it all! There's really not much to it, Petit Jules! We did it all! And many other things. Killing people. . . .
>
> Listen, Petit Jules, in order to kill a Vietminh, you pull out your knife and wham! You knock him down. And I say to my captain, I want to see blood flow and see it flow I did. Yes, I saw blood flow! And I saw buddies die six feet away from me, friends with whom we were drinking coffee a moment earlier and right afterward they are dead on the spot. And all this, what is it for? . . .

For nothing, for nothing, old buddy! And just as I am walking by your side . . . I am dead . . . a grenade blast. . . .

A shell explosion. Don't be afraid, Petit Jules! All I am saying is that in Indochina, that's how it is. I am walking by your side and suddenly I fall dead. What good is it? It's worthless, Petit Jules. Everything will be behind you, that's how life is.

None of this matters. We, we are not happy. Look at how happy those people over there are.

Up on their . . . whatever you call them [water skis] but they can . . . show themselves in public. None of this matters. Maybe these people are cowards. Me, I fought for the good of France and I am brave. I am a man! I have nothing, I am poor, but I am brave all the same. None of this matters, Petit Jules! I have no income. . . . Let's go home Petit Jules! None of this matters. Let's go back home![60]

The sequence culminates Ganda-Robinson's account of his experiences after he left home for the French army. In it, he equates his struggles in Treichville to just yet another struggle and thus part of "everything" that he had done after leaving home. As he recounts the deaths that he witnessed during battle, Ganda-Robinson adopts the persona and perspective of the hardened soldier who objectifies the enemy. Curiously, when he identifies with his fellow soldiers, he makes no mention of white or black comrades. Ganda-Robinson's account is raw and his tone defiant. Yet he also asserts a sense of accomplishment and resolve in the face of his experiences in Vietnam and Treichville. Even more curious is the fact that Ganda-Robinson's ongoing concerns about being happy like everyone else would soon be echoed at the start of Rouch and Edgar Morin's *Chronique d'un été*, when Marceline Loridan and Nadine Ballot ask people on the streets of Paris if they are happy.

Screened at the 1958 Cannes Film Festival, *Moi, un Noir* was awarded the Prix Louis Delluc, which film critic Jean de Baroncelli described as the cinematic equivalent of the Prix Goncourt in French literature.[61] Commercial release followed in March 1959 at art houses in Paris, where it was programmed with Resnais's *Le Chant du Styrène* (*The Song of Styrene*, 1958) and a short subject by Jean-Daniel Pollet. Writing in the Communist Party daily *L'Humanité*, Armand Monjo placed *Moi, un Noir* alongside Vautier's *Afrique 50* and Resnais and Marker's *Statues* as one of the very few films in which black Africans could be seen addressing realities of contemporary Africa beyond the commonplaces of slavery, racism, and colonialism.[62] The effect, Monjo wrote, opened a window onto black Africa by treating the miseries of black workers in Treichville on a par with those seen in Italian neorealist films and in documentaries by Robert Flaherty, Luis

Buñuel *(Las Hurdes)*, and Ivens and Storck *(Misère au Borinage)*. Jacques Doniol-Valcroze described *Moi, un Noir* as the first truly black African film, "a journey to the end of the night" in which all references to the white world had disappeared. It was thus a film for which conventional Western categories of documentary and exotic travelogue in the style of *Nanook of the North* (1922) simply failed to apply. Doniol-Valcroze's reference to Louis-Ferdinand Céline's *Journey to the End of the Night* anticipated the 1981 feature *Coup de Torchon (Clean Slate)*, in which, as Lynn Higgins notes, director Bertrand Tavernier relocated Céline's 1932 novel to French Western Africa on the eve of World War II.[63]

Nearly a decade after *Moi, un Noir*, the Senegalese writer and filmmaker Ousmane Sembène asked Rouch what he thought Europeans might do once Africans began making films on their own. Rouch answered that being a European was both an advantage and a liability because, when placed in front of a culture that was not his own, the European saw things that those within the culture did not always see. Sembène countered that, especially in the realm of cinema, one had to analyze as well as see. For example, instead of knowing merely that a man on-screen was walking, one needed to know where the man was coming from and where he was going:

> There's a film of yours that I like, that I have defended, and that I will continue to defend. It is *Moi, un Noir*. In principle, an African should have made it, but none of us at the time was in a position to do so. I think that a follow-up to *Moi, un Noir* is needed. To continue—I think about it all the time—the story of this boy who, after Indochina, no longer has a job and winds up in prison. What happens to him following independence? Would anything have changed for him? I don't think so. . . . In the end, for me there are only two films on Africa that count: yours, *Moi, un Noir*; and then there's *Come Back Africa*, that you do not like. And then a third that's somewhat one of a kind, since I mean *Les Statues meurent aussi*.[64]

Sembène's words cut two ways. While he seemed to acknowledge what Rouch had tried to do in *Moi, un Noir*, the anger that he directed toward ethnologists who studied Africans "as though they were insects" failed to exclude Rouch from the damage caused by American and European films that portrayed Africans negatively. These depictions were exactly what Deleuze would attribute in *Cinema 2* to the colonization of Africa by stories from the outside. Rouch's efforts to treat his local collaborators and those whom he filmed as equals did not protect him from Sembène's anger or influence his stance that Africans needed to make their own films.

Sembène's call for an African follow-up to *Moi, un Noir* did not go unheeded. Starting in 1966, Ganda made eight films of his own before he died in 1981 at the age of forty-five. One of the eight is a forty-five-minute feature, *Cabascabo*, released in 1968 and shown at the Cannes Film Festival the same year. *Cabascabo* (a word in a Zerma dialect that translates as "hard to cook") extended *Moi, un Noir* by depicting problems encountered by a young native of Niger who, much like Ganda-Robinson and Ganda himself, returns home after French military service in Indochina. Statements by Ganda during a December 1980 interview underscored his ongoing ambivalence concerning the collaboration with Rouch more than twenty years earlier:

> Personally I did not like this film very much for a number of reasons. First, at a certain point it all rang hollow. In addition, I thought that the way what I was thinking at the time was shown on-screen should have been different. Because if truth be told, I was also somewhat of a co-director of the film, I brought my own share to the film on a day-to-day basis. We were working together and then Rouch did the editing. . . .
>
> Rouch profited from my life experience. Besides, there was initially no question whatsoever of a film about an Indochina war veteran. It was supposed to be a film about immigrants from Niger. It was supposed to be called *Zazouman de Treichville*, a short subject. And we ended up with a feature-length film called *Moi, un Noir*. I tried in my first film to set things straight, to say almost the same things as I had seen them and with a lot more detail. And this is why I made *Cabascabo*, to express what I was feeling . . . because I did not have the means to do so earlier. . . .
>
> There are moments when Rouch went too far; for example when he stated in his commentary that my father had not tolerated the defeat in Indochina. This was an exaggeration. My father knew nothing about it; the war meant nothing to him.[65]

Ganda's openness about the differences between Rouch's concerns ("problems") and his own pointed to the singular ability of the filmmaker to record from a specific point of view that he or she made visible first by the physical placement of the movie camera and later through editing. Rouch wanted to convey what he took for the reality of the lives of *bozori* like Ganda. But he could do this only from a point of view that—by necessity—diverged from that of Ganda. Rouch's status as a "free" white European male filming in Africa under colonial rule also pointed to the question raised by Deleuze concerning the extent to which Rouch had succeeded in fleeing himself by becoming another, even if only temporarily.

The implicit critique of colonial society throughout *Moi, un Noir* had little if any impact on institutions and policies of colonial rule against which an individual such as Ganda was more or less powerless, even when afforded public venues in which to screen his film throughout Europe and the West. Rouch showed that he was aware of this bind when, in a notice published in January 1981, shortly after Ganda's death, he wrote:

> There was no word "end" to the story of the man who dreamt of being simultaneously Edward G. and Sugar Ray Robinson, an actor or a boxer but who, by moving to the other side of the camera, became quite simply a filmmaker. The "to be followed' were eight films that today are classics in the history of film: *Cabascabo, Le Wazzou polygame, Saïtine.* Or even his last film, his last adventure, *The Man in Exile,* about a diplomat who, just before dying, recounts with marvel the exemplary legends of an Africa forever lost.[66]

Cabascabo constituted a response to Sembène's call for an African continuation of *Moi, un Noir.* Ganda's depiction of the hard readaptation faced by a young native of Niger following French military service in Indochina yielded to a critical account of daily life in rural Africa dominated by predatory friends and exploitative working conditions. Once Cabascabo exhausted the small fortune that he had accumulated in Indochina, he found himself as much an outcast among his family, friends, and neighbors as he had been among French soldiers in Indochina. But unlike *Moi, un Noir*'s Ganda-Robinson, who leaves Niamey to seek a new life in Treichville, Cabascabo heads out in the film's last scene to work in the local fields because he realizes that he must remake himself among his peers before deciding where (in Sembène's formulation cited above) he is going and (Deleuze again) whom to become.

In a 1968 press release accompanying *Cabascabo*'s screening at the Cannes Film Festival, Michel Perez approached the film from another angle when he praised its unremitting critique of an African mentality that exploited the weaknesses of those who tried to buy their way back to acceptance among family and friends, who were all too happy to help returning veterans spend whatever wealth they had accumulated abroad.[67] Instead of seeing the return to nature and to the land at the end of the film as negative, Perez viewed the film's unblinking perspective and cinematic qualities as worthy of the work of certain American masters on which a new African cinema in the making ought to model itself.

Rouch's African films of the 1950s contained no explicit call for the end of colonial rule.[68] Instead, his efforts to balance fieldwork, narrative, and improvisation recast local informants as agents of narratives over which they exercised an unprecedented degree of control. Rouch often gave equipment to those whom he filmed so that they might make films of their own. Unlike Jean-Paul Sartre, who wrote the essay "Orphée noir"

("Black Orpheus") a decade earlier as an advocate for—and in place of—others, Rouch took actions that were closer to those of Michel Foucault, who, during the late 1960s and 1970s, consciously transferred powers of and rights to self-representation to prisoners in U.S. jails and others to whom they had formerly been denied. Despite the tensions and contradiction noted above, *Moi, un Noir* contributed to a cinematic practice for and by Africans to which Rouch and Ganda were committed, each in his own way.

Even if Rouch never succeeded in fleeing the West, *Moi, un Noir* prodded future African filmmakers such as Sembène and Ganda to make films on their own terms. In the context of late colonial Africa, *Moi, un Noir* marked a necessary phase in the progression toward autonomy and self-representation, which remains relevant both in relation to Rouch himself—see, for example, Manthia Diawara's *Rouch in Reverse* (1995)—and in conjunction with the new African cinema since the 1960s.

Transition III

The Group of Thirty

The Groupe des Trente (Group of Thirty, or G30) was a collective of French film directors, producers, critics, and technicians. It was formed in response to proposed changes in government funding policies that the collective's December 1953 declaration described as a threat to the unique art form of the short subject *(le court métrage)*. Even though the G30 eventually registered as an association under French law, its activities suggested a mix of artisanal guild, lobby, and agitprop collective. This activist dimension shaped by the force of circumstance explains the group's role in what is arguably a major test case of French state policy toward film—and, by extension, toward the performing arts and culture—during Fourth and early Fifth Republic France.

Debate surrounding the status and fate of the short subject spanned the better part of the 1950s. While the primary target of debate was government funding policies, the G30's defense of the short subject was grounded in a commitment to ensuring its survival as a unique art form in the service of culture.[1] This mission was all the more remarkable because the G30 was not a production company and never made films in its own name. Its impact resulted instead from its sustained defense of quality (more on this term to follow) in conjunction with state agencies and film industry organizations. Even though the G30 made no films in its own name, censorship difficulties encountered by group members Alain Resnais and Chris Marker pointed to state policies related to funding for production and distribution. Two frame grabs reproduced here illustrate how some members displayed their G30 affiliation in the credits of films on which they worked. The first appears in the opening credits of *Toute la mémoire du monde* (*All the World's Memory*, Alain Resnais, 1956). The second, from Chris Marker's *Dimanche à Pékin* (*Sunday in Peking*, 1956), conveys the group's name in the form of thirty abstract images of cats in a layout of six rows, each of which contains five cats.

My goal in what follows is to retrace the G30's formation and its evolving mission by exploring how the organization's two-part strategy of defense and promotion contributed to the renewal of short-subject and art house filmmaking in France from 1953 to 1963. In terms of promotion, screenings organized by the group in Iron Curtain capitals Prague, Moscow, and Leningrad from 1957 to 1960 expanded the scope of the G30's original mission from aesthetics centered on quality as a measure for funding to French and Cold War cultural politics during the Fourth and early Fifth Republics. The G30's interactions with Soviet bloc colleagues

Group of 30 designation (*Toute la mémoire du monde,* 1956).

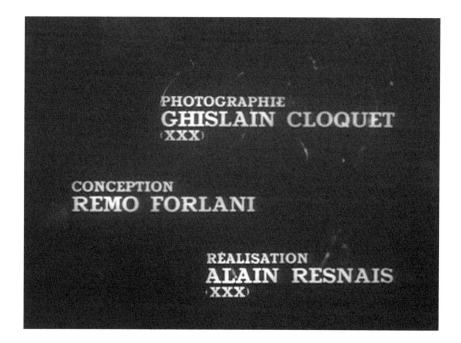

Visual pun: thirty cats for the Group of Thirty (*Dimanche à Pékin,* 1956).

recalled the ethos of the Popular Front–era Groupe Octobre (October Group), whose members Jacques and Pierre Prévert, Jean-Louis Barrault, and Sylvia Bataille had promoted the exchange of films between France and Russia some twenty years earlier. A second interwar precursor was the 1936–38 Ciné-Liberté cooperative, which produced Jean Renoir's *La Marseillaise* (1938) as a populist alternative to the commercial studio system.[2]

Direct links to these interwar antecedents appeared among signers of the G30's December 1953 declaration Pierre Braunberger, Jacques-Yves Cousteau, Georges Franju, Robert Hessens, Jean Lods, Jean Mitry, Jean Painlevé, Georges Rouquier, and Nicole Védrès, all of whom were born from 1902 to 1915. Alongside these film industry professionals, whose activities dated back to silent cinema and the transition to sound, younger signatories Alexandre Astruc, Ghislain Cloquet, Jacques Demy, Pierre Kast, Chris Marker, Alain Resnais, and Agnès Varda, all born 1920–30, would soon contribute to the French New Wave and Left Bank cinema.[3] The list of names expresses a commitment to collective action and governance among film professionals with a shared vision of the industry in which they worked. Solidarity across generations was in line with postwar efforts among filmmakers and critics to break with a so-called tradition of quality on the part of directors whose emphasis on literary adaptation often resulted in little more than filmed theater. In 1954, François Truffaut famously skewered the importance that interwar and postwar directors associated with this tradition placed on scriptwriting and fidelity to the source text of adaptation.[4] *Quality* was clearly a malleable term. The pejorative sense it had for Truffaut in his 1954 *Cahiers* article was incompatible with what it meant for members of the G30.

Equally important for understanding the G30 and its mission is the group's equation of short subject and documentary, which extended the collective's explicit defense of the former toward an implied defense of the latter. This equation existed in various forms as far back as Auguste and Louis Lumière's 1895 programs of shots *(vues)*, whose running time of fifty or so seconds resulted from the fifty-four-foot capacity of a film reel typically projected at eighteen frames per second.[5] The one-reel short was the de facto format of early films such as *La Sortie de l'usine Lumière à Lyon* (*Workers Leaving the Lumière Factory in Lyon*, 1895) and *L'Arrivée d'un train en gare de La Ciotat* (*Arrival of a Train at the La Ciotat Station*, 1896)—and this well before any stable distinction between fiction (narrative) and nonfiction (documentary) existed.

The equation of short subject and documentary also helps to account for the impact of early postwar documentaries by future G30 members Nicole Védrès (*Paris 1900*, 1947), Georges Franju (*Le Sang des bêtes*, 1949), and Alain Resnais (*Van Gogh*, 1948; *Gauguin*, 1950; and *Guernica*, 1950) on "young Turk" *Cahiers du Cinéma* critics-turned-filmmakers Truffaut and Jean-Luc Godard. If the urgency that first mobilized the G30 in 1953 took priority over questions of aesthetics and film theory, these questions nonetheless grounded the group's longer-term advocacy on behalf of the short subject in narrative and nonfiction filmmaking. Defense of the short subject as a unique art form focused on ensuring the material conditions of its survival.

The immediate prehistory of the G30 goes back to the early months of the 1940–44 Vichy regime, when an October 26, 1940, law set the regulatory maximum of the short subject at 1,300 meters, the equivalent of forty-seven minutes and twenty-nine seconds in the standard 35 mm commercial format.[6] The same law, instituted by the Comité d'Organisation de l'Industrie Cinématographique under the control of German occupying forces, dropped the double-feature program in favor of a single feature preceded by one or more short subjects. Finally, a subsidy provision required movie theater owners to turn over 3 percent of gross box-office receipts to help finance future short subjects. The 1940 law provided the short subject with a degree of programming stability and a guarantee of financial support it had never before received. Yet some theater owners maximized their profits by programming those short subjects they could acquire for screening at the lowest possible cost. As a result, award-winning films produced under Vichy by Marcel Ichac, René Lucot, and Georges Rouquier, all of whom joined the G30 a decade later, were rare exceptions to the norm of innocuous program fillers known as *docucus* (loosely translated as "dumb and silly"—or even "dumbed down"—documentaries). The *docucus* were reputedly so bad that some spectators timed their arrival at screenings to avoid them.[7]

Following the 1944–45 liberation of France, a September 1948 law enacted under the authority of the newly created Centre National de la Cinématographie extended the wartime status quo of the short subject. The situation remained unchanged until an August 6, 1953, law replaced the automatic support in effect since 1940 with a quality subsidy *(prime à la qualité)*. An early version of the law had responded to calls from film industry figures for such a subsidy as a supplement to automatic support. Questions immediately arose concerning the criteria that would determine quality and—more pointedly—who would be authorized to make this determination. A second law that passed just over two weeks later, on August 21, complicated matters by dropping the short subject as a required component of programming while offering theater owners who programmed "quality" short subjects a 1 percent bonus on box-office receipts.

This carrot-and-stick approach to financing reform was promoted by high-level CNC administrators Jacques Flaud and Jacques Chausserie-

Laprée, who agreed with many younger film professionals that without a radical change in policy, the short subject would never break with the mediocrity resulting from wartime legislation. Where the August 6 law held out promise for greater participation by film industry professionals in determining the financial well-being of the quality short subject, many filmmakers deemed the return to the double-feature format promulgated by the August 21 law intolerable. Defenders of the short subject soon protested the proposed reforms on a number of fronts. Reputedly led by Alain Resnais, whose 1948 documentary *Van Gogh* had earned a 1950 Oscar for best two-reel short, the G30 exploited the critical respect that group members had earned among peers and spectators within and outside France.

The new 1953 law based on competition for subsidies provided support for up to eighty films per year, with the films chosen by a committee *(jury)* composed of representatives of three state ministries, three members of the French Association of Film Critics, three directors of short subjects, three producers of short subjects, and the CNC's director general. The films eligible for support in any given year would be chosen from an initial pool of 150 films to be screened by the new committee. Accordingly, the goals set forth in the G30's December 1953 declaration in response to the proposed reform of financing were (1) to ensure that the interests of quality filmmaking, which the G30 upheld against the status quo of automatic subsidy, were duly represented; and (2) to defend the short subject against obsolescence by restoring it as an integral component of commercial programming.

Early support for the G30's declaration came from film industry professional groups such as the union of educational, documentary, and short-subject filmmakers under Marcel de Hubsch, the Fédération Française des Ciné-Clubs, and the left-wing activist Travail et Culture collective. Consensus among film industry colleagues was not, however, absolute. In February 1954, a rival group of independent producers and directors under the leadership of Louis Cuny called for a return to automatic support, contending that no individual or commission could presume to determine, much less legislate, quality, which Cuny and his followers deemed subject to public reception. After implementation of the August 1953 laws was placed on hold, debate pitted those in favor of competitive support based on committee-determined quality against those who preferred a return to automatic support.

Allegations against the G30 during this phase of debate cast the collective as a front for the interests of the French Communist Party–inspired Confédération Générale du Travail (General Confederation of Labor) trade union.[8] Not even André Bazin's insight that what separated the two sides was greed among too many film professionals all wanting "a slice of cake" was able to stem debate.[9] Ever judicious in his analysis of the situation, Bazin agreed with Flaud and Chausserie-Laprée when he wrote that even the complete disappearance of the short subject would be preferable to maintaining the status quo in which the documentary—note the slippage equating short subject and documentary—was often nothing more than a superfluous weight on commercial programming.

Notes taken at an October 1954 plenary meeting summarize the scope of activities undertaken by G30 task forces *(commissions)* as a four-point program to defend and promote the short subject by (1) resuming official interactions with ministers, Senate and National Assembly members, and responsible organizations; (2) returning to the exportation subsidy, retroactive to 1953; (3) implementing a realistic policy concerning distribution and promotion; and (4) maintaining closer contact with groups and associations involved with the short subject, notably the École Nationale de la Photographie et de Cinématographie, the Institut des Hautes Études Cinématographiques, the Cinémathèque Française, and the Fédération Française des Ciné-Clubs.[10] These activities continued in one form or another even after the August 1953 reforms were enacted in March 1955.

The triumph of the quality model of competitive financing allowed the G30 to shift its activities from defense to promotion. In January 1957, three of its members—Paul Grimault, Pierre Kast, and Jean Vidal—arrived in Prague for a week of short-subject screenings at the invitation of Czech film officials. Two months later, eleven days of screening in Moscow and Leningrad programmed twenty-five films, including Resnais's *Nuit et brouillard* (*Night and Fog,* 1955), Roger Leenhardt's *Victor Hugo* (1951), and Georges Rouquier's *Le Sel de la terre* (*Salt of the Earth,* 1950). In October 1958, Soviet filmmakers came to Paris for a weeklong festival of documentary and short-subject films. In May 1960, Marcel Ichac, Grimault, and Vidal returned to screen films in Moscow and Leningrad.

By 1962, the urgency that had brought the G30 together nearly a decade earlier eased up after government support of short subjects evolved again in 1959 to a two-step competition under the authority of the new Ministry of Culture (directed by André Malraux), which assumed state oversight of filmmaking in place of the Ministry of Industry and Culture. While many of the G30's early members—Franju, Resnais, Marker, Varda, and Demy—were making feature-length films, their 1950s efforts remained a point of pride among those for whom the collective had been a rallying point for the short subject during a "golden age" marked by what had come to be seen as an emergent French school of the short subject.[11]

Exactly what, then, did *quality* mean for the G30 in 1953? Consensus suggests little difficulty today in identifying "quality" documentaries, short subjects, and feature-length films by Rouquier, Védrès, Franju,

Marker, and Resnais that continue to attract attention among spectators, scholars, and critics. Yet from 1953 to 1959, when the G30 defended the interests of film industry professionals against state agencies, the determination of quality based on form and content engaged pressing issues of governance and control. Determining what quality was—and what it was *not*—was inseparable from the authority vested in those empowered to make the determination in question. *Quality* thus became a password that conveyed commitment to practices among those who wanted to support films on the basis of their merits rather than in conjunction with a policy of automatic support whose results between 1940 and 1953 had been more or less consistently mediocre.

The struggle for quality among French film professionals was a test case during the 1950s in at least two ways. Among those not directly involved with the film industry, it pointed to what was at stake for state agencies with legislative control over a practice linked to France's cultural heritage *(patrimoine)*. Among film professionals, it promoted a degree of autonomy in determining the financial conditions on the basis of which short-subject filmmaking might be practiced as an art and a livelihood.

A listing of films directed by G30 members during the 1950s discloses parallels between the idea of quality that the collective had defended in 1953 and the professional activities of individual members over the next decade. These parallels support my claim above concerning questions of aesthetics and theory as the unspoken basis of a defense of quality fully in line with models of the short subject and documentary at a remove from pre-1953 practices financed through automatic support. Prominent here in terms of the quality model were (mainly) short-subject documentaries by Alain Resnais (*Les Statues meurent aussi, Nuit et brouillard,* and *Toute la mémoire du monde*), Chris Marker (*Dimanche à Pékin* and *Lettre de Sibérie*), and Agnès Varda (*La Pointe-Courte, L'Opéra Mouffe,* and *Cléo de 5 à 7*), all of whom Roud would subsume in 1962 under the blanket designation of "Left Bank" cinema.

An inventory by topics such as painting, architecture, theater, literature, and film fully supports characterization of the short subject in the December 1953 declaration as a unique instrument of culture and an essential means of instruction. If the point seems self-evident today, the transfer of state oversight of filmmaking from the Ministry of Industry to the Ministry of Culture before the end of the 1950s integrated the G30's advocacy within state policy affecting graphic, plastic, and performing arts. Significant contributions by G30 members Nicole Védrès, Yannick Bellon, Jacqueline Jacoupy, and Agnès Varda likewise signaled a rise in the number of women filmmakers, which soon included Nadine Trintignant and Nelly Kaplan.[12]

A measure of the G30's prominence in the period 1953–59 can be seen in films by its members that address social issues ranging from decolonization and societies in transition to health and occupational safety. Films of the period by Resnais, Franju, Marker, and Varda replaced the blandness of placeholder short subjects with striking visual styles in line with what Jean Vigo had termed in 1930 a social cinema grounded in a documented point of view.[13] Over a longer duration, from the latter half of the 1940s through the latter half of the 1950s, relevant examples of innovative audiovisual style among G30 members include Franju's 1949 *Le Sang des bêtes,* the pointed use of newsreel and archival footage during the final ten minutes of Resnais and Marker's 1950–53 collaboration *Les Statues meurent aussi,* and Paul Grimault's animation sequence and the thrice-repeated sequence of the squinting Yakut in Marker's *Lettre de Sibérie.* A final measure of the G30's prominence between 1953 and 1963 involves the venues most likely to program films produced by its members. Known in French as *cinémas d'art et essai,* a first group of seven Parisian art houses dating back to the silent era comprises the Studio 28, the Studio des Ursulines, the Studio Cardinet, the Studio 43, the Studio Bernard, the Ranelagh, and the Studio Parnasse.[14] Additional Parisian venues, including the Champollion, the Panthéon, the Studio Raspail, and the Pagode, likewise provided alternatives to standard programming.

Some of these movie theaters still exist and feature a ciné-club atmosphere with screenings followed by roundtable discussions or question-and-answer sessions with directors and critics. Arnaud Chapuy and Jean-François Cornu go one step further when they factor in support of films directed by G30 members by producers such as Pierre Braunberger, Georges Beauregard, and Anatole Daumann in conjunction with a claim that the G30 constituted a New Wave before the fact *(une pré–Nouvelle Vague).*[15]

The films made by G30 members from 1953 to 1963—ending with Marker's *Le Joli Mai*—illustrate the extent to which the short subject and the documentary were not just phases of an apprenticeship but constituted a discrete platform that lent itself equally to formal experimentation and a critique of postwar modernization, sometimes both. Accordingly, the G30's activities, as well as the short subjects, documentaries, and feature-length films completed by its members from 1953 to 1963, were integral to a period of effervescence that contributed on a number of fronts to the sustainment of "quality" French films. Jacques Flaud made the point when he described the G30 as a catalyst whose advocacy of the quality subsidy incited state agencies and the general public to take the short subject and documentary with a new seriousness that soon extended as well to feature-length and narrative films.[16] Flaud's statement thus supports

Chapuy and Cornu's hypothesis concerning the G30 as a kind of French New Wave before the fact.

In retrospect, the French government's implementation of a quality subsidy in 1955 marked the institutional triumph of the G30's advocacy, the impact of which would extend over the following decade to films identified with the New Wave and Left Bank cinema. Perhaps inspired by the agitprop Groupe Octobre of the 1930s, the G30 remained an advocate of quality filmmaking during a decade when artists and intellectuals in the public sphere increasingly found ways to make culture a vehicle for protest and militancy on multiple fronts. As a rallying point for collective action, the G30's 1953 manifesto thus aligns with the 1960 Declaration of the 121, which supported young conscripts who refused the call to serve the French army in Algeria, and the call addressed to the French people signed by some 229 writers, artists, and intellectuals protesting the murderous police actions during the October 17, 1961, Paris demonstrations in support of an independent Algeria.[17]

5

Two Takes on Postwar Paris

You never know what you are filming.
　　　　—Chris Marker, *Le Fond de l'air est rouge* (*A Grin without a Cat*, 1977)

Scenes in a Library: *Toute la mémoire du monde* (Alain Resnais, 1956)

What interest might a 1956 documentary short about a library hold today for the historically minded spectator? In the pages that follow, I explore the place of Alain Resnais's 1956 documentary *Toute la mémoire du monde* (*All the World's Memory*) among the eight short subjects he directed before completing his first feature-length fiction film, *Hiroshima mon amour*, in 1959. In particular, I argue that *Toute la mémoire du monde* can rightly be seen as a supplement to *Nuit et brouillard* (*Night and Fog*), the thirty-minute documentary on Nazi concentration and death camps that Resnais completed a year earlier.[1] Within a somewhat longer duration, I also situate *Toute la mémoire du monde* within a corpus of documentaries that engage aspects of postwar modernization in France during a period of decolonization coincident with the emergence of an art and universe in the aftermath of the concentration camp.[2] Much as Edward Dimendberg has argued concerning *Le Chant du Styrène* (*The Song of Styrene*), I contend that a reconsideration of *Toute la mémoire du monde* rewards "close reading with a veritable return of repressed geopolitical relations" in late Fourth Republic France.[3]

My epigraph from Chris Marker's cinematic account of failed revolution following 1967 suggests that only in retrospect might one come to understand fully what one sees—or, in this case, films—in the heat of the moment. Marker's caution is especially apt with regard to the early postwar period, during which celluloid-based still photography and cinema necessitated a delay imposed by processes of chemical development. In *Blow-Up* (1966), Michelangelo Antonioni personified the consequences of this material-based delay in the characterization of the photographer Thomas (David Hemmings), who inadvertently witnesses a murder, which he sees only after he develops and enlarges shots he has taken at random in a London park. At stake for me in invoking this delayed disclosure is how best to account for a seemingly minor short subject such as *Toute la mémoire du monde*, whose complexity as text and document arguably develops to the point of clarity some sixty years after the fact. Here, then, are working questions that generate my remarks: What might inquiry into the genesis and production of *Toute la mémoire du monde* tell us today about the industrial, social, and political conditions in which the film was made? How did Resnais's film of scenes in a library disclose aspects of daily life during a decade marked increasingly by silence surrounding Vichy and by division concerning the fate of French Algeria? What assumptions concerning the concepts of library, archive, and memory might *Toute la mémoire du monde* question, given that its ostensible subject is a state agency of record whose mission is to collect and conserve printed materials and other objects whose inclusion qualifies them as national treasures?

The film historian Pierre Billard might have been thinking about *Toute la mémoire du monde* when he wrote in 1962 that one no longer volunteered for committed cinema in the way one used to enlist in the French Foreign Legion: "Social cinema has become less schematic and more ambiguous. What it has lost in ideological efficiency it has gained in sincerity and human truth."[4] Leo Bersani and Ulysse Dutoit likewise assert that, while Resnais is an improbable model of political engagement in art, the elision of the assumed distance between the viewing and documented subjects in films such as *Nuit et brouillard* (1955) arguably makes sensual formalism a measure of political seriousness.[5] Both remarks point to issues of film form and social mission for which the films Resnais made from 1948 to 1958 remain test cases.

Alain Resnais (1922–2014) helped to transform the French New Wave into a global phenomenon when *Hiroshima mon amour* won the International Critics' Prize at the Cannes Film Festival in 1959. *Hiroshima* was the first of some twenty feature-length films Resnais directed before he died in March 2014, but it was far from his first film. From 1936 through 1958, he undertook close to two dozen film projects. Some were never finished, others were unreleased, and yet others were lost. From 1947 to 1959, Resnais also worked as assistant and/or film editor on projects directed by Nicole Védrès, Paul Paviot, Agnès Varda, Jacques Doniol-Valcroze, William Klein, and François Reichenbach.[6] Among the eight documentaries Resnais completed from 1948 to 1958, *Nuit et brouillard* remains an object of debate whose emotional force is built on Resnais's skills as an editor adept at aligning shots and sequences. Period footage and photographs in black and white alternate with (mainly) color sequences filmed at sites of onetime concentration camps a decade after they were liberated by Allied forces in 1945. These visual materials are supplemented with a commentary by former deportee Jean Cayrol (read in voice-over by Michel Bouquet) and a musical score by political exile Hanns Eisler.[7]

Controversy following the completion of *Nuit et brouillard* centered on its insinuation that the Vichy regime had collaborated actively in deporting detainees held in France to camps under German command east of the Rhine. A prime catalyst here was an archival photo taken in April 1941 at the Pithiviers detention camp showing a guard dressed in the uniform of a *gendarme,* that is, a French soldier assigned to civilian duty.[8] More recently, controversy has centered on allegations that Resnais failed to identify the majority of detainees seen in the film as Jews. A working title of the film, *Résistance et déportation* (Resistance and deportation), arguably elided the specificity of Jewish victims within a program that targeted all those whom the Nazis perceived as enemies. Yet this sense of deportation was consistent with statements in the December 7, 1941, Nacht und Nebel Erlass (night and fog decree) that underground agents and *all others* (my emphasis) perceived as enemies of the Third Reich would vanish without a trace, as though into night and fog.[9]

Despite statements by Resnais as early as 1960 that he wanted to be making film musicals, he remains for many spectators "a filmmaker of the mourning heritage of the mass horrors of the twentieth century: Guernica, the Holocaust, Hiroshima."[10] In *Hiroshima mon amour,* the trauma of this horror is personified by an unnamed French woman (Emmanuelle Riva) who has a brief affair with a Japanese man (Eiji Okada) whom she meets in Hiroshima while acting in a film about the atomic bombing that occurred there in August 1945. A two-part sequence in the form of a pseudo-documentary is precipitated by the film's opening exchange: "You saw nothing in Hiroshima. Nothing." . . . "I saw everything. *Everything.*"[11] The first part of the sequence features shots of hospitalized victims of the 1945 bombing, whose gaze into the camera Antoine de Baecque has likened to a gesture of absolute witnessing.[12] Equally relevant to this returned gaze is the fact that when hospital patients in the sequence turn away from the camera, they are corroborating the film's opening assertion that those who had not witnessed the bombing firsthand had seen nothing.

A nine-minute follow-up sequence mixes period photographs and newsreel footage with reenactments, film clips, museum exhibits, and an "atomic tour" by bus through the city. The sequence's 136 shots include numerous instances of a visual style akin to that in earlier films by Resnais as far back as the late 1940s.[13] The sequences partially fulfill the initial request Resnais had received from French and Japanese producers for a documentary about the 1945 bombings, preferably along the lines of *Nuit et brouillard.* But if these sequences respond to the request for a

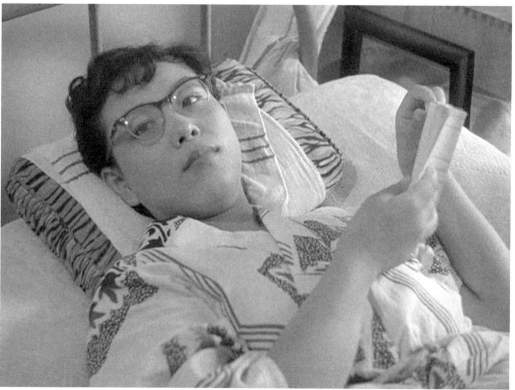

Returning the accusatory gaze in *Hiroshima mon amour* (1959).

documentary, they do so with a twist. For while Resnais opted in the end for a fiction film with a screenplay and dialogue by novelist Marguerite Duras, these two films-within-a-film blurred stable distinctions between fiction and nonfiction films in favor of a hybrid of the two.

Toute la mémoire du monde began as a commission from the French Ministry of Foreign Affairs for a short subject about the Bibliothèque Nationale (BN), the French national library on the rue de Richelieu in central Paris. The project was to be the fifth part of a filmed series called *The Encyclopedia of Paris,* with the national Radio et Télévision Françaises (RTF) listed as coproducer.[14] The origin of the commission in state agencies points to preproduction constraints in the form of sponsorship (national library, national radio and television services) as well as expectations grounded in film genre (documentary) and mode (reportage, educational "visit"). These constraints make it hard to dissociate the commission from an earlier project that set Resnais at odds with the state-run Centre National de la Cinématographie. As described in chapter 4, in 1953 the CNC refused to authorize the visa required for the commercial release of *Les Statues meurent aussi (Statues Also Die),* the documentary short on African art in European museums that Resnais had undertaken with Chris Marker in 1950 at the request of Alioune Diop, founding director of the Parisian publishing house and bookshop Présence Africaine and the journal of the same name.

The first volume of Marker's *Commentaires* includes the text of a July 31, 1953, letter from Henry de Segogne, president of the CNC's censorship commission, stating that the final ten of the film's thirty minutes had raised objections, the seriousness of which prevented members of the commission from approving the film for commercial distribution. Segogne added that the commission was reluctant to suggest specific cuts because it did not want to risk reproach for substituting itself for the film's authors. He concluded that Resnais and Marker's interests would be best served if they would decide for themselves on modifications and submit a revised version of the film that the commission might view favorably.[15] Members of the commission later thanked Marker for not mentioning the burning of villages in the film, adding that while things such as that could be stated in a book, journal, or newspaper, showing them in a film projected in a movie theater amounted to crowd rape *(viol de foule),* which was unacceptable.[16] The incident recalls René Vautier's *Afrique 50* (1950), in which sequences showing villages in French West Africa burned by order of colonial officials led to a prison term for Vautier after he smuggled the film into France in defiance of orders from the office of the colonial governor.

It is plausible to align the commission from the French Foreign Ministry for a film on the Bibliothèque Nationale with others Resnais had received from state agencies and private sponsors. The commission might also have been an anodyne project allowing Resnais to move beyond confrontations generated first by *Les Statues meurent aussi* and subsequently when *Nuit et brouillard* was withdrawn from the 1956 Cannes Film Festival after festival organizers feared that screening it might provoke protests from West Germany. A third possibility is that Resnais accepted the commission with the intention of portraying the national library and its operations in ways that undermined the expectations that administrators and others presumably had for the film. This last possibility is based on irresolution surrounding *Statues* that had set Resnais and Marker not only against government censors but also against Présence Africaine and the Tadié production company, who wanted to release a commercial version of the film shortened by a full third of its original length. Resnais and Marker agreed initially to this shortened version on the condition that it would begin with a disclaimer citing CNC censorship of the film they had first submitted. When no such disclaimer appeared in the version prepared by Tadié, Resnais and Marker had the film withdrawn. The resulting deadlock delayed commercial release of the film in its entirety until November 1968.

Conflicts setting Resnais against state censors date back as far as February 1950, when a CNC commission demanded that the word "German" in Paul Eluard's commentary for *Guernica* be replaced by the word "Nazi."[17] The request upheld French postwar policies that promoted West German reconstruction under Chancellor Konrad Adenauer by ascribing responsibility for wartime actions to Hitler and the National Socialist Party rather than to the German nation as a whole.[18] In March 1956, *Nuit et brouillard* was chosen by the Cannes Film Festival's selection committee to compete in the short-subject category. (The other film proposed was Albert Lamorisse's *Le Ballon rouge/The Red Balloon.*) The absence of Resnais's film from the list of official entries released by State Secretary of Industry and Commerce Maurice Lemaire the following month precipitated a flurry of written exchanges among diplomats, historians, film critics, and industry officials. (Three years later, *Hiroshima mon amour* was screened in an out-of-competition category at Cannes because festival officials claimed that its perspective on the atomic bombing might damage Franco-American relations.)

Among the exchanges surrounding *Nuit et brouillard,* a March 27, 1956, letter to the state secretary of industry and commerce from the Cannes Festival's chief delegate, Robert Favre le Bret, disclosed the mix of commercial and diplomatic issues at stake in the film's exclusion from regular competition at Cannes:

> *[Nuit et Brouillard]* is a film that personally moved me deeply and that deserves to be widely distributed, but . . . it is contrary to the very spirit of the Festival and would above all open the door to other evocations

or positions that would completely deform the appearance of this event by making it a field of passionate arguments, which it is necessary at all costs to avoid if the Festival is to CONTINUE.[19]

Several weeks later, German cultural attaché Bernhard van Tieschowitz wrote to Favre le Bret that the Cannes Festival was an unsuitable venue for the film, which he personally wanted to be shown throughout Germany in order to do full justice to the victims and martyrs of the Nazi terror. Cold War diplomacy thus trumped those who wanted the film to be screened in the regular competition at Cannes. (For the record, *Nuit et brouillard* was awarded the 1956 Prix Jean Vigo, the same prize *Les Statues meurent aussi* earned three years earlier despite the CNC's refusal to authorize it for commercial release.)

State interventions involving three short subjects by Resnais as well as *Hiroshima* illustrate the oversight to which filmmaking in postwar France was subject. A first gesture of resistance to this oversight appeared in *Toute la mémoire du monde*'s opening credits, in which the names of Resnais and his chief cinematographer, Ghislain Cloquet, were displayed over three *X*s enclosed within parentheses. The *X*s referred to the Groupe des Trente, created in December 1953 by directors, producers, and other industry

Book as prisoner (*Toute la mémoire du monde*, 1956).

professionals to defend the short-subject format against proposed changes in government funding policies. Resnais and Cloquet signed the group's manifesto, as did older colleagues Alexandre Astruc, Yannick Bellon, Pierre Braunberger, Jacques-Yves Cousteau, Georges Franju, Jean Painlevé, Georges Rouquier, and Nicole Védrès.[20]

Preliminary correspondence among individuals at the French Foreign Ministry, the RTF, and the Bibliothèque Nationale referred to a synopsis in three parts describing the library's physical and organizational structure *(contenant)*, the contents *(contenu)* of its six nominal collections, and its operations to store, conserve, and display holdings the film would characterize as treasures *(trésors)*.[21] The author of this first synopsis, Jacques Krier, was said to have based it on a synopsis he had written for a film project on L'Imprimerie Nationale (the State Print Shop). A February 5, 1955, memorandum addressed to the BN's director, Julien Cain, listed factual errors and faulted a tone it deemed more appropriate to advertising than to documentary reportage about a major government agency *(un grand organisme français)*.[22] The author of the memorandum concluded that a viable film could be made only if someone acting in the name and interests of the library were authorized to oversee a well-structured project.

Two months after the initial synopsis was rejected in October 1955, a memo by BN administrator Jacques Suffel described a visit by the head of the Films de la Pléiade production company, Pierre Braunberger, whose willingness to assume part of the film's financing led to Resnais's appointment as its director. This appointment, in turn, produced two new synopses by Remo Forlani (1927–2009), whom Resnais had met a decade earlier in Paris when both were involved with Travail et Culture, an activist group of left-wing Catholics to which film critic and theorist André Bazin also belonged.[23] Forlani's first synopsis set forth a utopian vision of the BN as the site of an archive that promoted knowledge in the form of a universal memory. To this end, he and Resnais planned sequences to be shot as if in a futuristic science fiction film and others whose absence of voice-over commentary and music were modeled on silent film. Interior shots from below were inspired by American prison films.

Forlani's first synopsis included a passage that anticipated the rapid access to information that electronics and digitization have since facilitated:

> Let's imagine a giant machine (a robot) capable of providing answers to every kind of question as easily as the machines in Métro stations that tell you instantly how much you weigh. With the help of television, it may be possible one day . . . simply by turning a knob to call up on a screen all the images and words summarizing human knowledge. It is imaginable that someday all the masterpieces of culture will be linked

together so that a continuous reading and a permanent access to all
memories will be possible. The world's memory will exist as a reality,
making the Bibliothèque Nationale not simply a storehouse but a museum or archive of civilization in its various written expressions: all the
world's memory.[24]

Bibliothèque
Nationale em-
ployee as prison
guard *(Toute
la mémoire du
monde)*.

Forlani recast this initial vision in a second synopsis in which he wrote
of "a secret concerning memory in the National Library, one of happiness
or of peace. These texts exist. But for the moment, the library's readers
are unable to see it."[25] Resnais discloses part of this secret during a sequence midway through the film that shows how the BN ensures the
continuous growth of its collections. Three uniformed men carry large
canvas sacks through a courtyard and down a staircase. A few bars of
Arthur Freed and Nacio Herb Brown's "Singin' in the Rain" in Maurice
Jarre's musical score convey a light touch, as though the workers might be
actors on the set of the Gene Kelly–Stanley Donen Hollywood musical.
Nearly four minutes of the film (9:40–13:20) follow a new acquisition as
it is received, stamped, cataloged, and shelved for future consultation.
The start of the sequence in an inner courtyard of the BN picks up on

previous stills and tracking shots of the library's dome and exterior. They also recall period photographs of concentration camp watchtowers in *Nuit et brouillard*. These visual parallels are strengthened by the assertion in Cayrol's commentary that "in Paris, words are imprisoned at the Bibliothèque Nationale."[26] Which is perhaps a dramatic way of stating that the BN is a noncirculating library.

Resnais had shown throughout *Nuit et brouillard* how tattoos and ledger entries reduced concentration camp prisoners to numbered objects. By contrast, *Toute la mémoire du monde* treated books as though they were human. And this to a point where Jacques Doniol-Valcroze wrote that Resnais had completed a film whose sense of enclosure extended an obsession with a concentration camp universe *(un univers concentrationnaire)* from one film to the next:

Nontraditional holdings *(Toute la mémoire du monde)*.

> His film . . . tells the story of a land where all the character-books are automatically imprisoned as soon as they are born. . . . Release is thereafter impossible. What is possible is simply to visit the prisoner after completing the written forms that allow authorities to be sure that you won't try to help the prisoner escape.[27]

An indication of what Resnais was trying to convey in the sequence was the fact that the book being processed was not a real book but a nonexistent title in the real Petite Planète (Little Planet) series of travel guides edited at the Éditions du Seuil publishing house by none other than Chris Marker. Physical details of the fake book seen in the film include a cover

Processing the new arrival (*Toute la mémoire du monde*).

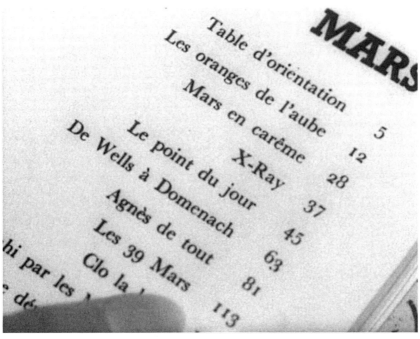

Dubious table of contents (*Toute la mémoire du monde*).

photograph of the Italian actress Lucia Bosé and an ersatz table of contents with possible references to André Breton's *Point du jour* (*Break of Day*, 1934), H. G. Wells (or Orson Welles), Jean-Marie Domenach, Agnès Varda, and Alfred Hitchcock's *The 39 Steps*.[28]

The fake book was more than an inside joke. Much like shots elsewhere in the film featuring comic-strip characters Mandrake the Magician, Dick Tracy, Terry and the Pirates, and pulp detective Harry Dickson, it expressed Resnais's lifelong interest in mass-market print cultures, including comic books and detective fiction.[29] The inclusion of these materials also raised questions concerning their physical and figurative place among the BN's collections. Were these materials part of the BN's collections? Or had Resnais placed them in his documentary as a provocation, in line with similar provocations in films by Luis Buñuel and Jean Vigo? Shots of the materials were so brief that many viewers could easily fail to notice them the first time around. Their inclusion expressed Resnais's personal take on the BN and its collections as a means of dislocating the vision of the library as a repository of national treasures that the French Foreign Ministry had presumably intended the film to convey.

A chilling detail in support of my claim concerning *Toute la mémoire du*

Guarding France's treasures (*Toute la mémoire du monde*).

French soldier at Pithiviers detention camp (*Nuit et brouillard,* 1955).

monde as a supplement to *Nuit et brouillard* can be seen during the film's final minute, after a tracking shot along tables in the main reading room cuts to a dark corner between two bookcases to reveal a barely visible figure whose uniform and cap identify him as a library guard. A medium close-up on the figure precedes a statement in the voice-over commentary to the effect that "the readers seated in front of their bits of universal memory will have placed end to end . . . the fragments of one and the same secret, one that goes by the name of Happiness."[30] The absence of camera movement notations in versions of Cayrol's commentary that I have consulted sustains a discrepancy between what the voice-over states and what the film shows. This discrepancy heightens the potential for split or multiple meanings in the form of mixed messages. The effect tempers explicit meanings in individual shots and connotations grounded in visual and verbal associations. In this instance, the two shots of the reading room guard recall the archival photograph in *Nuit et brouillard* of a figure whose uniform and cap identify him as a military guard at the Pithiviers detention camp. (This was the image that French censors had insisted on removing from the film.) Aligning the two photographs supports my sense that the happiness or peace to which *Toute la mémoire du monde's* commentary refers as the library's secret contains a second secret, seen in the film's final sequence as an agent of surveillance kept almost—but not completely—out of sight.

Far from isolated, the shadowy shots of the library guard—made possible by the use of high-speed Kodak Tri-X film—extend a visual tone first seen in the film's opening sequence in what appears to be the BN's basement. The three-minute sequence contains only five shots, four of them tracking shots with durations ranging from eight to thirty-eight seconds. All are set within a dimly lit space filled with piles of newspapers and topless crates of books. The disorder belowground contrasts with the ordered spaces that will soon be seen aboveground. What place do these disordered objects have among the BN's collections? Are they newly arrived items not yet processed? Are they rejects, somehow unworthy of the treasures on display above? In line with what Resnais had shown in *Nuit et brouillard,* are they akin to the more prosaic treasures confiscated from concentration camp prisoners? Or more pointedly, do these shots in the BN's basement draw on the footage of mass graves of concentration camp victims included by Resnais a year earlier in *Nuit et brouillard*?

Bibliothèque Nationale's basement holdings *(Toute la mémoire du monde).*

Empty shoes
(*Nuit et brouillard*).

Likewise striking in the opening sequence are shots of a movie camera, a microphone, and a carbon arc klieg light, as though to remind spectators that what they are seeing is not the BN but—following the logic of René Magritte's 1928–29 painting *La Trahison des images (The Treachery of Images)*, aka *Ceci n'est pas une pipe (This Is Not a Pipe)*—a film about the BN. The abruptness with which these objects appear in the underground space is heightened by Maurice Jarre's musical score and Georges Delerue's haunting orchestration of woodwinds, percussion instruments, and celesta. Voice-over commentary during the sequence is limited to three sentences. The first states that, because men have short memories, they have accumulated numerous devices to jog them. Additional sentences at the end of the sequence assert that "in front of these overloaded cargo holds men are frightened, frightened of being submerged by this multitude of writings, by this mass of words. So in order to ensure their freedom, they construct fortresses."[31] Production notes for the opening sequence disclose that what Resnais and Forlani had in mind was to establish the film's perspective in agreement with what the BN's head administrator and the department heads had requested:

> Visible to the spectator, the movie camera and microphone move across a dark basement revealing in a lightning flash of light from a guard's flashlight—piles of books, crates of newspapers, cases, statues, old vases, dusty manuscripts. This fantastic reserve, this basement of accumulated objects seemingly forgotten forever, this is the deepest basement of the BN: here we are in the presence of treasures, treasures that belong to us. These yellowed papers, these damaged objects are not lost. They are waiting there in expectation. The moment will come when they will be put back into circulation, when they will be of use once again. But what use will they likely serve, what will be the sense of restoring them, of drawing them back from oblivion?
>
> What use will this almost illegible old book in Latin have? Who will waste if only a second of time looking at this medal whose motif is more or less erased? Who will learn anything from this two-century-old manual? This daily newspaper from last year, who will even think about leafing through it?
>
> What's the use of making an effort to preserve these old things?
>
> And even this book, this medal, this pamphlet, this daily, we also need to identify them at first glance. But things get even *worse*.[32]

The production notes confirm the ambiance of uncertainty that the opening sequence establishes for Resnais's depiction of the library as an unfamiliar and disquieting space. Along with the shots of the reading room guard, the extent to which Resnais intended to instill his library film with a sense of mystery is akin to that in the silent films by Louis Feuillade featuring the archvillain Fantômas.[33] Is this what the French Foreign Ministry and the RTF had in mind when they commissioned the film? Had Resnais met the expectations of the commissioning sponsors? Or, to borrow the notion of *détournement* used at the time by members of the Situationist International under Guy Debord, had Resnais diverted (or even hijacked) the project by subverting the intentions of those who had commissioned it? Similar issues surrounding *Les Statues meurent aussi* strengthen this possibility.

Éric Rohmer once called *Toute la mémoire du monde* the most mysterious of all Resnais's short films ("both modern and disturbing") because it echoed a statement by Jean Renoir concerning a civilization of specialists. Jacques Rivette likewise declared that, because Resnais was someone for whom the age of science fiction had become a reality that was both frightening and human, the phrase "science fiction" lost its pejorative and childish associations.[34] For Christine Richardson, the opening sequence became an episode of spontaneous generation in which bowels transmutably deferred to the uterus, which gave birth to the viewer of films and the

reader of books through a singly mechanical conception of sensory processes.[35] With only minor exceptions, Resnais's film of scenes in a library
seems unjustly overlooked if not openly forgotten.

Other Scenes in a Library

The depiction of the BN in *Toute la mémoire du monde* shares little with
passages in Rainer Maria Rilke's 1910 novel *Die Aufzeichnungen des Malte
Laurids Brigge (The Notebooks of Malte Laurids Brigge)* in which the narrator
describes the national library as a haven where he can sit all day long
reading poetry among others doing the same.[36] A quarter of a century
later, Walter Benjamin mused on hearing the rustling of leaves painted on
the ceiling of a reading room while working at the BN on his *Passagenwerk
(Arcades Project)*. A characterization closer to that in Resnais's film occurs
in a passage of W. G. Sebald's 2001 *Austerlitz* in which the novel's title
character tells the narrator that several years after conducting research on
a daily basis at the library on the rue de Richelieu, he saw a short black-
and-white movie about the library. As the film showed messages racing
through pneumatic tubes as though along the library's nervous system,
it struck him that the scholars working there and the library apparatus
formed an immensely complex and evolving creature that had to be fed
with myriad words in order to bring forth even more words:

> I think that this film, which I saw only once but which assumed ever
> more monstrous and fantastic dimensions in my imagination, was en-
> titled *Toute la mémoire du monde* and was made by Alain Resnais. Even
> before then my mind often dwelt on the question of whether there in the
> reading room of the library, I was on the Islands of the Blest or, on the
> contrary, in a penal colony.[37]

Twenty pages later, Austerlitz tells the narrator about working at the new
Bibliothèque Nationale de France on the Left Bank, where birds sometimes killed themselves by flying into mirrored windows whose reflections
of trees planted in the library's courtyard they had mistaken for real trees:

> Sitting at my place in the reading room, said Austerlitz, I thought at
> length about the way in which such unforeseen accidents, the fall of a
> single creature to its death when diverted from its natural path, or the
> recurrent symptoms of paralysis affecting the electronic data retrieval
> system, relate to the Cartesian overall plan of the Bibliothèque Natio-
> nale, and I came to the conclusion that in any project we design and de-
> velop, the size and degree of complexity of the information and control

systems inscribed in it are the crucial factors, so that the all-embracing and absolute perfection of the concept can in practice coincide, indeed ultimately must coincide, with its chronic dysfunction and constitutional instability.[38]

Both passages from *Austerlitz* suggest how the historical moment depicted in *Toute la mémoire du monde* opens onto a decade of postwar modernization that the film's genesis and production disclose. This is the sense in which Sebald's words in 2001 state what Resnais had shown forty-five years earlier; namely, that the idealized vision of rapid access to universal knowledge entails control, surveillance, and exclusion that are best kept as much out of sight as possible. Three years before those of the hospitalized women in *Hiroshima mon amour*, the gaze of Lucia Bosé on the cover of the phony book looks out onto the afterlife of a concentration camp universe whose presence within state-supported modernization in early postwar France *Toute la mémoire du monde* makes visible. But rather than simply disclosing this presence as an essential truth that agencies and institutions of postwar modernization displace or suppress, Resnais's documentary shows the extent to which the conceptual grounding of the BN on reasoned inquiry linked to universal knowledge is inseparable from sites of mass production and mass annihilation for which World War II was a testing ground. It is thus possible to consider depictions of the laboratory and the art museum in *Les Statues meurent aussi*, the library in *Toute la mémoire du monde*, the factories in *Le Mystère de l'atelier 15* and *Le Chant du Styrène*, and the hospital in *Hiroshima mon amour* as variations of the concentration camp that Giorgio Agamben has called the secret matrix of postwar modernity's political space.[39] Along similar lines, one might extend Agamben's claim to the slaughterhouse sequences in Franju's *Le Sang des bêtes* (*Blood of the Beasts*, 1949) that show the blue-collar dignity of butchers whose labor in the service of industrial killing feeds survivors of World War II.[40]

Hubert Damisch has argued that a delay of ten to fifteen years occurred before films by Resnais and others engaged with images of the undifferentiated horror with which George Stevens, Samuel Fuller, and Orson Welles had contended (the former two in person as American soldiers) when they entered concentration and death camps starting in 1945.[41] This delay approximates what Henry Rousso has referred to as periods of unfinished mourning and repression following the end of World War II.[42] It also corresponds to what Damisch terms a work in the aftermath *(un travail dans l'après-coup)*, in line with my efforts to locate *Toute la mémoire du monde* and *Nuit et brouillard* within a postwar *art concentrationnaire*. It would be unjust and reductive to describe Resnais's goal in *Toute la mémoire du monde* as one of denunciation because the film's critique of postwar institutions of knowledge does not preclude the prospect of the happiness *(bonheur)* evoked in its final minute. If this invocation of happiness seems at odds with earlier sequences in the film—in particular, with the two shots of the library guard—it prefigures sequences at the start of Jean Rouch and Edgar Morin's *Chronique d'un été* (*Chronicle of a Summer,* 1961), during which Marceline Loridan and Nadine Ballot walk the streets of Paris to ask passersby if they are happy. Along the same lines, the female protagonist of Agnès Varda's *Cléo de 5 à 7* (*Cleo from 5 to 7,* 1962) states that, because she feels less alone after meeting a young soldier (Antoine Bourseiller) on leave from military duty in Algeria, she is happy despite the fact that she is about to undergo radiation treatment for cancer. Even Loridan's statement midway through *Chronique* that she was "almost happy" to be deported alongside her father suggests the uncanny imbrication of horror and happiness that the memory of the camps was capable of producing.

Among later films by Resnais, *Biarritz-bonheur* was the title he reputedly wanted for *Stavisky . . .* (1974), whose final shot of the gates of the Petite Roquette prison to which Arlette Stavisky has been sent recalls the fate of the processed book in *Toute la mémoire du monde* as well as that of men, women, and children seen in *Nuit et brouillard* on their way to concentration or death camps.[43] Once again, what is shown in *Toute la mémoire du monde* tends less toward suppressing or transcending the memory of horror than toward asserting possible happiness from which the aftermath and aftereffects of World War II are never absent. The association of the dream of happiness invoked at the end of *Toute la mémoire* and the prospect of universal knowledge seems incongruous with the film's depiction of the BN as a carceral space. Yet this very incongruity corresponds to an assertion by Chris Marker concerning the ability of film to convey in a flash a world altogether and absolutely familiar and completely foreign.[44] *Nuit et brouillard* forcefully discloses this flash in shot 74, when an assertion in voice-over—"First gaze on the camp; it is another planet"—accompanies an extreme close-up of the face of a man whose expression of shock appears in eyes that look directly at the camera.[45]

As arresting as these individual shots may be in themselves, they contribute to effects whose complexity recalls the practice of the *Denkbild* ("thought-picture" or "thought-image") associated with writings by social and cultural theorists Ernst Bloch, Siegfried Kracauer, Walter Benjamin, Theodor W. Adorno, and Max Horkheimer. Gerhard Richter describes the *Denkbild* as a brief, aphoristic prose text often combining elements of literature, philosophy, journalistic intervention, and cultural critique to focus on an everyday and seemingly negligible object, such as a gas

Another planet *(Nuit et brouillard).*

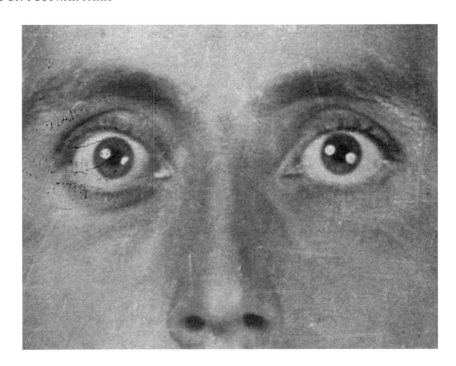

station or a telephone, or on affective states such as boredom.[46] In *Toute la mémoire du monde,* the progressive interaction of word, image, and music follows what Adorno identifies in the *Denkbild* as a practice in which form becomes content. Differences involving the material specificity of film are tempered by the kind of absorption Bersani and Dutoit note with reference to *Nuit et brouillard.* As with poetry and musical compositions, *Toute la mémoire du monde* lends itself to effects of progressive density promoted by association through montage across individual shots, sequences, and (even) films.

The nature of the *Denkbild* as a verbal construct does not preclude looking at *Toute la mémoire du monde* as a critical exercise—what I have been calling "scenes in a library"—devoted to a seemingly trivial aspect of daily life. In his writings for the *Frankfurter Zeitung* in the 1920s, Kracauer asserted, much as Georges Perec would assert a half century later in conjunction with the infra-ordinary, that the objective of this exercise was to decode surface phenomena all too often unnoticed: "We must rid ourselves of the delusion that it is the major events which have the most decisive influence on us. We are much more deeply and continuously influenced by the tiny catastrophes that make up daily life."[47] The relevance of the *Denkbild* for my remarks on *Toute la mémoire du monde* draws on the various ways Resnais overlays reportage with minor dislocations through subtle interactions of word, image, and music. These dislocations punctuate the film, whether or not spectators identify the fuller significance of the dislocations related to the BN's day-to-day practices between report-age and *Denk-* or *Momentbild.* The effect fashions *Toute la mémoire du monde* as an exercise in documentary reportage—with a difference.

A final sense of the inflection of reportage in *Toute la mémoire du monde* via the *Denkbild* draws on the nature of memory invoked by the film's title. The inclusiveness conveyed by the title's initial term is exaggerated in light of the BN's role as state archive of record, to which every book and news-paper printed in France must by law be submitted. Is the reference to all the world's memory a slippage grounded in assumptions of universality? If so, is this exaggeration to be understood as literal or figurative? The library's defining principle, to create an internal order in retaining col-lected materials with a view toward their future retrieval, extends earlier depictions of the museum and the concentration and death camp records seen, respectively, in *Les Statues meurent aussi* and *Nuit et brouillard.* This principle goes well beyond the BN's more mundane charge as a depository for all texts published in France. The ostensible gap between this charge and the entirety of the world's memory invokes the Enlightenment project of universal knowledge in the final sequences of the film.

Toute la mémoire du monde ends by invoking the prospect of universal memory as a safeguard against forgetting. But the still and moving images of concentration and death camps in *Nuit et brouillard* extend to—and can be seen as haunting—the depiction of the BN's daily operations. And this to a point where the projections of instant access to and total recall of universal knowledge seem instead an alibi for the silence surrounding World War II and the Algerian war that state censorship blocked Resnais from engaging openly. The fate of the fake book that *Toute la mémoire du monde* casts as a prisoner of the BN is a material link between the concen-tration camp universe seen in *Nuit et brouillard* and the seemingly anodyne aspects of daily life in late Fourth Republic Paris. More than sixty years later, this is a transposition that Resnais's film of scenes in a library has made irrefutable.

Paris Springtime Zero: *Le Joli Mai* (Chris Marker, 1963)

"Mes films suffisent"—"My films are enough," or perhaps "My films speak for themselves." As if his output of nonfiction and fiction writ-ings, films, videos, and digital projects were not daunting enough, Chris Marker (born Christian François Bouche-Villeneuve, 1921–2012) openly resisted efforts by others to contend with the full corpus of his writings, films, and digital works. Interviews with him were infrequent and subject to self-mythologizing. Bernard Eisenschitz cautions that Marker is rarely where one expects him to be and that one would do better to insist on the diversity of his projects rather than their unity.[48] Arnaud Lambert notes that dividing Marker's projects into distinct periods requires that the militant decade 1967–77 be treated differently from the 1950–62 period of essay films, the documentary period of the 1980s, and the digital works starting in the 1990s with *Level 5* and *Immemory*, both released in 1997.[49] Yet even Lambert's careful periodization seems to leave out the years between 1962 and 1967—that is, between what he calls Marker's essay film period and the militant decade.

In this chapter section I explore Marker's 1963 documentary feature *Le Joli Mai* in conjunction with what I consider to be his shift toward socially committed filmmaking that by 1967 openly engaged social and political issues within and outside France. This period—whose later years Lambert tags as "militant"—culminates in 1977 with *Le Fond de l'air est rouge (A Grin without a Cat)*, Marker's epic account of failed global revolution between 1967 and 1977. What, then, is the place of *Le Joli Mai* within the long decade between 1962 and 1977? In raising this question, I do not intend to fill in and be done with a perceived blank or blind spot. Instead, I propose to reconsider a film whose place within Marker's corpus tends to be overshadowed by *La Jetée*, the exercise in serialized still frames he undertook at the same time.

Le Joli Mai is a 144-minute black-and-white documentary composed mainly of interviews with Parisians in May 1962.[50] While the French title translates literally into English as "the lovely [or pretty] month of May," I prefer "the merry month of May" for its alliteration. Part survey *(enquête)* and part voice-over commentary, the film is divided into two parts: "Prière sur la Tour Eiffel" ("Prayer on the Eiffel Tower") and "Le Retour de Fantômas" ("The Return of Fantômas"). The first part, just under sixty minutes, comprises ten segments; the second, roughly eighty-six minutes, has twelve. Each segment starts with a superimposed title listing date, location, occupation, and initials of the interview subject or subjects. The effect recalls a similar chapter-by-chapter breakdown in Agnès Varda's *Cléo de 5 à 7*, likewise shot on location in Paris a year earlier. It also anticipates the time stamps often displayed on digital media and surveillance videos. The title of Part 1 draws from a section of the 1924 novel *Juliette au pays des hommes* (Juliette in the land of men), whose author, Jean Giraudoux, was the subject of a 1952 monograph by Marker. The title of Part 2 evokes the protagonist of more than forty-three crime novels by Marcel Allain and Pierre Souvestre, written mainly between 1911 and 1926.[51] Louis Feuillade adapted some of the early novels to film in a five-part series released in 1913. Seven adaptations to film followed from 1932 to 1966.

In *Le Joli Mai*, voice-over sequences frame and punctuate the interviews, whose subjects align along a continuum from self-centeredness to a willful concern with others. The result is a composite portrait or time capsule—let me call it *Paris 1962*, with a nod to Nicole Védrès's *Paris 1900*—that also fashions a self-portrait of Marker at age forty. The latter dimension is evident in the opening and closing sequences, in which the voice-overs sound more like prose poetry than expository reportage. Bookend voice-over sequences at the film's start and end recited in French by Yves Montand and in English by Simone Signoret center on how individual Parisians describe their personal priorities in May 1962.[52] Accordingly, much of what is seen on-screen draws on how individuals describe their daily lives and their interactions with others. Self-reflexive moments remind spectators that they are watching something more or other than reportage. Such moments occur in shots of a clapper slate to start a new sequence and of a lightweight movie camera. Others occur when the camera pans away from head shots of the interview subjects to focus on details such as a spider on a suit jacket or fidgeting hands.

Where the "man/woman in the street" format recalls Jean Rouch and Edgar Morin's 1961 *Chronique d'un été*, *Le Joli Mai* departs in intent and objective from Rouch and Morin's practices of cinéma vérité that provoked interview subjects in order to expose inner conflicts.[53] *Chronique* had built a loose chronology around interviews with a number of Morin's acquaintances in the leftist Arguments group. Marker sought instead to survey a cross-section of ordinary Parisians whose opinions were seldom, if ever, solicited. "Êtes-vous heureux?" (Are you happy?) Marker and his crew asked the same question Marceline Loridan and Nadine Ballot had asked of passersby two years earlier for *Chronique*. But Marker was raising it instead in conjunction with the March 1962 Évian Accords, which granted political autonomy to Algeria following 130 years of colonial occupation. In 1960, Rouch and Morin had skirted censorship related to Algeria by focusing on sub-Saharan Africa. Two years later, Marker openly addressed prejudice and racism directed toward North and sub-Saharan Africans living in France. This may help to explain why the commercial release of *Le Joli Mai* was delayed until May 1963.[54] It was likely that Marker remained under scrutiny in the wake of previous clashes with government censors in conjunction with documentaries he had completed over the previous decade, some on his own, such as *¡Cuba Sí!*, and others—*Les Statues meurent aussi* and *Nuit et brouillard*—with Alain Resnais.

The first line of voice-over commentary in *Le Joli Mai* announces Marker's engagement with Paris in the wake of Algerian independence by asserting that the film was shot during a period that some people referred to as the first springtime of peace. For supporters of an independent Algeria, the Évian Accords marked the start of a new era. Hence the title of this section, "Paris Springtime Zero," which I have based on Roberto Rossellini's 1948

Germania anno zero (Germany Year Zero), with a nod to Jean-Luc Godard's *Allemagne 90 neuf zéro (Germany Year 90 Nine Zero, 1991)*, in which the word *neuf* translates both as the noun "nine" and as the adjective "new." The importance of the spoken word in *Le Joli Mai*'s voice-over commentary, the voices of the interviewers (including that of Marker), and those of the inter-view subjects are matched visually by alternating long shots *(vues d'ensemble)* and close-ups *(plans rapprochés)*. An opening long shot of an individual

Showing the apparatus (*Le Joli Mai*, 1963).

climbing along the roof of a building recalls trick effects in Dziga Vertov's *Man with a Movie Camera* (1929) that dwarfed and isolated humans amid oversize camera equipment and epic-scale architecture in Soviet capitals. Telephoto lenses compress depth of field, lending abstract patterns to urban iconography seen at a distance. An aerial shot of the shadow of the Eiffel Tower across the Pont d'Iéna recalls the opening section of Guillaume Apollinaire's 1913 poem "Zone," looking out from the tower at panoramas of the

Long and telephoto shots of Paris (*Le Joli Mai*).

awakening city below, as well as the bird's-eye view of Michel-Étienne Turgot's 1734–36 map of the city in twenty-one sections. And when the voice-over states that Paris cannot be seen with a virgin eye but only as marked through previous interpretations, the assertion undermines Louis Aragon's efforts in his 1926 novel *Le Paysan de Paris* to approximate the experience of a first-time visitor who has come to the city from the provinces.

Le Joli Mai's first interview is with a small-shop merchant who describes happiness as the moment when the sale of a men's suit puts cash in the till. When asked if he goes to see movies like Alain Resnais's *L'Année dernière à Marienbad* (*Last Year at Marienbad,* 1961), he confesses that he never went beyond primary school and that he prefers films in which men shoot guns and use the telephone. To the man's credit, he has enough self-awareness to know that *Marienbad* is not his kind of film. Subsequent segments in Part 1 feature two architects thinking aloud about how to develop a new neighborhood on the outskirts of the city, a taxi driver talking about the abstract painting he does in his spare time, and a boy marveling at U.S. astronaut John Glenn's space capsule on display at a science museum.

A seven-minute segment features interviews with three women who live in Aubervilliers, the same town on the northern outskirts of Paris explored in Eli Lotar's 1946 documentary. Tracking and pan shots of ramshackle dwellings, narrow passageways, and an outdoor water spigot are enhanced by Michel Legrand's harpsichord composition, which competes on the sound track with an advertisement for a city-center luxury housing project blaring from a loudspeaker perched on the roof of a passing

Heavy shadow over the Seine (*Le Joli Mai*).

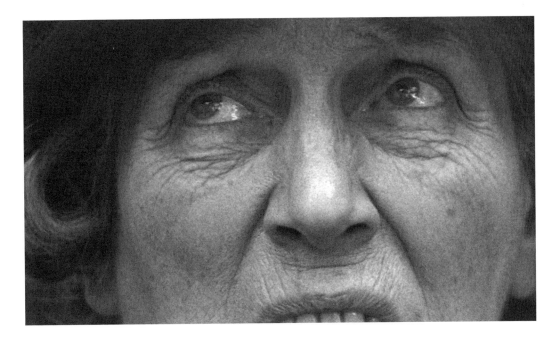

Face of anxiety, I
(Le Joli Mai).

car. (Legrand's composition echoes the main theme that Georges Delerue composed for François Truffaut's 1960 feature *Tirez sur le pianiste/Shoot the Piano Player*.) The first of the three women says that the neighborhood is filled with gossip before admitting that she would gladly leave if she had the chance. The second is filmed leaning out of her window, on whose sill she has planted pansies. As she talks about her flowers, Legrand's composition morphs into dissonant chords that accompany pans along deserted daytime streets before the camera stops on a handwritten sign announcing weekly reading courses for North Africans.

The third interviewee, Madame Langlois, has just learned from local authorities that she and her family of eleven will be relocated from the

In Aubervilliers
(Le Joli Mai).

Worried teen-
ager (Le Joli
Mai).

single room that they have been sharing for seven years to a three-bedroom apartment in a new housing development. Langlois is next seen showing the new apartment to some of her children, the eldest of whom, a teenage girl, looks out from the balcony with a sullen expression. A minute earlier, the girl had admitted being afraid to go out alone in her old neighborhood because of the *harkis* living nearby. The remark discloses a moment of embedded racism directed at Algerian Muslim loyalists who fled to France to escape reprisals after siding with the French colonizers, many of whom also fled as self-rule for Algeria approached.

It is hard to imagine that Marker filmed the Aubervilliers segment without having Lotar's documentary in mind. Even more significant is the visible presence of North Africans in slum areas that white proletariats and subproletariats such as Madame Langlois have left for state or locally financed low-rent housing. When, toward the end of Part 2, a young Algerian recounts in voice-over how immigration authorities had roused him early one morning while he was sleeping, tracking shots along dilapidated terraces and walkways resemble those seen in the earlier segment shot in Aubervilliers. *Le Joli Mai* suggests that little in the area has changed between 1946 and 1962 except for local demographics. This may have been Marker's understated way of acknowledging a shift in emphasis from the misery experienced by the poor white French Lotar had depicted to that of first-generation immigrants newly arrived from former colonial territories in North and sub-Saharan Africa.

The first part's closing sequence centers on a young couple engaged to be married. After some terse replies to initial questions, the two reveal

their shared hopes for the future. While the woman talks, the camera pans down to her gloved hands, which are kneading the bare hand of her fiancé. Is she simply nervous, or does her gesture express something else? The moment recorded by the pan can be seen as invasive and even somewhat cruel because it reveals more about the couple's unspoken concerns than do their efforts at candor. When the interviewer turns to questions of

Engaged couple *(Le Joli Mai).*

Nervous fidgeting *(Le Joli Mai).*

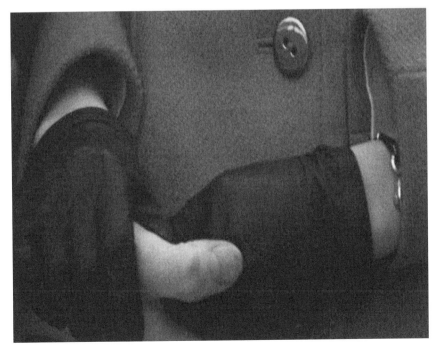

politics and Algeria, the man, who is dressed in a military uniform, says that he is shipping out in ten days for assignment in Algeria and that he prefers not to think or talk about it. The man's statement confirms the extent to which many Parisians whose opinions Marker and his crew were recording had submitted to a self-censorship that suppressed debate concerning France as a society and nation in favor of a focus on personal happiness. When asked outright how world events affect their thoughts about the future, the couple admit that they feel little solidarity with people whose lives are different from theirs. Cross-editing with clips from a raucous wedding reception enhances the couple's isolation from politics and social issues. When Marker returns to the couple, the woman says softly but with a smile of pride that everyone should be like them and steer clear of politics. As Legrand's waltz-time title theme fades in, the man says that he believes in eternal love. Lettering superimposed over the final shot states that the segment ends Part 1 of the film.

Filming on the streets of Paris a year earlier, Agnès Varda had depicted ninety minutes in the life of the female protagonist of *Cléo de 5 à 7* as she awaits the results of a medical exam she fears will confirm a diagnosis of stomach cancer. Walking alone in the Parc Montsouris, Cléo (Corinne Marchand) converses with a gregarious soldier who is about to return to Algeria. After she reveals her fear of cancer to him—something she had kept from her lover and her friends—he tries to calm her by saying, "There you are; the two of us are in a bubble. Do you feel better now?"[55] When the young couple in *Le Joli Mai* express their view of future happiness, Marker's crosscutting with a gaudy wedding reception suggests that the bubble of intimacy surrounding the couple isolates them from the misery of those less fortunate, toward whom they express neither empathy nor solidarity.

Part 2 of *Le Joli Mai* develops the divergence between personal happiness and the degrees of concern for and involvement with others with which Marker and cinematographer Pierre Lhomme increasingly identify. The shift is first announced with reference to urban myth embodied in the figure of Fantômas. Against a shot of headstones beneath a bridge, the voice-over commentary states that the "lord of the underworld," Fantômas, purportedly buried in the Montmartre cemetery, rose from his grave in 1962 to cast his enormous shadow over Paris. The assertion picks up on the image of the Eiffel Tower's shadow across the Pont d'Iéna in Part 1 and on the statement (16:17) that a threat *(menace)* is weighing on Paris. The allusion to threat aligns with a segment devoted to the public funerals of nine people who died in the underground Charonne Métro station in February 1962 when Paris police used violence to break up a demonstration against the right-wing Organisation de l'Armée Secrète (Secret Army Organization), which was opposed to Algerian independence. Marker filmed thousands of Parisians demonstrating in silence to protest police actions under the authority of onetime Vichy official Maurice Papon. Montand/Signoret's voice-over states that it was so quiet on the Place de la République at noon that one could hear birds singing. Forty years later, Marker reused clips from the segment in *Chats perchés* (*The Case of the Grinning Cat*, 2004). In

Cléo moving through Paris in *Cléo de 5 à 7* (1962).

January 2015, the Place de la République was the site of a mass demonstration honoring the victims of the *Charlie Hebdo* killings.

Marker conveys additional signs of menace in shots of locked doorways and graffiti that read as traces of dissent and militancy. Among these traces, the name Poujade is notable. Pierre Poujade (1920–2003) was a shopkeeper whose libertarian campaign against French tax policies launched a political career in which he cast himself as a defender of

Signs of struggle
(Le Joli Mai).

common men and women against government bureaucrats. In November 1953, he created the Union de Défense Commerçants et Artisans (UDCA; Defense Union of Businesspeople and Craftsmen) to organize tax protesters. In the 1956 legislative elections, the UDCA won fifty-two seats. Its youngest member of parliament was Jean-Marie Le Pen, then leader of the UDCA's youth branch and later the longtime leader of the Front National, a political party that remains a far-right-wing presence. A portrait of Poujade graced the March 19, 1956, cover of *Time* magazine, and Roland Barthes included a brief piece on him in his *Mythologies* (1957). Whether intentional or not (probably intentional), the inclusion of Poujade's name in *Le Joli Mai* conveys the political nature of the menace otherwise embodied in more abstract terms by Fantômas.[56]

Part 2 of *Le Joli Mai* increasingly sets Marker's predilection for positive

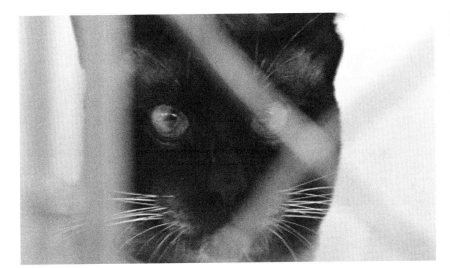

Feline editorializing (*Le Joli Mai*).

instances of involvement against depictions of disengaged positions, as when he presents—without commentary—a man who claims to hold the record for dancing the twist and three sisters who believe that women should have no say in political matters. In both instances, the statements by people on-screen suggest that they are so removed from the ethos of concerned involvement that Marker wants to promote that he inserts close-ups of cats to fashion an ironic cross-editing that mocks the views in

Filmmakers on location *(Le Joli Mai).*

question. Elsewhere, Marker turns to in-jokes to poke fun at some inter-viewees. A six-minute segment (1:25:11–1:31:22) records a dialogue between two men described as engineers but sounding more like futurologists who make pronouncements about technology, labor, leisure, and people whom they consider unproductive. At one point, one of the two asks pointedly, "Les gens qui travaillent, que font-ils?" (People who work, what do they do?) Once again without comment, Marker inserts brief clips of film-makers Edgar Morin and Jean Rouch seated at an outdoor café, Anna Karina and Jean-Luc Godard riding in a car, and directors Jacques Rivette and Alain Resnais on the streets of Paris.

Finally, a family of North Africans is shown in front of a television set watching a movie about flying saucers. Remarks on the third world by two futurologists seem to anticipate a segment showing a family of immigrants watching a science fiction film in their cramped dwelling on the outskirts of Paris is a suitable barb. Over sounds of family chatter, the voice-over states that in May 1962, the dreamed-of future is consumed ready-made and that, for many Parisians, television—"the only window that opens onto the rest of the world"—becomes all the more necessary as the home becomes smaller. The camera pans across the crowded room before linger-ing on a middle-aged man whose facial expression exudes a mix of pride and embarrassment. And this in contrast with that of a boy who mugs for the camera. The television program seen in the segment continues Marker's penchant for science fiction, comics, and extraterrestrials, which he shared with Alain Resnais. Toward the end of their 1950–53 collabo-ration on *Les Statues meurent aussi,* Marker had invoked extraterrestrials when he wrote of the white French settlers *(colons),* "Nous sommes les Martiens de l'Afrique" (We are the Martians of Africa).[57]

The segment centered on the North African family serves as a transi-tion to one-on-one interviews with an African from Dahomey, a militant worker-priest, and an Algerian teenager. These segments leave little doubt concerning the film's ideological orientation along a continuum from the labor union movement and working-class struggles to the populist left. The interview with R. O. from Dahomey (now Benin) features his acute grasp of differences between the whites he encountered as a child in colo-nial Africa and those he met later in France starting at the age of thirteen or fourteen. After R. O. states that as a child in Dahomey he came to think of the refrigerator as a sign of civilization, Marker cuts to a trade show where vendors hawk the newest kitchen appliances, including a new stove available in one model with a self-timer and another without. For R. O., the use value of these appliances is tempered by their symbolic value as object-badges linked to the ethos of postwar modernism modeled on conspicuous consumption imported from the United States. When asked what he thinks of the French, R. O. answers that after his grandmother told him to mistrust them, he equated all white French with the authority figure of the colonial governor. When he admits that his first impression of the French he encountered in France was quite different from what he had expected, the camera pans down to his hands on the table in front of him. Unlike those of the young woman seen earlier in the film standing with her fiancé on the Pont de Neuilly, R. O.'s hands do not fidget. When asked if he has any true friends among his (white) French acquaintances, he hesitates before softly but firmly answering, "No."

The interview with the worker-priest, a fiftyish-year-old man sitting with his arms folded on a table, is filmed mainly in medium shots. Natural lighting from a window to his right softens the man's features. Camera movement is minimal. When he is asked to describe his conversion, the spectator may expect to learn of his Catholic faith. Yet the man answers that he had understood as early as 1946 that committing to Communism meant committing to a world without God at a time when he still believed in God. Having first joined the labor union movement, he knew that his acceptance of a membership card in the French Communist Party–backed Confédération Générale du Travail was a life choice rather than a passing experiment. Forced by church officials to choose between the priesthood and the workers' struggle, he chose the latter because he believed it was the better way to transform society. As in the previous segment with R. O., shots show the man's hands held calmly and without fidgeting.

Three witnesses, three testimonials (Le Joli Mai).

The final interview features a young Algerian whose education and training as a technician had earned him employment as a skilled worker in a Parisian factory. Shot on a hillside with the interviewer often visible, the interview redirects questions the worker-priest addressed in terms of personal faith toward concrete issues of labor relations and racism. While the Algerian recounts how a coworker had thought it out of line *(anormal)* for an Algerian to be paid more than a (presumably white) Frenchman,

Marker intercuts to a crew of North Africans at work on a city street. The voice-over states that the working class in France extends downward toward a subproletariat typically made up of manual laborers from colonized territories. The inference that this hierarchy persists despite the independence of former colonies suggests that little has changed since a decade earlier, when René Vautier's *Afrique 50* denounced the exploitation of cheap manual labor under colonial regimes in French West Africa. It is as though practices of labor exploitation implemented in occupied overseas territories have been brought home.

When asked if he considers the factory incident a case of tacit or explicit racism, the Algerian replies that he did not confront his coworker because he believes that men were not made to hate each other. He adds that after he left the factory job following some unpleasantness *(des ennuis)*, members of the Direction de Surveillance du Territoire (Directorate of Territorial Surveillance) intelligence agency had barged unannounced into his room at 4:30 in the morning and roughed him up in front of his family. The young man states that the incident led to a hospital stay and his slow recovery from a mental breakdown. Asked outright how he sees his future, the Algerian says that while he is happy about Algeria's independence, he prefers to stay in France, where he is confident that the future will lead to a better fate *(destin)*. One wonders today if any of these three interviewees are still alive and, if so, what they might have to say about racial tensions that persist in the wake of violence such as the January 2015 attacks at the Paris offices of *Charlie Hebdo*.

The final nine minutes of *Le Joli Mai* are a counterpart to the opening segment's aerial perspective. Long shots of Paris, showing the Arc de Triomphe, the Champs-Élysées, the market area at the foot of the rue Mouffetard, and the interior of a train station, feature time-lapse effects that simulate a twenty-four-hour day-in-the-life cycle like those seen thirty years earlier in city symphonies including Alberto Cavalcanti's *Rien que les heures* (*Nothing but Time*, 1925), Walter Ruttmann's *Berlin: Sinfonie der Großstadt* (1927), and Dziga Vertov's *Man with a Movie Camera*.[58] The voice-over commentary recapitulates statistics for the month of May, including 3,762 births, 2,036 deaths, and the numbers of vehicles produced in Citroën, Simca, Renault, and Panhard automobile factories. A final assertion, that for the city's 5,066 prisoners, each day of the month is like all the others, provides a transition to an overhead shot of the Petite Roquette prison and to voice-over statements by a woman—presumably an inmate—who talks about daily life behind bars. The woman's voice is flat and without affect. When asked what prisoners think about when they think about the city, she says that they imagine two marvels: doors that open from the inside and steps that go in a straight line.

A phantom ride perspective in a vehicle traveling through the deserted streets of early morning Paris opens the film's final segment, following the assertion that Parisians outside the city's prisons carry prisons inside themselves. Street-level long shots facilitate identification of areas in the vicinity of the Arc de Triomphe. These are followed by close-ups and extreme close-ups of men and women. Compressed depth-of-field effects created through the use of telephoto lenses bring a dramatic flair to facial

Time-lapse shots of the Arc de Triomphe (*Le Joli Mai*).

expressions while the voice-over asks, "What's bothering you? What are you afraid of? What's the matter?" At one point, the voice-over interrogates these faces in the crowd directly: "Qu'est-ce qui ne va pas, visages?" (literally, "What's your problem, faces?"):

> Is it, as people often say, because you think too much about yourself? Or is it maybe instead that without knowing it you think too much about others? Maybe you think in some confused way that your fate is linked

Urban prison
(Le Joli Mai).

to that of others, that unhappiness and happiness are two secret societ-ies, so secret that you have inadvertently aligned yourself with them and that without hearing it, you harbor somewhere within yourself a voice that says: as long as misery exists, you are not rich, as long as distress exists, you are not happy, as long as prisons exist, you are not free.[59]

The soberness of the facial expressions seen is enhanced throughout the segment by the sound of a low drone and by the repeated phrase "as long as" *(tant que)*, which fashions a thematic progression from wealth and happiness to freedom. Marker's decision to cast all three clauses in the negative—not rich, not happy, not free—formulates a final critique of self-centered consumerism toward which the film has been building. The trope of anaphora formed by the repetition of "as long as" is a rhetorical flourish that further separates the critique of disengaged individuals im-plicit throughout the film from segments in the second part that depict others such as the former priest who display concern for others. In his films over the next decade, at least through *Le Fond de l'air est rouge,* Marker would continue to explore this concern in conjunction with social and political turmoil depicted in the heat of the moment *(à chaud)* as an alter-native to self-censored coverage by mainstream news agencies. In terms of personal practice, Marker would commit to sustained collaborations with militant groups, collectives, and cooperatives.

I want to return briefly to my initial claim that *Le Joli Mai* initiates a shift in Marker's filmmaking toward explicit activism and militancy. To be sure, the shift is less of a clean break with earlier films that Marker had com-pleted in different parts of the world from 1952 (Helsinki in *Olympia 52)* to 1961 (Cuba in *¡Cuba Sí!)* than a means of rethinking the assumptions and implications at work in these so-called hybrids of travel film and essay film. *Dimanche à Pékin (Sunday in Peking,* 1956) and *Lettre de Sibérie (Letter from Siberia,* 1958) match Marker's openness toward societies in transition with his curiosity concerning offshoots of Soviet Communism. Toward the end of *Dimanche à Pékin,* a young couple shown walking side by side on a crowded street are said to be tenderly talking about the latest five-year plan. In *Lettre de Sibérie,* an animated segment on prehistoric cave paint-ings includes a male portrait drawn in the elongated and heavily outlined style of the midcentury painter Bernard Buffet (1928–1999).[60] Another sequence parodies American mass culture with a phony ad for Arcady's Horn Flakes (read Kellogg's Corn Flakes) breakfast cereal, an owl puppet, and a portrait of *Mad* magazine mascot Alfred E. Neuman.

Both films of the mid-1950s soften social critique through irony and satire. Yet it is only in *Le Joli Mai* that depictions of a consumerist ethos are tempered by counterinstances of those who undertake individual and

Faces of anxiety,
II and III (Le Joli
Mai).

collective action for the benefit of others. The salesman hawking men's clothing outside his shop openly states that he is happiest when he has money in the till. Two messenger boys working at the Paris stock market think of little more than professional advancement and higher salaries. A young soldier and his fiancée steer clear of politics so that they can isolate themselves among those who share their values. These individuals personify an indifference to the suffering of others that the second part of *Le Joli*

Mai contrasts with the openness of the African R. O., the worker-priest, and the young Algerian committed to making a better life for himself in France. In 1966, Marker stated that he had made *Le Joli Mai* as

> a sort of call to make contact with others, and for both the people in the film and the spectators, it is the possibility of doing something with others that at one extreme creates a society or a civilization . . . but can simply provide love, friendship, sympathy.[61]

Fast-forward: the third pamphlet in the 1968 *États généraux du cinéma* series of short subjects includes a listing for *Le Joli Mois de mai (The Merry Month of May)*, a collective project shot—not, to my knowledge, by Marker—in May–June 1968. The pamphlet describes the film in the following terms:

> Power is in the street. Where the role of revolutionary violence is clearly demonstrated. The film illustrates the student movement, the break-down of [social] structures, the power vacuum, the return to power of the government (Gaullist demonstration on the Champs-Élysées). . . . Yes, but this is only the start.[62]

Yes, I would add, but perhaps only with the turn toward militancy that Marker had begun six years earlier in *Le Joli Mai.* By which I mean that the film's equation of a humane concern for others with collective activism marks a preliminary expression of a moral stance that Marker would re-direct over the following decade toward activism and militancy.

A Hard Left

A practical consequence of the shift initiated by *Le Joli Mai* was Marker's decision to work on multiple fronts and in multiple configurations. The decision produced a decade and a half of intense activity in which Marker's filmmaking—not only what he filmed but also how and with whom he filmed it—became openly politicized. Yet, as Catherine Lupton notes, the Chris Marker "who donned the collectivist mask of left-wing radical politics in 1967, and largely ceased to sign the films that he produced over the following decade, differs in emphasis, not in kind, from the Markers who preceded and came after him."[63]

Marker's filmmaking from 1962 to 1977 includes solo films such as *Le Mystère Koumiko (The Koumiko Mystery, 1965)* as well as collaborations with directors Joris Ivens, François Reichenbach, and Jorge Semprun. Other activities involved the Société pour le Lancement d'Œuvres Nouvelles (SLON; Society for the Launching of New Works), a production and distribution collective that Marker helped to launch in 1967.[64] Marker's initial effort for SLON brought together Jean-Luc Godard, Agnès Varda, Jacques Demy, Claude Lelouch, Joris Ivens, and William Klein for the anti–Vietnam War collective feature *Loin du Vietnam* (*Far from Vietnam*, 1967). In 1994, Varda wrote that she had proposed a segment *(sketch)* about a woman who mistook demolition work in an old part of Paris for the U.S. bombing of Hanoi. Varda's husband, Jacques Demy, had planned a contribution about a Puerto Rican U.S. soldier and a Vietnamese prostitute. Neither segment was retained in the final film.[65]

Marker's presence as producer and editor responsible for pre- and postproduction allowed him to "sandwich" documentary, fiction, and newsreel footage.[66] Thomas Waugh describes *Loin du Vietnam* as a test case and model of political filmmaking in France over the next decade. The film received mixed reviews in France, where it was considered a commercial failure. In the United States, its release amid intense debate surrounding antiwar and civil rights movements enhanced its visibility. A publicity poster for the release featured the slogan "No Vietnamese ever called me Nigger." The phrase was the title of a 1968 documentary by David Loeb Weiss in which it appeared on placards carried by participants during the 1967 antiwar Harlem Fall Mobilization March. The phrase is often attributed to the heavyweight boxing champion Muhammad Ali (born Cassius Marcellus Clay Jr., 1942–2016), who reputedly said, "I got nothing against no Viet Cong. No Vietnamese ever called me Nigger." A 1966 poem by Ali contains the following lines: "Keep asking me, no matter how long / On the war in Vietnam, I'll still sing this song / I ain't got no quarrel with no Viet Cong."

Despite the high visibility of *Loin du Vietnam* outside France, SLON members considered a lesser-known project undertaken during the same year to be more in line with practices of workers' cinema as far back as those of the mid-1930s Ciné-Liberté group. In March 1967, René Berchoud, who belonged to a popular culture organization in Besançon, wrote to ask Marker if he might consider a trip to Besançon, where "important things [were] happening."[67] Seven months later, *Loin du Vietnam* had its French premiere in Besançon. In the interim, Marker and *Le Joli Mai* production crew members Pierre Lhomme, Antoine Bonfanti, and Michèle Bouder worked in Besançon with codirector Mario Marret on *À bientôt, j'espère* (*Be Seeing You*, 1968), a forty-four minute documentary account of a recent strike during which three thousand workers occupied the Rhodiacéta textile factory. Much like Joris Ivens and Henri Storck's *Misère au Borinage* more than thirty years earlier, *À bientôt, j'espère* grew from a collaboration among filmmakers in support of striking workers whose experience had radicalized them toward activism and militancy. In 2005, Marker credited Marret, whom he later listed as codirector of *À bientôt, j'espère*, with creating a singular atmosphere of solidarity among filmmakers, militant workers, and the broad base of factory workers in and around Besançon:

> It is to [Marret] that we owe, through *À Bientôt, j'espère*, this atmosphere of perfect equality among filmmakers and their subjects *[entre filmeurs et filmés]* that I would surely never have been able to establish on my own and that earned us the honor of a personal comment from General de Gaulle, who apparently spent his time watching television, "What is all this about journalists on a first-name basis with workers *[ces journalistes qui tutoient les ouvriers]*?"[68]

In the final two minutes of the film (42:44–44:04), workers are seen gathered around a table where one of the strike organizers, Georges "Yoyo" Maurivard, recaps the productive effects of solidarity among coworkers:

> And I will tell the bosses that we will beat them *[on les aura]*, that's for sure, because of this solidarity and because they have no idea what's going on. We'll get you. . . . We no longer really hold a grudge against those who take themselves for bosses when they really aren't. But those of you who withhold capital, we'll get you. That's the way things are. That's nature and . . . be seeing you soon.

À bientôt, j'espère is significant for what it implies concerning the evolved nature of Marker's filmmaking as a collective—or even cooperative— activity. Over a longer duration, it can also be seen as pitting Marker against Jean-Luc Godard in a one-on-one debate about militant cinema. This confrontation was predictable because Marker's involvement with SLON and the Medvedkin Group from 1967 to 1974 coincided in large part with Godard's work for the 1968–75 Dziga Vertov Group, which he launched with Jean-Pierre Gorin.[69] In both cases, nominal affiliation with radical traditions of Soviet filmmaking between the wars served as a badge of renewed militancy.

The major issue faced by both filmmakers was how to go beyond reportage and documentation toward an authentic militant cinema made by and for workers. By extension, the issue transcended individual egos and raised the question of what was at stake among intellectuals who wanted to transcend class differences in the cause of productive collaboration. For Godard, the Besançon strike heightened differences between his stated goal to "make political cinema politically" and the position he ascribed to Marker's activities in relation to the strike.[70] The priority of production over distribution *(diffusion)* and reception was the basis of what Godard

Faces of resistance, II (*À bientôt, j'espère*, 1968).

sought from a militant cinema attuned to the specific conditions affecting a capitalist country under the yoke of imperialism.

Despite his work with Gorin during the Vertov Group period, Godard considered collective activity complex and tricky: "There always comes a moment when someone more qualified than another needs to take charge of collective work. One should not leave oneself vulnerable to the utopia of absolute egalitarianism."[71] When he asserted that the movie that really should have been made in France in 1968 was one about the strikes at Rhodiacéta, Godard acknowledged the seemingly unbridgeable gap between filmmakers who did not speak the language of strikes and workers who understood that strikers were "better at talking" on the picket lines than on film. And this, Godard concluded, even in films made with good intentions.[72] The swipe at Marker was hard to miss.

Elsewhere in the same interview, Godard described an inherent contradiction when he reiterated that a movie on the Rhodiacéta strike by a moviemaker would not have been the movie that should have been made:

> And if it were made by the workers themselves—who, from a technical point of view, could very well make it, if someone had given them a camera and a guy to help them out a bit—it still wouldn't give as accurate a picture of them, from the cultural point of view, as the one they give when they're on the picket-lines. That's where the gap lies.[73]

Whether or not Marker meant it as such (he probably did not), his involvement with SLON's short-term mission to help workers in Besançon make their own films was a response to Godard. This project's spirit of collaboration brought to mind Jean Rouch's efforts a decade earlier to provide those whom he had filmed in sub-Saharan Africa with the practical means to make their own films. In sum, the trajectory of Marker's filmmaking from 1962 to 1968—that is, from *Le Joli Mai* to *À bientôt, j'espère*—marks a movement toward collaborative activism and even militancy during the period leading to student and worker protests that would escalate to open revolt in 1968. As Marker would put it when looking back at this period a decade later in *Le Fond du ciel est rouge*, the true failure of global revolution occurred not in 1968 but in 1967.

Perhaps Marker acted so promptly on Berchoud's March 1967 invitation to see what was happening in Besançon because he was reminded of his early postwar ties with the activist groups Peuple et Culture and Travail et Culture, whose shared mission had been to bring literature, theater, and film to factories and other workers' groups. A major demand among Rhodiacéta strikers was for greater access to culture in conjunction with programs at the local Centre Culturel Populaire de Palente-les-Orchamps

(CCPPO; Popular Culture Center of Palente-les-Orchamps), which Berchoud and his wife had launched in 1959 with another Rhodiacéta worker, Pol Cèbe. By the time of the 1967 strike, CCPPO activities had included performances of plays by Bertolt Brecht, lectures on Pablo Picasso, an evening devoted to Jacques Prévert's Popular Front period work with the Groupe Octobre, and screenings of René Vautier's *Afrique 50*, as well as films by Godard, Eisenstein, and Ivens.[74]

Marker's postwar activism began in 1947 while he was a member of the theater center at Travail et Culture's Paris offices at 5 rue des Beaux-Arts, in whose film section he also worked as an assistant to the film critic André Bazin. Under the pseudonym Chris Villeneuve, Marker wrote for and edited the first issues of *DOC*, a publication that provided literary and musical materials for use in a popular education context.[75] Around the same time, he began to contribute fiction, poetry, reviews, and essays to *Espri*, a leftist Catholic monthly launched in 1932 under the leadership of Emmanuel Mounier. In 1952, Marker and Bénigno Cacérès coauthored *Regards neufs sur le movement ouvrier* (Another look at the workers' movement) as part of the Regards Neufs (Another look) series at the Éditions du Seuil. A year later, Marker contributed short entries on René Clair's *Entr'acte* (1924), Luis Buñuel and Salvador Dalí's *Un chien andalou* (1929), Jean Cocteau's *Le Sang d'un poète* (*The Blood of a Poet*, 1930), and Carl Theodor Dreyer's *La Passion de Jeanne d'Arc* (*The Passion of Joan of Arc*, 1928) to *Regards neufs sur le cinéma* (Another look at cinema) in the same series. These earlier activities help to explain why Berchoud's 1967 invitation allowed Marker not only to follow up on the implied militancy announced five years earlier in *Le Joli Mai* but also to reconnect with articles on interwar avant-garde filmmaking written more than a decade earlier. The result in 1967 amounted less to parallel activities in *Loin du Vietnam* and *À bientôt, j'espère* than a merging of activities on global and local fronts into a combined effort. Framing Marker's films from 1962 to 1967 within the 1962–77 militant period defined by Arnaud Lambert suggests that the origins of Marker's activism can be traced back to the seventy-three texts he published in *Esprit* from 1947 to 1954. Marker's move toward collaboration and militancy from 1962 to 1967 thus extends practices of social cinema and documentary between the wars, going back as far as the four late 1920s documentaries I have explored in earlier chapters in conjunction with a first wave of social documentary culminating in Vigo's *À propos de Nice* and "Toward a Social Cinema."

Afterthoughts

A Radical Lyricism

Writing this book has reinforced my sense that social documentary is less a discrete subgenre than a hybrid of experimental and nonfiction filmmaking whose trajectory in France can be traced from silent-era practices of the mid- and late 1920s through the long history of New Wave France from 1945 to 1963. This is the case as European avant-garde practices of the 1920s associated with medium-specific experimentation by René Clair, Jean Epstein, Walter Ruttmann, and Joris Ivens yielded to small-scale independent productions displaying various types and degrees of social engagement. For filmmaker André Sauvage, the advent of sound imposed a choice between working on large studio productions capable of absorbing the cost of new technologies or committing himself instead to independent projects commissioned on an ad hoc basis, and often through private sources. Sauvage's writings in 1929 and 1930 expressed his resistance to the new economic pressures associated with the transition to sound. His stance coincided with a shift toward socially engaged filmmaking on the part of Joris Ivens, Jean Vigo, and Luis Buñuel. But where Ivens, Vigo, and Buñuel continued their filmmaking, Sauvage retreated before dropping out.

The 1928–30 period I have examined in chapters 1 and 2 coincided with efforts among independent filmmakers in Europe, England, and the United States to create alternate networks through which to promote and distribute their films. An international film and photography exhibition held in Germany in May–June 1929 and filmmakers' congresses held in Switzerland (September 1929) and Belgium (December 1930) addressed the material and ideological issues on which these efforts were grounded. My treatment of films made by Vigo, Ivens, Henri Storck, and Eli Lotar during the 1930s points to the heightened importance of social concerns whose urgency Lotar's *Aubervilliers* (1946) addressed in the immediate aftermath of the 1940–44 German occupation of France. My treatment of films completed by Ivens, Storck, and Lotar, in various combinations and as collective actions, supports my claims concerning a critical mass or front over and beyond individual films and filmmakers.

The films that Alain Resnais and Chris Marker made together and on their own from 1950 to 1959 remain the initial points of reference from which the idea for *Critical Mass* first took form. As I considered the context of documentary practices within which Resnais and Marker were working, films such as Lotar's *Aubervilliers,* Nicole Védrès's *Paris 1900,* Georges Franju's *Le Sang des bêtes,* and René Vautier's *Afrique 50* emerged as early postwar antecedents. When a colleague asked if my corpus of postwar films drew on a radical tradition of documentaries such as the one launched among Soviet filmmakers of the 1920s, I realized that the four late silent-era films were united as much—if not even more—by an incipient engagement with social critique grounded in class distinctions. Documentaries by Georges Lacombe, Boris Kaufman, André Sauvage, and Marcel Carné filmed in and on the outskirts of Paris cast this engagement in conjunction with a human geography.

Vigo's 1930 "Toward a Social Cinema" remains a defining text for a first wave of documentaries completed in 1928–29 by Lacombe, Kaufman, Sauvage, and Carné in line with Vigo's sense of Buñuel and Dalí's *Un chien andalou.* A year later, Joris Ivens wrote "Reflections on the Avant-Garde Documentary," a six-point manifesto in which the turn toward independent practices took on an openly militant objective. For Ivens, the struggle between the avant-garde *cinéaste* and the big film production companies took the form of resistance to the technical progress of commercial cinema, which valued success grounded in the poor taste of a badly educated public over the social progress based in self-awareness and self-critique:

> Documentary film is the only positive means left the avant-garde *cinéaste* who wishes to commit himself fully to labor, insofar as he represents the expression of the masses or popular expression in his work. . . .
>
> In the current state of the cinema, documentary provides the best means of discovering the cinema's true paths. It's impossible for it to fall into theater, literature, or music hall entertainment, none of which is cinema.[1]

Ivens concluded by stating that his cinematic ideal of provoking latent actions and responses would be achieved "only in Russia, where the masses are accustomed to such activities daily and are able to understand the social truth of documentary."[2] In so doing, he identified an ideological position on the left that had been implicit in Vigo's call a year earlier for a social cinema that would open the spectator's eyes and put a certain world on trial.

Traces of Ivens's vision of a social cinema linked to revolutionary activism persisted among the films in my postwar corpus. This was especially the case for Vautier's *Afrique 50* and in Marker's trajectory of the 1960s, from *Le Joli Mai* to *À bientôt, j'espère.* Even so, elements of critique are visible among postwar films by Lotar, Jean Rouch, Resnais, and Marker. This plurality of practices fails to attain the consistency of a clear and stable school or movement. Instead, it promotes a sense of collective action I have tried to convey in terms of a critical mass.

Additions to the corpus of social documentary in France function less to fill in gaps than to map broader fields of avant-garde and documentary as a transnational phenomenon. For the 1930s, additional French-based films might include Buñuel's *Las Hurdes* (*Land without Bread*, 1933), Jean Renoir's *La Vie est à nous* (*Life Is Ours*, 1936), and André Malraux's *Espoir, Sierra de Teruel* (*Man's Hope*, 1945). For the 1940s, the likely additions are Georges Rouquier's *Farrebique* (1946), Védrès's *Paris 1900* (1947), and Franju's *Le Sang des bêtes* (*Blood of the Beasts*, 1949). For the 1950s, films that come to mind are Franju's *Hôtel des Invalides* (1952) and *Les Poussières* (*Dusts*, 1954), as well as Agnès Varda's *L'Opéra Mouffe* (1958) and perhaps even Resnais's *Le Mystère de l'atelier 15* (*The Mystery of Workshop 15*, 1957) and *Le Chant du Styrène* (*The Song of Styrene*, 1958). For the 1960s, Rouch and Edgar Morin's *Chronique d'un été* (*Chronicle of a Summer*, 1961) would initiate a trajectory leading from Chris Marker's *Le Joli Mai* (*The Merry Month of May*, 1963) and his *Loin du Vietnam* (*Far from Vietnam*, 1967) to the openly militant *Cinétracts* (1968), associated with the events of May 1968. Extending the corpus to the 1970s would allow for inclusion of Guy Debord's *La Société du spectacle* (*Society of the Spectacle*, 1974) as well as the prospect of considering Debord's films completed as far back as 1952. All of this is less to admit to the shortcomings of what I have hoped to accomplish in this book than to propose directions for future inquiry.

Scott MacDonald offers an alternate approach to the intersection of documentary and avant-garde cinemas in which city symphonies function as "crucial early instances of cinema's potential for experiment, for developing new forms, for moving beyond the commercial marketing of narrative melodrama, and for making an exploration of the cinematic apparatus the subject of film."[3] Setting the self-reflexive experimentation in Dziga Vertov's *Chelovek s kino-apparatom* (*Man with a Movie Camera*, 1929) alongside Alberto Cavalcanti's *Rien que les heures* (*Nothing but Time*, 1925) and Walter Ruttmann's *Berlin: Sinfonie der Großstadt* (*Berlin: Symphony of a World Capital*, 1927), MacDonald designates Charles Sheeler and Paul Strand's 1921 *Manhatta* as containing an important premonition of what later came to be called the city symphony. The relevance of MacDonald's remarks is threefold. In addition to identifying the city symphony as an early instance of the intersection of documentary and avant-garde practices, MacDonald asserts the link between photography and film that is central to my account of Eli Lotar's trajectory from his street photography of the late 1920s to filmmaking activities culminating a decade and a half later in *Aubervilliers*. Finally, the films cited by MacDonald support my sense of social documentary's origins in the 1920s as international and transatlantic. Strand's work as a freelance newsreel cameraman during the same period prepared him to turn to overtly political filmmaking a decade later in collaborations with Fred Zinnemann, the Austrian émigré who had worked on Robert Siodmak's *Menschen am Sonntag* (*People on Sunday*, 1930), and later with Ralph Steiner and Leo Hurwitz on Pare Lorentz's first New Deal documentary, *The Plow That Broke the Plains* (1936).[4]

A second organizing principle for this volume centers on documentaries that convey what Luc Sante, following Émile Zola, has aptly called "a strange city, with its distinct neighborhoods, its suburbs, its villages, its paths and its roads, its squares and its intersections," all radiating out from the central marketplace at Les Halles.[5] In *The Other Paris*, Sante notes that as the city grew in concentric circles as determined by successive walls from the thirteenth century to *la Zone* of the mid-nineteenth century and the ring roads *(boulevards périphériques)* completed in 1973, the center gradually moved. Villages that had once been part of the surrounding countryside were absorbed into the city, and "what had once been periphery was directed toward the middle."[6] Sante taps into the mix of populist and surrealist sensibilities in documentaries from Lacombe's *La Zone* (1928) and Sauvage's *Études sur Paris* (1929) of the late 1920s to Marker's invocation of Fantômas—whom he describes as "the consummate genius of evil"—nearly four decades later in *Le Joli Mai*. And this in conjunction with Sante's efforts to evoke what life was like in cities when they were "as vivid and savage and uncontrollable as they were for many centuries, as expressed by Paris, the most sublime of all of the world's great cities."[7]

Drawing from Michel de Certeau's "Walking in the City" chapter about aerial and street-level perspectives on the streets of Manhattan, Alastair Phillips writes that while Paris is irreducible to a metaphorical text, there is surely an analogy between one's viewing of the textual spaces of the cinematic narrative and the walker's encounter with the created spaces of the built city environment.[8] André Sauvage anticipated this very shift in perspective some fifty years earlier during the fifth and final section of *Études sur Paris* with a sequence of shots that progress from atop the Tour Saint-Jacques across the Seine to the Left Bank's Latin Quarter, between the Panthéon on the rue Soufflot and the Luxembourg Gardens just to the west of the Boulevard Saint-Michel. The films by Lacombe and Sauvage not only predate later critical takes by Sante, de Certeau, and Phillips, but they also tap into the surrealist sensibility of the 1920s for which Louis Aragon's *Le Paysan de Paris*, André Breton's *Nadja*, and Robert Desnos's *La Liberté ou l'amour!* serve as foundational narratives.

Ian Walker recapitulates the relevance of these 1920s narratives when he argues for revised perceptions that ascribe to documentary photography of the period its status as "a complex and multivalent genre that seeks to comment on issues of social and cultural importance without losing sight of the position from which that commentary is made."[9] In so doing, Walker helps to account for the trajectory taken by Eli Lotar from his early photographs of the same period under the tutelage of Germaine Krull to his work over the next twenty years as a cameraman for Luis Buñuel on *Las Hurdes* and finally as director of *Aubervilliers*, filmed in the summer of 1945. Traces of a surrealist feel for urban Paris extend to Alain Resnais's 1956 *Toute la mémoire du monde (All the World's Memory)*, in which the Bibliothèque Nationale takes on the qualities of a carceral space modeled on the wartime concentration camps Resnais had featured a year earlier in *Nuit et brouillard (Night and Fog)*. Even more to the point is the fact that Chris Marker ends *Le Joli Mai* with a sequence about Parisian men and women incarcerated in the city's prisons.

A final source for the Paris-based sections of this book is Jean-Paul Clébert's 1952 *Paris insolite (Paris Vagabond)*, whose first-person account of life among homeless and street people *(clochards)* was a gritty update of passages in Louis-Ferdinand Céline's *Journey to the End of the Night* devoted to Right Bank neighborhoods on either side of the northern city limits to be depicted some twenty years later by Didier Daeninckx. Clébert admitted that he acquired his experience of Paris at street level by hawking the daily paper *L'Intransigeant* along Right Bank Grands Boulevards and at Métro entrances. He described his Paris as inexhaustible, and his account of it as nothing less than baroque vagabonding:

> Now that I stride through the city from one end to the other knowin it like the back of my hand (though still making fresh discoveries every day), I nourish the naive hope that writing this book will bring me satisfaction; I should like it to be a sincere and exhaustive documentary account of the liveliest face of Paris and of all the marvels it harbors in their natural state, all the extraordinary characters who miraculously survive there.[10]

Much like Lacombe and Céline two decades earlier, Clébert was drawn to the borderlands between the city and its outskirts, on which, he noted, *la Zone* was gradually disappearing, "like a grease spot being vigorously rubbed," as it made way for a railroad-like trench for what would become the *boulevards périphériques*.[11]

A final lesson I learned from this project involves the links between experience and knowledge for which documentary filmmaking provides a singular opening onto the past and the present. Vigo's call for a social cinema that would be a kick in the pants to open people's eyes remains axiomatic for the kinds of films that would move audiences to new understanding not only of the past but of the present as well. The element of provocation is paired in some instances with modes of intervention formalized in voice-over in postwar films by Lotar, Vautier, Resnais, Marker, and Rouch. Equally open to this essayistic dimension are silent-era films by Lacombe, Kaufman, Sauvage, and Carné in which the absence of voice-over fails to preclude the potential to intervene in social issues on the basis of an associative logic grounded in images arranged through seriality and editing. Each in its own way, the films discussed in *Critical Mass* resist models of documentary based in factual representation in favor of practices in which—as Vigo stated in 1930—the viewpoint of the author is clearly supported. This kind of social documentary demands that the spectator take a position. Such a film may not persuade an artist, but at least it will compel a man. And that, Vigo concluded, is worth at least as much.

Acknowledgments

Many colleagues and friends have supported this project over the past decade. For their interest, feedback, and generosity, I thank Richard Abel, Juho Ahava, Paula Amad, Dudley Andrew, Jean-Pierre Bertin-Maghit, Dominique Bluher, Brett Bowles, Nicole Brenez, Francesco Casetti, Ivan Cerecina, Kate Conley, Tom Conley, Ludovic Cortade, Corey Creekmur, Monica Dall'Asta, Natacha Derycke, Sam Di Iorio, Roger Draper, Natasă Ďurovičová, Patrick Ferran, Marie Ferran-Wabbes, Paul Fileri, Claudia Gorbman, Nathaniel Greene, Tom Gunning, Lynn Higgins, Nathalie Hubert, Kate Ince, Hervé Joubert-Laurencin, Charles Jousselin, Jonathan Kahana, Michèle Lagny, Roxanne Lapidus, Addie Leak, Herman Lebovics, Sylvie Lindeperg, Robert Lord, Teresa Mangum, Ivone Margulies, Michel Marie, Florent Matic, Laurence Millereux, Keith Reader, Andrew Ritchey, D. N. Rodowick, Joel Strom, François Thomas, Thomas Tode, Margrit Troehler, Marc Vernet, Laura Vichi, Luce Vigo, Jennifer Wild, and Kathleen Woodward.

From January through June 2009, I had the privilege to be appointed Solomon Katz Distinguished Professor of the Humanities at the University of Washington–Seattle. In 2012, a John Simon Guggenheim Memorial Foundation Fellowship provided me with a year of uninterrupted research, during which the first draft of the project took shape. The University of Iowa's Office of the Vice-President for Research supported this project with timely Arts and Humanities Initiative grants in 2008 and 2012. A spring 2013 residency at the University of Iowa's Obermann Center for Advanced Studies allowed me to pursue my research in an environment of dialogue and exchange. I send special thanks to the staff at the UI Libraries for their patience in fulfilling my frequent requests.

In France, Pierrette Lemoigne screened rare footage for me at the Centre National de la Cinématographie's Archives Françaises du Cinéma in Bois d'Arcy. The Musée Nicéphore Niépce (Chalon-sur-Saone) provided me with an electronic copy of Gisèle Freund's article on the Bibliothèque Nationale in Paris, first published in *Vu*, number 463 (January 27, 1937). Researchers at the Maison du Cinéma in Paris facilitated access to archival materials in the reserve collections of the Bibliothèque du Film and

Cinémathèque Française. I benefited on numerous occasions from the collections of digitized films at the Forum des Images and the Bibliothèque Nationale de France in Paris. At the Centre Pompidou, Damarice Amao shared her doctoral dissertation on Eli Lotar with me and provided access to Lotar's photographs of the 1920s and 1930s. At the Ciné-Reflet and Librairie du Cinéma du Panthéon bookshops, Frédéric Damien unearthed materials that others told me were not to be found *(introuvables)*. Émile-Dominique Zinsou likewise offered me his collection of rare back issues of the Fédération Française des Ciné-Clubs monthly, *Cinéma*.

Jason Weidemann, Douglas Armato, Danielle Kasprzak, Anne Carter, Laura Westlund, and Judy Selhorst at the University of Minnesota Press were unstinting in their support of *Critical Mass* as far back as 2009. Special thanks to Emma Wilson and Peter Bloom for their feedback on early drafts of the manuscript and to Thomas K. Dean for his copyediting. Chang-Min Yu spent long hours preparing images for production.

I am from a family of film lovers. My parents, Egon and Lisbeth (née Feigel) Ungar, reminded me that some of their first encounters with the United States and France in their native Vienna occurred through movies. For my father, this meant seeing Wallace Beery in George W. Hill's *The Big House* (1930). For my mother, it was Jean Gabin in Julien Duvivier's *Pépé le Moko* (1937). (How did she know that *Pépé* would become one of my favorites?) In Chicago's Lakeview neighborhood, where I grew up, the Century, Covent, and Parkway movie theaters along North Clark Street were no more than a ten-minute walk from home. I dedicate this book to my brother, Tom Ungar (aka T. T. Ungar), with whom I laughed too often and too loud at Victor Mature's posturing in Carlo Ludovico Bragaglia's *Hannibal* (1959) and at Jerry Lewis's mugging in Frank Tashlin's *The Geisha Boy* (1958). It is also for students and colleagues at the University of Iowa, the University of Washington, and the Université de Paris-III whose questions and comments spurred me to greater clarity as this book took shape over the past decade. And once again, it is for Robin, my favorite moviegoing companion.

Declaration of the Group of Thirty

Paris, December 20, 1953

The short subject used to have a hard time of it, but it always managed to survive. Today, its death is decided.

The French school of the short subject is distinctive in style, in quality, and in the ambitious subjects it undertakes. French short subjects have often met favor with the public throughout the world. There is not a single international festival where they do not carve out a prominent place, almost always the first.

A recent law authorizing a return to double-feature programs signals the demise of the short subject and makes the financing of French feature-length films all the more difficult. If this law is not withdrawn and measures are not taken to ensure that the short subject receives its due importance, there is much to fear.

A unique instrument of culture, an essential means of teaching and of knowledge, a spectacle, and an art are thus targeted all at the same time. No one would ever think of measuring the artistic value of a literary work by its number of pages or a painting by its physical dimensions. Alongside the novel or the most substantial of literary works, the poem, the short story, and the essay are often sources of renewal because they supply fresh blood and energy.

This is the role the short subject continues to play. In the end, its death would entail that of cinema, because an art that fails to move is an art that is dying.

Without compromising in any way the diversity of tastes, opinions, and beliefs within it, a group of directors, producers, technicians, and

---

Translated by Steven Ungar from reprint in *Bref,* no. 20 (1994): 40 41; document originally published in *La Cinématographie Française,* no. 1550 (January 9, 1954).

friends of the short subject has decided not to yield passively to the perils that threaten the short subject.

The moviegoing public likes quality short subjects. It does not yet know that it risks the imminent loss of the pleasure it takes in them.

The short subject is a means *[intermédiaire]* of spreading culture and scientific teaching among various organizations that run the risk of no longer having films at their disposal. Deputies, senators, and ministers have a mission to oversee France's cultural heritage in which the short subject no longer needs to demonstrate its importance. We risk the imminent loss of this important element of our heritage.

Our group refuses to accept that it is too late. It calls out to the public, to responsible organizations, and to members of government on whose actions the existence of the French short-subject film depends.

[Signed] Arcady, Marcel Ascoli, Alexandre Astruc, Yannick Bellon, Pierre Braunberger, Ghislain Cloquet, Jacques-Yves Cousteau, Henri Fabiani, Georges Franju, Marcel Garand, Paul Grimault, Robert Hessens, Marcel Ichac, Jacqueline Jacoupy, Claude Jaeger, Pierre Kast, Étienne Lallier, Jean-Jacques Languepin, Jean Leduc, Jacques Lemoigne, Pierre Lévi, Jean Lods, Eli Lotar, René Lucot, Marc Magnin, Jean-Pierre Marchand, Mario Marret, Bernard Maurice, Robert Ménegoz, Jean Mitry, Jean Mousselle, Francis Nivoix, Fred Orain, Jean Painlevé, Paul Paviot, Alain Resnais, Paul Renty, Georges Rouquier, Edmond Séchan, Jean Tedesco, Nicole Védrès, Jean Venand, Jean Vidal

This declaration has been approved by:

—M. de Hubsch, in the name of the French Union of Educational Documentary and Short-Subject Producers
—The Union of Cinematographic Production Technicians
—The Benevolent Association of Former Students of the National School of Photography and Cinematography
—The French Association of Film and Television Critics
—The French Federation of Ciné-Clubs

The signers of the declaration are the initiators of the "Group of THIRTY." This group is open to all professionals, friends of the short subject, and all interested organizations. Following the publication of this manifesto, a delegation of the Group of THIRTY was received by Monsieur [Jacques] Flaud, director of the National Centre of Cinematography, and by Monsieur . . . Louvel, Minister of Commerce and Industry.

This delegation received formal promises that regulatory measures would be taken before the end of the month of January for the protection of the French short subject.

Administrative Office: Marcel Ichac, Pierre Kast, Marc Magnin, Jean-Pierre Marchand, Fred Orain, Paul Paviot, Georges Rouquier.

Correspondence: Paul Paviot, Secretary General, 61, rue Chardon-Lagache, Paris 16e—MIR 62–97.

Quality Subsidy Study

Short-Subject Advantages

Instituted by the law of August 6, 1953, the new system allocating development resources to short-subject films has been in effect for two years. Films authorized for commercial distribution during 1955 as well as those not selected for a subsidy in 1954 are encouraged to compete again and again for funding.

Henceforth the consequences of the new law can be understood as:

—The quality of films has improved. Festival juries agree unanimously that an abundance of entries worthy of inclusion in international competitions has made final choices more difficult each year.

—The prospect of a subsidy has stimulated many producers to take risks (more and more films in color) and to be less stingy with production costs.

The increase in rates for financial support of feature-length films produced in France coupled with an award-winning short subject has facilitated placing "quality" films, sometimes even before they are entered in competition. The result has led producers of feature-length films to display greater discernment in their programming, which is fully in keeping with the legislators' intentions.

Criticisms. After this positive summary, let us examine the criticisms sparked by the law of August 6, 1953. Some of these address the very basis of the law. It seems, however, that the inequalities, indeed the so-called "injustices" some see as resulting from decisions by a commission panel are infinitely less shocking than the blind mechanism of the old system

Translated by Steven Ungar from reprint in *Bref*, no. 20 (1994): 41; document originally published in *Le Cinématographe*, no. 20 (1956).

that used to reject nine out of ten quality short subjects meant to accompany a mediocre feature-length film (happy when it did not remain locked up in a drawer somewhere). The successful feature used to drag along a sickening short subject bought for next to nothing, but that could generate significant financial support it did not warrant. To the contrary, the vast majority of film industry professionals—from producers to technicians, directors, cameramen, etc.—strongly favor the current system as well as improvements to the framework of the law.

Principal criticisms concern the following points:

1. Excessively long delays between completion of the film and the awarding of festival prizes result in slowing down resultant benefits;
2. Complexity of selection operations;
3. Award jury decisions.

Any modification to this law would entail serious consequences. Confident in the stability of its principle and its application for more than two years (the law is in force until the end of 1957 and can be extended by law for two additional years), many producers have often opted for quality, thereby entailing significant financial sacrifices. Sales or licensing contracts often include a repeal clause benefiting the producer in the event that the film in question subsequently receives an award and thus generates an additional financial support for the producer of the feature-length film. The technicians, producers, and cameramen can also be affected directly by a percentage of the subsidy earned by films on which they have worked. All would find themselves plaintiffs deprived of advantages they are justifiably expecting.

The quality subsidy has markedly improved the average quality of films. It has normalized relations between producers of feature films and short subjects. It has raised the artistic level of programming. Its basis is excellent. Its application has led to criticisms, but these can be remedied. Challenging them is thus to challenge the future of the short-subject film in France.

[Editors' note: Examining of each of these points in detail and proposing a number of solutions to remedy the defects noted, this lengthy study— eight typed pages and two pages of diagrams/charts—concludes by stating the importance of not returning to the system of automatic support recommended by followers of the group surrounding Louis Cuny.]

The Group of Thirty
April 5, 1956

Notes

Introduction

1. Rick Altman, *Silent Cinema Sound* (New York: Columbia University Press, 2004), 6.

2. Védrès was initially slated to direct *Nuit et brouillard (Night and Fog)*. See Sylvie Lindeperg, *"Night and Fog": A Film in History*, trans. Tom Mes (Minneapolis: University of Minnesota Press, 2014), 35, 37. See also Paula Amad, "Film as the 'Skin of History': André Bazin and Death in Nicole Védrès's *Paris 1900* (1947)," *Representations* 130 (2015): 84–118. Laurent Véray's *Vedrès et le cinéma* (Paris: Nouvelles Éditions Place, 2018) appeared as this book went into production.

3. Luce Vigo, *Jean Vigo: Une vie engagée dans le cinéma* (Paris: Cahiers du Cinéma, 2002), 84.

4. See Jean Vigo, "Toward a Social Cinema (1930)," in *French Film Theory and Criticism: A History/Anthology, 1907–1939*, 2 vols., ed. Richard Abel (Princeton, N.J.: Princeton University Press, 1988), 2:60–63.

5. See Fernand Braudel, "History and the Social Sciences: The *Longue Durée*," in *On History*, trans. Sarah Matthews (Chicago: University of Chicago Press, 1980), 25–54. This work first appeared in *Annales E.S.C.*, no. 4 (October–December 1958).

6. Román Gubern and Paul Hammond, *Luis Buñuel: The Red Years, 1929–1939* (Madison: University of Wisconsin Press, 2012), 25–26. Reliable sources on the prehistory of this conversion include the two volumes of Richard Abel, ed., *French Film Theory and Criticism: A History/Anthology, 1907–1939* (Princeton, N.J.: Princeton University Press, 1988); and Charles O'Brien, *Cinema's Conversion to Sound: Technology and Film Style in France and the U.S.* (Bloomington: Indiana University Press, 2005).

7. See Tom Gunning, "Before Documentary: Early Nonfiction Films and the 'View' Aesthetic," in *Uncharted Territory: Essays on Early Nonfiction Film*, ed. Daan Hertogs and Nico de Klerk (Amsterdam: Stichting Nederlands Filmmuseum, 1997), 14, 22. I thank Paula Amad for mentioning this article to me.

8. Bill Nichols, "The Documentary and the Turn from Modernism," in *Joris Ivens and the Documentary Context*, ed. Kees Bakker (Amsterdam: Amsterdam University Press, 1999), 144.

9. François Porcile, *Défense du court métrage français* (Paris: Cerf, 1965), 81–82. The other films listed by Porcile are *Un tour au large (A Journey on the Open Sea*, Jean Grémillon, 1926), *Voyage au Congo (Journey to the Congo*, Marc Allégret and André Gide, 1928), *Étude cinégraphique sur une arabesque (Arabesque*,

Germaine Dulac, 1929), and *La Nuit électrique* (*Electric Night,* Eugène Deslaw, 1928).

10. Georges Sadoul, *Le Cinéma français* (Paris: Flammarion, 1962), 41–42.

11. Nicole Brenez, "*L'Atlantide,*" in *Jeune, dure et pure! Une histoire du cinéma d'avant-garde et expérimental en France,* ed. Nicole Brenez and Christian Lebrat (Paris: Cinémathèque Française/Mazzotta, 2001), 20.

12. Jean-Pierre Jeancolas, "D.N.W. 28: Calling the Witnesses," in *100 années Lumière: Rétrospective de l'oeuvre documentaire des grands cinéastes français, de Louis Lumière jusqu'à nos jours,* ed. Louis Marcorelles, Ian Burley, et al. (Paris: Intermédia, 1991), 20.

13. Bill Nichols, "Documentary Film and the Modernist Avant-Garde," *Critical Inquiry* 27, no. 4 (2001): 580.

14. Henri Langlois, "L'Avant-garde française," in *Trois Cents Ans de cinéma* (Paris: Cahiers du Cinéma, 1986), 227–28. The article first appeared in 1953; it was reprinted in *Cahiers du Cinéma* 202 (1968). Unless otherwise noted, all translations in this book are my own.

15. Luc Sante, *The Other Paris* (New York: Farrar, Straus and Giroux, 2015), 10.

16. Carl Plantinga, "What a Documentary Is, after All," *Journal of Aesthetics and Art Criticism* 63 (2005): 105–6. Plantinga considers documentary as a subset of nonfiction films characterized by a greater degree of aesthetic, social, rhetorical, and/or political ambition than in corporate or instructional films. After describing inadequacies in models of the documentary as indexical record and as assertion, Plantinga posits a model of "asserted veridical representation" in which filmmakers signal their intentions for spectators to adopt an attitude of belief toward images and sounds as reliable sources for the formation of beliefs about the subject matter of films understood as approximations of the sense or feel of the profilmic events they show. He casts all three models as characterizations rather than as definitions.

17. See Stephen Barber's accounts of these pre-Lumière inventions in *Projected Cities: Cinema and Urban Space* (London: Reaktion, 2002), 13–23; and *Muybridge: The Eye in Motion* (London: Reaktion, 2012), 141–68.

18. Philippe d'Hugues, "La Naissance du long métrage en France," *1895* 13 (1993): 74.

19. Guy Gauthier, *Un siècle de documentaires français: Des tourneurs de manivelle aux voltigeurs du multimédia* (Paris: Armand Colin, 2004), 10.

20. Brian Winston, *Claiming the Real: The Documentary Revisited* (London: British Film Institute, 1995), 8, see also 32–33, 36–37. Erik Barnouw traces Grierson's evolving politics and their impact on documentary filmmaking in *Documentary: A History of the Non-fiction Film,* 2nd rev. ed. (New York: Oxford University Press, 1993), 89–100.

21. Joris Ivens, *The Camera and I* (New York: International Publishers, 1969), 97.

22. Marcel Duchamp, *Notes* (Paris: Flammarion, 1999), 118.

23. Jennifer Wild, *The Parisian Avant-Garde in the Age of Cinema, 1900–1923* (Berkeley: University of California Press, 2015), 31.

24. See Emmanuelle Toulet, *Birth of the Motion Picture,* trans. Susan Emanuel (New York: Harry N. Abrams, 1995), 14; Jean-Louis Comolli, "Vérité et mensonge," *Cinéma documentaire: Manières de faire, formes de pensée,* ed. Catherine

Bizern (Crisnée, Belgium: Yellow Now, 2002), 89; and Tom Gunning, "An Aesthetic of Astonishment: Early Film and the (In)credulous Spectator," *Art & Text* 34 (1989): 31.

25. Martin Loiperdinger, "Lumière's Arrival of the Train: Cinema's Founding Myth," *Moving Image* 4, no. 1 (2004): 93–121. I thank Peter Bloom for pointing me to this article and for his productive comments on an early draft of the manuscript for this book.

26. Dai Vaughan, *For Documentary: Twelve Essays* (Berkeley: University of California Press, 1999), xiv, 58.

27. Ibid., 84–85.

28. Francesco Casetti, *Eye of the Century: Film, Experience, Modernity*, trans. Erin Larkin with Jennifer Pranolo (New York: Columbia University Press, 2008), 3–5; and Jonathan Crary, *Suspensions of Perception: Attention, Spectacle, and Modern Culture* (Cambridge: MIT Press, 2001), 74.

29. Philippe Lejeune, *Le Pacte autobiographique* (Paris: Seuil, 1975); and Philippe Lejeune, *On Autobiography*, trans. Katherine Leary (Minneapolis: University of Minnesota Press, 1989). Jean-Paul Colleyn invokes a variant of Lejeune's model when he writes of a narrative pact as a means of accounting for differences between fiction and documentary film. Jean-Paul Colleyn, *Le Regard documentaire* (Paris: Centre Georges Pompidou, 1993), 17. Lynn Higgins likewise lists a certain kind of gaze among features that constitute a film's documentary thrust. Lynn Anthony Higgins, *Bertrand Tavernier* (New York: Manchester University Press, 2012), 187.

30. Claire Devarrieux and Marie-Christine Navacelle's *Cinéma du reel* (Paris: Autrement, 1988) contains interviews with filmmakers Joris Ivens, Louis Malle, Jean Rouch, Henri Storck, and Agnès Varda, as well as selections from a ciné-journal by Raymond Depardon. Formed in 1992, the Association des Cinéastes Documentaires (Association of Documentary Filmmakers), known as Addoc, is open to all filmmakers working in documentary modes who want to consider and debate ethical, aesthetic, and political questions at the heart of *le cinéma du réel*. See Catherine Bizern, ed., *Cinéma documentaire: Manières de faire, forms de pensée* (Crisnée, Belgium: Yellow Now, 2002).

31. The best selection of period sources in English appears in the two volumes of Abel, *French Film Theory and Criticism*, esp., for the 1920s, 1:95–436. In French, see the Galerie Maeght's 1993 facsimile reprint of Jean Epstein's *Bonjour cinéma* (Paris: Sirène, 1921); and André Tchernia's selection of articles and reviews by Robert Desnos, published under the title *Cinéma* (Paris: Gallimard, 1966).

32. Richard Abel, *French Cinema: The First Wave, 1915–1929* (Princeton, N.J.: Princeton University Press, 1984), 249.

33. Prosper Hillairet, *"Coeur fidèle" de Jean Epstein* (Crisnée, Belgium: Yellow Now, 2008), 40. See also Abel, *French Cinema*, 359–66.

34. Moussinac's review of *Coeur fidèle* substantiates this realist dimension; cited in Abel, *French Cinema*, 249. On poetic realism, see Dudley Andrew, *Mists of Regret: Culture and Sensibility in Classic French Film* (Princeton, N.J.: Princeton University Press, 1995).

35. Chris Marker, "L'Avant-garde française," In *Regards neufs sur le cinema*, ed. Jacques Chevalier (Paris: Seuil, 1953), 250. This book was an initiative of

Peuple et Culture, an offshoot of the Travail et Culture group of postwar cultural activists to which I return later. A second edition published in 1963 under the same title contained substantial additions and deleted a number of articles, among which Marker's was one.

36. Malcolm Turvey, *The Filming of Modern Life: European Avant-Garde Film of the 1920s* (Cambridge: MIT Press, 2011), 100. Tom Conley uses the aerial perspective of Michel-Étienne Turgot's 1739 great map of Paris as a point of departure for a geographic-topographic reading of *Paris qui dort* that turns the Eiffel Tower into a ground zero of French history. See Tom Conley, "Icarian Cinema: *Paris qui dort*," in *Cartographic Cinema* (Minneapolis: University of Minnesota Press, 2007), 23–39.

37. Salvador Dalí, "Documentary—Paris 1929—I," in *Oui: The Paranoid-Critical Revolution, Writings 1927–1933*, ed. Robert Deschames, trans. Yvonne Shafir (Boston: Exact Change, 1998), 50, cited in Turvey, *The Filming of Modern Life*, 111–12.

38. Jacques B. Brunius, *En marge du cinéma français* (Paris: Arcanes, 1954), cited in Gauthier, *Un siècle de documentaires français*, 55.

39. Brunius, *En marge du cinéma français*, cited in Gauthier, *Un siècle de documentaires français*, 31–32. A translation of the passage into English as "Second Stage" appears in Abel, *French Film Theory and Criticism*, 1:371–72.

40. Antoine de Baecque, *La Cinéphilie: Invention d'un regard, histoire d'une culture, 1944–1968* (Paris: Fayard, 2003). On a collective change of gaze during the silent period, see Casetti, *Eye of the Century*. In a transatlantic context, the arrival of postwar French films in the United States exploited patterns of an import–export market centered in art house cinema in which French "product" played such a major role that France's government opened the French Film Office (FFO) in New York City in 1956. On the U.S. art house phenomenon, see Barbara Wilinsky, *Sure Seaters: The Emergence of Art House Cinema* (Minneapolis: University of Minnesota Press, 2001). On the FFO and the importation of French films to a U.S. market, see Vanessa R. Schwartz, *It's So French: Hollywood, Paris, and the Making of Cosmopolitan Film Culture* (Chicago: University of Chicago Press, 2007).

41. Antoine de Baecque, *La Nouvelle Vague: Portrait d'une génération* (Paris: Flammarion, 1998), 64. Richard Roud coined the designation in "The Left Bank," *Sight and Sound* 32, no. 1 (Winter 1962–63): 24–27; and provided a follow-up assessment a decade later in "Left Bank Cinema Revisited," *Sight and Sound* 46, no. 3 (Summer 1977): 143–45. See also Claire Clouzot's broader approach in *Le Cinéma français depuis la Nouvelle Vague* (Paris: Nathan, 1972), 46–80. References to the early postwar period as a golden age appear in Roger Odin, ed., *L'Âge d'or du documentaire*, 2 vols. (Paris: L'Harmattan, 1998); and in Dominique Bluher and François Thomas, eds., *Le Court Métrage français de 1945 à 1968: De l'âge d'or aux contrebandiers* (Rennes: Presses Universitaires de Rennes, 2005).

1. A First Wave

1. Norma Evenson, *Paris: A Century of Change, 1878–1978* (New Haven, Conn.: Yale University Press, 1979), 206.

2. Dominic Thomas, "Documenting the Periphery," in *Africa and France: Post-*

colonial Cultures, Migration, and Racism (Bloomington: Indiana University Press, 2012), 189.

3. Keith Reader, "The *Banlieue* in French Cinema of the 1930s," *French Cultural Studies* 25, nos. 3–4 (2014): 288.

4. English translations of Benjamin's essays appear in Walter Benjamin, *Selected Writings*, ed. Michael W. Jennings, Howard Eiland, and Gary Smith (Cambridge, Mass.: Harvard University Press, 1999), 2:52 and 3:108. See Ian Walker, *City Gorged with Dreams: Surrealism and Documentary Photography in Interwar Paris* (New York: Manchester University Press, 2002), 100. Reproductions of and commentary on the photographs in *Zoniers* appear in Molly Nesbit, *Atget's Seven Albums* (New Haven, Conn.: Yale University Press, 1992).

5. Louis-Ferdinand Céline, *Journey to the End of the Night*, trans. Ralph Manheim (New York: New Directions, 1983), 287–88.

6. Pierre Mac Orlan, *Masques sur mesure* (Paris: Gallimard, 1966). This collection includes a 1930 essay on Atget.

7. Adrian Rifkin, *Street Noises: Parisian Pleasure, 1900–1940* (New York: Manchester University Press, 1993), 190.

8. See Kelley Conway, *Chanteuse in the City: The Realist Singer in French Film* (Berkeley: University of California Press, 2004).

9. David Harvey, *Rebel Cities: From the Right to the City to the Urban Revolution* (New York: Verso, 2012), 8.

10. Rifkin, *Street Noises*, 196.

11. Anne Applebaum, *Gulag: A History* (New York, Anchor, 2004), cited in Geoff Dyer, *Zona: A Book about a Film about a Journey to a Room* (New York: Vintage, 2012), 17.

12. Yve-Alain Bois, "Zone," in Yve-Alain Bois and Rosalind Krauss, *Formless: A User's Guide* (New York: Zone Books, 1997), 224.

13. Pierre Nora edited three volumes of essays under the title *Les Lieux de mémoire* (Paris: Gallimard, 1984–92).

14. In 1952, Lacombe contributed to *Les Sept Péchés capitaux (The Seven Deadly Sins)*, a Franco-Italian coproduction also involving directors Yves Allégret, Claude Autant-Lara, Carlo Rim, Jean Dréville, Eduardo de Filippo, and Roberto Rossellini. Segments on pride, lust, sloth, envy, avarice, anger, and gluttony included appearances by Michèle Morgan, Françoise Rosay, Viviane Romance, Maurice Ronet, Louis de Funès, and Gérard Philipe. Lacombe is listed as director of the segment titled "The Eighth Sin."

15. Walter Benjamin, "The Paris of the Second Empire in Baudelaire," in *Selected Writings*, vol. 4, *1938–1940*, ed. Howard Eiland and Michael W. Jennings (Cambridge, Mass.: Harvard University Press, 2003), 48.

16. Brunius, *En marge du cinéma français,* cited in Gauthier, *Un siècle de documentaires français,* esp. 25–34. Louis Daquin identifies a 1919–25 period during which laboratory *experiments* (my emphasis) by Delluc, Dulac, Epstein, Abel Gance, and others led to visibility for a new generation of filmmakers, including Clair, Carné, Lacombe, Renoir, and Vigo. Louis Daquin, *Connaissance du cinéma* (Paris: Editeurs Français Réunis, 1960), 106–7. Malcolm Turvey classifies practices during the period under headings of *cinéma pur,* Dada, surrealism, and city symphonies. See Turvey, *The Filming of Modern Life.*

17. Gilles A. Tiberghien, "*La Zone*," in Brenez and Lebrat, *Jeune, dure et pure!*, 126. For an informed account of the Studio des Ursulines's programming of avant-garde silent films, see Abel, *French Cinema*, 267–68.

18. See Charles-Robert Ageron, "L'Exposition coloniale de 1931: Mythe républicain ou mythe impérial?," in *Les Lieux de mémoire*, vol. 1, *La République*, ed. Pierre Nora (Paris: Gallimard, 1984).

19. Daniel Abric, "*La Zone*: Petit film amusant," *Cinémonde* 17 (February 14, 1929), 14, cited in Margaret C. Flinn, "Documentary Limits and the Limits of Documentary: Georges Lacombe's *La Zone* and the '*Documentaire romancé*,'" *Contemporary French and Francophone Studies* 13 (2009): 410.

20. Naomi Schor, "*Cartes postales*: Representing Paris 1900," *Critical Inquiry* 18, no. 2 (1992): 188–244.

21. Mireille Rosello, "*Les Glaneurs et la glaneuse*: Portrait of the Artist as an Old Lady," *Studies in French Cinema* 1, no. 1 (2001): 29–36; and Kelley Conway, *Agnès Varda* (Urbana: University of Illinois Press, 2015), 71–88.

22. Walker, *City Gorged with Dreams*, 122–23. Walker includes Jacques-André Boiffard's photograph of Breton at the Saint-Ouen flea market, which Breton reproduced in *Nadja*.

23. Philippe Esnault, "Surprise de vues: Les vertiges de Geogres Franju," *France-Culture*, radio broadcast, August 16, 1983, cited in Gauthier, *Un siècle de documentaires français*, 104.

24. Flinn, "Documentary Limits and the Limits of Documentary," 405.

25. Tom Gunning, preface to *Jean Epstein: Critical Essays and New Translations*, ed. Sarah Keller and Jason N. Paul (Amsterdam: Amsterdam University Press, 2012), 20.

26. Quoted in Abel, *French Cinema*, 366.

27. Fernand Léger, "La Couleur dans la vie (Fragment d'une étude sur les valeurs plastiques nouvelles)," *Promenoir* 5 (n.d.), cited in Katie Kirtland, "The Cinema of the Kaleidoscope," in Keller and Paul, *Jean Epstein*, 93–94.

28. Waldemar George, *Les Arts à Paris*, November 1924, cited in Pierre Leprohon, *Jean Epstein* (Paris: Seghers, 1964), 160–61.

29. Léon Moussinac, "Le Cinéma: *Coeur fidèle*," in *L'Âge ingrat du cinéma* (Paris: Editeurs Français Réunis, 1967), cited in Abel, *French Cinema*, 359.

30. Leprohon, *Jean Epstein*, 71.

31. Henri Langlois, "Jean Epstein," in *Trois Cents Ans de cinéma*, 248.

32. See Michel de Certeau, *The Practice of Everyday Life*, trans. Steven Rendell (Berkeley: University of California Press, 1984); Alice Kaplan and Kristin Ross, eds., "Everyday Life," special issue, *Yale French Studies* 73 (1987); and Michael Sheringham, *Everyday Life: Theories and Practices from Surrealism to the Present* (New York: Oxford University Press, 2006).

33. Georges Perec, "Approaches to What?," in *Species of Spaces and Other Pieces*, ed. and trans. John Sturrock (New York: Penguin, 1997), 211. I have slightly altered Sturrock's translation. This essay was first published in the February 1975 issue of *Cause commune* and was reprinted in Georges Perec, *L'Infra-ordinaire* (Paris: Seuil, 1989). In 1980, Paul Virilio formulated a more personalized approach to the infra-ordinary by challenging himself and oth-

ers "to look at what you wouldn't listen to, to be attentive to the banal, the ordinary, the infra-ordinary." Paul Virilio, *The Aesthetics of Disappearance* (New York: Semiotext[e], 1991), 36–37.

34. Perec, "Approaches to What?," 210.

35. Ibid., 211.

36. Jean Marguet, "Les Présentations: *La Zone*," *Cinémagazine* 43 (October 26, 1928), quoted in Dimitri Vezyroglou, *Le Cinéma en France à la veille du parlant* (Paris: CNRS, 2011), 274.

37. Colin Jones, *Paris: Biography of a City* (New York: Viking, 2004), 166.

38. Jean-Clarence Lambert, "Pour le dépassement du documentaire," *L'Âge du cinéma* 6 (1951), cited in Alain Virmaux and Odette Virmaux, "Documentaire et avant-garde," in Brenez and Lebrat, *Jeune, dure et pure!*, 104.

39. The Forum des Images, whose collections include a restored copy of the film, lists its production date as 1927, as does Gauthier, *Un siècle de documentaires français*, 61. A date of 1929 appears in François Albéra, "*Les Halles* vues par les avant-gardes cinématographiques," in *Les Halles: Images d'un quartier*, ed. Jean-Louis Robert, Myriam Tsikounas, and Martine Tabeaud (Paris: Publications de la Sorbonne, 2004). An online filmography in the Internet Encyclopedia of Cinematographers (http://www.cinematographers.nl) includes a 1927 entry for *Les Halles centrales* attributed to Kaufman and a separate 1929 entry listing Kaufman and Galitzine. Both mention a running time of seven minutes.

40. Albéra, "*Les Halles* vues par les avant-gardes cinématographiques," 161.

41. Weegee was the pseudonym of photojournalist Ascher Fellig (1899–1968), whose rapid arrival at New York City crime scenes was purportedly facilitated by his listening to police communications on a dispatch receiver he had installed in the trunk of his car. Weegee dubbed New York "the naked city" and used the phrase as the title of a 1945 collection of his crime scene and street photographs, many of which first appeared in tabloids. Jules Dassin hired him as a visual consultant for his aptly titled 1948 police-procedure noir, *The Naked City.*

42. Gauthier, *Un siècle de documentaires français*, 62.

2. Visualizing Paris Anew

1. Myriam Juan, "Le Cinéma documentaire dans la rue parisienne," *Sociétés et Representations*, no. 17 (2004): 291–314.

2. *Paris-Express* was also known as *Souvenir de Paris (Memory of Paris)*. After Henri Langlois discovered seemingly lost segments of the film in 1958, the Prévert brothers and Duhamel considered how best to make a new version with music and commentary. At the suggestion of film producer Anatole Dauman, they included new sequences of contemporary Paris. The result was a twenty-four-minute short subject screened at the 1960 Cannes Film Festival, with color cinematography by Sacha Vierny, music by Louis Bessières, and voice-over commentary read by Jacques Prévert and Arletty. The title of the new film, *Paris la belle (Beautiful Paris)*, was intended to equate the beauty of the city with that of a woman. See Pierre Prévert, "Surréalisme et cinéma,"

Études Cinématographiques, nos. 38–39 (1965): 53. Prévert notes on the same page that he was unaware in 1928 that Sauvage, Lucie Derain, and others were involved with film projects on Paris similar to the one he, his brother Jacques, and Marcel Duhamel were shooting.

3. Tyler Stovall, *The Rise of the Paris Red Belt* (Berkeley: University of California Press, 1990), 169–70.

4. Nathaniel Greene, "Un poète à la caméra," in *André Sauvage, poète insoumis,* ed. Eric Le Roy (Paris: Carlotta Films, 2012), 11. Greene notes that the short-subject segments of *Études sur Paris* were programmed opposite domestic and foreign features, including Carmine Gallone's *Liebeshölle* (*Love's Hell,* 1928), Teinosuke Kinugasa's *Jûjiro* (*Slums of Tokyo,* 1928), and Friedrich Zelnik's *Die Weber* (*The Weavers,* 1927). His essay appears in a booklet commissioned for Carlotta Films' October 2012 DVD release of *Études sur Paris.* The DVD contains six bonus items, including rushes from Sauvage's first film, *La Traversée du Grépon* (*The Crossing of the Grépon,* 1923), and clips/cuts from his *Portrait de la Grèce* (*Portrait of Greece,* 1928). Sauvage produced two versions of each of the five short studies: one in black and white, the other tinted.

5. Paul Gilson, "Entre deux prises de vues dans Paris/André Sauvage nous dit . . . ," *L'Ami du peuple,* September 7, 1928.

6. See Mark Ovenden, *Paris Underground: The Maps, Stations, and Design of the Metro* (New York: Penguin, 2009).

7. André Breton, *Manifestoes of Surrealism,* trans. Richard Seaver and Helen R. Lane (Ann Arbor: University of Michigan Press, 1972), 20. The passage by Reverdy appeared in the March 1918 issue of *Nord-Sud.*

8. Delaunay and her husband, Robert, designed costumes and set decorations for films by Abel Gance, Marcel L'Herbier, and René Le Somptier. See Monique Schneider-Maunoury, "Les Delaunay flirtent avec le cinéma," in *Le Cinéma au rendez-vous des arts, années 20 et 30,* ed. Emmanuelle Toulet (Paris: Bibliothèque Nationale de France, 1995).

9. Céline, *Journey to the End of the Night,* 249.

10. See François Maspero and Anaïk Frantz, *Roissy Express: A Journey through the Paris Suburbs,* trans. Paul Jones (London: Verso, 1994). In *Journal du dehors,* Annie Ernaux narrates a loose chronicle of daily life in the planned urban community *(ville nouvelle)* of Cergy-Pontoise, where she lived at the time while commuting to and from Paris on the RER line. See Annie Ernaux, *Exteriors,* trans. Tanya Leslie (New York: Seven Stories Press, 1996). On a smaller geographic scale, anthropologist Marc Augé combines personal memoir and ethnographic essay in his account of a lifetime of trips on the Métropolitain public transport system, which plotted a second Paris beneath (and occasionally above) the streets of the city, in *In the Metro,* trans. Tom Conley (Minneapolis: University of Minnesota Press, 2002).

11. Isabelle Marinone, *André Sauvage, un cinéaste oublié: De "La Traversée du Grépon" à "La Croisière jaune"* (Paris: L'Harmattan, 2008), 167. Marinone reproduces five of Sauvage's articles originally published in *L'Ami du peuple* and cites a sixth. My remarks on the articles draw on Marinone's reproduction of hitherto unavailable materials in the Sauvage family collection.

12. André Sauvage, "Le Documentaire et le film parlant," in "Causerie du ven-dredi," *L'Ami du peuple,* May 30, 1930, cited in Marinone, *André Sauvage,* 217.

13. Ibid.

14. Marc Chavannes, "Lettre de Marc Chavannes (Paris) à André Sauvage (Paris, le 13 avril 1928)," cited in Marinone, *André Sauvage,* 78.

15. André Sauvage, "Panoramiques," *Du Cinéma,* no. 2 (February 1928), quoted in Marinone, *André Sauvage,* 207.

16. Paul Gilson, "*Études sur Paris,*" *L'Ami du peuple,* September 14, 1928, cited in Marinone, *André Sauvage,* 82.

17. J. P. Gelas, "Un film sur Paris digne de Paris," *L'Action française,* April 19, 1929, quoted in Marinone, *André Sauvage,* 83.

18. André Breton, *Nadja,* trans. Richard Howard (New York: Grove, 1960), 66.

19. Pierre Taminiaux, "Breton and Trotsky: The Revolutionary Memory of Sur-realism," *Yale French Studies* 109 (2006): 54. Breton's 1923 review of Trotsky's book on Lenin appears in André Breton, *What Is Surrealism? Selected Writings,* ed. Franklin Rosemont (New York: Monad Press, 1978).

20. Tom Conley, *The Graphic Unconscious in Early Modern French Writing* (New York: Cambridge University Press, 1992), 13.

21. See [Robert] Massin, *Letter and Image,* trans. Caroline Hillier and Vivienne Menkes (New York: Van Nostrand Reinhold, 1970).

22. Breton, *Manifestoes of Surrealism,* 29.

23. Breton, *Nadja,* 31.

24. See Katharine Conley's cogent account of this breakup in *Robert Desnos, Surre-alism, and the Marvelous in Everyday Life* (Lincoln: University of Nebraska Press, 2003).

25. Robert Desnos, *Liberty or Love!,* trans. Terry Hale (London: BCM Atlas, 1993), 7. I have slightly altered Hale's translation.

26. Ibid., 52–53.

27. Mary Ann Caws notes that Desnos described Bébé Cadum as a soap star and a better guide to Paris than the *Guide Michelin.* Mary Ann Caws, *The Surrealist Voice of Robert Desnos* (Amherst: University of Massachusetts Press, 1977), 45.

28. Marinone, *André Sauvage,* 98.

29. Eric Le Roy, "'Les Oeuvres naissent d'un appel,'" in Le Roy, *André Sauvage,* 37–38.

30. Michel Ciment, "Ombres blanches et nuits noires: Robert Desnos et le cinéma," in *Robert Desnos,* ed. Marie-Claire Dumas et al. (Paris: L'Herne, 1985), 197.

31. See Nathaniel Greene, "Jacques Brunius, ou l'art de travailler la matière film," in a pamphlet accompanying *Jacques-Bernard Brunius, un cinéaste surréaliste,* DVD (Paris: Doriane Films, 2010), n.p.

32. A second series of the monthly, directed by Auriol from 1946 to 1949, is con-sidered by many to be a precursor of the *Cahiers du Cinéma.* This lineage took on visual expression in 145 of the first 159 issues (April 1951–October 1964) of the *Cahiers,* whose cover layouts featured the same shade of canary yel-low seen on those of the postwar *Revue.* Contributors to the postwar series included André Bazin, Jacques Doniol-Valcroze, Jean Cocteau, Jean-Paul

Sartre, Federico Fellini, and Pierre Prévert. See *La Revue du Cinéma, anthologie* (Paris: Gallimard, 1992).

33. Robert Desnos, "Musique et sous-titres," in *Cinéma,* 98. The first volume of a facsimile edition of collected issues of *Documents* (Paris: Jean-Michel Place, 1991) includes *L'Inhumaine, Les Nuits de Chicago* (*Underworld,* Josef von Sternberg, 1927), *Les Damnés de l'océan* (*The Docks of New York,* Josef von Sternberg, 1928), and *Symphonie nuptiale* (*The Wedding March,* Erich von Stroheim, 1928).

34. Desnos, *Cinéma,* 189. The 1991 facsimile edition of *Documents* reproduces the article with still photographs from *L'Inhumaine, Les Nuits de Chicago, Les Damnés de l'océan,* and *Symphonie nuptiale* that were not included in the 1966 *Cinéma* collection.

35. Horst Bredekamp, "A Neglected Tradition? Art History as *Bildwissenschaft,*" *Critical Inquiry* 29, no. 1 (2003): 422.

36. Kurt Korff, "The Illustrated Magazine," in *The Weimar Republic Source Book,* ed. Anton Kaes, Martin Jay, and Edward Dimendberg (Berkeley: University of California Press, 1994), 646.

37. Jacques-Bernard Brunius, "*Nord-Sud,* André Sauvage," in Brenez and Lebrat, *Jeune, pure et dure!,* 125, originally published in *Revue du Cinéma,* no. 3 (May 1929).

38. Brunius, *En marge du cinéma français,* 123–24.

39. Jean-Georges Auriol, "On vient de présenter . . . l'oeuvre d'André Sauvage," *L'Ami du peuple,* March 1930, cited in Le Roy, "'Les Oeuvres naissent d'un appel,'" 31.

40. Cited in Marinone, *André Sauvage,* 135. Clips from both *La Croisière noire* and *La Croisière jaune* are available on YouTube. See "*La Croisière noire,*" posted December 5, 2013, https://www.youtube.com/watch?v=VDsajU7sQ-Y&t=11s; "*La Croisière jaune* de A Sauvage," posted April 17, 2017, https://www.youtube.com/watch?v=T70orDEUuig; and "*La Croisière jaune* Citroën," posted February 1, 2015, https://www.youtube.com/watch?v=lMtVSHhCzKg&t=64s.

41. René Daumal, "Un film assassiné," *Nouvelle Revue Française,* no. 248 (May 1934): 898.

42. André Sauvage, "Le Passage difficile," in "Considérations sur le film parlant," *L'Ami du peuple,* May 23, 1930, cited in Marinone, *André Sauvage,* 213.

43. André Sauvage, "Prééminence du documentaire," *L'Ami du peuple,* July 18, 1930, cited in Marinone, *André Sauvage,* 194.

44. André Sauvage, "L'Homme de documentaire," in "Causerie du vendredi," in *L'Ami du peuple,* July 25, 1930, cited in Marinone, *André Sauvage,* 226–27.

45. André Sauvage, "Le Speaker ou la fin du silence," in "Causerie du vendredi," in *L'Ami du peuple,* December 12, 1930, cited in Marinone, *André Sauvage,* 229.

46. Nicole Brenez, *Cinémas d'avant-garde* (Paris: Cahiers du Cinéma, 2006), 44.

47. Sauvage, "Le Documentaire et le film parlant," cited in Marinone, *André Sauvage,* 218.

48. Jeancolas, "D.N.W. 28," 26.

49. Edward Baron Turk, *Child of Paradise: Marcel Carné and the Golden Age of French Cinema* (Cambridge, Mass.: Harvard University Press, 1989), 21.

50. Carné contributed eleven articles to *Cinémagazine,* some of them under the

pen name Albert Cranche. Jean Quéval, *Marcel Carné* (London: British Film Institute, 1850), 6.

51. Turk, *Child of Paradise,* 19.

52. Marcel Carné, quoted in Jean Mitry, "La Naissance d'un cinéaste," *L'Avant-Scène Cinéma,* no. 81 (1968): 7.

53. Dziga Vertov, *Kino Eye: The Writings of Dziga Vertov,* ed. Annette Michelson (Berkeley: University of California Press, 1984), 41.

54. Gary Cross, "Vacations for All: The Leisure Question in the Era of the Popular Front," *Journal of Contemporary History* 24, no. 4 (1989): 603.

55. Turk, *Child of Paradise,* 21.

56. Quéval, *Marcel Carné,* 7.

57. Marcel Carné, *La Vie à belles dents* (Paris: Jean-Pierre Olivier, 1975), 30.

58. Raymond Bellour, *Les Hommes, le dimanche, de Robert Siodmak and Edgar G. Ulmer* (Crisnée, Belgium: Yellow Now, 2009), 29.

59. The movie theater still operates today in the Left Bank area just south of the Latin Quarter. In February 1928, the Studio des Ursulines had been the site of an infamous brawl after surrealists led by André Breton and Louis Aragon shouted down Germaine Dulac and Antonin Artaud's *La Coquille et le clergyman* at that film's premiere.

60. The first review was signed R. P. B. in *Le Figaro,* the second by René Jeanne in *Le Petit Journal,* and the third by Claude Jeantet in *L'Action française.* Excerpts from all three appear in *L'Avant-Scène Cinéma,* no. 81 (1968), 8.

61. Marcel Carné, "Cinema and the World," in Abel, *French Film Theory and Criticism,* 2:103, originally published as "Le Cinéma et le monde," *Cinémagazine* 12 (November 1932).

62. Ibid., 2:105.

63. Carné, *La Vie à belles dents,* 117.

64. See Jonathan Driskell, *Marcel Carné* (New York: Manchester University Press, 2012). Driskell notes that 1938 box-office receipts for *Le Quai des brumes* in France were second only to those for Walt Disney's *Snow White and the Seven Dwarfs.*

65. Marcel Carné, "When Will the Cinema Go Down into the Street?," in Abel, *French Film Theory and Criticism,* 2:127.

66. Carné worked with Feyder on three additional films, ending with *La Kermesse héroïque* (*Carnival in Flanders,* 1935).

67. Carné, "When Will the Cinema Go Down into the Street?," 2:129.

68. See Dudley Andrew and Steven Ungar, *Popular Front Paris and the Poetics of Culture* (Cambridge, Mass.: Harvard University Press, 2005), esp. 277–98.

69. See Alexandre Trauner, *Décors de cinéma* (Paris: Jade-Flammarion, 1988). Trauner designed sets for nine films by Carné, from *Drôle de drame* (*Bizarre, Bizarre,* 1937) to *Juliette, ou la clef des songes* (*Juliette, or the Dream Book,* 1951).

70. Andrew and Ungar, *Popular Front Paris,* 283.

71. For discussion of *Toni,* see Christopher Faulkner, *The Social Cinema of Jean Renoir* (Princeton, N.J.: Princeton University Press, 1986). On *Le Quai des brumes,* see Jonathan Buchsbaum, *Cinema Engagé: Film in the Popular Front* (Urbana: University of Illinois Press, 1988).

72. Andrew, *Mists of Regret,* 155.

Transition I

1. Malte Hagener, *Moving Forward, Looking Backward: The European Avant-Garde and the Invention of Film Culture, 1919–1939* (Amsterdam: Amsterdam University Press, 2007), 16.

2. Peter Wollen, "The Two Avant-Gardes" (1975), in *Readings and Writings: Semiotic Counter-strategies* (London: New Left Books, 1982), 92–104.

3. Beaumont Newhall, ed., *Photography: Essays and Images* (New York: Museum of Modern Art, 1980), 245.

4. Christian Bouqueret, *Des années folles aux années noires: La Nouvelle Vision photographique en France, 1920–1940* (Paris: Marval, 1997), 173. See also "The International Exhibition 'Film und Foto,' Stuttgart 1929: A Portfolio," in Newhall, *Photography*, 243–49.

5. Cited in Thomas Tode, "Trois Russes peuvent en cacher un autre: Dziga Vertov et le congrès de La Sarraz, 1929," *Archives* 84 (2000): 3.

6. Ibid., 13–14.

7. Ibid., 7.

8. Henri Storck, "Interview de Henri Storck: À propos du 2e Congrès du cinéma indépendant," by Raymonde Borde, in *Protocole du troisième Congrès international du cinéma indépendant* (Lausanne: SIDOC, 1964), 145.

9. Laura Vichi, *Henri Storck: De l'avant-garde au documentaire social* (Crisnée, Belgium: Yellow Now, 2002), 12–13. My account of the 1930 Brussels congress draws on research conducted by Vichi, to whom I am grateful for encouragement and archival leads.

10. André Cauvin, "Le IIe Congrès international du cinéma indépendant à Bruxelles, 1930," *Travelling* 55 (1979): 37, originally published in *Les Beaux-Arts*, December 12, 1930.

11. Ibid., 38.

12. Charles Dekeukeleire, in *Le Rouge et le noir*, December 3, 1930, 7, cited in Vichi, *Henri Storck*, 15.

13. Vichi, *Henri Storck*, 181n26.

14. Germaine Dulac, "La Nouvelle Evolution," in *Écrits sur le cinéma (1919–1937)* (Paris: Paris Expérimental, 1984), 137–41. The text transcribes a December 3, 1930, talk at the Salon d'Automne.

15. Tami Williams, *Germaine Dulac: A Cinema of Sensations* (Urbana: University of Illinois Press, 2014), 173.

16. Wollen, "The Two Avant-Gardes," 94.

3. "All the World's Misery"

1. See Jean-Patrick Manchette, "Interview, Polar (1980)," in *Chroniques* (Paris: Rivages/Noir, 2003), 12; Jean-Patrick Manchette, *Romans noirs* (Paris: Quarto, 2005); and Jean-Patrick Manchette, *Journal* (Paris: Gallimard, 2008). Alternate approaches linking the *roman noir* to the literary and cinematic antecedents of postwar film noir include Charles O'Brien, "Film Noir in France before the Liberation," *Iris* 21 (Spring 1996): 7–20; and James Naremore, *More Than Night: Film Noir in Its Contexts*, rev. ed. (Berkeley: University of California Press, 2008).

2. Anissa Belhadjin, "From Politics to the Roman Noir," *South Central Review* 27 (2010): 61.

3. Jean-Paul Liégeois, "Avant-propos pour mémoire," in Didier Daeninckx, *La Mémoire longue: Textes et images 1986–2008* (Paris: Cherche Midi, 2008), 9.

4. In the November 1961 issue (no. 186) of Jean-Paul Sartre's monthly, *Les Temps modernes*, some 229 writers, artists, and educators signed a petition calling for inquiry into police actions on October 17. Signatories of the call, which compared the brutal treatment of Algerians in Paris to that of Jews under the Vichy regime, included Robert Antelme, Simone de Beauvoir, Maurice Blanchot, André Breton, Claude Lanzmann, Michel Leiris, Dionys Mascolo, Jean Rouch, Georges Sadoul, Nathalie Sarraute, and Claude Simon. See Jean-Luc Einaudi, *La Bataille de Paris, 17 octobre 1961* (Paris: Seuil, 1991); and Kristin Ross, *May '68 and Its Afterlives* (Chicago: University of Chicago Press, 2002), esp. 44–45.

5. Didier Daeninckx, *"Aubervilliers,"* in Brenez and Lebrat, *Jeune, dure et pure!*, 164. In 1996, Daeninckx wrote that one reason he started out writing *romans noirs* was the proximity of the La Villette slaughterhouse complex, which, to his mind, was equaled only by the Chicago stockyards Upton Sinclair described in his 1906 novel *The Jungle*. See also Daeninckx, "L'Écriture des abattoirs" and "À Aubervilliers, comme ailleurs . . . ," both in *La Mémoire longue*.

6. Stovall, *The Rise of the Paris Red Belt*, 1–2.

7. Stephen Barber, "European Breakdown Zone: Paris Suburbia," in *Extreme Europe* (London: Reaktion, 2001), 89.

8. Michel de Certeau, "Spatial Stories," in *The Practice of Everyday Life*, 115.

9. Vigo, "Toward a Social Cinema," 2:60–63. A French-language version of this essay appears in Jean Vigo, *Oeuvre de cinéma*, ed. Pierre Lherminier (Paris: Cerf, 1985), 65–68.

10. Alexander Sesonske, *Jean Renoir: The French Films, 1924–1939* (Cambridge, Mass.: Harvard University Press, 1980), 42–43. See also Pierre Lherminier, *Jean Vigo: Un Cinéma singulier* (Paris: Ramsay, 2007), 164.

11. Williams, *Germaine Dulac*, 82–83.

12. Luce Vigo, "Jean Vigo et Les Amis du cinéma de Nice," *Archives*, nos. 90–91 (2002): 43. See also Vigo, *Jean Vigo: Une vie engagée dans le cinéma*, 28–29; and Lherminier, *Jean Vigo*, 151–52.

13. Vigo, "Toward a Social Cinema," 2:60.

14. Ibid., 2:62.

15. See, for example, Roger Caillois, introduction to *The College of Sociology, 1937–1939*, ed. Denis Hollier, trans. Betsy Wing (Minneapolis: University of Minnesota Press, 1988), 9–10. On the origins of effervescent assemblies, see Michèle H. Richman, *Sacred Revolutions: Durkheim and the Collège de Sociologie* (Minneapolis: University of Minnesota Press, 2002), 26–27, 40–47.

16. Andrew, *Mists of Regret*, 66.

17. Vigo, *Jean Vigo: Une vie engagée dans le cinema*, 38.

18. Michael Temple, *Jean Vigo* (Manchester: Manchester University Press, 2005), 13. Temple astutely notes the triple function of Vigo's documentary debut as a formal experiment, a social commitment, and an apprenticeship in filmmaking.

19. Boris Kaufman, "Un génie lucide," *Premier Plan*, no. 19 (1961): 28. The first part of this passage uses Michael Temple's English translation of this passage in his *Jean Vigo*, 17. Often cited as the older brother of Denis Kaufman, best known for the 1929 film *Man with a Movie Camera*, made under the pseudonym Dziga Vertov, Boris Kaufman (1897–1980) had a long career that included camera work in France on Marc Allégret's *Zouzou* (1934). His subsequent work in the United States included collaborations with Elia Kazan, Otto Preminger, and Sidney Lumet. In 1954, Kaufman won an Oscar for cinematography for Kazan's *On the Waterfront*. A decade later, he teamed up with Lumet on *The Pawnbroker*.

20. Vigo, "Toward a Social Cinema," 2:63.

21. The accordion accompaniment added to the version of *À propos de Nice* in Artificial Eye's DVD set *The Complete Jean Vigo* (2004) gives a sense of the contribution that music—which was often played live during silent film screenings—might have made to the tone of the film.

22. Temple, *Jean Vigo*, 24.

23. Ibid., 26.

24. Despite differences of visual style, Agnès Varda's 1958 documentary *Du côté de la côte* suggests how little the area had changed as a tourist venue for the idle rich during the nearly thirty years since Vigo made *À propos de Nice*. A literal English translation of Varda's title, *Over by the French Riviera*, fails to do justice to the sound play in the French original grounded in phonetic and graphic resemblance.

25. Buchsbaum, *Cinema Engagé*, 34. See also Nicole Racine, "L'Association des Écrivains et artistes révolutionnaires (A.E.A.R)," *Le Mouvement Social*, no. 54 (January–March 1966): 29–47.

26. On *Las Hurdes*, see Tom Conley, "Documenting Surrealism: On *Land without Bread*," *Dada/Surrealism*, no. 15 (1986): 176–98; James Lastra, "'Why Is This Absurd Picture Here?': Ethnology/Heterology/Buñuel," *October*, no. 89 (1999): 51–68; and Vivian Sobchack, "The Dialectical Imperative of LB's *Las Hurdes*," in *Documenting the Documentary*, ed. Barry Keith Grant and Jeannette Sloniowski (Detroit: Wayne State University Press, 1998), 70–82.

27. Bathélemy Amengual, "Monde et vision du monde dans l'oeuvre de Vigo," *Études Cinématographiques*, nos. 51–52 (1966): 49.

28. Román Gubern and Paul Hammond write that Daniel Abric and Michel Gorel's 1930 documentary *Paris-Bestiaux* appears to have been the blueprint for Franju's *Le Sang des bêtes*. Gubern and Hammond, *Luis Buñuel*, 50. Significantly, they add that the film, which no longer exists, may have been inspired by Lotar's 1929 series of photos at the La Villette slaughterhouse complex.

29. See Simon Baker, "A Corpse," in *Undercover Surrealism: Georges Bataille and Documents*, ed. Dawn Ades and Simon Baker (Cambridge: MIT Press, 2006), 82–83.

30. The narratives are Breton's *Nadja* (1928), Aragon's *Le Paysan de Paris* (*Paris Peasant*, 1926), and Desnos's *La Liberté ou l'amour!* (*Liberty or Love!*, 1927).

31. Walker, *City Gorged with Dreams*, 130.

32. Jean Gallotti, "La Photographie, est-elle un art? Eli Lotar," in *Les Documents de la modernité: Anthologie de texts sur la photographie de 1919 à 1939*, ed. Dominique

Baqué (1929; repr., Paris: Jacqueline Chambon, 1993), 388–89. My thanks to Damarice Amao for informing me that, despite its title, the photograph listed as *Somewhere in Paris* was shot at an unidentified location in the South of France.

33. *Somewhere in Paris* appeared in *L'Art vivant* 111 (August 1929) and in *Photo Graphie* 1 (1930). Images of laundry flapping in the wind, a staple of postwar European art cinema starting with Italian neorealism, recall sequences in Agnès Varda's 1954 directorial debut, *La Pointe-Courte*. *La Zone, Billancourt* had no press publication. References are from Alain Sayag and Annick Lionel-Marie, eds., *Eli Lotar* (Paris: Centre Georges Pompidou, 1993), 111.

34. Kim Sichel, *Germaine Krull: Photographer of Modernity* (Cambridge: MIT Press, 1999), 99.

35. Michel Frizot and Cédric de Veigy, *Vu: The Story of a Magazine*, trans. Ruth Sharman (London: Thames and Hudson, 2009), 7.

36. Alain Virmaux and Odette Virmaux, "Cinéma: L'Énigme d'une carrière prometteuse et inaboutie," in Sayag and Lionel-Marie, *Eli Lotar*, 97.

37. Erwan Cadoret, "Un Double Regard sur la misère: *Aubervilliers* d'Eli Lotar et Jacques Prévert," in *Le Court Métrage français de 1945 à 1968 (2): Documentaire, fictions: Alerts-retours*, ed. Antony Fiant and Roxane Hamery (Rennes: Presses Universitaires de Rennes, 2008), 262–63.

38. See Guy Cavagnac, ed., *"Une partie de campagne": Eli Lotar, photographies du tournage* (Montreuil: Éditions de l'Oeil, 2007). Others working on the film included the photographer Henri Cartier-Bresson and future directors Jacques Becker and Luchino Visconti. In 1960, assistant cameraman Albert Viguier would work and appear briefly during a crucial sequence in Jean Rouch and Edgar Morin's *Chronique d'un été*.

39. Greene, "Jacques Brunius, ou l'art de travailler la matière film."

40. Ivens, *The Camera and I*, 46. According to Hans Schoots, *We Are Building* tempered formal experimentation with a strict realism that demonstrated Ivens's sensitivity to the work process. Schoots also notes that the collaboration between Ivens and Lotar occurred only after a violent quarrel over the latter's romantic involvement with Krull. Hans Schoots, *Living Dangerously: A Biography of Joris Ivens* (Amsterdam: Amsterdam University Press, 2000), 53, 32.

41. Rosalind Delmar, *Joris Ivens: 50 Years of Film-making* (London: British Film Institute, 1979), 29.

42. See Jamie Miller, "Politics and the Mezhrabpom Studio," *Studies in Russian and Soviet Cinema* 6, no. 2 (2012): 257–69.

43. See Thomas H. R. Waugh, "Joris Ivens and the Evolution of the Radical Documentary, 1926–1946" (PhD diss., Columbia University, 1981).

44. Michèle Lagny, "*La Seine a rencontré Paris* and the Documentary in France in the Fifties," in Bakker, *Joris Ivens and the Documentary Context*, 114–24.

45. Kathleen Newman, "Notes on Transnational Film Theory: Decentered Subjectivity, Decentered Capitalism," in *World Cinemas, Transnational Perspectives*, ed. Nataša Ďurovičová and Kathleen Newman (New York: Routledge, 2010), 10.

46. Quoted in Jacqueline Aubenas, "Storck, Henri," in *Dic doc: Le Dictionnaire du documentaire, 191 réalisateurs*, ed. Jacqueline Aubenas (Brussels: Communauté Française de Belgique Wallonie-Bruxelles, 1999), 377–78.

47. Delmar, *Joris Ivens*, 26. See also Bert Hogenkamp and Henri Storck, eds., "*Le Borinage*: La Grève des mineurs de 1932 et le film de Joris Ivens et Henri Storck," *Revue Belge du Cinéma*, nos. 6–7 (1983–84), 3–129.

48. Damarice Amao, "Passion et désillusion, Eli Lotar (1905–1969): Contribution à une histoire des rapports entre les avant-gardes photographique et cinématographique à Paris dans l'entre-deux-guerres" (PhD diss., Université de Paris-IV, 2014), 1:371. I am grateful to Ms. Amao for sharing her dissertation with me. As I complete revisions to my manuscript in early 2018, I want to note that Amao's dissertation has appeared as a book under the title *Eli Lotar et le mouvement des images* (Paris: Textuel, 2017). See also Pia Viewing, "'Transfuge du cinéma': Eli Lotar and Documentary Film," in *Eli Lotar*, ed. Damarice Amao, Clément Chéroux, and Pia Viewing (Paris: Editions du Centre Pompidou, 2017), 199–208. This volume accompanied a February–May 2017 exhibition of Lotar's work at the Jeu de Paume in Paris.

49. Paul Strand, "*Les Maisons de la misère*" (1939), in *The Documentary Tradition*, 2nd ed., ed. Lewis Jacobs (New York: W. W. Norton, 1979), 129.

50. Georges Sadoul, *Écrits: Chroniques du cinéma français, vol. 1, 1939–1967* (Paris: Union Générale d'Éditions, 1979), 411. See also Alain Weber, *La Bataille du film, 1933–1945: Le Cinéma français, entre allégeance et résistance* (Paris: Ramsay, 2007).

51. See Philip Watts, *Allegories of the Purge: How Literature Responded to the Postwar Trials of Writers and Intellectuals in France* (Stanford, Calif.: Stanford University Press, 1998).

52. Newsreels are often far from neutral. Claude Chabrol's 1993 documentary feature *L'Oeil de Vichy (The Eye of Vichy)* offers a critical take on newsreels produced during 1940–44 for screening in movie theaters throughout occupied France. As stated in the film's opening sequence, *The Eye of Vichy* does not show France as Chabrol had seen it in person as a boy between the ages of ten and fourteen, but instead as Philippe Pétain and others in the Vichy regime had wanted it to be seen. Fifty years after the fact, Chabrol wanted spectators to see how the regime had openly sought to deceive the French.

53. Denis Marion, "*Aubervilliers*," *Combat*, March 30, 1946, n.p. See also Pol Gaillard, "*Aubervilliers* et *Le Voleurs des paratonnerres*," *L'Humanité*, April 13, 1946, n.p. A half century later, Samuel Lachize provided a more level-headed assessment of the film by noting that Aubervilliers in 1994 was no longer that of 1945 and that, while there were still problems to be addressed, the hope to resolve them remained as well. See Samuel Lachize, "Les Prolétaires ont-ils une âme?," *Cahiers de la Cinémathèque* 59–60 (February 1994): 33.

54. André Bazin, "*Battle of the Rails* and *Ivan the Terrible*," in *Bazin at Work: Major Essays and Reviews from the Forties and Fifties*, ed. Bert Cardullo, trans. Alain Piette and Bert Cardullo (New York: Routledge, 1997), 199. Bazin's review first appeared in the April 1946 issue of *Esprit*. An earlier review in *Gavroche* (January 31, 1946) is reprinted in André Bazin, *French Cinema of the Occupation and Resistance: The Birth of a Critical Esthetic*, trans. Stanley Hochman (New York: Frederick Ungar, 1981), 122–23. Additional references are Jean-Pierre Bertin-Maghit, "*La Bataille du rail*: De l'authenticité à la chanson de geste," *Revue d'histoire moderne et contemporaine* 33 (1986): 283–84; and Sylvie Linde-

perg, "Political and Narrative Ambiguities in *La Bataille du rail,*" *Historical Reflections/Réflexions historiques* 35, no. 2 (2009): 142–43.

55. Alex Ross, *The Rest Is Noise: Listening to the Twentieth Century* (New York: Picador, 2007), 209.

56. Amao, "Passion et désillusion," 1:374.

57. The song is Vincent Scotto's 1926 composition "Où est-il donc?," which translates as "Where is it now?" or "What's happened to it?," with lyrics by A. Decaye and Lucien Carol. On Duvivier's film, see Ginette Vincendeau, *Pépé le Moko* (London: British Film Institute, 1998).

58. "Gentils enfants d'Aubervilliers / Gentils enfants des prolétaires / Gentils enfants de la misère / Gentils enfants du monde entier." The lyrics transcribed as metered verse in Jacques Prévert, *Spectacles* (Paris: Gallimard, 1951), and reprinted in Jacques Prévert, *Oeuvres complètes,* vol. 1 (Paris: Gallimard, 1992), 335, differ slightly from those heard in the film. The refrain in the film and printed versions is the same. For the sake of mellifluence, I have preferred to translate *gentil* in this context as "sweet" rather than as the more usual "nice." A decade after *Aubervilliers,* Édouard Luntz's 1959 *Enfants des courants' d'air (Children Adrift)* offered an updated depiction of daily life in a shantytown setting on the outskirts of Paris. Luntz's fictionalized documentary was screened at the Cannes Film Festival. In 1960, it was awarded the Prix Jean Vigo. My thanks to Nathaniel Greene for pointing me to this remarkable twenty-four-minute film.

59. My translation is taken from subtitles in the 2011 Royal Belgian Film Archive's DVD/Blu-ray disc release of *Misère au Borinage, Les Maisons de la misère,* and *Le Patron est mort (The Boss Is Dead).*

60. Léon Bonneff, *Aubervilliers* (1912; repr., Paris: L'Esprit des Péninsules, 2000). Bonneff (1882–1914) self-identified as a proletarian writer. His articles deploring workplace health and safety hazards appeared in left-wing publications such as the antimilitarist weekly *La Guerre sociale* (whose director was none other than Jean Vigo's father, Eugène Bonaventure Jean-Baptiste Vigo) and the PCF daily, *L'Humanité.* Often collaborating with his brother, Maurice, Bonneff wrote *Les Métiers qui tuent* (Professions that kill, 1905), *La Vie tragique des travailleurs* (The tragic life of workers, 1908), and *Aubervilliers.* Sent to war in 1914, he died the same year of wounds suffered in Lorraine. Attesting to the novel's continued relevance is the fact that *Aubervilliers* continues to be reprinted, most recently in 2015. See also Sante, *The Other Paris,* 108–10.

61. I am thinking here of Renoir's *La Bête humaine* (*The Human Beast,* 1938) and Carné's *Hôtel du Nord* (1938).

62. André Bazin, "*M. le maudit,*" *Radio, Cinéma, Télévision* 110 (February 24, 1952), n.p. See also Daeninckx, "*Aubervilliers,*" 164, cited in Amao, "Passion et désillusion," 1:378.

63. Amao, "Passion et désillusion," 1:385–86. Erwan Cadoret states the point somewhat differently by describing *Aubervilliers* as the synthesis of Lotar's career as a photographer and cameraman *(opérateur de prises de vues).* Cadoret describes this career as twenty-five years long. Cadoret, "Un Double Regard sur la misère." But if one starts with Lotar's training under Germaine Krull beginning in 1927, the duration is closer to eighteen. All of this suggests that (1) a key to understanding *Aubervilliers* can be found in aspects of Lotar's

early photography, and (2) as Damarice Amao puts it, *Aubervilliers* is a film of the 1930s that circumstances forced Lotar to put off until 1945. See Amao, "Passion et désillusion," 1:378.

64. Georges Bataille, "Abattoirs," *Documents,* no. 6 (November 1929): 328. In English, see "Slaughterhouse," in Georges Bataille, Michel Leiris, Marcel Griaule, et al., *Encyclopaedia Acephalica* (London: Atlas Press, 1995), 72.

65. "La Viande: Huit photos prises à l'abattoir par Eli Lotar," *Variétés* 2, no. 12 (April 1930); the portfolio was placed between pages 320 and 321. My account of the reproductions of Lotar's *La Villette, Abattoir* series draws extensively on Émilie Lesage, "La Série *Aux Abattoirs de la Villette* (1929): Le Point de vue du photographe Eli Lotar par-delà la revue *Documents* et la philosophie de Georges Bataille" (master's thesis, Université de Montréal, 2009).

66. Walker, *City Gorged with Dreams,* 131.

67. See Hollier, *The College of Sociology*; and Richman, *Sacred Revolutions.*

68. Georges Didi-Huberman, *La Ressemblance informe ou le gai savoir selon Georges Bataille* (Paris: Macula, 1995), 163.

69. Ibid., 162.

70. Yve-Alain Bois, "Abattoir," in Bois and Krauss, *Formless,* 46.

71. Walker, *City Gorged with Dreams,* 127. This account contradicts Didi-Huberman's assertion that Lotar had taken the photos in order to illustrate ("aux fins d'illustrer") Bataille's article. Didi-Huberman, *La Ressemblance informe,* 159.

72. Bois, "Abattoir," 43, 46.

73. Charles Baudelaire, "L'Héautontimoroumenos," in *Oeuvres complètes,* ed. Claude Pichois, vol. 1 (Paris: Bibliothèque de la Pléiade, 1975), 78–79. The English version is from Charles Baudelaire, *Les Fleurs du mal,* trans. Richard Howard (Boston: Godine, 1983), 79–80. The poem continues: "Je suis la plaie et le couteau! / Je suis le soufflet et la joue! / Je suis les membres et la roue, / Et la victime et le bourreau!" (I am the knife and the wound it deals, / I am the slap and the cheek, / I am the wheel and the broken limbs, / Hangman and victim both!)

74. Carlo Rim, "La Villette rouge," *Vu,* no. 166 (May 20, 1931): 698. A facsimile of the article appears in Frizot and de Veigy, *Vu,* 106–8.

75. Rim, "La Villette rouge," in Frizot and de Veigy, *Vu,* 107–8.

76. See Gérard Ponthieu and Elisabeth Philipp, *La Villette, les années 30: Un certain âge d'or* (Paris: Atlas, 1987). The book reproduces the same photograph (123) of the master horse butcher le Père Macquart seen forty years earlier in Franju's *Le Sang des bêtes.*

77. Lotar, "Ici, on ne s'amuse pas," *Jazz* 11 (November 15, 1929): n.p., cited in Sayag and Lionel-Marie, *Eli Lotar,* 20.

78. For an informed commentary on Lotar's 1930s trajectory as a filmmaker, see Viewing, "'Transfuge du cinéma,'" 38–51, 199–208.

Transition II

1. On Gaumont-Franco-Film-Aubert's bankruptcy, see François Garçon, *Gaumont: A Century of French Cinema,* trans. Bruce Alderman and Jonathan

Dickinson (New York: Harry N. Abrams, 1994), 41–47. On Pathé-Natan, see Marc-Antoine Robert, "L'Affaire Natan," in *Pathé: Premier Empire du cinéma,* ed. Jacques Kermabon (Paris: Centre Pompidou, 1994), 260–66.

2. Colin Crisp, *The Classic French Cinema: 1930–1960* (Bloomington: Indiana University Press, 1997), 34. See also Paul Léglise, *Histoire de la politique du cinéma français,* vol. 1, *La IIIe République* (Paris: Pichon et Durand-Auzias, 1970), 105–13; and Jacques Choukroun, "Aux origines de 'l'exception française'? Des études d'experts au 'Rapport Petsche' (1933–1935)," *1895* 44 (2004): 5–27.

3. Léglise, *Histoire de la politique du cinéma français,* 1:133.

4. Quoted in Crisp, *The Classic French Cinema,* 38. See also Léglise, *Histoire de la politique du cinéma français,* 1:179–98; and Georges Sadoul, "En marge de l'affaire Pathé-Natan" (1939), in *Écrits,* 37–38.

5. Alan Williams, *Republic of Images: A History of French Filmmaking* (Cambridge, Mass.: Harvard University Press, 1992), 249.

6. Evelyn Ehrlich, *Cinema of Paradox: French Filmmaking under the German Occupation* (New York: Columbia University Press, 1985), 22. For a literary perspective on the charged notions of cultural and political health, see Jean Paulhan, *Les Fleurs de Tarbes ou la terreur dans les lettres* (Paris: Gallimard, 1941). Informed accounts of the literary press and book publishing during Vichy include Pascal Fouché, *L'Édition française sous l'occupation (1940–1944),* 2 vols. (Paris: Bibliothèque de la Littérature Française Contemporaine de l'Université Paris-VII, 1987); Pierre Hebey, *La "Nouvelle Revue Française" des années sombres, juin 1940-juin 1941: Les Intellectuels à la dérive* (Paris: Gallimard, 1992); Anne Simonin, *Les Éditions de Minuit, 1942–1955: Le Devoir d'insoumission* (Paris: IMEC, 1994); and Gisèle Sapiro, *La Guerre des écrivains, 1940–1953* (Paris: Fayard, 1999).

7. Paul Léglise, *Histoire de la politique du cinéma français,* vol. 2, *Entre deux républiques, 1940–1946* (Paris: Filméditions-Lherminier, 1977), 29.

8. Colin Crisp, "Business: Anarchy and Order in the Classic Cinema Industry," in *The French Cinema Book,* ed. Michael Temple and Michael Witt (London: British Film Institute, 2004), 122.

9. Quoted in Ehrlich, *Cinema of Paradox,* 18, translation slightly altered.

10. François Garçon, *De Blum à Pétain: Cinéma et société française, 1936–1944* (Paris: Cerf, 1984), 39.

11. Williams, *Republic of Images,* 250.

12. Ehrlich, *Cinema of Paradox,* x, 14. For an openly polemical take on recent debate, see Jean-Marc Lalanne, "Un cinéma très occupé," *Cahiers du Cinéma* 564 (January 2002): 84–85; and Sylvie Lindeperg, "L'Évaporation du sens de l'histoire," *Cahiers du Cinéma* 565 (February 2002): 50–51. Both were written in conjunction with the commercial release of *Laissez-Passer (Safe Conduct),* Bertrand Tavernier's 2002 feature on filmmaking during Vichy France.

13. Pierre Braunberger, *Pierre Braunberger, producteur: Cinémamémoire,* ed. Jacques Gerber (Paris: Centre Georges Pompidou/Centre Nationale de la Cinématographie, 1987), 132.

14. Léglise, *Histoire de la politique du cinéma français,* 2:52.

15. On the term *Israélite,* see Pierre Birnbaum, *Sur la corde raide: Parcours Juif entre exil et citoyenneté* (Paris: Flammarion, 2002); and Jean-Pierre Bertin-Maghit,

Le Cinéma français sous l'occupation (Paris: Presses Universitaires de France, 1994), 30.

16. Crisp, *The Classic French Cinema*, 57.
17. Crisp, "Business," 123.
18. Ehrlich, *Cinema of Paradox*, 57–58.
19. Léglise, *Histoire de la politique du cinéma français*, 2:110.
20. Bertin-Maghit, *Le Cinéma français*, 109. See also Olivier Barrot, *L'Écran français, 1943–1953: Histoire d'un journal et d'une époque* (Paris: Éditeurs Français Réunis, 1979), esp. 11–27.
21. Ehrlich, *Cinema of Paradox*, 172.
22. Léglise, *Histoire de la politique du cinéma français*, 2:147. See also the text of the October 25, 1946, law, based on the version in the French government's *Journal Officiel* for that date, in ibid., 2:203–6.
23. Crisp, *The Classic French Cinema*, 65.
24. Bertin-Maghit, *Le Cinéma français*, 123.
25. Crisp, *The Classic French Cinema*, 74–75; see also Léglise, *Histoire de la politique du cinéma français*, 2:165–73.
26. Crisp, *The Classic French Cinema*, 203. In 1964, the ETPC was renamed the Lycée Technique d'Etat Louis Lumière. See also the ETPC's courses listed in André Lang, *Le Tableau blanc* (Paris: Horizons de France, 1948), 207–9.
27. Crisp, *The Classic French Cinema*, 205.
28. Léglise, *Histoire de la politique du cinéma français*, 1:225–26, 2:74. See also Lang, *Le Tableau blanc*, 204. L'Herbier's official title was founder. IDHEC's first director, Pierre Gelin, was replaced in October 1947 by Léon Moussinac.
29. *Annuaire des anciens élèves de l'IDHEC* (Paris: IDHEC, 1965), n.p. Others listed among the first ten entering classes included cinematographer Ghislain Cloquet, director Jacques Rozier, and filmmaker-critic Noël Burch.
30. Agnès Varda, *Varda par Agnès* (Paris: Cahiers du Cinéma, 1994), 40. Varda's status as a woman filmmaker who financed her own early films may explain why it took until 1964 for her to receive her professional card. In the interim she made three short subjects and three feature-length films. For each, she needed to apply to the CNC for special dispensation. She adds that she holds card number 2197, and that if there had been separate numbers for men and women, she would have been among the first ten women listed. She asks pointedly whether Germaine Dulac (1882–1942) ever needed a card.
31. Crisp, *The Classic French Cinema*, 208.
32. Rémy Tessoneau, *L'Enseignement à l'IDHEC* (Paris: IDHEC, 1958), n.p., document RES1146, Bibliothèque du Film, Cinémathèque Française, Paris.
33. Léglise, *Histoire de la politique du cinéma français*, 2:72.
34. Ibid., 2:178–79. The characterization of IDHEC as a brokerage house appears in Dudley Andrew, *André Bazin* (New York: Oxford University Press, 1978), 84.
35. Lang, *Le Tableau blanc*, 207. The indices and related IDHEC research materials are housed in the Cinémathèque Française collections at the Bibliothèque du Film at the Maison du Cinéma, 51 rue de Bercy, Paris 75012.
36. See the chapter sections on wartime and early postwar periods in Laurent Mannoni, *Histoire de la Cinémathèque Française* (Paris: Gallimard, 2007),

78–166. For detailed accounts of Bazin's efforts on behalf of Travail et Culture, see Andrew, *André Bazin*, 85–94; and de Baecque, *La Cinéphilie*, 34–35, 38. Some of Bazin's writings on film under the aegis of the Peuple et Culture association are reprinted in Jacques Chevalier, *Regards neufs sur le cinéma*. See also *Travail et Culture: Eléments d'historique TEC, période 1944–1949* (Paris: n.d.). I thank Sam Di Iorio for providing access to this documentation from the Institut National de la Jeunesse et de l'Éducation Populaire.

37. For differing assessments of the postwar purges, see Tony Judt, *Past Imperfect: French Intellectuals, 1954–1966* (Berkeley: University of California Press, 1992); and Watts, *Allegories of the Purge*.

38. Bluher and Thomas, *Le Court Métrage français*.

4. Colonial Cinema and Its Discontents

1. David Henry Slavin, *Colonial Cinema and Imperial France, 1919–1939: White Blind Spots, Male Fantasies, Settler Myths* (Baltimore: Johns Hopkins University Press, 2001), xi.

2. Peter J. Bloom, *French Colonial Documentary: Mythologies of Humanitarianism* (Minneapolis: University of Minnesota Press, 2007), vii.

3. Pierre Boulanger, *Le Cinéma colonial: De "L'Atlantide" à "Lawrence d'Arabie"* (Paris: Seghers, 1975). Thirty years earlier, Pierre Leprohon published one of the first studies to document a range of fiction and nonfiction practices personified by what the subtitle of his book referred to as "image hunters out to conquer the world." Pierre Leprohon, *L'Exotisme et le cinéma: Les "Chasseurs d'images" à la conquête du monde* (Paris: J. Susse, 1945).

4. Bluher and Thomas, *Le Court Métrage français*. Sources since the mid-1990s that revise Leprohon's and Boulanger's respective accounts include Dina Sherzer, ed., *Cinema, Colonialism, Postcolonialism: Perspectives from the French and Francophone Worlds* (Austin: University of Texas Press, 1996); Matthew Bernstein and Gaylyn Studlar, eds., *Visions of the East: Orientalism in Film* (New Brunswick, N.J.: Rutgers University Press, 1997); and Abdelkader Benali, *Le Cinéma colonial au Maghreb* (Paris: Cerf, 1998).

5. René Vautier, *Caméra citoyenne* (Rennes: Apogée, 1998).

6. I have translated Vautier's expression *cinéma anti-colonialiste* as "anticolonial," which I take to be a more elegant English formulation than "anticolonialist." At the same time, I recognize that this decision on my part may not convey the full extent of opposition to colonial policies or principles that the suffix *-iste* implies. Vautier's filmography includes *Algérie en flammes* (*Algeria in Flames*, 1958); *J'ai huit ans* (*I Am Eight Years Old*, 1961, with Yann Le Masson); *Le Glas* (*The Knell*, 1964); and *Avoir 20 ans dans les Aurès* (*To Be 20 Years Old in the Aurès*, 1972).

7. Paulin S. Vieyra, "Propos sur le cinéma africain," *Présence Africaine*, no. 23 (1958): 107–10, cited in Manthia Diawara, *African Cinema: Politics and Culture* (Bloomington: Indiana University Press, 1992), 22; and in Alison J. Murray Levine, *Framing the Nation: Documentary Film in Interwar France* (New York: Continuum, 2010), 77.

8. Vautier, *Caméra citoyenne*, 33–34.

9. Ibid., 47. Peter Bloom has pointed out that Côte d'Ivoire was a key site in establishing the Françafrique system under Jacques Foccart, especially in conjunction with Félix Houphouët-Boigny's complicity as a reliable ally in establishing the system. The 1949–50 massacres marked the start of a long-standing system of French intervention. In fact, Houphouët-Boigny coined the term *Françafrique,* equated with French–African cooperation.

10. On *Chronique,* see Ivone Margulies, *"Chronicle of a Summer* (1960) as Auto-critique (1959): A Transition in the French Left," *Quarterly Review of Film and Video* 21 (2004): 173–85; Sam Di Iorio, "Total Cinema: *Chronique d'un été* and the End of Bazinian Film Theory," *Screen* 48, no. 1 (Spring 2007): 25–43; and Steven Ungar, " 'In the Thick of Things': Rouch and Morin's *Chronique d'un été* Reconsidered," *French Cultural Studies* 14, no. 1 (2003): 5–22.

11. "Si tu ne plies pas, on te casse." Vautier, *Caméra citoyenne,* 27.

12. Émile Breton, *"Afrique 50,"* in *Une encyclopédie du court métrage français,* ed. Jacky Evrard and Jacques Kermabon (Crisnée, Belgium: Yellow Now, 2004), 13.

13. Critical approaches to these practices include Fatimah Tobing Rony, *The Third Eye: Race, Cinema, and Ethnographic Spectacle* (Durham, N.C.: Duke University Press, 1996); François Laplantine, *La Description ethnographique* (Paris: Nathan, 1998); and Alison Griffiths, *Wondrous Difference: Cinema, Anthropology, and Turn-of-the-Century Visual Culture* (New York: Columbia University Press, 2002).

14. René Vautier, *Afrique 50* (Paris: Cahiers de Paris Expérimental, 2001), 7. This pamphlet includes stills and an English translation by Tami L. Williams; further citations refer to this translation. On occasion, I have slightly modified Williams's translation. My thanks to Nicole Brenez for providing me with a copy of *Afrique 50* during her fall 2001 stay in Iowa City. Tellingly, the copy was recorded from a broadcast hosted by Vautier on Algerian television. In 2013, the audiovisual cooperative Les Mutins de Panagée released a combination DVD containing *Afrique 50,* an updated short called *Du sang et du sable (Blood and Sand),* and a one-hundred-plus-page booklet. A year later, the same cooperative released a four-CD boxed set, *Vautier en Algérie,* which includes films dating from 1954 to 1988.

15. Vautier, *Afrique 50,* 21.

16. Ibid., 37.

17. The SPCA was founded in 1915. On the role of its offshoots in support of French colonial rule in postwar Algeria, see Sébastien Denis, *Le Cinéma et la guerre d'Algérie: La Propagande à l'écran (1945–1962)* (Paris: Nouveau Monde, 2009).

18. The term appears in François-Xavier Verschave, *La Françafrique: Le Plus Long Scandale de la république* (Paris: Stock, 1999).

19. Quoted in Nicole Brenez, "Définition et principes pour le cinéma d'intervention sociale, par René Vautier, Cancale, 2003," in *Cinémas d'avant-garde,* 84.

20. Jean-Pierre Jeancolas, "Colonisation et engagement (ou défaut d'engagement) du cinéma français, 1945–1965," in *Cinéma et engagement,* ed. Graeme Hayes and Martin O'Shaughnessy (Paris: L'Harmattan, 2005), 35.

21. Sam Di Iorio, "The Fragile Present: *Statues Also Die* with *Night and Fog*," *South Central Review* 33, no. 2 (2016): 20. Di Iorio helpfully tracks down the origins of footage in the last reel shot during a 1933 clash between police and striking steelworkers in Ambridge, Pennsylvania. A second recycled clip showed Sugar Ray Robinson knocking down Jean Walzack during a middleweight boxing match in Liège, Belgium. The latter footage anticipates the role of fantasy figure Robinson would soon play for Oumarou Ganda's Edward G. Robinson in Jean Rouch's *Moi, un Noir*.

22. Bennetta Rosette-Jules, *Black Paris: The African Writer's Landscape* (Urbana: University of Illinois Press, 1998), 6.

23. Extensive listings of Marker's writings and film work appear in *Théorème*, no. 6 (2002); and in Catherine Lupton, *Chris Marker: Memories of the Future* (London: Reaktion, 2005). As *Critical Mass* goes to press, the Cinémathèque Française has announced a May–July 2018 exhibition on Marker, which is likely to include commentary on materials received by the organization following Marker's death in July 2012.

24. De Baecque, *La Cinéphilie*, 38. While most Resnais filmographies start with the 1948 *Van Gogh* short subject, James Monaco goes back to *L'Aventure de Guy* (*Guy's Adventure*, with a script by Gaston Modot), an unfinished *Fantômas* (1935), and assorted shorts during the mid-1940s with collaborators including Marcel Marceau, Gérard Philipe, and Remo Forlani. See James Monaco, *Alain Resnais* (New York: Oxford University Press, 1978), 216–17. To my knowledge, there is no consensus concerning a definitive Resnais filmography.

25. Marker included the letter in his *Commentaires* (Paris: Seuil, 1961), n.p. It is reprinted in André Cornand, "*Les Statues meurent aussi*," *Image et Son*, no. 233 (December 1969): 194–95.

26. Cornaud, "*Les Statues meurent aussi*," 195.

27. Gil J. Wolman, "Methods of Détournement," in *Situationist International Anthology*, rev. and expanded ed., trans. and ed. Ken Knabb (Detroit: Bureau of Public Secrets, 2008), originally published in the eighth issue of the Belgian journal *Les Lèvres nues* (May 1956). See also Jean-Marie Apostolidès, *Les Tombeaux de Guy Debord* (Paris: Flammarion, 2006), 152–54.

28. Marker, *Commentaires*, 9.

29. Alain Resnais, "*Les Statues meurent aussi* et les ciseaux d'Anastasie," interview by René Vautier and Nicole Le Garrec (1972), in *Ode au grand art africain: "Les Statues meurent aussi*," ed. Elena Martinez-Jacquet (Paris: Primedia, 2010), 35–36.

30. On activism among writers, artists, and intellectuals opposed to postwar French policies concerning Algeria, see Joël Roman, ed., *Esprit: Écrire contre la guerre d'Algérie, 1947–1962* (Paris: Hachette, 2002); Goulven Bouldic, *Esprit, 1944–1982: Les Métamorphoses d'une revue* (Paris: IMEC, 2005); and Farid Laroussi, "Anticolonialism," in *The Columbia History of Twentieth-Century French Thought*, ed. Lawrence D. Kritzman (New York: Columbia University Press), 140–43.

31. Marker, *Commentaires*, 11.

32. Ibid., 20.

33. Marcel Martin, "*Les Statues meurent aussi*: Un Chef-d'œuvre mutilé," *Lettres Françaises* 21–27 (1961).

34. Alain Resnais, "Entretien avec Alain Resnais: Propos recueillis par Guy Gauthier," *Image et Son*, nos. 161–62 (1963): 52.

35. Marker, *Commentaires*, 15.

36. Ibid., 21.

37. Peter J. Bloom, "La Subversion des hiérarchies du savoir dans *Les Statues meurent aussi*," in *Zoos humains: De la vénus hottentote aux reality shows*, ed. Nicolas Bancel, Pascal Blanchard, Gilles Boetsch, Éric Deroo, and Sandrine Lemaire (Paris: La Découverte, 2002), 359.

38. Paulin Soumanou Vieyra, *Le Cinéma et l'Afrique* (Paris: Présence Africaine, 1969); Paulin Soumanou Vieyra, *Le Cinéma africain* (Paris: Présence Africaine, 1975).

39. Vieyra, *Le Cinéma et l'Afrique*, 42.

40. Ibid., 179. See also Vieyra's remarks on documentary in his *Réflexions d'un cinéaste africain* (Brussels: Organisation Catholique Internationale du Cinéma et de l'Audiovisuel, 1990), 62–64.

41. Alain Resnais, "Le Public avait envie de respirer un autre air," in *Que reste-t-il de la Nouvelle Vague?*, ed. Aldo Tassone (Paris: Stock, 2003), 222.

42. Quoted in Kwame Anthony Appiah, "Whose Culture Is It?," *New York Review of Books*, February 9, 2006, 39.

43. Ibid.

44. Gilles Deleuze, *Cinema 2: The Time-Image*, trans. Hugh Tomlinson and Robert Galeta (Minneapolis: University of Minnesota Press, 1985), 223. I follow Deleuze by capitalizing the term *Noir* in line with period usage despite my sense that doing so equates identity and race. The relevant difference here is between *un Noir* (a black man) and *un Africain* (an African).

45. Jean-Luc Godard, "Étonnant, Jean Rouch, *Moi, un Noir*," in *Jean-Luc Godard par Jean-Luc Godard*, vol. 1, *1950–1984* (Paris: Cahiers du Cinéma, 1985), 177. The review first appeared in *Arts*, no. 713 (March 11, 1959). The sentence in French reads, "Un Français libre qui pose librement un regard libre sur un monde libre." Godard's early enthusiasm for *Moi, un Noir* centered on Rouch's ability to transform his collaborators into characters who played out their lives—both real and idealized—in front of the movie camera. Twenty years later, Godard's enthusiasm had not waned: "*Moi, un Noir*, it affected me a lot. It's somewhat like [Robert] Flaherty: making fiction out of lived experience. Take characters from real life and make fiction with them." Jean-Luc Godard, "Entretien avec Jean-Luc Godard," by Jean-Luc Drouin and A. Remond, in *La Nouvelle Vague 25 ans après*, ed. Jean-Luc Drouin and A. Remond (Paris: Cerf, 1983), 179. Following the 1960 release of *Breathless*, filmmaker Luc Moullet referred to Godard as the "Jean Rouch of contemporary France." Quoted in François Nemer, *Godard (le cinéma)* (Paris: Gallimard, 2006), 19.

46. Paul Henley, *The Adventure of the Real: Jean Rouch and the Craft of Ethnographic Cinema* (Chicago: University of Chicago Press, 2009), 75.

47. Colleyn, *Le Regard documentaire*, 21.

48. Philip Dine, *Images of the Algerian War: French Fiction and Film, 1954–1962* (Oxford: Oxford University Press, 1984), 178.

49. Guy Gauthier, "Jean Rouch, gourou nouvelle vague," *CinémAction*, no. 104 (2002): 72.

50. Gary Wilder, *The French Imperial Nation-State: Negritude and Colonial Humanism between the Two World Wars* (Chicago: University of Chicago Press), 8–9.

51. My remarks on voice-over do not extend to what Deleuze, drawing on the writings of Jean Mitry and Pier Paolo Pasolini, explores as free indirect images. See Louis-Georges Schwartz, "Typewriter: Free Indirect Discourse in Deleuze's *Cinema 1*," *SubStance*, no. 108 (2005): 107–35.

52. Edward G. Robinson (1893–1973) was the stage name of Emanuel Goldenberg, who was born in Bucharest, Romania. Walker Smith Jr. changed his name to Sugar Ray Robinson (1921–1989) in 1940, when he became a professional boxer. Dorothy Lamour (1914–1996), who played in more than fifty feature films, is best remembered as Bing Crosby and Bob Hope's sarong-clad costar in seven *Road to . . .* movies made from 1940 to 1962. Lamour was her birth name.

53. "*Moi, un Noir*," *L'Avant-Scène Cinéma*, no. 265 (April 1981): 8–9. Further citations refer to this source as Rouch, "*Moi, un Noir*."

54. Jacques Rancière, "La Fiction documentaire: Marker et la fiction de mémoire," in *La Fable cinématographique* (Paris: Seuil, 2001), 202–3.

55. Jean Rouch, "'Parole interdite,' parole sous contrôle . . . ," interview by Colette Piault, *CinémAction*, no. 81 (1996): 144.

56. Rouch, "*Moi, un Noir*," 22.

57. Ibid., 24.

58. Ibid., 30.

59. Ibid., 34.

60. Ibid., 35–36.

61. Jean de Baroncelli, "*Moi, un Noir*," *Le Monde*, March 18, 1959. Despite this praise, Baroncelli wrote that the film approached farce in its tone and drama, but with moments of lyricism that recalled the novelty and purity in paintings by Henri Rousseau.

62. Armand Monjo, "*Moi, un Noir*: Une fenêtre ouverte sur l'Afrique noire," *L'Humanité*, March 24, 1959.

63. See Jacques Doniol-Valcroze, "Le Premier film authentiquement africain," *France-Observateur*, March 18, 1959; and Higgins, *Bertrand Tavernier*, 166. Godard describes Ganda-Robinson's monologue on his wartime experience in Indochina as part Céline and part (Jacques) Audiberti. Godard, "Étonnant, Jean Rouch, *Moi, un Noir*," 178.

64. Quoted in Albert Cervoni, "Une Confrontation historique en 1965 entre Jean Rouch et Sembène Ousmane: 'Tu nous regardes comme des insectes,'" *CinémAction*, no. 81 (1996): 104–6. *Come Back Africa* is a 1959 feature-length film directed by Lionel Rogosin (1924–2000). Although the film was scripted, Rogosin's use of nonprofessional actors recruited among street people earned it mention alongside *Moi, un Noir* as an example of docu-fiction and, for some, cinéma vérité.

65. Oumarou Ganda, in Pierre Haeffner, "Les Avis de cinq cinéastes d'Afrique noire: Entretiens avec Pierre Haeffner," *CinémAction*, no. 81 (1995): 97–98. Ganda's account of his interactions with Rouch differed markedly from what

Rouch stated in a 1990 interview with Lucien Taylor. See Jean Rouch, "Life on the Edge of Anthropology and Film," in *Ciné-Ethnography* (Minneapolis: University of Minnesota Press, 2003), 139–40.

66. Rouch, *"Moi, un Noir,"* 40. The notice was published originally in *Le Monde*, January 10, 1981.

67. Michel Perez, "L'Afrique est dans l'Afrique: Leçons d'un cinéma en devenir," *Semaine Internationale de la Critique/XXIIᵉ Festival de Cannes* (1968), n.p.

68. Sam Di Iorio, "Jean Rouch: The Anthropologist as Auteur," *Film Comment* 41, no. 3 (2005): 60.

Transition III

1. Roger Odin, "Vitalité du court métrage: Le Groupe des Trente," *CinémAction* 104 (2002): 30.

2. On Ciné-Liberté, see Ginette Vincendeau and Keith Reader, eds., *La Vie est à nous: French Cinema of the Popular Front, 1935–1938* (London: National Film Theatre/British Film Institute, 1986); Buchsbaum, *Cinema Engagé*; and Andrew, *Mists of Regret*. On the Groupe Octobre, see Michel Fauré, *Le Groupe Octobre* (Paris: Christian Bourgois, 1977).

3. Françoise Giroud is credited with using the expression "New Wave" in 1957 in reference to the generation born between the world wars. Her survey of this generation in a series of articles in the mass-circulation weekly *L'Express* was reprinted as *La Nouvelle Vague: Portraits de la jeunesse* (Paris: Gallimard, 1958). As noted previously, Richard Roud coined the notion of the Left Bank group of filmmakers in his article "The Left Bank" in the winter 1962–63 issue of *Sight and Sound*. Concerning the Groupe des Trente's name, Paul Paviot recalled that an early meeting organized to draft a collective declaration was attended by "at least thirty people." See Luce Vigo, "Le Groupe des Trente (1953–1970)," in Evrard and Kermabon, *Une encyclopédie du court métrage français*, 207. The declaration, dated December 20, 1953, and published on January 9, 1954, in issue no. 1550 of *La Cinématographie Française*, carried forty-three signatures. A reprint of the declaration appeared in *Bref*, no. 20 (1994): 40–41. The English translation in Appendix A of this book is mine. The names of Jacques Demy, Chris Marker, and Agnès Varda, listed by Roger Odin and his research team as G30 members, are not among those in the January 1954 publication. Roger Odin et al., "Le Cinéma documentaire et le Groupe des Trente," in Odin, *L'Âge d'or du documentaire*, 1:22. Paul Grimault (1905–1994), whose lifelong commitment to animated film earned him the unofficial title of "the French Walt Disney," is the only individual I have been able to identify as a member of both the Groupe Octobre and the G30.

4. François Truffaut, "Une certaine tendance du cinéma français," *Cahiers du Cinéma*, no. 31 (1954). The article appears in English translation as "A Certain Tendency in French Cinema," in *The French New Wave: Critical Landmarks*, ed. Peter Graham and Ginette Vincendeau (New York: British Film Institute/Palgrave Macmillan, 2009), 39–63. See also Michel Marie, *The French New Wave: An Artistic School*, trans. Richard Neupert (Malden, Mass.: Blackwell,

2003); and Richard Neupert, *A History of the French New Wave* (Madison: University of Wisconsin Press, 2002).

5. Thierry Méranger, *Le Court Métrage* (Cahiers du Cinéma, 2007), 7–8. The equation can also be found in Odin et al., "Le Cinéma documentaire."

6. François Thomas, "Avant-propos," in Bluher and Thomas, *Le Court Métrage français*, 9.

7. A productive comparison for understanding the double bind affecting the wartime short subject in France is the U.S. and British phenomenon of the B picture, which was typically screened as the second half *(complément de programme)* of a double feature and sold on the basis of a flat fee. Much like U.S. and British B pictures of the 1930s to 1950s, the exhibition category of accompanying feature bestowed on short subjects by the October 1940 law resulted in smaller production budgets than those assigned to feature-length equivalents of the A picture. From the 1940s to the 1980s, a similar discrepancy held true for 78 rpm and later 45 rpm vinyl music recordings, which were marketed with flip-side "filler" equivalent to the B film.

8. See the text of a February 18, 1954, letter addressed to CNC director Jacques Flaud from the Syndicat Autonome du Cinéma Français, reproduced in *Bref*, no. 20 (1994): 29.

9. André Bazin, "La Longue Misère du court-métrage," *Arts*, no. 500 (January 26, 1955), cited in Porcile, *Défense du court métrage français*, 24. A second article on the topic by Bazin appeared in *France-Observateur*, February 3, 1955.

10. Cited in Odin et al., "Le Cinéma documentaire," 1:23. The École Nationale de la Photographie et de Cinématographie (National School of Photography and Cinematography) and IDHEC were state-run professional schools. Henri Langlois, Georges Franju, Paul-Auguste Harlé, and Jean Mitry launched the Cinémathèque Française in 1936 to preserve, restore, study, and screen French and international films. The Fédération Française des Ciné-clubs was part of the worldwide film society movement following World War II.

11. Luce Vigo and Émile Breton, "Le Groupe des Trente, un âge d'or du court métrage?," *Bref*, no. 20 (1994): 23–42. Porcile's *Défense du court métrage français* remains an informed and reliable resource. Elena Von Kassel Siambini astutely cites Eli Lotar's *Aubervilliers* and the critical stir surrounding its February 1946 release as one of the first clear signs of where postwar French documentary was going. At the same time, her emphasis on films by G30 members understates the ideological implications of the group's championing of exchanges with Soviet bloc filmmakers. See Elena Von Kassel Siambini, "Le Groupe des Trente: The Poetic Tradition," in *The Documentary Film Book*, ed. Brian Winston (London: British Film Institute/Palgrave/Macmillan, 2013), 180–88.

12. Odin et al., "Le Cinéma documentaire," 1:38.

13. Vigo, "Toward a Social Cinema," 2:60–62.

14. Philippe Pilard, "Paris ciné 50," *Bref*, no. 20 (1994): 24.

15. Arnaud Chapuy and Jean-François Cornu, "Les Producteurs du Groupe des Trente, fondateurs d'une pré–Nouvelle Vague?," in Bluher and Thomas, *Le Court Métrage français*, 47–58. See also Braunberger, *Pierre Braunberger,*

producteur; and Jacques Gerber, *Anatole Dauman: Pictures of a Producer,* trans. Paul Willemen (London: British Film Institute, 1992).

16. Jacques Flaud, "Les Années-passion: Jacques Flaud raconte," *Bref,* no. 20 (1994): 28.

17. An English translation of the Declaration Concerning the Right to Insubordination in the Algerian War (often called the Declaration of the 121) was published in *Evergreen Review,* no. 15 (1961). An editorial titled "La Bataille de Paris" (The battle of Paris), followed by a call to the French people, appeared in issue no. 186 (November 1961) of Jean-Paul Sartre's monthly, *Les Temps Modernes.*

5. Two Takes on Postwar Paris

1. Resnais's six other documentaries of the period are *Van Gogh* (1948), *Gauguin* (1950), *Guernica* (1950), *Les Statues meurent aussi* (*Statues Also Die,* 1953), *Le Mystère de l'atelier 15* (*The Mystery of Workshop 15,* 1957), and *Le Chant du Styrène* (*The Song of Styrene,* 1958).

2. See David Rousset, *L'Univers concentrationnaire* (Paris: Seuil, 1965); and Jean Cayrol, "*Nuit et brouillard*: Commentaire," in *Oeuvre lazaréenne* (Paris: Seuil, 2007), 991–1001. Rousset's book was first published in 1946, and Cayrol's commentary in 1997.

3. Edward Dimendberg, "These Are Not Exercises in Style," *October,* no. 112 (2005): 65.

4. Quoted in Jean-Michel Frodon, *L'Âge moderne du cinéma français: De la Nouvelle Vague à nos jours* (Paris: Cahiers du Cinéma, 2010), 44.

5. Leo Bersani and Ulysse Dutoit, *Arts of Impoverishment: Beckett, Rothko, Resnais* (Cambridge, Mass.: Harvard University Press, 1993), 181–86.

6. René Prédal, "Filmographie," *Études Cinématographiques,* nos. 64–68 (1968), 171. *Van Gogh* won the 1950 Oscar for best short (two-reel) subject from the Academy of Motion Picture Arts and Sciences. Nine years later, the screenplay Marguerite Duras wrote for *Hiroshima* was nominated for an Oscar.

7. Eisler (1898–1962) studied musical composition with Anton Webern and Arnold Schoenberg before turning to political themes in collaborations with Bertolt Brecht. After living in Vienna, Berlin, and Moscow, Eisler immigrated to the United States in 1938 to teach at the New School for Social Research in New York. Four years later, he moved to Los Angeles, where he worked again with Brecht. His book *Composing for the Films,* cowritten with Theodor W. Adorno, was published in 1947. After World War II, Eisler was among the first in the U.S. film industry to be called to testify before the House Un-American Activities Committee. In 1948, he left the United States for Europe to avoid deportation.

8. See Richard Raskin, *Nuit et brouillard* (Aarhus, Denmark: Aarhus University Press, 1987), 14–24; and Lindeperg, "*Night and Fog,*" 153–55.

9. For background on the decree and the origins of the expression "Nacht und Nebel" in Richard Wagner's 1869 opera *Das Rheingold,* see Raskin, *Nuit et brouillard,* 14–24; and Lindeperg, "*Night and Fog,*" 67.

10. Emma Wilson, *Alain Resnais* (New York: St. Martin's Press, 2006), 16.

11. Marguerite Duras, *Hiroshima Mon Amour,* trans. Richard Seaver (New York: Grove, 1960), 15.

12. Antoine de Baecque, *L'Histoire-caméra* (Paris: Gallimard, 2008), 56–58.

13. Dominique Noguez, "Jeunesse d'*Hiroshima,*" in *Tu n'as rien vu à Hiroshima,* ed. Marie-Christine de Navacelle (Paris: Gallimard, 2009), 40. The pseudo-documentary also contains a clip from Hideo Sekigawa's 1953 feature film *Hiroshima.*

14. Suzanne Liandrat-Guignes and Jean-Louis Leutrat, *Alain Resnais: Liaisons secrètes, accords vagabonds* (Paris: Cahiers du Cinéma, 2006), 40. The role of the RTF is discussed at length in Alain Carou's "Entre la commande et l'utopie," *1895,* no. 52 (2007): 116–40; my account of the genesis of *Toute la mémoire du monde* draws extensively from Carou's article.

15. Marker, *Commentaires,* n.p.

16. Cited in Jean-Luc Douin, *Dictionnaire de la censure au cinéma* (Paris: Presses Universitaires de France, 2001), 382.

17. *L'Avant-Scène Cinéma,* no. 38 (1964): 8–10.

18. Lindeperg, *"Night and Fog,"* 146.

19. Quoted in ibid., 166.

20. Vigo and Breton, "Le Groupe des Trente."

21. Carou, "Entre la commande et l'utopie," 118.

22. Julien Cain (1887–1964) directed the BN from 1930 to 1964. During World War II, he was deported to Buchenwald because he was Jewish and was replaced by Bernard Faÿ, who openly collaborated with Vichy and German officials. Richard Raskin writes that, as head of the Commission d'Histoire de la Déportation section of the Comité d'Histoire de la Deuxième Guerre Mondiale, Cain assembled the materials that formed the basis of Henri Michel and Olga Wormser's anthology *Tragédie de la déportation, 1940–1945* (Paris: Hachette, 1955), a major exhibition at the Institut Pédagogique National, and the initial outline for the narrative organization of *Nuit et brouillard.* Raskin, *Nuit et brouillard,* 25–26.

23. Carou, "Entre la commande et l'utopie," 123. Braunberger, whom Suffel's memo identified erroneously as Serge Bomberger, had worked with Resnais on *Van Gogh* and *Guernica.* After *Toute la mémoire du monde,* he produced *Le Chant du Styrène.* Braunberger, *Pierre Braunberger, producteur,* 146. See also Robert Benayoun, "Entretien avec Remo Forlani," in *Alain Resnais, arpenteur de l'imaginaire* (Paris: Ramsay, 1985), 273–78. Forlani writes in *Toujours vif et joyeux* (Paris: Denoël, 2003) that the commentary for *Toute la mémoire du monde* bearing his name was broadly rewritten by Chris Marker. Resnais was appointed after efforts to recruit Braunberger's initial choice for director, Jacques Baratier, fell through.

24. Quoted in Carou, "Entre la commande et l'utopie," 125.

25. Quoted in ibid., 133.

26. *L'Avant-Scène du Cinéma,* no. 52 (1965): 66.

27. Jacques Doniol-Valcroze, "La Prisonnière Lucia," *Cahiers du Cinéma,* no. 77 (1958): 59–60.

28. Bosé (born 1931) has had a long career as an actress. Her film work includes roles in Michelangelo Antonioni's *Cronaca di un amore* (*Chronicle of a Love,*

1950), Juan Antonio Bardem's *Muerte de un ciclista* (*Death of a Bicyclist*, 1955), Federico Fellini's *Satyricon* (1969), and Marguerite Duras's *Nathalie Granger* (1972). André Breton's *Point du jour* was published in 1934. H. G. Wells (1866–1946) was author of *The War of the Worlds* (1898), which Orson Welles adapted as a radio drama first broadcast on October 30, 1938. Domenach (1922–1997), editor of the left-wing Catholic monthly *Esprit* from 1957 to 1975, militated openly in favor of Algerian independence. "Agnès de tout" in the table of contents may be a veiled allusion to the filmmaker Agnès Varda, who, toward the end of *Toute la mémoire du monde*, is seen briefly seated at the far left of a long table in the BN's main reading room. Her name appears in the film's credits. Alfred Hitchcock adapted his 1935 feature film *The 39 Steps* from John Buchan's 1915 novel of the same name. The word *Martiens* (Martians), following a partially obscured word—possibly *trahi* (betrayed) or *envahi* (invaded)—may express Resnais and Marker's shared interests in science fiction. The phrase "Nous sommes les Martiens de l'Afrique" (We are the Martians of Africa) appears in the commentary of *Les Statues meurent aussi*; see Marker, *Commentaires*, 21. See also Karen Beckman's discussion of the *Mars* book segment in "Animating the *Cinéfils*: Alain Resnais and the Cinema of Discovery," *Cinema Journal* 54, no. 4 (Summer 2015): 14.

29. On Resnais's uncompleted project for a film devoted to Harry Dickson, see Frédéric Towarnicki, *Les Aventures de Harry Dickson: Scénario de Frédéric de Towarnicki pour un film (non réalisé) par Alain Resnais* (Nantes, France: Capricci, 2007). See also Beckman's remarks on *Toute la mémoire du monde* in conjunction with a "cartoon-friendly Resnais" in "Animating the *Cinéfils*," 10–16.

30. *L'Avant-Scène du Cinéma*, no. 52 (1965): 72.

31. Ibid., 65.

32. Facsimile of production notes in Jean-Luc Douin, *Alain Resnais* (Paris: La Martinière, 2013), 44.

33. Liandrat-Guignes and Leutrat, *Alain Resnais*, 244.

34. Jean Domarchi, Jacques Doniol-Valcroze, Jean-Luc Godard, Pierre Kast, Jacques Rivette, and Éric Rohmer, "Hiroshima, notre amour," in *Cahiers du Cinéma*, vol. 1, ed. Jim Hiller (Cambridge, Mass.: Harvard University Press, 1986), 60. Was Resnais's inclusion of the camera, microphone, and klieg lights a nod to Welles and *Citizen Kane* (1941)? Alain Carou invokes this possibility in "Les Souterrains de Xanadu: *Toute la mémoire du monde*, d'Alain Resnais," *Revue de la Bibliothèque Nationale de France*, no. 27 (2007): 50–57.

35. Christine Richardson, "*All the Memory of the World*: In Retrospect," *Enclitic* 3, no. 1 (1979): 63.

36. Rainer Maria Rilke, *The Notebooks of Malte Laurids Brigge*, trans. Stephen Mitchell (New York: Vintage, 1990), 38.

37. W. G. Sebald, *Austerlitz*, trans. Anthea Bell (New York: Modern Library, 2001), 261.

38. Ibid., 281.

39. Cyril Neyrat, "Horreur/bonheur: Métamorphose," in *Positif: Revue de cinéma: Alain Resnais*, ed. Stéphane Goudet (Paris: Gallimard, 2002), 50–51. The factory model extends to the photographer Gisèle Freund (1908–2000), whose first professional assignment was a commission from BN director Julien Cain

to take photographs in all the libraries in Paris. Some of these photographs were included in "Un Grand Reportage de *Vu* à la Bibliothèque Nationale, la première usine intellectuelle du monde," *Vu,* no. 463 (January 27, 1937); see Gisèle Freund, *Photographie et sociéte* (Paris: Seuil, 1974), 119.

40. Noa Steimatsky, "Visuality and Viscera," in *The Five Senses of Cinema,* ed. Alice Auteliano et al. (Udine, Italy: Forum, 2005), 138.

41. Hubert Damisch, *Ciné fil* (Paris: Seuil, 2008), 158.

42. Henry Rousso, *The Vichy Syndrome: History and Memory in France since 1944,* trans. Arthur Goldhammer (Cambridge, Mass.: Harvard University Press, 1991). Louisa Rice replaces Rousso's modifier "unfinished" with "selective" to characterize this mourning as a product of Gaullist policies that sought to hide the fact that the Vichy regime was one during which Frenchmen had murdered each other. Louisa Rice, "The Voice of Silence: Alain Resnais' *Night and Fog* and Collective Memory in Post-Holocaust France, 1944–1974," *Film & History* 32, no. 1 (2002): 23.

43. Liandrat-Guignes and Leutrat, *Alain Resnais,* 66. Midway through *Stavisky...,* Serge Alexandre (played by Jean-Paul Belmondo) escorts Erna Wolfgang (Silvia Badesco) from his Empire Theater, where she has come to audition. Recognizing her as a fellow Jew and refugee, he tells her with a mix of candor and flirtation that he would give a lot to ensure that she has a happy life before adding that he could offer all the pleasures of Paris to her. Wolfgang replies that she prefers happiness. Jorge Semprun, *Stavisky...,* trans. Sabine Destrée (New York: Viking, 1975), 46.

44. Chris Marker, *Giraudoux par lui-même* (Paris: Seuil, 1952), 43. I have translated Marker's final word in the passage, *étranger,* as "foreign" rather than "strange." An alternate translation might be "alien."

45. Raskin, *Nuit et brouillard,* 84.

46. Gerhard Richter, *Thought-Images: Frankfurt School Writers' Reflections from Damaged Life* (Stanford, Calif.: Stanford University Press, 2007), 7–8. In its emphasis on everyday objects and experiences, the *Denkbild* can be seen as a precursor of the short texts by Roland Barthes republished in *Mythologies* (Paris: Seuil, 1957).

47. Siegfried Kracauer, *The Mass Ornament: Weimar Essays,* trans. Thomas Y. Levin (Cambridge, Mass.: Harvard University Press, 1995), 7–8.

48. Bernard Eisenschitz, "Marker Mémoire," *Programme de la Cinémathèque française,* January 1998, 14–15.

49. Arnaud Lambert, *Also Known as Chris Marker* (Paris: Le Point du Jour, 2008), 9.

50. I am working with the 2013 restoration overseen by Pierre Lhomme, who was chief cinematographer and Marker's codirector when the film was shot fifty-one years earlier. Earlier versions ran between 165 and 180 minutes, edited down from some fifty-five hours of initial footage. See Nathalie Mary, "*Le Joli Mai* ou les prémices d'une révolution," *Vertigo* 46 (2013): 18.

51. Marcel Allain (1885–1969) and Pierre Souvestre (1874–1914) cowrote thirty-two novels around the figure of Fantômas. After Souvestre's death, Allain wrote an additional nine, the last of which was published in 1963. A 1980 television series of four episodes included two stories each by New Wave-era stalwart Claude Chabrol and Luis Buñuel's son Juan Luis. Comic books

produced in France, Mexico, and the United States from 1941 through 2009 attest to the ongoing appeal of the Fantômas myth a century after the character first appeared in print. On what has come to be known as the Fantômas cycle, see Patrice Gauthier and Francis Lacassin, *Louis Feuillade: Maître du cinéma populaire* (Paris: Gallimard, 2006); and Philippe Azoury and Jean-Marc Lalanne, *Fantômas, style moderne* (Crisnée, Belgium: Yellow Now, 2002).

52. Marker met Signoret (née Simone Kaminker) in 1936 while both were students at neighboring lycées in Neuilly. Montand was among early actor acquaintances whom Marker recruited to do voice-overs for his films. In 1974, Marker completed a fifty-nine-minute documentary on Montand, *La Solitude du chanteur de fond (The Loneliness of the Long Distance Singer)*. The title plays on that of the 1962 feature film *The Loneliness of the Long Distance Runner*, which director Tony Richardson adapted from Allan Sillitoe's 1959 novel.

53. See Margulies, "*Chronicle of a Summer* (1960) as *Autocritique* (1959)"; and Di Iorio, "Total Cinema."

54. Cynthia Marker, "Self-Censorship and Chris Marker's *Le Joli Mai*," *French Cultural Studies* 12 (2001): 24. Cynthia Marker quotes part of a letter from government minister Louis Terrenoire, who had supported the banning of Chris Marker's 1961 film *¡Cuba Sí!*: "No film of ideological propaganda is eligible for authorization, if only because of the risks that this kind of production entails for public order. In the specific case of Cuba, you are perhaps unaware that the press and radio in that country frequently attack the elected officials and populations of our overseas administrative territories *[départements]* in Martinique and Guadeloupe. To offer, under these conditions, a film audience to the Cuban leaders strikes me as inappropriate."

55. Agnès Varda, *Cléo de 5 à 7: Scénario* (Paris: Gallimard, 1962), 92. In French, the final sentence is "Eh bien voilà, on est deux dans une bulle."

56. The graffito naming Poujade that appears in *Le Joli Mai* reads "Poujade nous l'avait dit . . . nous sommes trahis" (Poujade told us . . . we have been betrayed).

57. Marker, *Commentaires*, 21.

58. Nora Alter sees the mix of fictional narrative and documentary fact in Alfred Döblin's 1927 modernist novel *Berlin Alexanderplatz* as an antecedent of Marker's efforts in *Le Joli Mai* to represent the spectrum of political perspectives bearing on this first spring of peace in the immediate aftermath of the Évian Accords. Nora M. Alter, *Chris Marker* (Urbana: University of Illinois Press, 2006), 79. Döblin's novel was adapted for film in 1931 by Phil Jutzi and again in 1980 in a fourteen-part television series directed by Rainer Werner Fassbinder.

59. "Est-ce, comme on le dit beaucoup, que vous pensez trop à vous? Ou n'est-ce pas plutôt qu'à votre insu vous pensez trop aux autres? Peut-être sentez-vous confusément que votre sort est lié à celui des autres, que le malheur et le bonheur sont deux sociétés secrètes, si secrètes que vous y êtes affiliés sans le savoir et que, sans l'entendre, vous abritez quelque part cette qui vous dit: tant que la misère existe, vous n'êtes pas riches, tant que la détresse existe, vous n'êtes pas heureux, tant que les prisons existent, vous n'êtes pas libres."

60. The inclusion of animated sequences by Paul Grimault is yet another desta-

bilizing factor because it departs from conventions of travelogue and non-fiction reportage. It is also significant because Grimault (1905–1994) was a member of the interwar Groupe Octobre and the postwar Groupe des Trente.

61. Chris Marker, "L'Objectivité passionnée," *Jeune Cinéma* 15 (May 1966): 14, quoted and translated in Lupton, *Chris Marker*, 80.

62. *Le Cinéma au service de la révolution: États généraux du cinéma*, no. 3 (Paris: Le Terrain Vague, 1968), 18.

63. Lupton, *Chris Marker*, 109.

64. In 1974, SLON transferred operations from Belgium to France under the new name ISKRA, an acronym for Image, Son, Kinescope, Réalisation, Audio-visuelle. Alter, *Chris Marker*, 84. See also Myriam Villain, "Le Montage est toujours révolutionnaire: À propos de la série *On vous parle de . . .* (1969–1973)," *Eclipses* 46 (2007): 142–49. Marker may have chosen the name ISKRA in homage to an early twentieth-century publication that became the official organ of the Russian Social Democratic Labor Party and whose managing editor from 1900 to 1903 was none other than Vladimir Lenin. In light of Marker's predilection for wordplay and animals, it is worth noting that *slon* and *iskra* are the respective terms in Russian for "elephant" and "spark."

65. Varda, *Varda par Agnès*, 92.

66. William F. Van Wert, "Chris Marker: The SLON Films," *Film Quarterly* 32 (1979): 38; Thomas Waugh, "*Loin du Vietnam* (1967), Joris Ivens, and Left Bank Documentary," *Jump Cut* 53 (Summer 2011). Marker was involved in other collective projects in various formats as well, in conjunction with workers' groups in the Besançon Medvedkin Group, *cinétracts* coverage of the 1968 student and worker protests in Paris, and a 1969–73 series of documentary shorts under the blanket title *On vous parle de . . .* (Speaking to you from . . .) shot in Brazil, Paris, Prague, and Chile.

67. Min Lee, "Red Skies: Joining Forces with the Militant Collective SLON," *Film Comment* 39, no. 4 (2003): 39. My account of Marker's involvement with SLON draws on Lee's article as well as on Trevor Stark's "Cinema in the Hands of the People: Chris Marker, the Medvedkin Group, and the Potential of Militant Film," *October*, no. 139 (Winter 2012): 117–50; and *Les Groupes Medvedkine: Le Film est une arme* [The Medvedkin Groups: Film is a weapon], a booklet included in the 2006 ISKRA/Éditions de Montparnasse DVD release of *Les Groupes Medvedkine*.

68. Chris Marker, "Pour Mario," in *Les Groupes Medvedkine*, 15.

69. Some historians and critics place the end of the Dziga Vertov Group in 1972, others in 1975. I base my decision to follow the latter date on Jean-Michel Frodon, "From Pen to Camera: Another Critic," in *A Companion to Jean-Luc Godard*, ed. Tom Conley and T. Jefferson Kline (Malden, Mass.: Wiley-Blackwell, 2014), 15.

70. Jean-Luc Godard, "Le Groupe 'Dziga Vertov,'" in *Jean-Luc Godard par Jean-Luc Godard*, 1:342. This essay was first published in *Cinéma* 151 (December 1970). That was well before Godard became disenchanted with the Dziga Vertov Group following the critical and commercial failure of *Tout va bien* (*Everything's Going Fine*, 1972).

71. Ibid., 1:348.

72. Jean-Luc Godard, "Struggle on Two Fronts: A Conversation with Jean-Luc Godard," *Film Quarterly* 21, no. 2 (1968–69): 21–22.

73. Ibid., 22.

74. Stark, "Cinema in the Hands of the People," 120.

75. Lupton, *Chris Marker*, 25.

Afterthoughts

1. Joris Ivens, "Reflections on the Avant-Garde Documentary" (1931), in Abel, *French Film Theory and Criticism*, 2:79.

2. Ibid., 80.

3. Scott MacDonald, "Introduction," in *Avant-Doc: Intersections of Documentary and Avant-Garde Cinema* (New York: Oxford University Press, 2015), 5.

4. Charles Wolfe, "Straight Shots and Crooked Plots: Social Documentary and the Avant-Garde in the 1930s," in *The Documentary Film Reader: History, Theory, Criticism,* ed. Jonathan Kahana (New York: Oxford University Press, 2016), 234.

5. Sante, *The Other Paris*, 9.

6. Ibid., 7.

7. Ibid., 17.

8. Alastair Phillips, *City of Darkness, City of Light: Émigré Filmmakers in Paris, 1929–1939* (Amsterdam: Amsterdam University Press, 2004), 11. De Certeau's "Walking in the City" appears in *The Practice of Everyday Life*, 91–110.

9. Walker, *City Gorged with Dreams*, 4.

10. Jean-Paul Clébert, *Paris Vagabond*, trans. Donald Nicholson-Smith (New York: New York Review of Books, 2016), 21.

11. Ibid., 81.

Filmography

Years refer to initial releases.

1895
L'Arrivée d'un train en gare de La Ciotat (Arrival of a Train at the La Ciotat Station),
     Auguste and Louis Lumière
La Sortie de l'usine Lumière à Lyon (Workers Leaving the Lumière Factory in Lyons),
     Auguste and Louis Lumière

1902
Le Voyage dans la lune (A Trip to the Moon), Georges Méliès

1912
La Conquête du Pôle (The Conquest of the Pole), Georges Méliès
Zigomar contre Nick Carter (Zigomar versus Nick Carter), Victorin-Hyppolite Jasset

1913
Fantômas, Louis Feuillade

1914
In the Land of the Head Hunters, Edward S. Curtis

1915
La Folie du docteur Tube (The Madness of Doctor Tube), Abel Gance

1920
Das Cabinet des Dr. Caligari (The Cabinet of Dr. Caligari), Robert Wiene

1921
L'Atlantide (Lost Atlantis), Jacques Feyder
Manhatta, Charles Sheeler and Paul Strand

1922
Nanook of the North, Robert J. Flaherty

1923

Coeur fidèle (True Heart, aka *The Faithful Heart)*, Jean Epstein
   Paris qui dort (The Crazy Ray), René Clair
Simba, King of the Jungle, Martin and Osa Johnson
La Traversée du Grépon (The Crossing of the Grépon), André Sauvage

1924

Ballet mécanique (Mechanical Ballet), Georges Antheil, Dudley Murphy, and
   Fernand Léger
Entr'acte (Intermission), René Clair
L'Inhumaine (The Inhuman Woman), Marcel L'Herbier
Schatten—Eine nächtliche Halluzination (Warning Shadows), Arthur Robison
The Thief of Bagdad, Raoul Walsh

1925

Les Aventures de Robert Macaire (The Adventures of Robert Macaire), Jean Epstein
Bronenosets Potyomkin (Battleship Potemkin), Sergei Eisenstein
Jeux des reflets et de la vitesse (Plays of Reflections and Speed), Henri Chomette
Rien que les heures (Nothing but Time), Alberto Cavalcanti

1926

Anémic Cinéma (Anemic Cinema), Marcel Duchamp
La Croisère noire (The Black Cruise), Léon Poirier
Moana, Robert J. Flaherty
Un tour au large (A Journey on the Open Sea), Jean Grémillon

1927

Berlin: Sinfonie der Großstadt (Berlin: Symphony of a World Capital), Walter
   Ruttmann
Chang, Ernest B. Schoedsack and Merian C. Cooper
The Docks of New York (Les Damnés de l'océan), Josef von Sternberg
Études des mouvements à Paris (Study of Traffic Circulation in Paris), Joris Ivens
Harmonies de Paris (Paris Harmonies), Lucie Derain
Rachmaninoff's Prelude in C Sharp Minor, Castleton Knight
Underworld (Les Nuits de Chicago), Josef von Sternberg
Die Weber (The Weavers), Friedrich Zelnik

1928

Aujourd'hui/24 heures en 30 minutes (Today/24 Hours in 30 Minutes), Jean Lods
De brug (The Bridge), Joris Ivens
Champs-Élysées, Jean Lods

La Coquille et le clergyman (The Seashell and the Clergyman), Germaine Dulac

The Crowd, Charles Vidor

Emak Bakia (Leave Me Alone), Fernand Léger

L'Étoile de mer (The Starfish), Man Ray

The Fall of the House of Usher, James Sibley Watson and Melville Webber

A Girl in Every Port, Howard Hawks

Les Halles centrales (The Central Covered Markets), Boris Kaufman

Jûjiro (Slums of Tokyo, aka *Crossroads)*, Teinosuke Kinugasa

Liebeshölle (Love's Hell, aka *Pawns of Passion)*, Carmine Gallone

The Love of Zero, Robert Florey

La Marche des machines (The March of the Machines), Eugène Deslaw

Montparnasse, Eugène Deslaw

La Nuit électrique (Electric Night), Eugène Deslaw

Paris-Cinéma, Pierre Chenal

Paris-Express, Marcel Duhamel and Jacques Prévert

La Passion de Jeanne d'Arc (The Passion of Joan of Arc), Carl Theodor Dreyer

La Petite Marchande d'allumettes (The Little Match Girl), Jean Renoir

Portrait de la Grèce (Portrait of Greece), André Sauvage

Romance of the Underworld, Irving Cummings

Tire au flanc (The Sad Sack), Jean Renoir

Visages de Paris (Faces of Paris), René Moreau

Voyage au Congo (Journey to the Congo), Marc Allégret and André Gide

The Wedding March (La Symphonie nuptiale), Erich von Stroheim

La Zone: Au pays des chiffonniers (The Zone: In the Land of the Ragpickers), Georges
Lacombe

1929

Chelovek s kino-apparatom (Man with a Movie Camera), Dziga Vertov

Un chien andalou (An Andalusian Dog), Luis Buñuel and Salvador Dalí

Drifters, John Grierson

Étude cinégraphique sur une arabesque (Arabesque), Germaine Dulac

Études sur Paris (Studies of Paris), André Sauvage

Gratte-ciel (Skyscraper Symphony), Robert Florey

Hallelujah, King Vidor

Impressionen vom alten marseiller Hafen (Impressions of the Old Marseille Harbor),
László Moholy-Nagy

Melodie der Welt (Melody of the World), Walter Ruttmann

Les Mystères du Château du Dé (The Mysteries of the Chateau of the Dice), Man Ray

Nogent, Eldorado du dimanche (Nogent, Sunday's Eldorado), Marcel Carné

Les Nouveaux Messieurs (The New Gentlemen), Jacques Feyder

Regen (Rain), Joris Ivens

Staroye i novoye (The General Line), Sergei Eisenstein
Thunder, William Nigh
Les Trois Masques (The Three Masks), André Hugon
Vendanges (Wine Harvests), Georges Rouquier

1930

L'Âge d'or (The Golden Age), Luis Buñuel and Salvador Dalí
À propos de Nice (Concerning Nice), Jean Vigo
L'Équipe/L'Étoile du nord (The Team/Northern Star), Jean Lods
Images d'Ostende (Ostend Images), Henri Storck
Menschen am Sonntag (People on Sunday), Robert Siodmak
Morocco, Josef von Sternberg
La Route est belle (The Road Is Beautiful), Robert Florey
Le Sang d'un poète (The Blood of a Poet), Jean Cocteau
Sous les toits de Paris (Under the Rooftops of Paris), René Clair
Wij bouwen (We Are Building), Joris Ivens
Zemlya (Earth), Alexander Dovzhenko
Zuydersee, Joris Ivens

1931

Pesn o Gerojach (Komosol, or Song of Heroes), Joris Ivens
Philips-Radio/Symphonie industrielle, Joris Ivens
Putyovka v zhizn (The Road to Life), Nikolai Ekk
Taris, ou la natation (Taris, or Swimming), Jean Vigo
La Vie d'un fleuve: La Seine (The Life of a River: The Seine), Jean Lods

1932

L'Affaire est dans le sac (It's in the Bag), Pierre Prévert
Boudu sauvé des eaux (Boudu Saved from Drowning), Jean Renoir
Coeur de lilas (Lilac), Anatole Litvak
Kuhle Wampe, Slatan Dudow
Les Petits Métiers de Paris: Scènes de la vie parisienne (Minor Professions of Paris: Scenes of Parisian Life), Pierre Chenal
Prix et profits, la pomme de terre (Prices and Profits, the Potato), Yves Allégret

1933

Las Hurdes, aka *Tierra sin pan (Land without Bread)*, Luis Buñuel
King Kong, Ernest B. Schoedsack and Merian C. Cooper
Misère au Borinage (Misery in Borinage), Joris Ivens and Henri Storck
Ténérife, Yves Allégret and Eli Lotar
Travaux du tunnel sous l'Escaut (Tunnel Work beneath the Escaut), Henri Storck
Zéro de conduite (Zero for Conduct), Jean Vigo

1934

L'Atalante, aka *Le Chaland qui passe (The Passing Barge)*, Jean Vigo and Boris
    Kaufman

La Croisière jaune (The Yellow Cruise), André Sauvage and Léon Poirier

Zouzou, Marc Allégret

1935

The Bride of Frankenstein, James Whale

Justin de Marseille, Maurice Tourneur

La Kermesse héroïque (Carnival in Flanders), Jacques Feyder

The 39 Steps, Alfred Hitchcock

Toni, Jean Renoir

1936

Housing Problems, Arthur Elton and Edgar Anstey

Une partie de campagne (A Day in the Country), Jean Renoir

The Plow That Broke the Plains, Pare Lorentz

La Vie est à nous (Life Is Ours, aka *The People of France)*, Jean Renoir

1937

Drôle de drame (Bizarre, Bizarre), Marcel Carné

La Grande Illusion (Grand Illusion), Jean Renoir

Les Maisons de la misère (The Houses of Misery), Henri Storck and Eli Lotar

Pépé le Moko, Julien Duvivier

Records 37, Jacques-Bernard Brunius

Snow White and the Seven Dwarfs, David Hand

The Spanish Earth, Joris Ivens

1938

La Bête humaine (The Human Beast), Jean Renoir

Café de Paris, Georges Lacombe

La France est un empire (France Is an Empire), Emmanuel Bourcier et al.

Hôtel du Nord, Marcel Carné

La Marseillaise, Jean Renoir

Le Quai des brumes (Port of Shadows), Marcel Carné

1939

The 400 Million, Joris Ivens

Gone with the Wind, Victor Fleming

Le Jour se lève (Daybreak), Marcel Carné

Violon d'Ingres (Hobbies across the Sea), Jacques-Bernard Brunius

1940
Power and the Land, Joris Ivens

1941
Citizen Kane, Orson Welles
Montmartre-sur-Seine, Georges Lacombe

1943
Hangmen Also Die, Fritz Lang and Bertolt Brecht

1944
Le Voleur des paratonnerres (The Lightning Rod Thief), Paul Grimault

1945
Les Enfants du paradis (Children of Paradise), Marcel Carné
Espoir, Sierra de Teruel (Man's Hope), André Malraux

1946
Aubervilliers, Eli Lotar
La Bataille du rail (The Battle of the Rails), René Clément
Farrebique, Georges Rouquier

1947
The Long Night, Anatole Litvak
Paris 1900, Nicole Védrès

1948
Germania anno zero (Germany Year Zero), Roberto Rossellini
The Naked City, Jules Dassin
Van Gogh, Alain Resnais

1949
Le Sang des bêtes (Blood of the Beasts), Georges Franju

1950
Afrique 50 (Africa 50), René Vautier
Cronaca di un amore (Chronicle of a Love), Michelangelo Antonioni
Gauguin, Alain Resnais
Guernica, Alain Resnais

1951

Juliette, ou la clef des songes (Juliette, or the Dream Book, aka *Juliette, or Key of Dreams),* Marcel Carné

1952

Bois d'Afrique (Wood from Africa), Eli Lotar
Hôtel des Invalides, Georges Franju
Les Jeux interdits (Forbidden Games), René Clément
Olympia 52, Chris Marker
Les Sept Péchés capitaux (The Seven Deadly Sins), Georges Lacombe et al.

1953

Hiroshima, Hideo Sekigawa
Les Statues meurent aussi (Statues Also Die), Alain Resnais and Chris Marker

1954

Les Maîtres fous (The Mad Masters), Jean Rouch
On the Waterfront, Elia Kazan
La Pointe-Courte, Agnès Varda
Les Poussières (Dusts), Georges Franju

1955

Afrique sur Seine (Africa on the Banks of the Seine), Paulin Soumanou Vieyra
Muerte de un ciclista (Death of a Bicyclist), Juan Antonio Bardem
Nuit et brouillard (Night and Fog), Alain Resnais

1956

Le Ballon rouge (The Red Balloon), Albert Lamorisse
Dimanche à Pékin (Sunday in Peking), Chris Marker
Toute la mémoire du monde (All the World's Memory), Alain Resnais

1957

Le Mystère de l'atelier 15 (The Mystery of Workshop 15), Alain Resnais
La Seine a rencontré Paris (The Seine Met Paris, aka *The Seine Meets Paris),* Joris Ivens

1958

Algérie en flammes (Algeria in Flames), René Vautier
Le Chant du Styrène (The Song of Styrene), Alain Resnais
Du côté de la côte (Over by the French Riviera), Agnès Varda
Lettre de Sibérie (Letter from Siberia), Chris Marker

Moi, un Noir (I, a Black Man, aka *I, a Negro)*, Jean Rouch
Mon oncle (My Uncle), Jacques Tati
L'Opéra Mouffe, Agnès Varda

1959
Come Back Africa, Lionel Rogosin
Enfants des courants d'air (Children Adrift), Édouard Luntz
Hiroshima mon amour, Alain Resnais

1960
Breathless, Jean-Luc Godard
Tirez sur le pianiste (Shoot the Piano Player), François Truffaut

1961
L'Année dernière à Marienbad (Last Year at Marienbad), Alain Resnais
Chronique d'un été (Chronicle of a Summer), Jean Rouch and Edgar Morin
¡Cuba Sí!, Chris Marker
J'ai huit ans (I Am Eight Years Old), René Vautier and Yann Le Masson
La Pyramide humaine (The Human Pyramid), Jean Rouch

1962
Cléo de 5 à 7 (Cleo from 5 to 7), Agnès Varda
La Jetée, Chris Marker
Lawrence of Arabia, David Lean
The Loneliness of the Long Distance Runner, Tony Richardson

1963
Le Joli Mai (The Merry Month of May, aka *The Lovely Month of May)*, Chris Marker
Salut les Cubains (Hi There, Cubans), Agnès Varda

1964
Le Glas (The Knell), René Vautier
The Pawnbroker, Sidney Lumet

1965
Le Mystère Koumiko (The Koumiko Mystery), Chris Marker

1966
La battaglia di Algeri (The Battle of Algiers), Gillo Pontecorvo
Blow-Up, Michelangelo Antonioni
La Noire de . . . (Black Girl), Ousmane Sembène

1967
Loin du Vietnam (Far from Vietnam), Chris Marker et al.

1968
À bientôt, j'espère (Be Seeing You), Chris Marker
Cabascabo, Oumarou Ganda
Cinétracts, Chris Marker
Jaguar, Jean Rouch

1969
Satyricon, Federico Fellini

1972
Avoir 20 ans dans les Aurès (To Be 20 Years Old in the Aurès), René Vautier
Nathalie Granger, Marguerite Duras
Tout va bien (Everything's Going Fine), Jean-Luc Godard

1974
La Société du spectacle (Society of the Spectacle), Guy Debord
La Solitude du chanteur de fond (The Loneliness of the Long Distance Singer), Chris
    Marker
Stavisky . . . , Alain Resnais

1977
Le Fond de l'air est rouge (A Grin without a Cat), Chris Marker

1981
Coup de Torchon (Clean Slate), Bertrand Tavernier

1988
Chocolat, Claire Denis

1990
Outremer (Overseas), Brigitte Roüan

1991
Allemagne 90 neuf zéro (Germany Year 90 Nine Zero), Jean-Luc Godard

1993
L'Oeil de Vichy (The Eye of Vichy), Claude Chabrol

1994
Les Silences du palais (The Silences of the Palace), Moufida Tlatli

1995
La Haine (Hate), Mathieu Kassovitz
Rouch in Reverse, Manthia Diawara

1996
Chacun cherche son chat (When the Cat's Away), Cédric Klapisch

1997
Immemory, Chris Marker
Level 5, Chris Marker

2000
Les Glâneurs et la glâneuse (The Gleaners and I), Agnès Varda

2001
Le Fabuleux Destin d'Amélie Poulian (Amélie), Jean-Pierre Jeunet

2002
Laissez-Passer (Safe Conduct), Bertrand Tavernier

2003
L'Esquive (Games of Love and Chance), Abdellatif Kechiche

2004
Chats perchés (The Case of the Grinning Cat), Chris Marker

2007
Le Voyage du ballon rouge (Flight of the Red Balloon), Hou Hsiao-Hsien

Index

Page numbers in italics refer to figures.

Steven Ungar is professor of cinematic arts, French, and comparative literature at the University of Iowa. His books include *Scandal and Aftereffect: Blanchot and France since 1930* (Minnesota, 1995), *Identity Papers: Contested Nationhood in Twentieth-Century France* (coedited with Tom Conley, Minnesota, 1996), *Popular Front Paris and the Poetics of Culture* (coauthored with Dudley Andrew), *Roland Barthes: The Professor of Desire,* and *Cléo de 5 à 7.*